(Continued from front flap)

for beginning to re-view our social system. The workplace reveals the meaning of democratic and liberal institutions that is obscured elsewhere.

The insights gained from the factory case-study are confirmed and enriched in a final section of *Working for Capitali$m* through Pfeffer's discussion of six of the best, recent books about work and workers in the United States, ranging from the H.E.W. task force report *Work in America,* to Studs Terkel's *Working,* to Harry Braverman's *Labor and Monopoly Capital.*

It is through this synthesis of theory with direct experience and observation that Pfeffer comes to understand work as a fundamental aspect of our lives and as the embodiment of the essential nature and purposes of our society. The conclusions about capitalist work and capitalist America that he draws from this understanding are neither pleasant nor easy to dismiss.

Richard M. Pfeffer is an associate professor at The Johns Hopkins University, a member of the New York Bar, and the author and editor of books and articles about China and the United States.

D1154476

Working for Capitali$m

WORKING FOR CAPITALI$M

Richard M. Pfeffer

Columbia University Press
New York
1979

The Following Publishers Have Kindly Given Permission To Reprint Various Extracts

From *Working: People Talk About What They Do All Day and How They Feel About What They Do,* by Studs Terkel. Copyright © 1972, 1974 by Studs Terkel. Reprinted by permission of Pantheon Books, a Division of Random House, Inc., and by Wildwood House, London.

From *The Hidden Injuries of Class,* by Richard Sennett and Jonathan Cobb. Copyright © 1972 by Richard Sennett and Jonathan Cobb. Reprinted by permission of Alfred A. Knopf, Inc.

From *Labor and Monopoly Capital* by Harry Braverman. Copyright © 1974 by Harry Braverman. Reprinted by permission of Monthly Review Press.

From *Work in America* by the Department of Health, Education, and Welfare. Copyright © 1973. Reprinted by permission of the MIT Press.

From *Clockwork,* by Richard Balzer. Copyright © 1976 by Richard Balzer. Reprinted by permission of Doubleday & Company, Inc. and David Obst Books.

From *All The Livelong Day,* by Barbara Garson. Copyright © 1972, 1973, 1974, 1975 by Barbara Garson. Reprinted by permission of Doubleday & Company, Inc. and International Creative Management.

From the song "It Don't Worry Me," by Keith Carradine. Copyright © 1975 by American Broadcasting Music, Inc./Lion's Gate/Easy Music. Used by permission only. All rights reserved.

LIBRARY OF CONGRESS CATALOGING IN PUBLICATION DATA

PFEFFER, RICHARD M
  WORKING FOR CAPITALI$M.

  INCLUDES INDEX.
  1. LABOR AND LABORING CLASSES—MARYLAND—BALTIMORE—
CASE STUDIES. 2. FACTORY SYSTEM—MARYLAND—BALTIMORE—
CASE STUDIES. 3. INDUSTRIAL RELATIONS—MARYLAND—
BALTIMORE—CASE STUDIES. 4. CAPITALISM. 5. LIBERAL-
ISM. 6. MARXIAN SCHOOL OF SOCIOLOGY. I. TITLE.
HD8085.B33P46   301.44'42'097526   78-23345
ISBN 0-231-04426-7
ISBN 0-231-04427-5 PBK.

COLUMBIA UNIVERSITY PRESS
NEW YORK/GUILDFORD, SURREY

COPYRIGHT © 1979 BY RICHARD M. PFEFFER
ALL RIGHTS RESERVED
PRINTED IN THE UNITED STATES OF AMERICA

*To the men and women
      who helped me to understand.
I hope this book
      helps them understand.*

Contents

Acknowledgments

THIS book has been at the center of my life for nearly four years. It has been affected by and has affected my relations with people and events.

In mid-1974 I temporarily stopped teaching at The Johns Hopkins University and went to work in a factory. In February 1975 I returned to the university to try in solitude to make sense of the factory experience; then to read what others have had to say about working; and finally to revise and complete this manuscript. While doing so, during 1977 and 1978, the question of whether I would be awarded tenure or terminated engulfed me and became a heated campus issue.

The book that has come through these events could not have been written without the support and help of many people, in particular those acknowledged below.

In every sense this book could not have been written without the men and women with whom I worked in the factory.

I was sustained throughout by my wife, Elinor Bacon, who shared in some of the achievements, paid many of the costs, and grew in her own womanly strength.

I could not have worked in the factory without fake job references from my Uncle Charlie (Sigman, for whom as a child I worked part time in his and Aunt Esther's grocery store, before it failed) and from my close friend Allan Chasanoff, who often has helped me untangle my emotions and ideas about work and life.

David Harvey made some valuable suggestions on an early, incomplete draft of this book, as did several former students, especially Andrew G. Walder, Stephen C. Smith, and Carolyn Hock. A few old friends from the China field, Jim Peck and Molly Coye, provided useful comments, as did Rod Aya.

Richard Cone's, Jane Harrison's and David Harvey's friendship and generous help during the tenure struggle saw me through that ordeal. The unlimited support of Tom Thompson, of Student Council leaders Dave Chesanow and Jerry Spada, and of student activists Rita Chang, Kevin Cleary, Mark Hertsgaard, Liam Schwartz, Chris Taylor, and Mary Waters was more than anyone has a right to expect.

Knowing Stelios and Pauline Spiliadis made a difference. So did Joy Joffe and Rosemary Maguire. And being able daily to see and talk with Evelyn Scheulen and Evelyn Stroller and to have their, and especially Catherine Grover's, aid in typing this manuscript was important.

Finally, I wish to thank the deceased Harry Braverman and Monthly Review Press, Richard Sennett and Jonathan Cobb, Barbara Garson, Richard Balzer, Studs Terkel, and the authors of *Work in America* for allowing me to quote extensively from and to comment upon their books.

Baltimore, Maryland   Ric Pfeffer
March 1978

ACKNOWLEDGMENTS

Working for Capitali$m

Prologue

THIS book is what it is, in part, because of who I am. I am the product of American society, which socialized me, and of my particular experiences and personality. To some extent, therefore, this book inevitably involves a personal statement.

But I believe it is much more than that. For one, it is a modest effort to bridge the gap known as the "division of labor," which among other things systematically separates mental work and workers from manual work and workers. When I chose to spend seven months in 1974–75 of my sabbatical leave from The Johns Hopkins University faculty operating a forklift truck in a Baltimore factory, I violated that system. The violation is at the core of this book, since the practical experience in the factory led me to a new understanding of work in America, of the relation between work and societal life, and of American society as a whole.

Prior to the 1970s I had not really thought at all about the nature of work in the United States or about its meaning for American society. Never in my public school career or in my education at so-called elite universities—B.A., Yale University; LL.B., Harvard Law School; Ph.D. in Government, Harvard University—did any of my courses seriously consider the topic of work and its implications. If you think about it, this in itself is an exposé of our educational system. It was not, in fact, until shortly before I started to work in the factory that I belatedly began to understand the social and human significance of work.

This tentative understanding was reinforced and enriched by the experience of working in a factory. I now realize that work is one, if not the, central component of societal life. As such, the quality of work in a particular society cannot be understood simply as marginally related, or related by mere coincidence, to the broader society. *The quality of work, rather, is determined by and in turn determines the nature of society. Thus, for any society, if we understand the essential quality of its work, we will better understand the essential nature and purposes of its social organization; and if we understand the essential nature and purposes of its social organization, we will better understand the essential quality of its work.*

This book, about work in the United States, is then also about American society. The point seems unexceptionable. But many of us may be made uncomfortable by the proposition that work and societal life reflect and determine each other. The problem is that if the descriptions of work offered here are representative, and if work and society are so intimately related, then we must draw conclusions about America that are congruous with the conclusions about work. In short, if work in America is as destructive as it is portrayed in this book, and if the quality of work in any society is indicative of the true nature of that society, then life in America in some substantial sense must be destructive, like work in America.

I no longer doubt that almost every ideal and institution in the United States is subordinated to the right of a small minority among us to make large profits. That subordination and the resulting desecration of our values and lives are only most blatant and most undeniable in our workplaces. Work, then, because it is at once so central and so relatively unadorned, is a good place to begin re-viewing and reconsidering the nature of our social system.

The undeniable and generally accepted truth concerning work in the United States today is that, on the whole, it is extremely confining, dehumanized, and meaningless for those who perform it. To explain this, some say simply that work by nature is a necessary evil, which we experience in a form determined by the inevitable development of technological forces. Others say, No, work in our system is more inhumane than it needs to be; therefore we can and should carry out reforms to make work more satisfying. Taken together, these prevailing views mean that the quality of work in the United States, at worst, cannot be improved at all and at best, can only be improved somewhat and within the system. Their common, silent message is that no other form of social organization can offer hope of radical improvement in work.

With these nearly unchallenged conventional views I strongly disagree. That is to say, I disagree with the ideas most of you already have about work. As to the potential for humanizing work, I support meaningful reform, but *I do not believe the work process can be radically improved through reforms within the American system.*

We have great difficulty taking seriously the possibility that work can be very different, that technology can be developed and applied very differently, and that the United States can be very different. We have this difficulty because our experience and our consciousness have confined, within the boundaries imposed by our present social existence, our understanding of why we are what we are and our related understanding of what we can become and how. There is, of course, nothing unusual in this. Most people in every age have believed that the society in which they lived represented not only what was but, in some substantial sense, what could be. The prevailing set of beliefs in every age, therefore, has functioned as a major obstacle to understanding social reality, just as the prevailing set of beliefs about work, the United States, and humankind today functions as a major obstacle to understanding our own reality.

In writing this book I have sought to expose reality by exploring a strikingly different way of understanding, which I am only beginning to develop within myself. I have tried to write something that might help me and other people to understand our lives more fully. Therefore I have tried to write about work in a way that, on the one hand, is not so abstracted in its theory as to appear irrelevant to nonacademics, nor on the other, so limited to a description of what is as to suggest nothing about why our lives are the way they are.

It is grounded in large part in a common practical experience, the very texture and structure of which reflects and embodies central aspects of our social system. My message is that the almost imperceptible meaning and patterns of events in the small in daily work life must be understood. This is crucial, I believe, because *the nature and structure of daily life is socially "determined," not coincidental. And since daily life is what shapes us into what we are, if we do not understand these patterns, their sources and their purposes, we cannot hope to change them and change what we are.*

My own commitment to change was created slowly over decades during which I (and countless others) became deeply disillusioned and skeptical about American politics—its leaders, its values, and its institutions. I began to wonder whether "politics," as it is conventionally and narrowly understood here, really was the problem. I began to question whether the problem might not be buried deeper, in our economy and in the class system, culture, ideology, and institutions that are its essence and provide its support.

This questioning attitude, drawn from my own experiences in the 1960s, was reinforced by my professional study and teaching about the People's Republic of China. The Chinese Revolution suggested two things to me. First, a radically different way of understanding the world existed; and second, a radically different way of organizing society, based upon that understanding, was possible. As I lived in the United States and studied China, my changing understanding of the United States affected how I perceived China's system, even as my changing understanding of China affected how I perceived our system. Belatedly, in the early 1970s, I came to what for me then was a shocking conclusion: the success China had achieved in creating a just and egalitarian society might be intimately related to socialism; and the fundamental failure of the United States to create such a society might be intimately related to capitalism.

My trip to China in early 1972 was a turning point in my own development. My month-long visit challenged me intellectually, politically, ideologically, and psychologically. I became aware, as if for the first time, of my own individualism, and began more seriously to question its mainsprings, liberalism and capitalism. I started to think about how societies like China and the United States were created, maintained, and changed. And, confronting Chinese slogans urging everyone to "serve the people," I began to wonder not only who was served by the Chinese social system but who was served by the American system. Experiencing the observable and explicit integration of "politics" and "economics" in China, I realized that, contrary to what I had been taught and thought, these are in every system but aspects of an integrated whole that variously interpenetrate and shape each other and therefore cannot properly be understood in separation from one another.

Up to that time, my life had been characteristic of what the Chinese call a "three-gate cadre": someone who has moved from the gate of the family, through the gate of school, and then on through the gate of work unscathed by any prolonged experience of the sort of labor common to most members of the society. My lack of such experience, I saw, did indeed separate me from the lives of most Americans, and my teaching and research at Johns Hopkins reflected that removal from dominant social realities.

I also was beginning to find liberal analyses and proposed remedies for the profound and glaring failures of American society inadequate and ideological. Half-consciously, I began to search for a better framework within which to understand China and the United States. Having read Mao Tse-tung's *Selected Works* earlier, I turned haltingly and anxiously to the writings of Karl Marx. Haltingly, because I had gotten the American message inscribed in our school texts, our mass media, and our minds that Marx has been proven wrong time and again. Anxiously, because I had been made aware in my political and professional socialization that Marx's ideas somehow are unacceptable, even dangerous, and that, in the context of a still virulent if subterranean anti-communism, those who take Marxism seriously are likely to be ridiculed, vilified and punished.

As I began to read Marx in 1972 and to struggle to understand his profound and subtle analyses, I was shaken by a recognition. The underlying nature of our capitalist system, which liberal ideology and liberal social science had hidden from view, was increasingly exposed. Reading Marx confirmed and explained what I had previously only suspected—that America's fundamental problem is capitalism. It also sharpened my feeling that my own work life in the university was so separated from the work lives of the majority of Americans as to impede my understanding of the problems our brand of capitalism creates for them. Without a better understanding of these problems, I was unlikely to be in a position to make any contribution to resolving them. So for intellectual and political reasons I felt I had to become more familiar with the American working class and its problems.

Two other reasons lay behind my decision to go to work in a factory. First, I wanted to test myself. I wanted to see how I would react in a setting in which I was denied my accustomed elite status as professor, lawyer, and cosmopolition. And second, I needed for professional purposes, if I was not to "perish" at Johns Hopkins where I do not have tenure, to publish another book.

However, there was one problem with my decision to work in a factory. I was afraid to act upon it. Never before having done factory labor, I was afraid of the unknown and of failing. And I was afraid, too, of "succeeding"—afraid of what "success" working in a factory might mean for my future in the university. Working in a factory, even when labeled in academic jargon as "participant observation," was not a course of action likely to impress my colleagues in political science with my professionalism. Nor, I feared, was the kind of book I wanted to write likely to meet with the professional approval of those colleagues, who would decide whether, even after publishing, I would perish.

Troubled by all these matters, I sought to reduce my fears by hedging my bets. I applied in the fall of 1973 for grants for the following year, more to legitimate my project than to subsidize it. As an alternative, I also applied for a year-long sabbatical leave at half-pay from Johns Hopkins. My applications for grants were rejected, but my sabbatical request was approved by Hopkins' maverick Dean of Arts and Sciences, George Owen, to whom I am grateful. I do not know whether I would have had the courage to interrupt my academic career without that leave. With the sabbatical to work in a factory and write a book about it approved, I was assured of some funding and, much more important, I would carry with me a frail presumption of academic legitimacy.

When the 1974 spring term ended, I began to look for a job (chapter 1). Once on this road, I started to gather materials for and to think about this book. At the outset, I made two decisions. First, I decided that I would keep a daily journal as the raw material for writing this book. Second, I decided that, although I was essentially a stranger to the social science literature on work, I would write up my work experience before I allowed myself to read anything specifically about work in America.

Having made those decisions, I then encountered several problems I had not anticipated. To keep an accurate journal, I learned, I had to be able to take notes on events and conversations during the day. While I was looking for a job such note taking was not a problem, since I could jot down notes after each job interview. But on a job all day I would need some privacy. Fortunately for me, the job I finally got and held for seven months until I was laid off involved dumping trash into a compactor that was housed in a separate room of the factory. The room afforded me needed privacy. Fortunately, also, the trash job required that I keep a record of the number of industrial hoppers I dumped each day into the compactor, which provided me with an inconspicuous opportunity to record daily events. Whenever necessary, I simply noted relevant events and bits of conversations on the back of the same time cards on whose face I recorded the hoppers dumped. On many days I filled six or seven such cards with twenty to thirty entries of notes. As I filled each card, I folded it and stuffed it into my pants pocket. Then, every day when I returned home after work I spent from thirty to sixty minutes typing up, organizing, and commenting upon the noted experiences while they were still fresh in my mind. By the time I was terminated in February 1975, I had nearly three hundred pages of typed notes.

The bulk of this book (parts I and II) concerns events in the factory in which I worked, which I take as representative of the American political economy of work. The last part of the book (part III) goes well beyond that case study to bring out the nature and scope of the existing consensus on the quality of work in America as reflected in six of the best, recent books about work and workers. It is an exploration, because I did not and do not have any neat, fully worked out theories about how all these aspects of capitalism relate one to another. What I am trying to do above all else in this part is to indicate how vital and how difficult it is simply to understand as the source of the problem the very system that shapes us in so many subtle ways. And I am trying also to indicate the directions in which useful analysis should move.

The book that has emerged remains vulnerable to a number of misunderstandings and criticisms relating especially to my factory case study. For various reasons, I decided quite early in my factory term that I would limit my relations with co-workers to the workplace and to union meetings. I did not socialize with workers after work, although on several occasions I was given a chance to do so. That decision limited my experience. The decision, moreover, may be misunderstood by readers as evidence of a lack of feelings of affection and respect on my part for my co-workers. If so, I regret it. Because I do not dwell on these aspects, a reader might not realize from this book how much I liked and respected many of the people with whom I worked, how often I enjoyed the bull sessions at breaks and meals, and how fondly I have thought back to and miss the sense of camaraderie, fragile but real, that exists in the factory. My efforts to cross over the division of labor succeeded only partially and temporarily. Now that division once again separates my life from the lives of my co-workers.

A second, related regret is that I had to hide my identity from my co-workers. I hid it in order to survive, just as in this manuscript I have disguised the identity of other workers for their protection. I am certain that if word ever had gotten out that I was a professor on leave I would have been fired immediately. Moreover, in the highly unlikely event that I survived such exposure, workers, with knowledge of my background and purposes, probably would have treated me differently. So under the circumstances I do not see that there was a better way to achieve what I sought.

While in the factory I functioned in three different roles. My assumption of each of these roles raises its own questions. For one thing, I was a worker, initially a worker learning how to do a job that was wholly new to him. My role as a worker determined my work life throughout the term in the factory, but it was especially dominant during the first few months. That fact is reflected in part I, which is about the work itself.

In the factory I also functioned in the role of observer, intellectual, and "social scientist." I did not simply do my job. I also tried to probe, to report on, and to understand what working meant: what my job was like and why; what it demanded of and did to me; how coworkers worked and felt about their jobs; how certain jobs were interrelated with other jobs and certain workers with other workers; how management managed; how the union operated; and how these and other facets of working relate to capitalism, of which they are aspects. My role as analyst is reflected in the entire manuscript.

Finally, as a worker, union member, and human being, I functioned also as an activist in the factory. Faced during the term with serious shared problems in work and with the prospects of a new contract and union elections, I might have chosen not to participate in trying to shape events. I chose otherwise. If I am not certain I chose correctly, I am certain that, however I chose, the choice would have affected this manuscript. As it is, part II reflects what I learned in no small part because of my activist role.

There are criticisms that can be made of my assuming each of these roles. With regard to my role as a factory worker, for example, some friends have criticized my having taken a factory job in the first place on grounds that during a period of high unemployment I deprived someone of a needed job. I cannot deny that simple and awful truth. I can only hope that what I write here can somehow compensate for it by contributing in a small way to a long-term transformation of our society that will eliminate the manmade calamity of unemployment.

Most of the serious criticisms of which I am aware focus not upon my role as worker, however, but upon my roles as intellectual and activist in the factory context. They boil down to two questions that raise the specter of elitism and bad faith. First, there is the question whether in going into the factory not only to learn from but also to "teach" experienced workers and others to understand their work lives I was not being condescending. And second, there is the question whether, as a professional who intended to abandon the factory after a time and to return to a waiting job, I had the "right" to become active in politics within the factory.

PROLOGUE

Although I find both of these questions troubling, the second is most difficult. As to whether I have been condescending, I do not think I have been. On the one hand, I know that I learned more from the experience and from my co-workers than they are likely ever to learn from me. For instance, I learned some of the realities behind abstract concepts like "division of labor" and "relations of production." On the other hand, I know that whatever I may be able to return to my co-workers and others is the result, ironically, of the division of labor in the United States. That division has allowed me to develop a trained and disciplined mind, has encouraged me to take a larger view of society; and once I decided to violate its mandate, it has afforded me upon my return to the university the time to reflect on, read, and write about the factory work experience. Many of my co-workers, I am convinced, could have done at least as well, were they with me on this side of the great social divide.

As to the question of my right under the circumstances to become an activist, the charge implicit in the question, of course, is that so long as I was not in the same position as my co-workers I did not run the same risks as they did. Therefore, I was freer to advocate action to improve our work situations. For instance, if I encouraged workers not to accept a company offer for a new contract, thereby risking a strike, or if I encouraged workers to try to transform the union, the possible consequences of those acts—say, the loss of wages while on strike, or the loss of job for being a troublemaker—would be more bearable for me than for many workers.

This is true enough. Nevertheless, the issue of my activism must be put in a still broader perspective. To focus, as I sometimes mistakenly have myself, on a single individual as if he or she alone has the capacity to significantly change the course of events is a form of glorification of the individual, whether this takes the form of praise or condemnation. Whatever I did as an activist could only be one small part of a situation in which many others also were acting. Whether I was active or not, the forces that dominate the factory still would have acted to maintain their domination. Had I been passive, there simply would have been one less person opposing those forces. In the face of the half-truths, propaganda, and outright lies not infrequently perpetrated on workers by the forces that rule the factory, which my background and experience equipped me to expose, would silence and inaction on my part have been ethically and politically superior to activism? I am not confident of the answer, but I doubt it.

In any event, it is not clear that my arguments would have been more likely to be correct had my material interests and future possibilities been the same as other workers. Had I shared the same risks as they, been as dependent upon the factory job as they, doubtless I would have been more intimidated from expressing what I understood. But would I have been more likely to be correct in that understanding? I think not.

Finally, although the nature of the risks confronting me has been different, I too have faced serious risks, both inside and outside the factory. For one thing, I was more overtly active inside the factory than all but a handful of workers. That made me a prime target for retaliation. For another, if I was less materially dependent upon holding the factory job than most of my co-workers, I did not take lightly the prospect of losing it, either. During most of my term in the factory, maintaining that job, as this prologue should have made clear, was vitally important to my life, for intellectual, political, psychological, and career reasons. When, for example, after four months on the job, one of my fabricated job references was contacted by my employer for verification, I became extremely fearful that the jig was up and I would lose my job. Moreover, if it is true that by the time I finally was terminated I was more or less ready to leave and therefore did not experience the job loss as a calamity, still, today, back in the university, I continue to bear risks related to my purposes in going into the factory, to the roles I performed while there, and to what I learned.

Indeed, just after this manuscript had been accepted for publication by both Columbia University Press and by Monthly Review Press, the majority of the Political Science Department voted to deny me tenure. The department denied me tenure expressly because it does not appreciate this book, and without, as is customary, seeking evaluations of my scholarship from leading scholars in my fields outside Johns Hopkins.

In response to my appeal to approve the setting up of an ad hoc committee to solicit such outside references, the Academic Council of the Faculty of Arts and Sciences, which never has granted an appeal from a departmental denial, upheld the department's decision out of respect for "departmental autonomy." Only after an exhausting, and, for Johns Hopkins, unprecedented struggle, which began in the spring and ended in mid-November of 1977, was an ad hoc committee finally appointed. In the course of that struggle over 60 percent of Johns Hopkins undergraduates in a Student–Council–sponsored referendum voted 1,268 to 53 in favor of my receiving a "fair hearing"; approximately 25 percent of the full professors on campus petitioned the Academic Council to approve such a committee; assurances were given privately by university officials that if I were found to be "promotable" I would be awarded a position outside the Political Science Department; the Academic Council on its own initiative reconsidered my case and deadlocked in a tie vote; and two high-placed university administrators offered their resignations.

At the time of this writing I know that the ad hoc committee has been appointed, but I do not know what my chances for tenure are. The committee's composition, deliberations, and recommendations to the Academic Council all are secret. It is no secret, however, that given the furor my case has created on this extremely sedate and narrowly professionalized campus, given the nature of my scholarship and politics, and given the tightness of the academic job market, I am all too likely to be unemployed in the near future.

So, if risk is to be taken as the main measure of good faith, I believe I have demonstrated good faith. Be that as it may, and whatever my mistakes, I have done what I felt I had to. What is good in the book, like what is bad in it, is a product of that total experience.

Not everything that happened in the factory, of course, has been (or could or should be) included in this book. It is organized around a fundamental critique of our political economy of work and takes an extremely critical view of related liberal institutions and their impact on the workplace. It understands liberal institutions—including those, like elections, which we usually think of as most anti-authoritarian and democratic—primarily as highly sophisticated control mechanisms.

Because of this emphasis, I probably do not do justice to the secondary aspects of these institutions, which are better known and generally treated reverentially as if they were primary. In my criticism of institutions like unions, collective bargaining contracts, and grievance procedures, for example, I do not sufficiently emphasize the other side of these institutions. They are the product of partially successful workers' struggles. And their creation at the time constituted significant progress, just as their continued existence today still provides certain very important safeguards for workers.

Consequently, to take the case of unions, even if they were all as bad as the one I experienced, which they are not, my strong criticism of them should not be construed to mean that I favor their abolition. On the contrary, since unions are the only potentially mass organization workers have, I favor the expansion of unions, but of transformed unions that fight aggressively for workers' overall interests and encourage worker activism in union and work affairs.

In any event, I have not tried to write a "balanced" book. I have tried to write a book from which I and others could learn what our world is like, so we could be better prepared to change it. Conditions in the factory, even more obviously than most other places in our society, are hardly balanced. The few rule and are generally well served, while the many are ruled and labor in dismal jobs to make a living. There is nothing "natural" or technologically ordained about these conditions. They were not always as they are today; nor will they remain so into the indefinite future. These conditions are manmade, and they can and must be changed by the actions of men and women.

Most workers in our society today do not and cannot work to significantly improve their lives, because they do not understand why their lives are what they are or realize that collectively they can transform them. As it is, they do not and cannot work with any sense of higher purpose or achieve much sense of fulfillment. They are just "making a living." That is as it must be, since workers still are enthralled, materially and ideologically. They are, after all, working for capitalism.

I
The Work Process

I

Looking for a Job

"Safety Is Contagious; Let's Have an Epidemic"
"Courtesy Is Contagious; Let's Have an Epidemic"
and
"Safety First,"
said the signs hung on the plywood-paneled walls, alongside the poster-advertisements for the company's product, sophisticated trenchcoats worn by beautiful people. But no one in the crowded personnel office seemed to take notice as they sat and waited.

Most of those waiting were between 18 and 25 years old, though a few were middle-aged. Nearly all were black; most were women, many fat to the point of obesity. Beautiful people, they were not. If hired, they would be producing for the chic and wealthy and for those who aspired to such status.

The Londontown company, it was known, employed women almost exclusively in production. As an employer it was reputed to be one of the lowest paying larger plants in the city. Men, given a choice, did not want such jobs. Nor could they easily get them, since women were considered more dextrous on sewing machines.

The people waiting that morning to be interviewed for jobs, about twenty in all, did not, except for the few young blacks who seemed to be acquainted, talk to each other. Nor did they read while waiting, though two of the twenty were leafing through old issues of *U.S. News and World Report*, provided no doubt by the company. When a new person entered the room, no one advised the entrant what procedures to follow, even when several newcomers sat down without first asking the receptionist for job application forms.

Mostly, those waiting simply stared vacantly into space. Their eyes rarely met each others'. They did not smile at or respond observably to the few who were active. On their faces were fixed, blank looks. They were there for one purpose, to get a job. That meant they had to wait until they were called for an interview. They had all waited many times before, it seemed, in other personnel offices. They had been called to interview before. And most probably had worked before.

No one knew, I learned, how many jobs were available at this factory, or what kind of jobs were open. No one knew exactly what the pay would be, or what working conditions were like. And no one seemed too concerned to find out. I wondered about that.

I had filled out my job application the day before, so I only had to wait for one and one-half hours on this day to be called in for the interview. Although most of those ahead of me had been called by their first names, I was not. The interviewer, a white woman, was very nice. She gave the impression of being concerned with my well-being.

She explained that all available jobs paid $2 per hour, for a gross of about $4,000 a year for a 40-hour week. I nodded, somewhat afraid that talking too much might expose me as a pretender. Looking at my falsified employment record, which indicated that after graduating from a Long Island, New York, high school I had worked there, first as a delivery truck driver for a grocery store for fifteen years, and then as a general maintenance worker for a construction firm for five years, she asked if I knew how to maintain machines or if I could drive tractor trailers. I answered no.

As she questioned me, the interviewer began phoning around to find out about warehousing jobs with the company, but the man in charge was unavailable. She did not invite me to try the manual dexterity test on her desk, which I concluded was used to test prospective female production workers.

Before completing the interview, the woman asked why I had moved to Baltimore. I answered, as I had been coached by friends who knew the factory interview circuit, that my wife had relatives here. She asked if I intended to stay in the city. I answered yes, which seemed to satisfy her. She closed the interview saying she would follow up on the warehouse job and get back to me at home. I never heard from her again. Nor did I myself follow up on the possibility.

The experience at Londontown in many ways was typical of the weeks spent looking for a job. It was also, I later realized, portentous of what was to come. On the other days I looked for a job, I pursued classified ads on the phone and in person and stopped in at large corporations on the chance they might be hiring unskilled production workers.

My initial experience searching for a job had been in response to an anonymous ad in the *Baltimore Sunday Sun*. I had called to find out what and where the factory was, and learned it was a firm called Bio Quest, located in an industrial park about twenty minutes outside the city. I drove out and waited in the lobby for approximately two hours to get a job application, which I filled out in an office upstairs. I then had a five-minute interview with the man I had spoken with on the phone, who informed me that all the job openings had been filled.

On the day following, I drove out to Bethlehem Steel's huge Sparrow's Point plant. I was not prepared for the bleak, almost charred moonscape quality of the land at "The Point," although some years earlier I had toured a steel mill in Gary, Indiana. The employment office was crowded with men lined up before desks. I got a job application and, with some trouble, filled it out. The difficulty lay in trying to respond to questions like what salary I wanted. Since I didn't know what jobs were open, I didn't know what to say. While on line waiting to hand in my application, I heard by word of mouth that Bethlehem was hiring for the coke ovens, hot and dangerous work.

I need not have been anxious, however, for when I got to the desk after a brief wait the secretary-receptionist told me that indeed they were hiring, but from the February waiting list; that if I was not called within two months and wanted my file to remain active, I should come down again and fill out another application.

On the way home from Sparrow's Point, I stopped off at the

LOOKING FOR A JOB

local GM factory. Although the personnel office was empty, no one working there seemed to notice me. My asking for an application appeared to constitute an unwarranted interruption. Perhaps that was partly because GM had been laying off and was not hiring. But GM outer office personnel employees treated job seekers in a way not very different from what I had experienced elsewhere, making them feel insignificant, beneath notice.

All told, I spent about two weeks full time and one week part time looking for a job before I had any success. During that time I increasingly came to feel "unemployed" in a literal sense. That feeling of being unemployed, even without the economic distress that normally accompanies it, was troublesome psychologically. What would it have been like, I tried to imagine, had I desperately needed the wages to support my family? The feelings of failure would have been overwhelming.

As the period wore on, I found myself avoiding looking for jobs. I tried to find other things I "had to do." I did not want to be rejected again. But it wasn't just the fear of another rejection that haunted me. It also was the fear of being offered a job and being unable to choose rationally whether to accept the particular offer. How, I asked myself, was I to make such a decision? How to know whether to accept an offered job when the meaning of taking that job was obscure, when what the job really was like could not be known in advance? And the magnitude of that decision was compounded by my realization that once I took a job I would be tied down, making it that much harder to look for and find another job. But then I wondered, did it really make any difference what kind of a job I had? Had the unemployed I encountered in hiring offices acted as if the choice were crucial to them? I wasn't certain.

In any event, these feelings and questions daily came to seem increasingly irrelevant. As I looked for a good job, the experiential message I received louder and clearer was: "We don't need you. There are plenty more where you come from. Be grateful for whatever you can get." It was as if all these separate experiences had been organized by some powerful and invisible hand to teach each job seeker that as an individual worker s/he is powerless, even worthless.

THE WORK PROCESS

"Cherish any job we throw to you," experience said, though no company personnel employee had put it so crudely. On the other hand, no company as yet had called back either. I renewed my efforts to get a job, any job.

Several employers I spoke to on the phone were impressed by my seeming steadiness when I told them I had worked on prior jobs for fifteen and five years respectively. But they were embarrassed to tell me their jobs paid $2 an hour, which one self-consciously informed me was insufficient to support a family. They were looking, they said, for younger unmarried people to whom they could pay such wages and whom they could train. I understood.

During the last weekend before finding a job, I was very edgey. Looking through the Sunday classified ads for unskilled factory work, I found very few openings. I decided to try warehousing, for a while at least. The next morning I drove half an hour outside the city to the large Maryland Cup (Sweetheart Cup) plant, which had been advertising for warehousing jobs. I entered the hiring office and read the sign explaining what to do, filled out the application with the stubby pencil reminiscent of high school hearing tests, and sat down to wait with the others, mostly young blacks.

I was called in for a brief and pleasant interview for a warehousing job that paid $2.84 an hour. The main catch in the job was that the warehouse, which now was located near my home, was soon to be moved to Columbia, Maryland, thirty miles out of Baltimore. The move was the reason there were openings, since a number of the present employees at the warehouse planned to quit rather than commute that distance. I assured the interviewer I didn't mind the commute. He sent me down to be interviewed by the foreman at the warehouse, who also inquired about the commute. The foreman seemed satisfied with my response and sent me, in turn, for a physical exam at a business-supported, private downtown clinic, where efficiently and perfunctorily they checked my eyes, hearing, and blood pressure, took a urine sample and examined me for possible hernia. So far, so good. Was I really going to get a job, I anxiously wondered, trying to restrain my premature elation?

Not wanting to put all my eggs in the Maryland Cup, and wanting to see what employment agencies are like, I stopped off on my way home from the clinic at the Silver Employment Agency. The agency was in a ghetto slum; all the others waiting to be interviewed were very young black males, who looked like first-timers on the job market. The interviewer was white; the secretaries were black. Through a glass panel in the partition separating the interviewer from the secretary-receptionist, we could see one-half of the interview, the white interviewer. But we could not see the black interviewee, who was out of the frame, invisible, though obviously a part of the scene.

I waited for an hour to be interviewed, while a variety of blacks preceded me. In the interim I realized to my surprise that I had learned to stare vacantly. And as I stared vacantly I felt vacant, somehow absent, not really involved in this painful and boring process. When I was called by the receptionist and entered the interviewer's office, one of the first things he said to me was, "You look like a schoolteacher." Trying to recover from my dismay, I feebly but quickly responded, "I should live so long." And then, trying to move the conversation away from that subject, I said, "Most people tell me I look like Arnie on TV," of whom he had never heard. With the informalities completed, instead of offering me factory work, he suggested I interview the next day for forklift operator at Alban Tractor Co., where I could work the 3:00 P.M. to 11:00 P.M. shift, and earn $3.20 an hour.

After indicating my interest, I was sent into the back room where a secretary had me fill out the agreement with the employment agency. Under that agreement I was obligated if I got the job to pay to the agency over a fifteen-week period a "permanent placement fee" of $300, which would be deducted by my employer from my weekly wages. In the event my employment was terminated within ninety days, however, I was obligated instead to pay a "temporary placement fee," the amount to be determined by how much I had earned and whether the termination was my fault. If I was terminated through no fault of my own, or if I voluntarily left the job with "just cause," that temporary fee was not to exceed 20 percent of my total wages received or 75 percent of $300, whichever was less. But if, as would be more likely, I was discharged "for cause" or left the job without "just

THE WORK PROCESS

cause" within ninety days, then I was liable for up to 75 percent of the permanent placement fee, for $225.

The contract seemed to me a form of extortion, a modern indenture. But I badly wanted a job and could personally tolerate the economic conditions the agency imposed. I pliantly signed and left.

After a quick lunch, I returned to Maryland Cup and waited expectantly for what seemed a long time, because the secretary was unwilling to take the initiative to advise the personnel man I was there. Finally he came out himself and asked why I was waiting. When I told him, it was clear from his response that I had the job. I had a job! He sent me to someone who prepared all my papers and gave me a packet of information. In the packet was a letter signed by the President of Maryland Cup, one "Mort Gliden," who welcomed me to the "Maryland Cup team." "Mort," apparently was just another member of "the team." Whatever, by now I was delighted to join up.

With my papers prepared, I was sent to another part of the plant to have my picture taken for my ID badge and to have my hearing tested. For the hearing test, I was given earphones, placed in a booth, and told to press a button whenever I heard the tones of varying frequency. As I concentrated to listen for the barely audible tones, I began to hold my breath, so my breathing wouldn't interfere with my hearing. I wanted the job very badly, but wasn't sure I was passing the test. Repeatedly, I didn't know whether I had heard a tone or whether the ringing was in my ears. I left the booth dejected, feeling I might well have blown it. But the tester checked my polygraph and assured me that I had very sensitive hearing, especially at high frequencies. I felt relieved. I still had the job.

So by the end of the day I had one job that was to start the following Monday and the possibility of another through the upcoming interview set up by the employment agency. Both jobs involved driving a forklift, which was OK with me, but the Maryland Cup job would soon mean commuting about an hour each way, and the Alban Tractor job, if it came through, would mean not only commuting but also working the night shift, a prospect to which neither I nor my wife Elinor looked forward. At my wife's strong urging, I therefore went down the following morning to look for a job at Blancs.* Blancs, friends who work in factories had told us, regularly hires new people, because its turnover rate is high and because it is expanding. Coincidentally, Elinor had passed one of Blancs' South Baltimore plants on the previous Saturday. That had prompted her recommendation that I give it a try.

The employment office at Blancs was a largish room with rows of elementary-school-type desk-chairs. From twelve to fifteen people were waiting there when I arrived, mostly black, mostly young, and mostly male. I filled out the application the secretary-receptionist gave me and attached my reference letter. While waiting to be called, I had one of my first conversations with another job-seeker during the three weeks I had spent waiting in employment offices. He was black, around my age, and had been looking for a job for six months without success. He was trained as a molder, but had no idea what was available at Blancs and said he was ready to take about anything. He was called first, and came out a few minutes later with a referral to one of the plant's shops. Then I was called.

The personnel interviewer, who looked to be around 55, was very personable, as usual. Of all the questions he might have asked, he asked only why my wife's last name was different from mine. Apparently satisfied with my answer, he launched into a brief, concerned introductory speech about how he sometimes felt like he was playing God. He then proceeded to inform me that a man he had just hired as a forklift driver and sent for a physical had failed his blood pressure test and might become a stroke victim if he drove a fork. Would I like the job, he asked, at $3.47 an hour? Yes, I emphatically answered. It was a day-shift job. Blancs was only about fifteen or twenty minutes' drive from my home. The salary was the best I had yet been offered. And I remembered that someone once had remarked to me that Blancs might be an interesting place to work.

The personnel officer, Mr. Smith, then sent me with a visitors' badge and a referral slip to wait at the guardhouse at the main gate to the plant. At the guardhouse I was given a pair of plastic safety glasses

---

* Blancs is not the real name of this company, where I finally worked. I have forgone using the real name at the request of my publisher.

THE WORK PROCESS

to be put on when I entered the plant. After waiting fifteen minutes, I was told to go to meet a dour, white secretary standing fifty yards away. I followed her into a high-ceilinged, one-story building, and into the air-conditioned, partitioned-off office area.

There I sat and waited for about an hour for the superintendent. During that time no one said a word to me. I was nervous as hell, not knowing what to expect. As I looked around, I could see the office obviously was a trouble-shooting–type outfit, receiving equipment parts, doing installations and repairs. The man I was waiting for came by with two other well-dressed men whom he obviously was showing around. He was tall and very imposing looking, with blondish-red hair, a ramrod straight, navy posture and a well-managed pot belly. He exuded self-confidence, efficiency, purposefulness, coolness, and ambition. He saw me and said crisply he'd be with me in a few minutes. I said OK.

A half hour later he returned to the interview and told me about the job. Basically I was to be the plant trashman, picking up and dumping hoppers full of industrial waste. Somewhat nervously I asked how long it would take to learn to operate a forklift. The superintendent, Ron Merritt, facilely replied that, since I had driven trucks before, it would take only about fifteen minutes. I was quietly skeptical. He then told me I was expected to work overtime, perhaps a couple of hours each day, either before 8:00 A.M. or after 4:30 P.M. I was also expected, he informed me, to work Saturdays. He said the plant was open seven days a week all year long. I would receive time-and-a-half for most overtime and double-time for Sundays. He emphasized that I should get to work every day on time. Blancs, he stressed, wasn't interested in "part-time help."

Although I was less than delighted to learn I was to work Saturdays, I tried not to show it. I assured Merritt I would be on time and was reliable. Merritt concluded the interview explaining to me that in the heat of the summer some of the trash I would be picking up got "very ripe." It therefore had to be collected and dumped in the compactor every day. On some days, he told me, I might have to work later, until 6:30, even 8:00 P.M. The interview concluded, I was sent back to Mr. Smith, who told me to report for my physical at the

LOOKING FOR A JOB

plant at 1:30 P.M. the following day. He reminded me to be on time, and said I would start the next Monday.

As I left the office, I felt anxious about everything: about doing damage with the forklift; about whether I was physically capable of lifting heavy things; about hurting myself; about being exposed as a fraud. The job sounded like I would be working pretty much on my own, which was very different from my original conception of the sort of work I wanted, assembly-line work. But I thought that I would take it. It would be a start.

I debated whether to go for the employment-agency-arranged interview at Alban Tractor and decided to go, if only for the experience. At Alban Tractor I had a very pleasant interview with a man who told me about the company and the opportunities for advancement. He was the only interviewer during the entire period who bothered to do that. He also said that he had a lot of young guys driving forks for him and could use an older, steadier man around. He admitted third shift was a hard one to staff. I told him, half truthfully, that the thing holding me back was whether my wife would agree to my working that shift. I was embarrassed wasting his time, since I had largely decided to take the Blancs' job if I passed the physical. I said I'd get back to him about the job, which I subsequently did.

Thus in two days my situation had changed radically. It seemed likely after three weeks with no success that I would have three job offers, all driving forks in one capacity or another. Each offer seemed to present some opportunities and to entail its own problems. That night when I returned home to discuss the choice with my wife, we quarreled badly. Elinor was glad for me that I might get a job I though I'd like, *but* she was displeased about the prospect of my having to work both Saturdays and a lot of daily overtime. More hours meant that she would have added house-related burdens and that I would be around less. Most particularly, it meant that if, as I hoped, Soren, my ten-year-old son from a former marriage, came to live with us for the coming school year, Elinor would have the added burden of having to care for my son before and/or after school while I might still be at work. I didn't know what to say. Her feelings and anxieties were so reasonable. We agreed, at least, that on no account would I take a job that required working third shift. Elinor seemed a bit relieved. It was obvious, however, that whichever of the three jobs I took would seriously impinge on our family life. I knew millions of other Americans had to accept and tolerate those incursions, but that didn't make it any easier for us. It's especially hard on the family, I realized, if there are children, if both spouses work and if neither is a martyr, as in our case.

The next afternoon I returned to Blancs with a new worry and a new decision to be made. The insurance form I had had to fill out for Blancs threatened to expose my true background through my Johns Hopkins University Blue Cross/Blue Shield affiliation. If I admitted to being insured by Johns Hopkins, the jig surely would be up. So I decided to state on the form that I carried no insurance, a gamble that paid off.

Upon arriving at the Blancs' guardhouse at 1:25 P.M., I was directed to the plant medical center. Two men were already waiting there, one the man I had spoken with the day before. Both were friendly. I was given an eye test and an ear test. And then we just waited. Soon there were eight of us, and we waited for more than an hour. I was getting angry at being kept waiting for so long once again. I guess I took it personally, as if this occasion was being used yet again to tell me that I didn't matter.

Finally the doctor, who I later learned didn't go on duty til 3:00 P.M., arrived. He took us into his office in groups of four. In my group we each stripped to the waist. He lined us up and proceeded to check our heartbeat with a stethoscope. Then he checked us each for hernia, checking our testicles with his hand, without washing between examinations. I almost complained, but decided I wouldn't be the first. No one else spoke up. Then we were told to urinate on a plastic strip with two color patches on it. We did so in the bathroom, where it became clear that the other men also were very angry at the way the doctor had handled us, politely, but as if we were dumb animals. "Like being in the army," one said.

Before completing the physical, the doctor examined my hands and noticed my bad finger. He had me sign a waiver so that the company couldn't he held liable for prior damage should there be any further injury to the finger while I worked for Blancs.

After the physical we went back to Smith in personnel, where we were given a packet of information about working for Blancs, including a bound copy of our union's contract with the company. Like children, we were advised to put our employment slips in our wallets so we wouldn't lose them. And then Smith mechanically read us information about safety, safety shoes, injury reports, the union—it's a union shop—and so forth. He barely looked at us while he read. Finished, he asked if there were any questions. There were none.

My search for a job was over. While looking, I had learned several things. First, that companies consistently show a lack of concern about making prospective employees wait. The only time that counts is company time. Second, that whatever differences may have existed between the way I previously had been socialized to think and feel about work and the way most Americans who have to seek and hold so-called blue- and lower-white-collar jobs have been socialized, the common experience of looking for a job willy-nilly subjects all to an intimidating introduction to the facts of work life. Although I imagined I had not been socialized by my prior life to accept so little, after only three weeks I was close to accepting whatever I could get. By then I dimly sensed what those I had seen staring vacantly in numerous personnel offices may have understood all too well: that the power to make crucial life decisions about work was in someone else's hands. The unavoidable message of the experience of looking for a job is that what you are worth and what you will do is not something men and women like you will decide. You can only decide whether to accept or decline what is offered you. Powerless and in need, it is hardly surprising that job seekers respond to these conditions by staring vacantly. Separation of the self from the experience is one of the few forms of self-protection available.

If this is what looking for a job is like, is there, I wondered, any relation between that experience and the experience of working on the job itself? I would soon know. In three days, on Monday, July 8, at 8:00 A.M., I was to start work.

THE WORK PROCESS

II

Being Broken In:
The First Two Weeks

THE first two weeks at Blancs primarily were spent learning the routine, trying frantically to catch up on missed years of working-class socialization and experiences with machines, coping with a variety of disruptive events, meeting fellow employees, and trying to manage the intense emotions generated in me by these phenomena.

I reported for my first day on the job after a nervous weekend during which I had indulged my fear of the unknown. Picking up my badge at the guardhouse, I went to Ron Merritt's office in the Service Department, where my superintendent introduced me to my foreman, Sam Leonard, who had me wait a few minutes and then, in turn, introduced me to the current trashman, Bryan Morton. Morton, as he was called, was to break me in. When Sam told him to teach me the routine, Morton asked if he should let me operate the fork on the first day. Sam answered yes. By so doing, Morton later confided to me, he shifted the responsibility for whatever damage I might do with the fork to Sam.

From that initial brief talk with Sam, the main message that stuck in my mind, which Morton reinforced by repeating several times during the morning, was, "Watch out for the rings." Piston rings in all sizes are what the plant daily produces by the thousands. The rings in process are simply piled up on the floor or stacked on racks of several sorts and deposited all over the plant's main production and inspection areas. Viewed from the vantage point of a fork driver's seat, these main areas look like a sea of stacked rings, crisscrossed by more open but crowded aisles as wide as 15 feet, and dotted with a variety of workbenches and one-person machines, the tops of which, along with the heads of workers, are visible at a distance over the rings.

Morton began breaking me in by showing me where to sign in and out each morning and afternoon. Then he took me to First Aid to get my own pair of safety glasses, which were to be worn at all times in the production and inspection areas of the plant. Finally, he led me to the fork I was to drive. The good fork, he explained, was broken, so we had to use the older, bigger one, which doesn't have an automatic clutch. That fork, number 116, like most, has one gear in forward and one in reverse, plus a low gear for going up inclines and carrying heavy loads. The other levers on the towmotor adjust the height and pitch of the two fork blades. After demonstrating how to operate it, Morton quickly got me up in the operator's seat. For the rest of the day he continued to give me instructions, advice, and warnings on what to do and what not to do, as well as directions on where to go next. But from perhaps ten o'clock on I did much of the driving. In learning the routine I encountered four main difficulties, some of which were overcome with time but others of which persisted.

First, I had to learn to operate the fork, which was largely a matter of practice and experience. Although its operation could not be mastered in fifteen minutes, as the superintendent had seemed to suggest, the simple mechanics of operating it could be learned quickly and then routinized. The art of driving it could be acquired within a few months. In learning to operate the fork I had to cope with several problems. Compared to a car, the fork had an incredibly small turning radius; it could turn on a dime. That meant, however, that the back end of the fork, if not controlled, could swing out wildly while the five-foot blades in the front mowed down anything in their path. In addition, frontal vision was somewhat obstructed even when the blades were empty, and when I was carrying a hopper up front, vision could be badly obstructed. Consequently, it was often necessary to drive the fork backward when it was loaded, which not only improved vision but also increased maneuverability. Getting

THE WORK PROCESS

accustomed to driving backward took a while. Finally, clearances between the fork and its load, on the one hand, and walls, machines,
employees, and goods waiting to be processed, on the other, were
frequently only an inch or two on either side.

Second, I had to learn the route to be followed to get to each of
my twenty or so Honda-Civic-sized hoppers. The hoppers were located both inside and outside of the various buildings that were
joined together essentially into two elongated structures, set one on
each side of an internal, outdoor 250-yard roadway that bisected the
entire plant. The inside hoppers were located off one of a number of
aisles, some set at open intersections, others perpendicular or parallel
to walls, and still others tucked into quite inaccessible corners. On
that first day, as I followed Morton's directions, I completely lost any
sense of where I was, feeling as if I were being directed in one
overhead door and out another through a complicated maze of aisles.
By lunch I felt I had been in and out of 15 separate buildings, and I
knew at that moment that I would have been unable to find one-half
of the hoppers I had dumped that morning. Sam had said it would
take about a week to learn the route. Morton reassured me that I was
doing OK and that by midweek I would get the route down.

Third, I had to learn how to dump the hoppers into the compactor and how to pack the 12-ton container so it could be taken out
when full, dumped, and returned empty. Dumping the hoppers
required driving the fork up the short, narrow compactor ramp while
raising the blades with the hopper on them, then parking the fork,
tilting the blades down toward the compactor bin, and finally getting
off the fork and improvising with a two-by-four to lift the hopper's
release lever so the hopper would dump. Often, because hoppers
were imbalanced and would not dump, I had to push them over bod-
ily. The dumping task was further complicated by the several sizes of
hoppers, by the absence of an emergency brake on the fork I was
operating (which meant it had to be left in gear), and by the absence
of its ignition key so that the fork had to be started and turned off
with a rasp inserted into the ignition, a makeshift that repeatedly fell
out at crucial moments.

Fourth, I had to learn to avoid the omnipresent stacks of rings.

THE FIRST TWO WEEKS

The stacks, I was told, toppled easily and the rings were easily nicked and damaged. If they became so damaged that they had to be melted down and reproduced, the cost, I was told, could run into thousands of dollars. On that first day, I remember vividly, the rings were what terrorized me most. The thought of smashing into a stack as I painfully maneuvered my fork to make a pickup or dropoff intimidated me every minute of the day. Compared to this newly inculcated and overwhelming concern for the rings, my concern for the safety of pedestrians seemed almost marginal. Just beep, I was told by several coworkers, and pedestrians will get out of your way.

The essence of the trashman's job is keeping the hoppers empty. In seven months on the job I dumped at least 3000 hoppers. The task of dumping is more complicated than it might sound. At the risk of belaboring it, let me describe the process. One hopper I had to dump early each day was located up front in a building on the opposite side of the road from the compactor building. To get to it, I followed Morton that first morning down the road toward the main gate, turned left around an outside ring-storage area, went down a narrower road, passed the company gas pump, made a left through another outside storage area, and then came to one of the seven or eight large overhead doors that were my means of ingress and egress from buildings. At that point, Morton had me get down while he demonstrated how to get the hopper. It required the following steps: turning the fork around; backing through the door with the empty hopper I had carried there; executing a 90-degree turn to the left, being careful to avoid the sides of the door and whatever else might be in the doorway area; backing about twenty yards down a narrow aisle dotted with stacks of rings that seemed to have been deposited along its length helter-skelter; raising the hopper to avoid hitting rings that could not be cleared; lowering the hopper to avoid hitting overhead fluorescent lights; backing down a ramp and into a tight corner to the left of the full hopper that was to be picked up; making a difficult turn into the aisle perpendicular to the one I backed down; dropping the empty hopper nearby in that second aisle; backing up carefully to avoid the pillar and stacks of rings on two sides in the aisle; making a sharp left turn to approach the full hopper; maneuver-

THE WORK PROCESS

ing the fork and lowering the blades to insert them into the bottom of the full hopper; tilting and lifting the blades to pick up the full hopper; backing up so as to position the fork to drive out forward, up the aisle by which I entered; driving up that aisle a few yards and dropping the full hopper; disengaging the fork from that hopper; backing up and turning into the perpendicular aisle to approach the empty hopper; picking up that hopper; backing up to the position opposite where the hopper had to be deposited; turning and driving forward to get to the position to drop the empty hopper; dropping the hopper and disengaging; backing up to the corner opposite the hopper, still being very careful; turning left and going forward up the ramp and the entrance aisle; picking up the full hopper and continuing up the entrance aisle, raising and lowering the hopper to avoid both rings and ceiling lights, respectively; executing a very tight left turn out the overhead; and then driving the fork with the loaded hopper back to and halfway up the main road away from the front gate; making a left turn through another overhead into the building where the compactor is; driving down the main aisle through the Final Inspections Department; making a left near the end of that aisle; driving forward and through another internal overhead door; making a sharp right into the compactor room; driving up the ramp to the compactor; putting on my gloves; dumping the hopper; turning on the compactor until the materials were pressed into the outside container; switching off the compactor; throwing some chemical salts into the empty hopper to cover trash odors; taking off my gloves; starting the fork and backing it down the ramp; and then going off to dump another hopper.

That particular process, which might be considered challenging but hardly rewarding, had to be repeated, with variations, about twenty times a day. It could be done in an average of, say, 20 minutes. In those first days it took me more like 45. Although not all the other hoppers involved such an intricate routine, each hopper involved its own distinctive routine with its peculiar difficulties. Many hoppers, in their own way, were at least as difficult to manage as the one described.

During that first day, needless to say, I felt extremely harried. I

THE FIRST TWO WEEKS

hardly wanted to take the two 10-minute breaks allowed during the day, one at 9:20 A.M. and the other at 2:20 P.M. I wasn't hungry at lunch, for which we were allotted an unpaid half-hour between 12:20 and 12:50. By lunch time we had picked up and dumped seven or eight hoppers, but I knew we still had to clean out the two cafeterias after lunch and then dump the remaining hoppers. I had to force myself to take the entire lunch hour, spending the first 25 minutes in one of the crowded, blistering hot cafeterias eating and observing, and the last 5 minutes back in the Service Department, where a number of my co-workers were playing a few snatched minutes of cards; bidwhist, I think it was.

After lunch, Morton and I began to clear out the empty cartons and to clean out the six or eight trashcans and garbage pails in each cafeteria. Although the cafeterias had not been serviced since Saturday, cleaning them in no sense was obnoxious. For the trashcans, the process involved lifting the outside of each trashcan up and off its inside container and removing the large plastic bag inside the container. All the trash-filled bags, cartons, and garbage pails were dumped in hoppers outside the cafeterias. Both cafeterias were to be cleaned out and their hoppers dumped by two o'clock or so, Morton told me, so that we could then return to finish off the rest of the plant's hoppers.

The afternoon seemed a bit easier than the morning, as I began to get the feel of it. Several men approached me to talk, one of whom had held the job before. He indicated it was a dead-end job, not easy to get off of. He also told me that to do the job I'd have to figure out my own pace and system. Soon after, Morton unantagonistically advised me not to talk much to other guys during working time unless I was ahead of schedule.

The last part of the afternoon passed fairly easily. It was very hot and humid, but for some reason it didn't bother me too much. I just kept drinking a lot of water and sweating. During the final hours of the first day I was mostly on my own, with Morton just telling me where to go and what hoppers to pick up or re-pick up. He'd meet me where I was supposed to go and then meet me again someplace else when I was done dumping the hopper. About 4:00 we knocked

THE WORK PROCESS

off, and he began filling out our time cards. Work officially stopped at 4:20. But after 4:00 we just killed time, standing around near the compactor, talking a bit. Morton had been on the fork for about a year and, as soon as I was trained, would move up a grade to his new job as machine oiler. At the end of the day I thanked Morton, who didn't seem to want my thanks. He said he was just doing what Sam, our foreman, told him to do. At 4:20 we went back to Sam's office to ask for a locker for me. Sam told Morton to show me where the lockers were, which he did, and then we split. As my final act of the day, I went to First Aid to order a pair of safety shoes, the cost of which would be deducted from my wages and for which, I was told, I would have to wait about two weeks.

All in all, it had been a hard but decent first day. It certainly could have been much worse. Morton, I could see, got his job done reasonably efficiently and with as little effort and time spent on it as possible in order to have some time to hide when he got ahead of schedule.

I began work the next day at 6:00 A.M. My hours, I learned, would be 8:00 A.M. to 4:30 P.M. Monday, 6:00 A.M. to 4:30 P.M. Tuesday through Friday, and 6:00 A.M. to 2:30 P.M. Saturday. It was unlikely I would have to work more than those hours, Morton informed me, since additional hours would involve getting paid double-time, and "the company don't want to pay a trashman double-time." Thank God! Fifty-six hours a week was quite enough for me.

Beginning work at 6:00 A.M. was good, though it meant getting up five days a week at 4:40 and leaving the house without any contact with my wife and son. At that time of the morning it was cool, the plant was fairly empty, and it was easier to get around to do the job. Besides, getting in a couple of productive early morning hours made me feel like I had a jump on the day. By eight o'clock it was already hot as the devil. The fans inside the plant moved the hot air around some, and it wasn't at all bad while I was up on the fork moving. But, in any event, I was concentrating on the job too much to pay much attention to the heat. By eleven o'clock, five hours into the day's job, I was wishing it was lunch time, though I was coming along all right

THE FIRST TWO WEEKS

with the fork. Morton even complimented me. A stranger watching me move around in a tight spot spontaneously said to me, "Good work." That felt fine.

I still had to learn the maze, however. As I got a little time to think about the job, I wondered why we didn't pick up the hoppers in the tightest areas early in the morning before most machine operators, truckers, and other fork drivers get in. That thought, I realized somewhat later, was the beginning of working out my own system for doing the job.

I had lunch with one of the muscled, young, black guys who had undergone the physical exam with me. He was from Alabama and we talked about the differences between the North and the South, which he said was less violent. After lunch Marbles, a union official, who worked as a janitor in the plant, called me over to his table to say my shop steward would be contacting me by the twentieth of the month to sign me up for the union. I said OK, though my lunch mate had indicated he wasn't eager to give up the compulsory $25 union initiation fee and the $8.50 a month in checkoff dues.

By around three o'clock our container at the compactor was filled, so we couldn't dump any more trash in the compactor. Thereafter we just moved around for a while and then sat down outside on benches along the roadway with a bunch of other guys who also were waiting in the heat for the work day to end. For many, work simply stopped before time was up, and men sat, stood, and chatted, looking from time to time to see whether their foreman or superintendent was coming.

While we were sitting another stranger came over to me and in a friendly way told me I hadn't put my fork blades down right. I went to the fork and put them down, following another guy's directions about getting them flat so no one would trip on them. As Morton came by, one of the men told him he should have showed me how to leave the blades. Morton said he had showed me, though I didn't recall, and later told him so. He repeated he had told me; I let it go, realizing that Morton doesn't make mistakes.

The next day was another scorcher, well into the 90s. That morning I began to write out the route and the routine of how to handle each hopper, no doubt an intellectual's response to a laborer's task. As I went through the routine, I got angry at myself for getting into jams with the fork and having to rely a few times on Morton to get me out. I also got angry at some undefined "others" for leaving rings in the aisle, swearing out loud to an unkind fate. At times I felt I wanted to throw up my hands in total frustration with the conditions of the work process. Morton seemed able to make the fork go anywhere. I could not. For myself, I realized that it frequently was worth the trouble and time to check out an area first before I came into it with the fork, moving what obstacles I could out of the way so I would have a relatively unobstructed ingress and egress. The problem was that moving stacks of rings myself was still nerve-wracking, and if I wanted the truckers to move them I had to ask them, which, having their own work to do, they didn't always appreciate.

That morning, like many others thereafter, just wasn't my morning. For the first time, I knocked down some rings. The rings shouldn't have been where they were, but Morton had just shouted, "Watch out," as my back wheel went over the bottom of the stand on which the rings were stacked. Morton was angry, but after my first feelings of deep apprehension, I was actually a bit relieved since I had expected the wrath of the gods to descend upon me, what with all the fuss everyone had made about hitting rings. We picked them up, apparently undamaged, and had the rest of the rings moved out of the way. I dutifully reported the incident to Sam, who was unperturbed.

Shortly thereafter, as I was passing through the overhead door leading toward the compactor area, the sliding, rippled metal door crashed down on the fork's protective frame above my seat. Apparently, unnoticed, one of the pull-chains hanging down on either side of the overhead had gotten caught in the fork frame, and my moving forward had jerked the chain, bringing the door down over me. Fortunately, the door didn't jam, and with some help from others I extricated the fork after the door had been raised. I considered putting a plastic covering over the fork frame to prevent a chain from getting caught again in the frame.

Just after that, as I was making a sharp swing outside on the road with a hopper on the front of the fork, the hopper flew off the blades.

THE FIRST TWO WEEKS

It scared the hell out of me since someone could have been seriously hurt or something badly damaged. I had neglected to tilt the blades back far enough to prevent the hopper from becoming dislodged as I swung around. I resolved to be more careful and alert after that.

By lunch time I was feeling better, less inadequate, as the routine went more smoothly. The afternoon passed quickly. I worked hard and more efficiently. I dumped about 22 hoppers in the compactor that day, about average. When I had 40 in the compactor I called Sam, who then called Robb Tyler, Inc., the container service company, which later sent a truck to pick up, dump, and return the empty container.

In those early days everything was new to me, the particular physical tasks, doing manual labor, being a trashman, everything. My reactions to these aspects of the job were intense. With each hopper I dumped efficiently, I felt a sharp sense of tangible accomplishment and, as hopper followed hopper, a growing capacity to handle the job. Far from bothering me, the physical work actually gave me pleasure and I felt joy in becoming aware of my body again after so many years. By contrast, I did not like hiding and standing around looking busy, and resolved to adjust Morton's schedule to cut the hiding time to enable me to do my job more cautiously. As one kind of experience in a lifetime, I was rather enjoying the job, notwithstanding the frustrations, anxieties, and demands on my time. But to have to do this for a lifetime, to know that one's life would be measured out in trash hoppers, seemed inconceivable to me in those first days on the job.

During that day I had learned a few very simple things about the fork: how much air to put in the tires, which deflated almost overnight; where and how to get gas for the fork, and where to put it. I looked forward to getting the regular fork back, since it was smaller, supposedly easier to handle, and had an emergency brake and an automatic clutch. But in retrospect I was not sorry to have been broken in on the clumsier, older fork, expecting that shifting from the 116 to the regular fork, like swinging a regular bat after swinging the heavier lead-weighted bat in baseball, would make the smaller fork seem that much more manageable.

THE WORK PROCESS

By the fourth day I was relying more on my notes regarding the route and details for dumping each hopper than on Morton directly. I didn't need his help much that day, so we talked more about working for Blancs. Morton told me the union was lousy, a "company union," he called it. Union meetings, which are held once a month on Sunday mornings, are "bullshit," he said. There had been a short strike last November and might be another this year. The reason the union was after me to sign up fast, he declared, was so that if I got fired during my 60-day probationary period with the company, it could still get its cut out of me.

Some time later in the day Sam ordered us to take an empty hopper over to where several men were sweeping up street trash, to wait until it was filled and then to dump it. At first I resented the interruption in the routine, the performance of which I saw as my responsibility. Morton, however, did not seem to mind the interruption at all. For him, working time was working time. And he knew better than I that our foreman was, indeed, our boss: that what Sam said went, and that as long as we followed Sam's orders we were covered.

Friday, like the day before, passed rather smoothly. The only events of note were Morton's wanting to deliver the compactor key to me in front of Sam so the transfer of responsibility would be official, and my advising Sam that the big hopper from the Chrome Department was very difficult to dump. Morton had been having trouble dumping that hopper but had never complained. He said that when we got the regular forklift back the hopper would dump OK. But in the interim I was afraid of injuring myself while trying to push the hopper over to dump it. In response to my telling Sam the hopper didn't work right, Sam called Morton in alone and, according to Morton, chewed him out. Morton apparently didn't back me up, saying he had been able to dump it all right. As a consequence, Sam confronted me, asking how come Morton could dump the hopper and I couldn't. He said he wanted to see the hopper the following day. I told Morton he should have backed me up, called him a "motherfucker," and was cool to him for the rest of the day.

On Saturday, I had to dump all the hoppers in eight hours instead of the usual ten. Fortunately Morton offered to help out with another fork. The five or six hoppers he leisurely dumped eased the burden considerably. He seemed to regret not having backed me up the day before, and we had a good day together. At lunchtime he introduced me formally to the heads of the two cafeterias. With him leaving, he said for the first time, I would get free snacks and free lunches there—trashman's perquisites. He also got a pickax and chopped out the quick-dry cement that had solidified in the bottom of the foul-smelling Chrome hopper, making it so difficult to dump.

Morton knew his job well. Although he didn't express ideas or even directions with any clarity, he was able to show me how to do various routine tasks and how to cope with whatever concrete problems came up during the week. He also gave me more general advice about not taking on work that wasn't my responsibility, since, he warned, if I started to do so everyone would take advantage of me. Morton was my only teacher on the job and he taught me well, almost exclusively through practical, on-the-job training. But whatever problems had not arisen while carrying out the routine during that first week, I realized even then, would be problems that in the future I would not know how to deal with.

With this awareness, I encouraged Morton on Saturday to notify Sam that the fork seemed to be losing power. When I first noticed the loss, I wondered what it might be. I didn't know anything about machines, but I didn't want to advertise my total ignorance to my foreman. On the other hand, I also didn't want to simply wait for the fork to break down if there was something that could be done to revive it. I thought perhaps I had been operating the fork incorrectly, that I might have been driving it in low or something. On checking with Morton, however, that proved not to be the case. It worried me that I might come in on Monday, more or less on my own, and find the fork dead. So, shortly after Morton mentioned the problem to Sam, I stopped by the office and told Sam I thought we were going to have trouble with the fork. Sam responded, almost offhandedly, that we were having trouble with everything, as if he couldn't be bothered with the problems of my fork. From his perspective I'm sure he had other more pressing breakdowns and responsibilities, but from my perspective as a new and inexperienced worker nothing could have been more pressing than being assured of having a working forklift. My needs, however, were subordinated in the nature of things to my foreman's. That day I began to suspect repairs were not likely to be made on the fork until it actually broke down. I worried about that over the weekend.

The weekend didn't begin until three o'clock Saturday afternoon when I arrived home from work. It passed as if it had never existed, without giving me time to really relax, to feel away from the routine. This reinforced my dominant impression of the week. Working 56 hours a week on the job, plus 3 hours of unpaid lunch hours, plus about 50 minutes a day commuting, and another half hour every day cleaning up after work, I was putting 67 *hours a week into work*. I had to get up about 2 hours before my wife on 5 days of the week and leave the house without seeing her or my son. And by the time I came home, cleaned up, and spent a half-hour typing up my notes for the day, I was too tired after supper to do anything but stare at the tube until eight-thirty or nine o'clock, when I often fell asleep.

It was no way to nourish a marriage, no way to raise a family, or for that matter, to do anything else. Except for shopping at super- markets that are open all kinds of hours, I could hardly run errands, go see a doctor, or do anything in the community. I found myself unable or unwilling to read newspapers, though I had been accus- tomed for years to reading the *New York Times* every day. I found myself torn between spending those few precious hours of waking leisure with my son, with my wife, or by myself. I found myself, in short and with some important differences no doubt, trying to live with drastically curtailed and compressed free time, as millions of American workers have learned to live, snatching moments of per- sonal satisfaction largely from time not sold to others. And my family found itself struggling to adjust to a situation that repeatedly threat- ened to effectively turn me into an absentee father and an absentee husband.

With the abbreviated weekend over, the second week on the job began as expected. The fork was "down," marking a poor beginning to what turned out to be one of my worst weeks at work. I killed time until the fork was repaired by the company mechanics, walking my route, checking the hoppers, and wondering when I could get back to work. At morning break I spoke to a middle-aged black worker who had been with the company for some years. He said the only way he could make ends meet was to work overtime, that he couldn't hack it on 40 hours. He was angry and dissatisfied with his lot, saying he had in the past voted for a strike every chance he had. He hoped we would have another strike this year.

By ten-thirty I was back at work. I worked entirely on my own all day. Despite the delay, the routine went fairly well. I dumped about seventeen hoppers, which is adequate for a Monday, the slowest day of the week on trash.

Tuesday began deceptively well, but as I was going through the overhead door near the compactor room, the pullchains must have caught again in the fork's top frame, and the overhead door crashed down on the frame, this time jamming badly. I tried to fix it, with the gracious help of the foreman in the area, but the door wouldn't unjam. I called Sam to report it, and he reacted like a sonofabitch. He asked me, "How come all these things have started to happen since you're here?" It was hardly a question I could answer, and I told him the problem with the door wasn't my fault. He hung up on me. I went over to the office to talk to him, where he had me sit and cool my heels, talking to me intermittently when he wasn't otherwise occupied, which was rare. We had a long, interrupted talk in which I said I tried to do my job and wasn't lazy or especially weak. "What about the Chrome hopper you complained about?" he retorted. Morton, he said, had been there for a year and had had no complaints. Then he put it to me: "If you don't like the job," he flatly stated, "now is the time to tell me." I felt abused and cornered, blamed for two things that weren't my fault, and responded angrily striking out at the absent Morton, which was stupid and unfair. Morton, I said, didn't know enough to come in from the rain. Sam got madder, saying Morton had done a good job for him. I apologized and indicated I thought Morton had done a good job training me, but that I was using the old, clumsy fork. Many of the hoppers in fact didn't dump well, I said, but I hadn't complained about them. The Chrome hopper really was too tough to dump and therefore a safety risk. Sam conceded that the hoppers were built in such a way that if loaded incorrectly they could be very hard to tilt. I said I understood, but that the Chrome hopper's problem was beyond that. Then he shifted the topic somewhat, asking me about the fork's having lost power, which turned out to be due to a slipped clutch. Again he appeared to blame me. I was incredulous and incensed. How, I asked, could I have done all that damage to that old machine in six days? He said the engine was idling too fast and I therefore probably had to play the clutch more than I should have. I should have told him, he said, about the idle. I replied that I'd never driven a fork before, and was concentrating on other things that first week. He said I had driven a motorcycle and a car and should have known. And so it went.

Sam ended the conversation indicating he was merely trying to find out why all these things had happened. He denied being sarcastic. I told him that asking someone why all these things are happening now that you're here is not exactly a question one can answer. I was pissed off, but only half showed it. Why, I wondered to myself, was he intent on blaming me for these mishaps? And was it really true that these breakdowns began when I took the job?

No matter, I was depressed for most of the remainder of the day. Sam sent a man over to fix the pullchains, who told me the fork I was using was higher than the one normally used, which is why the chain got caught in it. To try to prevent a reoccurrence, the man repaired and raised the chain. Later in the day the container was picked up, which cost me more time.

The daily mishaps, along with my foreman's disapproval, were getting me down. Nevertheless, I realized, despite such interruptions I could do the job adequately within the allotted time. So that wasn't the main problem. The hardest thing seemed to be adjusting emotionally to that endless series of disruptions in my routine, many of which were beyond my control. Breakdowns, added tasks, delays, obstructions. And no one really to blame, including myself. That's the way the job is, I realized intellectually. No sooner did I think I had the routine knocked, then something else went wrong. And as often

THE FIRST TWO WEEKS

44

as not when I took a problem to my foreman, the man to whom I was supposed to take job problems, he seemed too busy to be bothered, though not too busy to note it for later use against me.

As the day passed, I tried to assess how many of my difficulties were of my own making. I might well have contributed marginally to the deterioration of the clutch, for example. I did tend to complain more often than others. I probably did have an "I-rate-special-treatment," complaining approach to the job and life. I resolved to try to discipline myself, to lay low and cover myself. Talking about the problems with a fellow worker, I was reminded both that I had no rights while I was on probation, and, on the other hand, that my foreman had not as yet given me any warning slips. Still, I was skating on thin ice during this 60-day probation period and, Elinor and I agreed when I got home that evening, I might just get fired.

The following day was a relief. Few problems. The routine went well. By eleven o'clock I had nearly completed the morning routine and was trying to kill some time, which in those first weeks didn't come easy to me. Finishing up before lunch, I barely tapped a wall that looked like any other wall until a woman came out from behind it to explain that on the other side of that wall were rings hanging on nails in the wall. Again I was reminded that there is no telling when and from what sources trouble can come. Constant alertness is required, and yet the tasks must be routinized, making it difficult to keep alert.

During the day I spoke to two co-workers. One, a young movement type, warned me to watch out for certain workers like Marbles, the union committeeman who had earlier approached me. Those guys, he claimed, in effect spy for the company. The other, as we were talking about my problems with Sam, gave me advice I subsequently heard over and over again on the job: generally avoid all foremen. Sam, this man claimed, liked to exercise his authority and power, whether a worker was at fault or not. Partly out of my own exasperation and partly to see the response, I asked, "But what do they want from us, blood?" "They want it all," he replied.

Them and us. Whatever the complexities of the relationship between workers and management, it was becoming clear to me, as never before, that indeed it was them against us. And by the middle of my second week on the job I could see that many of my co-workers almost unavoidably saw the work world as divided in the same way.

I came in to work the next day determined to work efficiently and to avoid calling my foreman's attention to me. After dumping three hoppers, I drove over to get the hopper outside the service shop. As I approached the hopper, one of the men taking an early break nearby informed me that there were no lug nuts on my front left wheel. I got down from the fork with a sinking feeling in my stomach. All six of the lug nuts were off. One man speculated they had been stolen; another that a mechanic who had fixed the tire at some point might have neglected to replace the nuts. A third thought it was sabotage, perhaps directed against me personally. In any event, the fork was unsafe to drive.

I dreaded telling Sam when he came in around 7:40. At the suggestion of one of the workers, I retraced the route looking for the lug nuts. I found two or three of them, where they had obviously rolled away from the moving fork. The company mechanic gave me another couple, though he doubted they would fit my wheel. They didn't. So there was no alternative.

When Sam came in, I went over and told him. He turned around without speaking and walked away. Later, in talking with one of the mechanics, I was told Sam had blamed me for this problem, too, saying I had probably been driving too fast, that I was working the old fork too hard, both of which were untrue and nothing short of ridiculous as explanations for the lug nuts coming off. Sam seemed to want to blame someone. The dominant fact, however, was that the fork hadn't been kept up decently and was in lousy shape.

But I knew, on the other hand, that I was not completely free of fault. Earlier that morning as I had been picking up my first hopper I had heard a sound as if something metal had hit the ground. I had ignored it, assuming the sound had been caused by my running over some piece of metal on the pavement. Then, as I was cleaning up around the hopper, I saw two large nuts and assuming they had produced the noise, but thinking nothing else about them, I threw

THE FIRST TWO WEEKS

them into the trash. If I had had more experience with machines, I probably would have recognized them for what they were and checked my own wheels. Needless to say, I did not confess this to Sam or anyone else. And anyway, why had six lug nuts almost simultaneously come loose in the first place? No way I could be to blame for that.

But self-righteousness was no defense against the events of the day, which quickly went from bad to worse. The front wheel rim, it turned out, was damaged and could not be fixed, because the holes for the hub bolts had become elongated. One mechanic at the garage assured me that the problem was of long standing and the lug nuts had probably worked themselves loose over time. Regardless, I had to wait for an outside mechanic to come in to do the repair job. When he arrived, he casually informed me that there "wasn't much left of the tire either," a characterization that seemed more broadly descriptive of the state of most of our equipment. Shortly after my fork went, another fork in the department also broke down.

I had to spend the rest of the day killing time, loafing. It was very hard for me, not even being able to perform as a trashman. I moved around the plant from spot to spot, not knowing many workers, and at times feeling as out of place as a leper. I continued to worry, with new cause, that Sam might fire me. At one point when my super, Ron Merritt, called me over, I thought, "This is it," but it wasn't. He merely wanted to inquire whether a set of keys that had been found was mine. It was. I thanked him and simultaneously recognized the loss of the keys as symptomatic of my disorientation.

The only good thing about not being able to do my job that day was that it freed me to talk more to other employees. Feeling badly, I sometimes sought their sympathy and advice. Several assured me there was no way Sam could blame me for the loss of the lug nuts, but my impression was that he did, which really bothered me. The fact, hidden from my fellow workers, that I had somewhat contributed to the loss, also bothered me, making me feel incompetent. I feared my mistake being exposed, and relatedly and more profoundly I continued to fear being exposed myself as an imposter. I felt very vulnerable. In dealing with authority figures in the exercise of their power and authority over me in the past, I had relied heavily for protection upon my own capacity to perform competently and upon my related sense of independence. In this job, however, I was very dependent upon factors beyond my control and often beyond my understanding and competence.

My problems in dealing with power holders, however, obviously were not unique. One worker who had been at the plant for more than five years said he had had trouble with Sam for about three years until he decided to simply do whatever Sam told him to. "If Sam says jump off the roof, I'll do it," he says, "since I'm getting paid to obey Sam."

More than that, the demoralization I felt after only nine days on the job seemed to be widely felt. As several of us that day discussed working, one worker who had been with the company more than 20 years said that "that's 20 years too long, but it's too late to do anything else." In talking about the equipment, he said that in all the time he'd been there he'd seen the plant buy only a couple of brand-new forks. Instead, they bought second-hand forks, and the Service Department often got hand-me-down forks from other departments no longer willing to use them. About the very crowded conditions in the plant, he said that each time the plant was expanded, conditions quickly seemed to get more crowded than before.

The discussion tentatively confirmed a suspicion that had been growing day by day in me. Given the conditions, the trick in working is to not care about doing a good job. Do what you have to. Getting by is what counts, and practically speaking, that's all there is for most workers. By contrast, trying to do a good job is too frustrating and not rewarding. Put in your hours. Don't become too involved in your work. And try to leave the work world behind you as soon as you go out the gate.

Trouble is, the next day there it is again. And my next day began as the last one had ended, with my fork still out of commission and no way to know when it would be operational again. I walked my route, planning which hoppers to dump first, while half expecting at any moment to get the ax from Sam.

About eight-thirty I was paged and told by Sam to use a rented

THE FIRST TWO WEEKS

forklift. When I asked for someone to show me how to operate it, Sam did. He then made a little joke about my having had to "hump the trash on my back" the day before, which made me feel a bit less tense about the job. I adjusted to the new fork fairly quickly. Using a different fork, however, interfered in small but tangible ways with my routine. Different forks have different specifications and personalities, different turning radii, different widths, different blade sizes, and different positioning and modes of operation of levers. Since routine is the heart of the trashman's job, such interference with the routine is not only mildly troublesome, it also increases the probability of accidents.

Moreover, the horn on the rental fork was out of order. I angrily drove it that way for a brief period, anxious all the while that someone would pop out of one of the blind aisle crossings and walk in front of my moving fork. But what could I do? No way I would bother Sam with the problem if I could help it. Concerned with my predicament, I asked advice from a savvy fellow worker, who said I definitely should tell Sam, to put the responsibility on him, not me, if something happened. I could see he was right, so I told Sam, who took it in stride and told me, perfunctorily, I thought, to use the fork but to be careful at cross aisles. I drove as carefully as I could, but driving without a horn down crowded factory aisles is dangerous per se. At lunch another worker I told about the situation said I had been right to lay it on Sam. Then he swore at the Union Safety Committee, which apparently was supposed to check equipment out before we used it. I got through the rest of the day without any other mishaps.

Saturday morning Elinor, who needed the car, got up early and drove me down to work. When I arrived, I learned from Sam that I hadn't been posted to work that Saturday. Then I understood why he had asked me to work two extra hours of overtime the evening before. Nevertheless, I was delighted to have the day off. As I left the plant, the guard at the gate asked me where I was going. I told him I had the day off, naively surprised that they checked up on employees leaving the plant at odd hours, like truant officers checking to see if kids are playing hookey.

THE WORK PROCESS

That was how my first two weeks at Blancs ended. The plant was about to begin its two-week summer shutdown, during which it would be out of production and most employees would be taking their vacations. Those working were mostly either Service Department employees, who would be doing maintenance and cleanup and moving heavy machinery, or other workers who hadn't been on the job long enough to have earned vacations. Either way, I would work the next two weeks.

Would the coming weeks be significantly different from the first two? The experience of working those first weeks had reinforced the experience of looking for a job. The same fundamental message was hammered home in both processes: *what you think or care about is essentially irrelevant and ignored, because the basic purposes of the processes to which you are being subjected have been determined without your participation and are primarily for another's benefit. You are nobody—hands to be used.* As a worker, your principal responsibilities are: do your job; obey your foreman. On probation with the company and not yet a member of the union, you as a new worker in particular are nearly as powerless and as lacking in substantial rights, autonomy and control as you were as a job seeker.

Under such conditions it is understandable that workers learn to respond in kind, in the shared spirit of expediency, trying to "get by," and trying in whatever small ways they can to assert some control over their lives as workers.

THE FIRST TWO WEEKS

III

The Dictates of the
Production System

MY job, it turned out, was not in essence different from most jobs in our society. Most are characterized by certain common features determined by the nature of the society-wide organization of production. Each kind of job also has qualities that distinguish it at least somewhat from other kinds of jobs. These particular qualities are determined by how the kind of job is integrated into the production process. The job of trashman, for example, is different from the job of lathe operator, because each performs a different function in production. All jobs have their own rhythms and qualities, and these are determined both by the nature of the society-wide organization of production and by how the particular job is integrated into the production process.

In my job, some of the resulting rhythms and qualities were observable from the very first—say, the hours of work and the physical interference of the manufactured commodities with the process of dumping the waste byproducts of production. Others at first either were not observable or not observed. Still others were observed but not understood, as they must be, in their subordination to the dictates of the production system.

The rhythms and qualities of the job can best be understood as different facets of a single integrated system. Although there is room for some variation, the latitude for variation under the same regime of property is confined strictly by the nature of that regime.

As this regime shapes technology and determines production and the job, so the job in turn overwhelmingly dominates the worker. That is the primary aspect of working.

The worker, in response, devises strategies and tactics to try within very narrow confines to control all aspects of the job as much as s/he needs to and can. That is the secondary aspect of working. The patterns of work-time social relations for a trashman, as for other workers, flow from all the above.

What, then, is it like being the plant trashman? The job, it hardly needs to be said, is a low-grade position, graded 9 in the plant's formalized hierarchical ordering of jobs from 1 down to 11. Although in the plant there are few jobs graded as 11, many are graded as 9 and 10. But most of these are production jobs that carry production bonuses, which of course makes them monetarily more desirable. The trashman, on the other hand, only brings home more than his base pay by working overtime, as I was expected to do five out of six days a week. For this job, the tradeoff between more money and longer hours is the name of the game. So the job of trashman is one of the least desired positions in the plant. Still, it is not viewed by other workers as demeaning labor in the way that, say, that of municipal garbageman is viewed by professionals. With one reservation, the plant trashman basically is seen as just another employee.

That reservation is the byproduct of a second, informal hierarchy of jobs in the plant, a racial hierarchy. The racial hierarchy tends to put whites in the most desired jobs and blacks in the least. All jobs graded 11 and most 10s and 9s, in other words, are black jobs, while nearly all jobs graded 1 through 6 are white jobs. I, for example, was the lowest-grade white man in the Service Department and, except for production workers, one of the lowest-grade whites in the plant. My job was on the boundary line between white and black jobs. The three prior trashmen for the plant had been white, black, and white, in that order. Those still earlier had been mostly black.

Although I quickly became aware of the ambiguity of my racial status, and sometimes even felt some self-consciousness about it, generally my status as low white man on the totem pole did not bother me. On the contrary, I often felt more comfortable associating with black workers, whom I found consistently to have better senses of humor about their predicament, as well as more observable rage.

As trashman, I did basically the same things every day. Performing these daily tasks involved two kinds of relations, both of which were crucially shaped by the production system: relations with physical objects, like rings and hoppers; and relations with employees, who themselves related to these and other physical objects in doing their jobs. My working relations with other employees were directly caused and mediated by my and their relationships largely to things. If, for example, rings were blocking my hopper, it was because they had been put there by some other worker. And in that case I could choose either to remove them myself, which was not my job, or to ask a foreman or another worker to do it. If, on the other hand, a hopper were full and another worker had to dump more trash in it, I might be asked by that worker or summoned through the foreman network to dump the hopper.

When things go smoothly the job is performed by the trashman working alone and directly relating only with inanimate objects. Although the tasks always necessarily incorporate in the objects to be moved interdependent social relations, actual face-to-face cooperation during smooth periods is virtually nonexistent. Performance of the job therefore appears to focus almost exclusively on relations to things and to be deceptively individualistic.*

The trashman's job, like most production jobs under the current division of labor in the United States, provides the worker with only fragmented experiences. Like other American workers, I learned as a matter of course only about those aspects of production my job incorporated. Neither the trashman's functions, nor the union, nor management facilitated learning anything else. Other aspects of production, and how and why production is organized and coordinated as it is, were a mystery and a mystification. As trashman, I learned about waste as I encountered it in a particular phase of production. I

* To some extent, it is true, the job is more "individualistic" than most production jobs. Within the limits imposed by the production system, the trashman to an unusual degree does work out his own schedule, his own techniques, tactics, and strategies. Visual supervision is minimal and in the nature of the job, which demands working all over the plant, must remain so.

THE WORK PROCESS

learned, for example, that essentially good packaging cartons that are mislabeled or the wrong size are thrown away, apparently because it is cheaper to waste them than to return them to the producer for correction or to correct and store them in the plant for future use.

Veteran workers who have been in the plant for many years and held many jobs of course know much more about different aspects of production. But their vision, like mine, reflects the limited nature of their experiences. It is a composite of many fragmented work experiences rather than an organic appreciation of how and why production is organized in the way it is.

Fragmented work is generally repetitious. The trashman's job is repetitious, picking up and dumping hoppers. But, relative to other jobs, not nearly so monotonous, since (as indicated) each hopper has its own personality and has to be correspondingly handled. Nevertheless there is a Sisyphian quality to the work, as day after day the trashman confronts the waves of trash that wash through the plant, and day after day he empties the filled hoppers. Each day he finds the hoppers filled once again, and each day he gains a reduced sense of tangible accomplishment from once again emptying them.

Given the nature of the job, very little happens in the working life of a trashman that is spectacular. Neither the rare and very minor achievements and successes, nor the repeated small failures and indignities are worthy of much note as individual incidents. The patterned cumulation of these small events, however, sets the tone of work life.

Trashman work is not overly demanding physically, though in conjunction with long hours in particular it can be quite tiring, tiring enough to have made me feel for the first time in years that I was truly earning my bread. At first the responsibilities do not appear to be psychologically taxing. And yet the responsibilities are relentlessly there, and become exhausting as day grinds into day, over a 56-hour week, and week grinds into week: always having to watch out for careless pedestrians, who of necessity travel in the same crowded aisles as the forks (imagine driving an auto on city streets where there were no sidewalks and pedestrians walked in the roads); straining to see one's path in the face of numerous obstructions; always worrying about keeping up with the flood of trash; and repeatedly having to maneuver through the obstacle course of the aisles and blocked hoppers to get the job done.

In carrying out the daily duties of the job I was confronted, like all workers, by numerous workaday problems. Some were more or less manageable; others were more or less unmanageable. The ones that were more or less manageable were those over which I could exercise a certain degree of control through fixing a routine in my working methods. The problems that were more or less unmanageable involved factors that were less regularized and almost totally beyond my control. These problems I either had to learn to accept or tolerate, or else, finding myself unable to do so, I had to work feeling their intrusion as intolerable, which I too often did.

Among the problems I could manage were such matters as the compactor setup, which was determined by four linked components: (1) the ramp up which the loaded fork was driven; (2) the binlike opening into which trash was dumped; (3) the adjoining container outside the plant into which trash was stuffed; and (4) the huge motor-driven metal slab that inexorably pushed dumped trash out of the bin and compacted it in the container. Over the ramp were fluorescent lights. Over the bin was a pipe. On each side of the ramp were railings. The ramp itself consisted partly of an inclined plane and partly of a flat plane, the flat part just before the bin.

Although the compactor was provided almost exclusively for the fork-lift dumping of trash, mostly by the trashman, the setup was peculiarly ill fitted to the job. In the first place, the ramp was too narrow for good maneuverability. Although it had been widened at least once before, clearances on either side were measured in inches. Second, the bin was too short, so that when large items like barrels were dumped, they frequently got stuck. Third, overhead lights and the pipe were too low. In the process of dumping, the largest of the hoppers came perilously close to the pipe even when dumped perfectly. And finally, the lead-in, inclined ramp approached too closely to the hopper, so that the fork, when dumping, instead of being on a level place often was tilted slightly backward, thus precisely interfering

THE WORK PROCESS

with the dumping process, which required imbalancing the hopper forward.

All these shortcomings in the compactor setup, however unnecessary and exasperating, could be compensated for. What they required was patience, additional care, and at times greater physical exertion. With experience, for example, I learned how to dump the largest hoppers in a way that cleared the overhead pipe by several inches. I learned which hoppers posed problems in terms of that pipe and dumped them with extreme care. But, whenever I was distracted or careless, I increased the risk of tapping the pipe, which I did on several occasions, always thereafter thanking my good fortune it had not broken. The same was true of the other difficulties associated with the compactor. In each case they were constants, wholly predictable and knowable, and therefore manageable as a part of my routine.

Of another sort entirely were problems that cropped up every day, which were largely beyond my control and made manifest my dependence upon a variety of people and things. Since neither the particular occurrence of these difficulties nor their extent usually could be specifically predicted, the most I could do to defend against their intrusion was to try to get ahead in my work schedule so as to be able to better absorb the time losses they entailed. Once they intruded, my concerns boiled down to two: first, trying under the circumstances to "make do" in performing the job; and second, trying to control my own frustrations in the face of being unable to carry out the job, and, worse still, while normally not knowing when those circumstances would be altered. Given both my dependence on others and what may be my exaggerated sense of responsibility, the ambiguity about what (if anything) actually was being done to rectify the problems and the uncertainty regarding when they would be rectified often depressed and infuriated me.

As time passed, I tried to confront the reality of my own lack of control over the factors necessary to do the job well. I tried to reduce or eliminate my sense of responsibility for conditions impeding my performance through no fault of my own, the responsibility for which

DICTATES OF PRODUCTION SYSTEM

56

rested elsewhere. Although I came to believe I was applying in my factory work a standard of responsibility appropriate only to situations in which the person has greater control over his/her work environment, these internal struggles continued on a somewhat moderated scale until my last day at work.

Take the container pickup schedule, for example. In the routine for pickup I would call my foreman when the container had forty hoppers in it, continuing to dump hoppers into it until the container either was full or the outside pickup service came to take it away. Since the container (depending upon who else was dumping trash into it and how much) could hold sixty to seventy hoppers of trash, I could under the best of conditions continue working until the container was picked up. Then I would have to wait to dump again for only an hour or so. But frequently and for reasons I never understood, pickup was delayed for hours; not infrequently it was delayed for a day; and sometimes for two or even three days.

On such days I was unable to dump trash. The best I could do was to manage the trash: exchanging the few empty hoppers I had stowed away for other hoppers that were overflowing; lining up full hoppers on the internal roadway for rapid dumping; packing out the cafeterias by hand; and piling cafeteria trash ceiling high in the compactor bin. These managerial tactics, however, were quickly exhausted, and then there was nothing left to do but sit and wait—watching the trash pile up in and around the hoppers, watching the compactor room fill up with boxes and trash barrels that laborers and others had had to leave because the compactor was full, and trying to respond maturely to requests and complaints about the trash situation.

It may be difficult to understand how I could have been gripped by a job intrinsically so purposeless and meaningless on every level except one—just doing the job well for its own sake. But I never really felt I had any other choice. Believing generally in the potential meaningfulness of work and profoundly indoctrinated in the American work ethic in particular, I could not allow myself to become numb to the job, accepting its meaninglessness and merely putting in the time. Although other workers often gave the impression that they coped with the problem in that way, and although such a response would have been understandable and rational, their behavior at other times suggests their inner feelings and struggles are much more complex. In any event, I could not resign myself; nor were the pressures on me to do so that great, for this was not my life's career.

In order to do a good job, throughout most of the seven months on the job I waged a constant struggle to control small aspects of the uncontrollable system in an effort to minimize the effect that uncontrollable factors could have upon my work and me. Like most workers, I came to understand the rhythms of the job—for example, which hoppers normally filled up fastest—and tried to accommodate those rhythms to the extent possible to routines. To the degree I was able to organize the job into routines and stick to them, the likelihood of doing a good job was increased. Fixing routines not only gave me a sense of some control over the job, it allowed me also to organize my time so that as I became more efficient I could reserve some free time. In the event of disruptions that free time gave me the capacity to absorb the disruption without throwing off my entire schedule. In the event of a trouble-free workday, I had time to talk to other workers or to hide.

As I came to understand the job, I came also to expect a wide variety of disruptions in routines and tried to devise tactics and strategies to cope with them. In the process, although I keenly felt frustrations, anger, and helplessness, I also felt some elation in coping in small concrete ways with the daily manifestations of the contradiction between our work ethic and the conditions under which we work.

The basic rhythm of the job is determined by the flow of trash, which in turn is purely a function of production. Most hoppers have to be dumped every day; some have to be dumped more than once a day. The cafeterias have to be cleaned out every day. Production and its related modes of wasting therefore determined the number of hours I worked a day, when I began work, and the number of days I worked.

Within this context, each day had a definite beginning and end, as did each week. Since trash was handled essentially on a daily cycle, the more work I could get done in the three-hours-plus before morning break, the easier the rest of the day was likely to be. Morning break was a kind of landmark in the day, in much the same way that lunch half-hour and afternoon break were. The three breaks affected the rhythm of the day in two ways. First, as themselves part of the day's rhythms, they happily broke the work rhythm, affording a little time for relaxation and more extended socializing than was possible from the seat of a forklift truck. Second, they functioned as measuring rods of how the routine was going. If, for example, I had dumped thirteen to fifteen hoppers by lunch time, as I frequently had, I knew that in terms of work the rest of the day would be relatively smooth sailing, as long as my routine was not interrupted. I was likely then to be able to make extra break time, even to find a chance to read the newspaper.

Despite the fact that the tasks to be done each day were mostly the same, the rhythms of the days were somewhat different for both objective and subjective reasons. Objectively, on one level there were at least three kinds of days. First, there was the normal day, during which my minimal schedule was adequately met. On such days I neither had to rush nor was I able to create much additional break time for myself. Second, there were catchup days, during which I worked at peak pace to catch up because something had disrupted my routine a day or two earlier or sometime early in the day. Those were the days I worked the hardest; they also were the most fulfilling days in terms of my sense of self as a worker. And finally there were the days on which I got ahead of schedule, either because the trash load was relatively light, because I had worked particularly hard and efficiently early in the day, or because my routine had been going well on the immediately preceding days, enabling me to do in advance the few tasks that were performed on a weekly or semi-weekly basis, thereby freeing time later in the week.

In addition to these objective factors affecting daily rhythms, there were subjective ones. Some of these were intimately related to objective work conditions; others were not. Certain week days, for example, were more likely to feel like good days than others, no matter what the particular trash situation. As a general rule, Mondays were bad days, since they augured nothing but five more days of work thereafter. Tuesdays were slightly less bad, since at least one day of the week had already passed. Friday, by contrast, was a good day, especially as later in my factory working life I did not work many Saturdays. The quality of Fridays as the last work day of the normal work week and as payday, when the job's rewards were realized, was epitomized by the atmosphere in the locker room around four-thirty. It was like a mini-liberation—the joking, the planning for the weekend, the workers' sense of release from their cages, the pure joy. On several Fridays I actually yelled out loud knowing I would have no contact with the plant for two whole days. Although perhaps somewhat more demonstrative, I was hardly alone in those feelings.

Beyond such mixed objective-subjective factors, there were other factors that in terms of job time were still more purely subjective. There were days I felt badly for reasons that had little directly to do with the job. My bad feelings on those days, like my good ones on other days, affected how I experienced the rhythms and qualities of work. But usually when I felt badly, if my work routine went all right, doing the routine settled me down, unless my bad feelings were themselves a product of something that had happened on the job.

The other determinants of job rhythms, which under one set of circumstances can contribute to the regularity of rhythms and under another set can disrupt the day's rhythms, have been mentioned. The servicing of the full container, for example, could either coincidentally mesh well with the job's duties, in which case the day's rhythms were maintained, or, if the dumping of the container was four or five hours late, it could slow down those normal rhythms, creating other resultant rhythms and emotions. When servicing was several days late it simply eliminated the normal job rhythms, simultaneously creating conditions for the future in which once the container was serviced, the rhythms of the job immediately thereafter were much accelerated and much more intense.

The state of the equipment, particularly the fork, presented a similar opportunity/problem. On days when it worked reasonably well, the job was more likely to be performed efficiently and gracefully. Then the fork contributed to the regularity of the job's rhythms. But on those many days when it stalled out, got a flat, badly overheated, lost its brakes, wouldn't start, or broke down in endless

DICTATES OF PRODUCTION SYSTEM

ways, the rhythms of the routine were halted. Then, except for packing out the cafeteria by hand, nothing could be done. On such days I waited, not knowing when the fork would be fixed, until I was paged by my foreman to pick up the machine at the garage.

The state of the hoppers also affected the job rhythms, although not as drastically. On many days, for example, the hopper out front in the parking lot by the print shop was surrounded by plastic garbage bags and cartons filled with heavy thrown-out computer printouts, rolls of carbon paper, magazines, and the like. On days I could not pile these bags and cartons upon the already full hopper there, I had to bring out another hopper to accommodate the extra trash. Having to clean up around the hopper and dumping two hoppers instead of one meant I fell twenty to thirty minutes behind my routine.

Similarly, certain hoppers are inaccessible, say, 50 percent of the time. Regarding one such hopper, I regularly had to climb down from my fork to clear the approach aisle of the five to ten stacks of rings obstructing it before I could even approach the hopper with the fork. Although the piling up of trash around a full hopper made extra work for the trashman, the blocking of aisles by rings left there by other employees seemed less excusable, even provocative. At times it made me angry to the point that I wanted to scream at other employees, even strike out at them. Sometimes I did get angry at fellow workers, who may have forgotten that through their immediate relationship to things they also related to other workers.

Another factor that affected the job rhythms was the weather and the seasons. When it rained or snowed, transporting the hoppers outside was inconvenient and riskier. The normal fork, the 173, tended to slide badly at any speed under wet conditions. Rain and snow, like cold weather in general, also meant that overhead doors into the plant were closed, which added two additional steps to the job, pulling the up-chain upon approaching the doors and the down-chain after passing through them. My commonsensical response to rain and snow, therefore, was to try to minimize the time I had to spend outside by rearranging my routine to do what inside work I could until the weather improved.

Among all the factors affecting the job rhythms, the most crucial

THE WORK PROCESS

disrupting factor was equipment breakdown. Let me illustrate the problem in greater detail. The fork I generally used, the 173, an old Yale towmotor, had been in poor shape from long before I took the job as trashman. Its engine was "burned out." It ran extremely hot— the former trashman and myself were scalded by the radiator erupting. Its exhaust smoked terribly. It stalled frequently; it had no zip; its various parts were in a state of advanced deterioration. One day the battery would go; another day the alternator; another day the tires. In short, it was noxious and wholly unreliable. The prior trashman knew it. My foreman knew it. The superintendent knew it. The employeees in areas through which I drove knew it. They repeatedly complained to management about exhaust pollution. But it took me a while to learn it, since my foreman at first seemed to blame me for the problems, as if I had created them.

For a long time nothing was done to change the situation. Breakdowns were repaired piecemeal. The goal obviously was simply to keep the fork moving for as long and as cheaply as possible. Any problems its unreliability might create for the trashman, who had to use it, were of only marginal concern to management. After some months of these conditions persisting and of my complaints, I was told by my foreman that an application had been made to upper management to approve a major overhaul of the fork, but that getting approval would take some time. In the meantime, of course, only absolutely necessary repairs would be made since it would be foolish to make other repairs in light of the expected, eventual investment in the full overhaul.

This was the situation as it existed from July to early October. In three months, the 173 by conservative estimate had been down for one reason or another 10–15 percent of the time. Then, on October 11, a veteran worker tried to use the 173 in conjunction with another fork to move an extremely heavy piece of machinery. At the time I warned him and my foreman that the fork wasn't up to it, but pressed by demands to produce results, they went ahead anyway. The more experienced worker had a terrible time with the fork: it smoked, stalled, and finally ceased to turn over. At first he turned to me for help in operating the fork, which gratified me, particularly as I was able to coax it into action on several occasions when he was not. All too soon, though, nothing could be done with the fork. It was dead.

The other worker, I gathered, subsequently complained to my foreman about the condition of the fork. That galvanized Sam to authorize a minor overhaul for the fork "to get us over the hump" until the required approval of upper-level management for a major overhaul was received. In the interim, I was to use another fork. The next day, Saturday, we borrowed a rented fork from the Stores and Receiving Department. It was larger than the 173, but worked reasonably well. Despite the interference with my routine that driving a different fork imposed, I was grateful to be operating a reliable one.

Monday I was back on 173, which notwithstanding its "minor overhaul" was operating terribly. It repeatedly stalled, and increasingly became difficult to restart. When I informed my foreman, he advised me to try to operate the fork without turning it off until a new battery could be obtained and installed. I tried to follow his instructions, but was almost immediately confronted by one of the few active union Safety Committee members, who informed me that a number of workers had recently complained about the 173's exhaust. I sympathized with the complaints and tried to summarize the situation for her. I told her I would be delighted if the Safety Committee could break the logjam about the 173, since I didn't like driving it any better than workers liked smelling it.

The next day the 173 broke down again. The battery and alternator, I was told, had to be replaced. I used the Stores Department rental again, while awaiting the rental that the Service Department was supposed to have ordered. From my past experience, I was not confident one actually had been ordered. By the time the fork borrowed from Stores had to be returned, the 173 had been repaired. I returned to it and worked for a time until Sam told me to park it and to wait to resume my work until we got our own rental fork. Although at the time I did not know and was not told, the 173 had been "red-tagged" by a federal Occupational Safety and Health Administration (OSHA) inspector who had come into the plant that morning and had heard complaints about the fork. For all our sakes, the fork should have been shut down months earlier.

THE WORK PROCESS

With the 173 shut down, Sam told me to use the old 116, the large fork on which I had first been trained. I did as ordered but was not pleased to be using still another fork, this time one that was obviously too clumsy to do the job efficiently and safely.

Wednesday brought me full circle. At 6:10 A.M. the 116 wouldn't start either. Rather than just doing nothing until Sam would come in an hour and a half later, I decided for the time being to use the 173. The Safety Committeewoman asked me why it was in operation again, and unaware of the OSHA order, I explained it was only temporary, until the rental came in or Sam provided me with an alternative. The 173 was stalling a lot. Since it was raining, its wheels spun, too. At slow speed, I literally could not get the fork up the very slightly inclined plane leading into one of the overhead doors. With the necessary running start, I risked skidding into the door frame.

Still, whatever its multitudinous failings, the 173 at least was the right-size fork for the job. I decided to use it to pick up the inside hoppers with the most difficult approaches, so that when I was able to return to the 116 those would be behind me. As I was picking up a tightly wedged-in hopper, Sam on his way in saw me. He ordered me, in no uncertain terms, to get the 173 out of the plant, saying it had been red-tagged. That was the first I had heard the phrase and did not know for certain what it meant. But I assumed then the fork had been put out of service by OSHA. I responded that the 116 wouldn't start. He said he didn't care; that I'd have to wait for the rental to come in.

I was terribly angry and fed up. How was I supposed to do the job with such miserable equipment? In frustration, I went to Sam's office, told him I wanted to do a good job but couldn't with the equipment provided, and that what he needed was workers who didn't care about doing a good job. I said I wanted a transfer to another job. He could have cared less, and gave me permission to request a transfer from Ron, the superintendent. I was furious and insulted, accurately feeling both stymied and wholly unappreciated.

Fortunately, the rental arrived very soon thereafter. It was a decent-looking Hyster fork, like the rental we had borrowed, bigger than the 173 but smaller than the 116. Not bad at all for the job. But this was the fourth fork I had driven since Saturday, and I was disoriented both by the objective conditions and by my subjective state. Then to make matters worse, not wanting to rely on the rental's gas gauge, I decided to fill up the gas tank and mistakenly poured a small amount of gas into the radiator before I found out that the gas tank on this fork was hidden under the seat! The routine completely disrupted, I was, as once before after my second week on the job, ready to quit.

But there was still more to come. I had heard from many workers that rented forks often were in even worse states of repair than company forks, but given my good experience with the Stores Department rental I did not fully credit those stories. So it was, that at eleven o'clock on Thursday, I braked routinely to stop the rental, and to my surprise and horror, my foot went to the floor with little effect on the fork's forward momentum. The brakes on the rental had gone in less than one day. I was lucky not to have hit anyone or anything. But now what was I to do? The 116's hydraulic lift, I learned, was broken. The 173 had been banished.

With self-righteousness, I went to tell Sam the latest good news. When I arrived at his office, others were there. Sam described the situation with the forks to the assorted crowd. In response, another foreman asked why the company didn't just buy a whole new fleet of forks and in the long run save all the money it laid out for repairs, rentals, and lost labor time. Sam, as usual, tried to shift the blame to the employees, saying they abused the equipment. Since I had been trying to cope with the lousy equipment the company provided for months, and since most of the problems with equipment were the result of defective equipment and not my fault, I wanted to punch him one.

The rental was fixed by a Hyster serviceman who came in. I halfheartedly returned to my routine for a short while, until a fellow worker who needed a fork whose blades could be raised higher than his fork's asked to borrow it for a job. Reluctantly, since I was behind in my routine, I agreed. I used his fork briefly in the interim. That made the fifth fork I had had to use in five days. My routine was a wreck, and so was I.

THE WORK PROCESS

And that wasn't all. On the following Monday, I was warned by the worker who did the trashman's job on the Saturdays I didn't work that he thought the rental was leaking oil. That leak, I knew by then, might be motor oil, hydraulic fluid, or brake fluid. The horn on the rental also didn't work. While I waited for the fork to be serviced again, I used the 210, which I had operated once before that week. Then back to the serviced rental. On Thursday the rental simply stopped moving. Each of my back wheels, I was advised, by an onlooking, slightly amused fellow worker, was pointing in a different direction. The tie rods for the steering mechanism had broken. The brakes also seemed to be going again. Sam angrily complained to the rental agency. By afternoon another rental fork had been delivered. That fork was the sixth I had had to drive in less than two weeks.

Those two weeks in October 1974, although not typical, epitomized the problems I had been having with equipment. Those weeks also marked the end of an era for me, because the sixth fork proved to be the first good one I had been privileged to operate on the job. Aside from relatively minor problems, like a wholly unreliable horn, it performed consistently for the rest of my career as a factory worker, over three months.

Other sorts of incidents that broke the routines in small ways included orders from above, accidents, and a variety of consequences of my relations with fellow employees. At any time during the work day I might be assigned by my foreman or my superintendent to do a special job. In addition, other foremen might ask me to do things or tell me to do tasks differently, though they could not directly order me. Usually the jobs my bosses gave me were added trashman's work; on other occasions they were less differentiated, common labor. On one day in October, for example, my superintendent, who was usually quite polite with me, said, as I was about to disappear to hide out, that "if you get a chance," go over to the boiler room to get rid of the junk and 55-gallon cans accumulated outside the door. On another day he asked me to help other men move by hand 80-pound bags of salt from a skid into the boiler room. On my last day of work,

DICTATES OF PRODUCTION SYSTEM

when I was rushing because all overtime in the plant had been cut and because my last working hour was to be devoted to my "exit interview" in the personnel department, Ron called me during my morning break and asked me to take a hopper into the tool room. Since I had maneuvered a hopper in and out of the tool room only the day before and since on my last day I was not eager to undertake any extra work in an already tightly compressed schedule, I advised him that if I did that I would fall behind in my routine and explained I was particularly rushed that day. Totally unconcerned with a trashman's problems, he made it clear that I was to do what he said. Behind the polite form he normally used in asking me to do jobs, I realized, had always been the cutting edge of power and authority, which remained sheathed except when needed. Once drawn, it cut through any remaining illusions about mutual respect in management-worker relations.

Minor accidents and mishaps also broke my routine in small ways, repeatedly reminding me that I could not afford to be distracted for a moment while working. Some of these incidents I handled well. Those did not prove very disruptive. Others I handled less well, a few poorly. On five or six occasions during the seven months in the factory I hit stacks of rings. When that happened, I had to stop to pick them up, restack them, and calm myself down. In the early months I notified my foreman of these mishaps. He always took it well. On the last few occasions, however, if I had not been otherwise detected I did not notify him. By then I was thinking, like most workers I knew, that I shouldn't stick my neck out for no good reason.

One day, very early in the morning, my fork blade got stuck under a hopper in a way that prevented me from getting the hopper off the blade. After trying unsuccessfully for 15 minutes to scrape the hopper off on various curbs, much as one tries to clean one's shoes after stepping in what a healthy dog has left behind, one of the few other fork drivers who came in at 6:00 A.M. helped me to get it off.

On still another day, as I was broken-field driving down a ramp to get a hopper, I hit a pallet with some iron bars on it that had been left in the aisle. I hadn't seen it, and got very angry at myself and at whoever was responsible for having left it in the aisle. I turned upon another fork driver with whom I had previously had good relations. Typically, he denied any responsibility and retorted that he had been able to get by in the aisle without hitting the pallet, implying, I thought at the time, some incompetence on my part. That was all I needed. We went after each other verbally. Later I calmed down and the next day apologized to him. But my reaction to the accident, to which my carelessness had been a contributing but not the sole cause, also was typical. Anger at myself easily was projected onto others who had their own problems and didn't appreciate being the butt of someone else's fury, whether they in fact shared the responsibility or not. Such confrontations were fairly common in the plant. I came to understand they were built into the working conditions.

Two or three times during the seven months, I hit the fluorescent lights hanging over the compactor ramp. Once in January 1975 a box sticking up out of a full hopper tapped one of the fluorescent tubes and sent it crashing down around me. Thereafter my main anxiety that day, since Sam and I had been having trouble over my not wanting to work Saturdays, was to get the light replaced as inconspicuously as possible, without letting Sam or anyone in management know about the accident. A friend helped me out, replacing it near the end of the day.

Near the end of that month, while driving the fork backward, I developed a bad stiff neck. Favoring it one day while driving backward, I barely missed smashing into an overhead door when my foot, which was out of its normal position, came down on the gas pedal instead of the brake. Again and again the importance for safety of strictly maintaining my routine was impressed upon me. The smallest variations dramatically increased risks of accidents.

Other interruptions in my routine, serious or minor, were the result of a variety of patterned encounters with co-workers. Some made extra work for me; some helped me to do certain of my jobs; others asked me to help them; some even sought what might be called trash patronage.

There were days when I would come in before the sun was up ready to begin the routine and find, to my dismay, that my fork was not where I had left it the afternoon before. The first time that hap-

DICTATES OF PRODUCTION SYSTEM

68

pened, I impatiently searched for a half hour before finding it back in the foundry. Someone on night shift obviously had used it and, I soon found out, had left the fork with a flat tire. That meant I had to wait for the outside tire repair service to send a truck in to repair it, which delayed my work for some hours. The next time my fork was missing I didn't panic, since by then I had an idea what had happened to it. I simply walked back to the foundry and found a worker from the graveyard shift still operating the fork. Realizing that he had his orders just as I had mine, I didn't get irritated, but just told him that when he used my fork at night he should return it by 6:00 A.M. He understood.

I found that I very much enjoyed helping other workers out, though at first I was uneasy taking time away from my own routine. Early one day in December, before I had even begun my work, the carpenters asked me to move outside some new pallets they had made and to move in some stacks of broken boxes to be repaired. I hesitated momentarily, thinking that helping them out meant I would fall behind. Fortunately, I quickly overcame that hesitation and in fifteen minutes got the job done, with good feelings and no appreciable effect on my routine.

Meeting requests by employees to provide them with materials available to me as trashman was even less disruptive, because I could satisfy those requests in ways and at times that fitted within the rhythms of my routine. Thus, when workers asked me to get a few of the plastic bags I used in the cafeterias, to save refuse cardboard container lids, or to deliver the carpenter shop's hopper filled with waste wood that could be used at home as kindling wood, I was glad to dole out what patronage I could. Even the trashman, I learned, can do things for others, either in his capacity as a forklift driver or as the person immediately in charge of trash.

So, I half-consciously tried to devise tactics and strategies for various encounters with things and people to make my relations with things more manageable, to maintain and improve my relations with people, and to achieve whatever other job-related and personal goals I could. Sometimes, minor successes in one realm meant failure in another. At other times, tactics chosen failed to achieve anything

THE WORK PROCESS

positive. This was more likely to be the case, I came to realize, the more the conditions I confronted as a problem constituted integral parts of the existing organization of production. In such cases, whatever the expenditure of effort and/or good will on my part, I was unable to improve the situation.

Take the hopper up front in the Final Inspections Department. That hopper, located on a busy corner astride both the main aisle in Plant 3 and the aisle leading to the men's and women's bathrooms and the cafeteria, was quite difficult to dump under the crowded conditions that persisted in the plant. Behind the hopper and on its right were stacks of rings, often deposited within four inches of the hopper. To the left of the hopper was the main aisle, which sometimes also was partially blocked by rings deposited on this third side of the hopper. And before the hopper was the cafeteria aisle, which usually was obstructed by 55-gallon metal cans deposited on the far side of that aisle away from the hopper. What made the approach to this hopper still more difficult was that opposite the hopper on the cafeteria aisle, in front of the metal cans, was a small wooden office whose partitions extended up to the main and cafeteria aisles. To the left of that office in the main aisle, other stacks of rings invariably were deposited.

Consequently to get the hopper out, the trashman had to drive down the main aisle, swing hard right at the end of the rings beside the office, maneuver to get the fork blades under the hopper, and then back out with the hopper, without hitting the rings, the cans, the office, or the pedestrians passing by. As a general rule, the procedure was manageable so long as not too many of the obstructions were simultaneously present. If, for example, the rings around the hopper's back and right sides were a foot or more away, that allowed much more room for manuevering. If, for example, the metal cans were not in the cafeteria aisle, even though the hopper might be fairly tightly surrounded on two sides it could often be extricated. But as obstructions accumulated, the hopper became increasingly inaccessible.

At first I tried to deal with this problem by asking workers in the immediate area not to block the hopper. But I generally was told that it was the truckers who moved and deposited rings, not those who worked in the area. Then I tried to talk to the truckers, who for the most part either denied they had placed the particular rings in the obstructing position, or (if they conceded they had) countered that they had to put the rings someplace. I then spoke to foremen in the area, who likewise told me they had a job to do and were also short of space. Then I advised my own foreman, complaining to him repeatedly with no results. The conditions of production in the factory thus put me into conflict with those who had to deposit their rings somewhere and, given the shortage of space, could hardly avoid interfering with someone's job. They happened to choose mine. At the time I did not fully understand these implications of the system. I simply wanted to resolve my problem with the hopper. As my efforts at persuasion had failed totally to achieve any results, I decided in frustration to use my single, punitive weapon.

The next day I let the hopper fill up and did not dump it. On the second morning it was overflowing. I continued to ignore it. At lunch a trucker friend of mine called it to my attention. I told him I would not dump the hopper until the foremen with jurisdiction over the rings in the area asked me to, whereupon I planned to tell them I would be glad to dump it as soon as I got some cooperation in keeping the area unobstructed. Immediately after lunch, the area was cleared. Momentarily, I thought the tactic had succeeded, but I should have known better, for my tactic in this case was aimed at making foremen do what they probably could not do—finding places to put rings that would be both convenient for them and nonobstructive for me. As it turned out, my trucker friend had told his foreman he thought I couldn't get to the hopper to dump it and had himself moved the barrels and other obstructions temporarily out of the way, thereby relieving the foremen of the need to seriously consider the underlying crowding problem and its effect on my routine.

My delay in dumping the hopper had only created antagonism against me among a few workers in the area and had not contributed to resolving the conflict on any long-term basis. To achieve success, I should have recognized that the tactics and strategies employed cannot conflict with the given organization of production. That organization, as indicated earlier, dominates all jobs and all workers. Tac-

THE WORK PROCESS

tics and strategies have to be devised that accept that given and seek within its framework of hard reality to achieve whatever can be achieved.

To recognize and understand the implications of the demands of production on the work process and on other workers is a necessary first step in being able to cope with various problems and having decent relations with co-workers. Not to devise any tactics and strategies for dealing with manageable matters, on the other hand, means a worker is totally dominated by production and the job. If most things under the present regime of production are not amenable to a worker's control, some are. To abdicate in those areas makes all aspects of the job uncontrolled and insufferable from the worker's point of view.

Thus, if the trashman cannot even infinitesimally improve the crowded conditions under which he performs his job, he still can influence how his work and rest time are arranged. If he cannot determine when the outside container service will come to collect the full container, at least he can manage the trash once the container is full. More than that, the trashman can (if he concludes on the basis of experience that the service company's truck is not likely to come when the container will be filled, say, on a Saturday) prematurely "call in" the container as having forty hoppers in it, thereby increasing the probability that it will be emptied without undue delay but before it is completely full.

Small accommodations are all that is possible as long as one sells one's labor to another, who thereby becomes its owner and organizer.

IV

Doin' Time:
Working Men's and Women's Attitudes
toward Work and Time

THE rhythms of a particular job, the day of the work week, and the success in managing a day's routines influence how most employees daily experience time and work. Related factors profoundly affect how they appreciate normal work time, overtime, break or "free" time, lunch time, leisure time, vacation time, and expected retirement. A tipoff to the quality of this experience lies in the fact that retirement, which comes at the end of one's working life, is not, like work-related and work-punctuated time, referred to as "retirement time" but simply as retirement—as if to suggest that time in retirement is appreciated differently.

During a working life the salient factor shaping the experience of time for most employees is that time itself, even more than labor power, is what workers are conscious of selling on an hourly basis to the employing company for wages. Hourly employees, which is to say the majority of American workers, are paid at a certain rate for each hour they work in a standard work week. To the extent production bonuses are incorporated into total wages, a worker's sense of selling his/her time is supplemented by the more accurate consciousness that what actually is being sold is not simply time, but more particularly the use of the worker's labor power—the ability to produce—during a certain period of time.

What one sells one no longer owns. The company, not the worker, becomes the owner of the worker's working hours and, within very broad limits, determines how that time shall be spent. In determining, with employee compliance, whether and when a man or woman will work, for how many hours, at which site, doing what, and for what wages, companies determine generally an employee's work life. They also greatly influence how that portion of life left over after work can and will be spent. The worker repeatedly sells his/her labor power during a working life to earn the money required to satisfy nonwork needs. The company buys the employee's labor, just as it buys other factors of production, as cheaply as it can for use in satisfying the company's need to generate profits.

The way businesses in the United States appreciate time reflects the nature of the broader capitalist system of which they are the central component. This in turn shapes workers' appreciations and their reactions. Companies, I learned during the weeks spent looking for a job, care only about time they pay for. They are, for example, largely unconcerned with the "free time" of those in search of jobs, who often wait in personnel offices for hours only to be told there are no jobs available. From the moment a person's "free" time is about to become "company time," however, unconcern changes to concern. Thus in the initial interview with my superintendent at Blancs, he sternly advised that I should get to work every day on time, that the company wasn't interested in "part time help." And when I returned immediately thereafter to the company employment office, the interviewer reminded me to report on time for the scheduled physical the following day, even though he should have known I would face more than an hour's wait for the doctor.

Work began every day with an obeisance to time. Each morning when I reported to work at 6:00 I signed in. Workers who too often reported in 10 to 15 minutes late were warned by the foreman. Workers who missed a few days during a several-month period, unless because of sickness or accident, also were warned. If they continued to have imperfect attendance records, they were fired for "missing time," though the company does not pay wages for missed time. Time missed for any personal reason other than sickness or accident can be counted against the worker, one foreman told a worker in the presence of the worker's union committeeman. No matter that the particular worker was under subpoena to appear in court; or that another's child might be sick. Company time comes first. The convenience and satisfaction of valid human needs comes second.

Company time is for production. Men and women produce at Blancs in three shifts, 24 hours a day, six days a week. If you want a job, you work where and when the company needs you—even if it is third shift, from 4:00 P.M. to midnight, which usually means a man or woman barely gets to see his/her family during the week. While on the job, workers are repeatedly reminded that they are there for only one purpose, to produce for the company. Production workers are subjected periodically to time studies, in which an employee's rate of production at minimum acceptable levels of quality is measured. From these measurements management determines the employee's standard for production and his/her total wages, which is to say much of his/her life. I had been in the plant about six weeks when for the first time I noticed a time-study functionary holding a stopwatch on a woman machining piston rings and then jotting down his findings. Watching him brought home to me with a jar how these notations would henceforward dog that woman, as long as she worked at Blancs.

Management's attitude toward workers' time is epitomized by its reactions to two quite separate events that coincidentally happened on a single day in November 1974. That morning I had caught up with my schedule for dumping hoppers and had time to relax. As I was driving some place to hide, I passed a fellow worker, stopped, and entered into a conversation with him. For about 20 to 25 minutes we talked in full view of everyone who passed. Shortly after the conversation ended, I went to lunch. While eating, I was paged by my foreman who somewhat apologetically told me that the container service truck was coming in and asked that I go over immediately to prepare the trash container to be taken away. Although it was my unpaid lunch half-hour, I said OK and did as asked, especially as my foreman correctly and decently added that any lost lunch time should be made up during afternoon break. I thought little more of having

THE WORK PROCESS

had my lunch time interrupted until later in the day when I was
called into the office and told that I had been spotted by someone in
management that morning talking to another worker for what was
called an "excessive" period of time. My foreman, with some embarrassment, thereupon gave me a formal "oral warning" for "talking too
much," which went onto my record. When I asked him point blank
whether he, in fact, had any complaints about how I was doing my
job, he said no. It was just that I had been flagrantly talking, apparently enjoying myself, on company time. Company time, I realized, is company time. Workers' lunch time, on the other hand, is
generally to be respected, but "if necessary," can be interfered with
for the convenience of the company.

Consciousness of time as a factory worker was a new experience
for me after my very different life in an elite university. In the university, where so little of a professor's time is programmed—time during
which s/he must must be doing a particular task at a particular time,
like teaching every Monday morning, for example—the passage of
time tends to be measured in terms of that programmed time. Vacations are periods when teachers have no programmed time, when
time passes still more diffusely. In the long view, unprogrammed
time in the elite university is a function of the demand for writing
and publishing, which is the main form of production there. Because
the kind of production demanded in this sort of university is so different from a factory, an average service industry, or for that matter a
public school, time and one's relation to the job are experienced very
differently in the university.

Although to be successful in the university one has to produce
in accordance with "professional" standards, which in fact are defined by interlocking ideological and economic markets, academic
production in the United States allows the intellectual producer tremendous freedom to choose how s/he will spend his/her nonpro-
grammed productive time. Most hours in an academic's day are arranged by the academic worker at his/her convenience, seemingly to
produce only what the individual conceives of as good scholarship or
good teaching. Because professors are not paid on an hourly basis,
nor strictly on a piecework basis for each publication, they are not

very conscious of selling their time or even of selling the use of their labor power. Professors tend to feel as if they are producing for themselves, though they are acutely conscious that they must produce and that their production must be of the sort that is appreciated by superiors if they are to survive in the university. Still, because they do not feel as if they are simply being paid to do someone else's work for the profit of someone else, professors feel by and large that they are engaged in their own, purposeful work.

The sense of time and work in most other jobs in the United States, especially in factory work, is as different from this as day is from night. Most work time in the factory is programmed. Employees report when told, go home when told, and, in effect, work overtime when told. Their tasks are set for them. They are closely supervised. Although they do it, it is not their work they do. It is work for someone else, for another's profit. They sell their labor so they can earn enough money to live. Factory work, like most work in the United States, has no other purpose. For most workers the relation to work is reduced to a single factor, money wages.

Despite the fact that I had other reasons for being in the factory and consciously chose to be there, I experienced time and work rather like other workers. Work time was the driving force of my life. I was acutely aware of time passing. I counted hoppers, hours, days, weeks, and months. Generally, time passed neither slowly nor quickly, but relentlessly, like production and trash itself. Time seemed stamped out, in discrete units, but always inexorably pushing onward. One day's 4:30 in the afternoon turned into the next morning's 6:00 A.M. One Saturday's 2:30 into the following Monday's 8:00 A.M. Sandwiched in between were a few snatched hours of my nonwork life.

True, I worked longer hours than most of my co-workers. But that only intensified my experience of time being ground out and life being squeezed in. And if I worked more hours a week than most, I would work many fewer weeks in the factory than they, since the rest of my life would not be so consumed. While on the job, although my sense of time was undoubtedly influenced by my other purposes in working and by the related actions I had to take to achieve those purposes—daily note taking in preparation for this book, for example—still, after a certain period, I began to lose much of that sense of ulterior purpose. By late January 1975, as I increasingly felt I was no longer learning much on the job and as it became clear that my other aspirations relating to the job would be frustrated, I became daily more depressed, even at times almost resigned about work. I began to feel as if I was working just to make enough money to pay for some needed home repairs. I came to feel about work and time, in short, exactly the way most workers feel about them. Shorn of any values and fantasies I had imposed upon it, the job became simply a way to make a minimal living, nothing more.

As early as one month into the job I found myself beginning to count the days of the week, eagerly anticipating my day off. I was not quite certain why I was counting, because I did not particularly dislike my job. It was not the sort of job, like assembly line work, I had previously conceived of as especially alienating, and yet there I was counting. I began then to wonder whether, and if so why, other workers were counting time. Whether even workers who had been there for years were still counting? Workers who operated machines, workers in the foundry, maintenance people? Were they all counting, no matter how long each had been there and no matter what sort of job each did? The answer, as far as I could tell, is yes, nearly everyone in the plant was counting time.

It first came out one Monday at lunch when a young fork driver I hardly knew said irascibly, "Only four and a half more days of this bullshit." A week later I asked an employee who had worked in the plant for more than 20 years whether he still counted the days. "No," he immediately said, "it don't do no good to count." But on numerous occasions thereafter, I saw him counting minutes until the end of his lunch hour, counting days until Saturday when he could go out and "tie one on," and counting months until his vacation time came round again. The only time he didn't count was the years until retirement, because he didn't plan to retire. He'd worked all his life and wasn't willing to pinch pennies trying to make it on what the company plus Social Security would give him for retirement. He said he'd work until he died. By contrast, another employee who also had been in the factory for over 20 years did plan to retire as soon as he reached 62. That was what he thought about nearly every day. In talking about it, he said, each day he looked forward to the 12:30 whistle, signaling the end of his lunch half-hour and his return to work, because that meant the date he would retire, in 1982, was one day closer.

Counting time was only one symptom of how negatively most employees felt about their jobs. The exuberance and release expressed in the plant locker rooms at the end of the work week were another. One young black worker who had been with the company for only a few months expressed his feelings about the job this way. He said he couldn't accomplish anything on his job, so "just being here is work." "I put in my eight," he said, but did as little as he could get away with. Still another employee, a man who had been with the company for years and, like many old-timers, had been laid off and rehired several times over the years, indicated that he had not intended to return after one of the layoffs. As a younger man, he said, he had enjoyed drinking and "assing around," but finally he had had to choose between settling down and working, on the one hand, or jail. Given that choice, he chose to do his time on the job.

The two men with different attitudes toward retirement expressed more generally the range of outward reactions to work as well. The one who planned to retire as soon as he felt financially able always complained about the job. The other rarely complained. The one had not really adjusted to his work life and didn't seem to want to adjust. Basically he wasn't satisfied with what he'd settled for. Complaining to fellow workers was his main way of expressing that dissatisfaction, because otherwise he was fairly timid. The other was "well adjusted." He had learned to expect nothing from his job but money. He treated the company the way the company treated him, coldly and with calculation. When, for example, too few machine operators came in on a Saturday for him to make much production bonus, he simply didn't work hard. When, after more than two decades on the job, he received his annual merit report, he just signed and ignored it. "They're always the same," he said. They said he needed to improve and take better care of the equipment. But, "how," he asked

THE WORK PROCESS

rhetorically, "can you take better care of 40-year-old equipment?" He didn't appreciate being treated like a child by the company, but he didn't fight back or complain much any more. He just hung in there, doing his job, earning his bread and regularly refilling the refrigerator he had at home reserved exclusively for beer.

Thus the experiencing of time is closely related both to how the company treats workers and to how men and women feel about their jobs and the company. The vast majority of workers with whom I had contact felt very negatively about their jobs. A middle-aged black man, graded as a 7, believed he was qualified to move up to 6. The company, he said, refused to promote him because of race prejudice. He claimed to take it coolly, but declared he had ways to get back at the company. He refused to work overtime when they needed him. A black, middle-aged woman who often worked 10 hours a day and in addition some Saturdays said she wasn't going to work herself to death. She said that certain women "hold in their pee, to get extra rings out to make bonus, but I won't bust my ass." She said she often did less than 65 percent of her standard, but she wasn't going to ask to have the standard restudied. Let the company initiate a restudy if it wanted. A young black machine operator, gazing at company posters that sought to instill a pride in work, when asked if he had pride in his work, only laughed and retorted, "you mean out on the streets?" An older white worker, who remembered the company 15 years ago as a "good place to work," now said he "hated to come in every day."

This palpable negativism of employees about their jobs exists across the board in nearly all job categories, largely independently of the degree of technological routinization attaching to the particular job. Although Americans have been led to believe that the degree of alienation among workers is much higher among those, like assembly line workers, technologically condemned to the narrowest of jobs, I found little or no evidence at Blancs that machine operators engaged in very simple, repetitive tasks were appreciably more negative about their jobs than say lower level maintenance personnel with equivalent weekly wages, whose jobs involved greater flexibility and scope. In any event, hardly anyone I knew in the factory, with the exception of a handful of craftsmen, had any substantial positive commitment to his/her job as a "career." When asked in casual conversation what they thought of their jobs, workers nearly universally responded, "it's a job."

With such an attitude about their jobs and work time, it is hardly surprising that most workers have reduced motivation to do a particularly good job or to work hard. Nor is it surprising that workers try to make free time for themselves so they can hide.

One day in July when my container was filled, I was sitting with two young workers on top of a pile of unassembled cardboard cartons in the shipping department, dangling my feet over the sides, and looking out the overhead doors where large trucks dock to let off and take on cargo. We were smoking; it was hot. I was reminded of nothing so much as Huckleberry Finn playing hookey from a distasteful school.

That same day a savvy fellow worker had advised me, "to be able to get yours, you have to understand how management works. You do your job according to how you get paid. Most important is to be there every day on time, so your foreman can work you if he really needs you. But generally just do your job and make some free time for yourself."

Workers, to the extent feasible, seek to gain some control of their time at work. I worked with a past master for a few days. An older black man, he had worked during the 1930s for a dollar for a 10-hour day, so to him the job at Blancs isn't too bad. Still, he talked about how hard it was in these times for him and his wife, who also worked, to make ends meet. "No poor man ever got rich working," he said, "with the government taking so much out of the poor man's wages in taxes." In manifest appreciation of his feelings for his job, he paced himself in each task. Between tasks he hid on the edges of the plant and rested a half-hour. He wasn't lazy, you could see that from how he worked when he wasn't resting. He just gave his job exactly the effort it deserved. He was working for $3.34 an hour.

The underlying battle for control of time between workers and the company is reflected also in the oral warning I had received for talking too long to a fellow employee. The company was asserting control over what it had paid for. Employees I barely knew indicated they understood that. Two days after I had been warned, while I was assuming the position in front of a latrine, a night fork operator razzed me inquiring whether I had asked Sam if I could "take a piss." He said that soon we wouldn't "be allowed to piss during company time, only during breaks."

Employee attitudes toward work time and the job, as well as company attitudes and practices toward employees, were reflected clearly in the matter of overtime. Perhaps because of the intense ambivalences on the part of both labor and management about overtime, consideration of this issue reveals much about the reality of factory life. My own experience regarding overtime was somewhat different than most other employees' because I was in a position to refuse it. But my experience may illuminate certain aspects of the problem theirs does not.

I was hired with the explicit understanding that I was to work a substantial amount of overtime each week. Although the union contract under which I was hired made overtime technically voluntary, for all intents and purposes I was given no choice if I wanted the job. At the outset I did not want to work any overtime. Unlike most other workers, I did not feel an economic need to work overtime. Although the added wages at time-and-a-half would be appreciated, my family could maintain itself at a good standard of living without it. But as I got into the job, my feelings about overtime became more complex. To get my job done properly I came to feel I often needed to work nine or ten hours each weekday with the trash. This meant that the best way for me to reduce the excessive work hours would be to eliminate Saturday work, a step my son and wife increasingly supported.

During my first sixty days on the job, the probationary period, I worked a six-day, 56-hour week every week, with the exception of the two weeks during plant shutdown, when I only worked a five-day week. During shutdown the issue of my working Saturdays, muted in tone, first came up. New to the plant, I had not realized I was supposed to check the shop bulletin board every week to see if I was posted for Saturday work. I simply expected, as told, to be working Saturdays. So, when on the Friday before plant shutdown my foreman asked me part way through the day if I would work a few additional hours of overtime that night, I assented without drawing any inferences about working the following day. I worked twelve hours that Friday and reported for work the next morning at 6:00, to be told that I had not been posted for Saturday work. I realized it was my mistake and was delighted to get the free time.

By contrast, during the final week of shutdown, as I had been wanting to get away to see my parents for a weekend, I asked my foreman if he would need me that Saturday. He said no, so I told him I would make other plans for the weekend, which I did. For a variety of reasons unrelated to me, the trash situation that week deteriorated. Late Friday afternoon, Sam paged me to say, "I just wanted to make sure you knew you were working tomorrow." I responded tartly, "I don't and I can't." I reminded him that I had checked with him earlier in the week about Saturday and that, as I told him, I had made plans to visit my parents in New York. Sam got someone else to dump the trash that Saturday.

Thereafter, to the best of my recollection, I worked every Saturday up to September 14. But I increasingly resented the intrusion upon my family and outside life generally. At the end of my probation in early September, the foreman came to me and said I didn't have to work every Saturday, that I was entitled to one out of four Saturdays off, during which another worker who knew the routine quite well would fill in. In response I told him that my family was on my back about all the hours and days I had to put in, whereupon he suggested that I might alternate on weekday mornings, coming in on some days at 6:00 A.M. and on others at 8:00 A.M. The suggestion, in effect, was for me to get the same job done daily in fewer hours. Since I was nervous about getting the job done in eight hours during the week and since my family and I especially wanted a free weekend, I suggested that I'd rather work alternate Saturdays. In my mind this was a step toward fully eliminating Saturday work, but I did not then make that explicit to my foreman, who no doubt saw the request simply as an effort to reduce Saturday work. On such a basis at least, he assented.

During the weeks following September 14, which had been my first Saturday off since August 3, I was concerned that the pattern of alternating Saturdays be established. My foreman, who understandably had more important things to think about, was much less concerned with but not insensitive to my wishes. On Saturday, September 28, after not having been alternated, I spoke to Sam about having the next two Saturdays off to do some things. He assented readily and said he had thought of giving me that day off so I would be alternating as requested, but that he had been short of manpower and so had had to post me for work. He assured me that I would be alternating Saturdays from then on. I was very pleased, even grateful.

Thereafter for some time I more or less worked alternate Saturdays, except that when Sam said he especially needed me I would work and when I had some special reason to get off he would usually agree even if the Saturday was not a scheduled one. But increasingly my family and I felt all Saturday work to be intolerable, and as time passed I tried repeatedly to communicate this fact to Sam. I told him frankly that I was having family problems about working so many hours and increasingly openly indicated I wished to work as few Saturdays as possible.

Then, in November the union signed a new contract with the company that experimentally changed the rules about overtime. Therefore, although overtime according to the old contract technically had been voluntary, if an employee refused to take overtime on Saturdays, the company had been entitled to deprive the employee of all other overtime. In other words, under the former contract the employee was faced with an all-or-nothing proposition, either "voluntarily" accept the overtime the company wanted him/her to work or risk losing it all. Under the new contract, an employee had the right to turn down Saturday overtime either on a blanket basis or Saturday-by-Saturday without forfeiting his/her option to work a contractually determined minimum part of whatever weekday overtime was required by the company.

That was the situation when the issue about my working Saturdays began to come to a head. Since I had worked the Saturday before the Thanksgiving holidays, during which the plant was closed down for a four-day weekend, I felt entitled to get off on the next working Saturday, December 7, which was my birthday. On Friday,

December 6, however, I noticed that my name was posted to work Saturday. I didn't want to have a hassle about it, but I also didn't want to work on my birthday. I told my foreman that I would rather not work the next day. He said he needed me; that he wouldn't have posted me if he hadn't needed me. He said he needed all the men he could get that Saturday. I said, "but it's my birthday." He said he couldn't help it; he needed me, and that if he could have scheduled me off he would have. But then he suggested that I might work just part day on that Saturday, say four hours—the minimum number of hours for which the company has to pay a worker for coming in to work. He further suggested I just hit the hoppers that needed it most. I agreed. It seemed the only possible compromise under the circumstances. I appreciated his belated efforts to take my needs into account somewhat, although I recognized the company would get all it wanted in the first place from the "compromise," while I would have to be in to work at 6:00 A.M. as usual.

The incident made me more determined to continue to cut back on Saturdays. Shortly thereafter I again informed the foreman that I would only work Saturdays when he really needed me, that otherwise I did not want to work Saturdays at all. Nevertheless, during the remaining two weeks in December before Christmas I was posted for each Saturday. On each Thursday evening or Friday morning after I saw the list, I informed my foreman that I did not wish to work that Saturday. It was getting a bit sticky, but I finally was getting my message across, I thought.

I returned to Blancs on Thursday, January 2, after a spectacular nine-day Christmas vacation, which under the new contract was a paid vacation, to find I had thought wrong. I had been looking forward to spending the coming Saturday with my son Soren, who had spent Christmas vacation in New York with his mother and who was having his eleventh birthday that day. But once again my name was posted to work Saturday, just as it had been posted for every week since the week before Thanksgiving.

I was angry at Sam; felt abused by him. He must know by now how I felt about Saturday work, I thought. Why didn't he just get Victor to dump the trash that day as he does whenever I'm not in?

THE WORK PROCESS

Why did Sam keep hassling me about Saturdays? Was my working that Saturday really "necessary"? Or merely "convenient"? Or, conceivably, was this process of repeatedly posting me to work Saturdays after I had told him in no uncertain terms I did not wish to work unless he really needed me an effort to make me more malleable? I did not and do not know. I only knew then that I had hoped not to have any further trouble with Sam about Saturday work, particularly as my six-month merit review was due soon. But there it was again.

I went up to Sam and told him I didn't want to work Saturday. He seemed displeased, and we began to exchange words. I said I had told him often that if at all possible I did not want to work Saturdays. He responded that he needed me. I retorted that he had posted me every Saturday since before Thanksgiving. Had he "needed me" every Saturday? Seemingly not understanding what I had said, he answered that Victor had handled the trash on several recent Saturdays. To which I responded that that was not because he hadn't posted me but because I had come to him each of those weeks and said I didn't want to work. We were both getting angrier.

I said that this Saturday was my son's birthday. He said he didn't care. I responded bitterly, "I know you don't care, but I do!" I said I had worked my own birthday only because he said he needed me. He said, too bad, but that he had had to work his birthday, too. I said that was his prerogative, but I had not wanted to work on my birthday. He then asked, almost rhetorically, did I then not want to work any Saturdays. I said, "Right!" I had repeatedly told him, I said, that I would be delighted not to work any Saturdays and would only work when he was in a jam. Whereupon he said, "Okay; start coming in at eight from now on every day during the week."

I was stunned. Although I was not wholly opposed, by any means, to giving up all my overtime, I feared the job could not be handled in eight hours. Moreover, the punitive nature of his declaration infuriated me. I resented his trying to punish me for not wanting to work Saturdays by taking away my weekday overtime. I said so. I also said that under the new contract, by then already in force for more than two months, Saturday overtime was voluntary, and that he had no right to punish me for refusing it. We parted on that note.

DOIN' TIME

I immediately looked for my union representatives, neither of whom was around at the time. But I did see my superintendent, Ron Merritt. I went up to him and in a fury began recounting the events. He said in his usual cool, detached way that if I wanted to discuss the matter with him I would have to stop yelling. I apologized, saying I was very angry about what had just happened. I told him I had repeatedly told Sam I didn't want to work Saturdays and that I had explained to him it was because of trouble with my family about working so many hours. I also told Ron that 48 hours a week was enough for me. That I didn't need to work 56 hours a week. With his usual poker face, Ron said Sam probably needed me. I told him Sam had posted me for every working Saturday since November 21, and that under the new contract I had a right not to work Saturdays. I ended up saying that if Sam tried to punish me by taking away my weekday overtime I would file a grievance and win it.

Merritt said he would talk it over with Sam. I felt terrible. It was the worst fight I had had with Sam in all the time I had been in the factory. But I was determined not to give in. I reported for work the next day, Friday, at 6:00 A.M. as usual. I never heard another thing about the matter. The irony of the situation was that two weeks later, with serious cutbacks in production, all overtime in the plant was eliminated.

That was an extremely serious blow to other workers in the plant, many of whom had made 30–50 percent of their total weekly wages through overtime work. Although other employees did not enjoy working overtime any more than I did, their situation was fundamentally different from mine. The difference lay in their dependence upon the money they made by working overtime.

In many cases overtime was necessary to enable workers to support their families at minimally decent standards of living. For those employees maximum hours legislation is a sham, since economic compulsion demands that they "voluntarily" work overtime. One employee, who had been with the company for nearly ten years, said he could not make ends meet without overtime. He made it clear he would like to avoid overtime work since he had no time to himself, but with money so tight he felt he had to work whenever he could.

THE WORK PROCESS

Still another worker, who was rarely given the option of overtime, moonlighted on another job when he could. He said one day at morning break that it was hard to "make it" on 40 hours. A fellow worker sitting nearby agreed and added bitterly, "We should be able to make a living on 40 hours a week."

Do these men voluntarily work overtime? Do other employees, indoctrinated with the consumption ethic, who live at a higher standard of living and work to keep up their various payments, voluntarily work overtime? What of the man who had worked 13 hours on Sunday, earning over $120 for his double-time, and who was so dog-tired on Monday he was having trouble doing his work? He had worked Sunday while his wife had waited for him right up to 7:30 P.M. so the family could go out to the country. That man felt he couldn't afford to take off a day later in the week to rest up.

Did the two employees at quitting time on that day in late August voluntarily choose to work overtime? We were all standing around that day ready to leave when Ron came in and half-jokingly said to the worker who that past Sunday had worked 13 hours, "I thought you said you were done with the job in heat treat."

"I am," replied the worker.

"No, you're not," said Ron, smiling; such-and-such was broken and needed a cable replaced. The worker, somewhat exasperated, said it was quitting time, and he had worked 13 hours the Sunday before and wasn't about to work any more. Ron, only slightly nonplussed, then asked for volunteers. There were none. Then he turned to another employee and began to cajole him. He coaxed, while the worker strung out the conversation without actually saying yes or no. Finally, before giving a direct answer, the worker turned to another man who worked as his helper and asked if he was working. The latter also was evasive. Ron waited and watched. Both finally worked, for two extra hours. Faced with the authority and power of management and with economic pressures on them, how "free" was their choice?

It is not just economic rewards/compulsions, then, that make men and women work overtime. It is a complex of reasons. Workers, for instance, know that it is risky too often to deny a foreman's or superintendent's request. Such denials can be taken to reflect a "bad attitude." Workers with "attitude problems" are less likely to get promoted, less likely to be well treated by management, and more likely to be held strictly to rules that others can quietly violate with near-impunity. External economic pressures to accept overtime when the company offers it thus are reinforced by internal pressures personified in the company's agent who directs worker's lives on the job, the foreman (and the superintendent).

And once overtime becomes something not to be avoided and even to be sought, then the allocation of overtime itself is transformed into another instrument of management for rewarding and punishing employees. A worker who filed a grievance some time ago believes that as punishment for grieving he has been deprived by his foreman of equal overtime. My foreman, as recounted above, tried to punish me by eliminating my weekday overtime. Although in my case he failed, the deterrence effect nonetheless was felt by other workers.

Thus for many reasons it is not easy to refuse to work overtime. But of course it is not supposed to be easy. The worker is on the job to serve the needs of the company to produce for a profit. When production is booming, the company demand for overtime is strong and, for the most part, men and women will and must work overtime, whatever else they might rather do. When production is lagging, overtime will be cut drastically, almost without effective notice and without regard for the economic needs of employees who have been encouraged by society to build up obligations on the basis of their overtime earnings. If production goes into a tailspin, layoffs (the opposite of overtime) will follow, with workers' lives taking up the production slack. Through it all, the worker is taught to be compliant to the demands of capitalist production as determined, interpreted, and enforced by management.

Consider the matter of vacations, for example. By and large for those many junior employees who have not earned more than two weeks yearly vacation, the choice of when they take their vacation is effectively made by the company. For most of those in production or production-connected jobs, their week or two weeks of vacation will be taken during the company shutdown, when the company does not want their services. By contrast, vacation for most of those in maintenance work, cannot be taken during those two summer weeks, because the company desperately needs their services then to get the plant back into good working shape.

Or take, again, the matter of overtime. Not infrequently, employees are "asked" late in the day, to do overtime, sometimes as they are about to leave for home. One day I know of it went beyond that. As we were leaving that day in early February, it was snowing lightly. Weather reports predicted about four inches of snow. By 4:30 P.M. the likelihood was strong that some snow would stick and accumulate. Yet service workers were not then asked to come in early the next morning to shovel snow. Instead, most were called at their homes that night, some as late as 11:45 P.M., and asked/told to report in at 5:00 A.M. to help clear the snow. Predictably, nearly all acquiesced and came in. Perhaps it was simply an oversight that resulted in such an egregious if unspectacular interference by the company in workers' private lives. Perhaps, on the other hand, the foreman waited till the evening to notify workers because he did not want to allocate overtime until he was certain it was necessary and would be useful from the company's point of view. I do not know.

The point is that the demands of capitalist production come first. What is left over after these demands are met is the residual time and capacity workers have to do everything meaningful in life. That time, time for living, thus is constricted, vulnerable, and manipulated. As a final illustration, consider the matter of union meetings. Since the plant worked on three shifts, and many workers normally worked on Saturdays, it was nearly impossible to find a single time for union meetings that did not conflict with production time, thereby precluding many workers from attending union meetings. Aside from the inconceivable choice of Saturday night, the only time available for union meetings that workers on all shifts could attend was Sunday. But Sunday is the prime day for "livin'." That, of course, was the day, once a month, we had our union meetings. And predictably, the overwhelming majority of workers chose each month not to attend. In so doing, they chose their private lives at the expense of the only institution they had to defend their collective interests at work, the union. That choice doubtless suited the company and union leaders.

V

Workplace Authoritarianism
Part I: Management

EMPLOYEES in American factories work under an authoritarian regime, based upon private ownership of the means of production, whose main function is to produce for the profit of owners. The attitudes and practices of the managers of this system of production toward workers reflect its purpose, as do workers' responses to management and to their jobs.

The authoritarian quality of production relations at work is central, rather than coincidental, to the American political culture, which is a liberal-capitalist culture. Some of the society's nonwork institutions serve to obscure, soften, and distract Americans from that fundamental authoritarian reality so crudely exposed in the workplace. But it is hard to imagine that the shaping to which workers are subject when they look for jobs and on the job itself could be as effective as it is if Americans before they entered the job market had not, for example, been taught to be deferential to authority, to treat consumption as an end, and to respond individually rather than collectively. The authoritarian relation in the factory could not be maintained, in short, if it were not supported by other institutions in our political economy to legitimate, facilitate, and enforce the continuing existence and development of capitalist relations in production.

Capitalism means, in part, that working men and working women are treated as a factor of production, like land and raw materials, to be purchased as cheaply as possible and exploited as much as possible under the circumstances to produce profit. Management's main task within this system is to manipulate the factors of production to maximize profit. This requires that management use its authority and power over workers to mold them to its own ends.

Exercise of power by some over others is predicated upon relative strength. In American factories it is predicated upon the weak bargaining position of individual workers, upon workers' feeling dependent on management for a livelihood, and upon their consequent sense of vulnerability. Power in American factories generally is seen as legitimately held by management. Rather than challenging managers' orders and forcing managers to exercise their power directly, therefore, workers, while keenly aware of that power, obey management directives in no small part because they accept management's authority to give direction. This acceptance implies deference by workers to management in the belief that in some sense management and the property owners it represents have the "right" in very broad areas to make decisions that affect workers' lives. From the point of view of those who rule the factory, exercising authority rather than power is a more efficient and satisfying means to achieve their ends. The exercise of authority normally avoids open struggle and confrontation, allowing power to be conserved and hidden until needed.

Power and authority are organized hierarchically, with management engaged in tasks that incorporate more power and authority. Partly in reflection of this allocation of power and authority and partly in support of it, there are observable patterned differences in the command behavior of managerial personnel at different levels.

Take my foreman and superintendent for example, the only managerial figures with whom I had much contact. My foreman, Sam, like foremen in general, was the link between producers and managers. He was the lowest-level line employee in management and the person immediately in charge of all manual laborers within his department. As a crucial middleman, he had to face both ways: down, in personally directing and coordinating the work of those below him, and up in dealing with Ron Merritt, the superintendent, and higher levels of management to develop and implement their directives. As a man required to spend most of his time with workers in order to direct them in their tasks, he needed to be someone who could relate reasonably well to workers. As the lowest rung on the managerial ladder of power and authority, one who did not spend much time in committee meetings and dealing with outside businessmen, he did not need to be too sophisticated or polished.

In fact, my foreman, like most foremen I know, gave the appearance on the job of being "working class." Although I sensed that he might have had some technical training and perhaps some higher education, his style, even as he exercised power and authority over us, was working class. He dressed more or less like a worker—no tie or jacket—mingled easily with workers, cracked jokes, got angry, swore, typically used slang, and as a personality seemed fairly open. His outward behavior, however, obscured important facets of his managerial role that he nonetheless performed. Like other foremen, for example, he no doubt kept information from workers that might well have dramatically affected their lives, such as future layoffs, for they were conceived as having no right to such information.

By contrast, my super, Ron, gave the appearance of being decidedly ruling, not working, class. He oozed quiet confidence, almost to the point of arrogance, walked ramrod erect, was extremely courteous, spoke crisply and dressed formally, and rarely if ever observably lost his cool. Although he related reasonably well to workers, always it was at a measured distance and openly instrumentally. If he spent considerable time with workers and foremen, he spent considerable time also with upper-level management and with men from outside the plant who came in to discuss business. If Sam's outward bearing obscured central aspects of his managerial role, Ron's epitomized his role as manager. Like a military officer, he gave off the aura of self-discipline and command. Like other successful business, academic, and political entrepreneurs, he gave the intimidating impression without actually ever saying so that it was his time that was most valuable, and that it was his judgment that most mattered. He was (I realized only after seeing Al Pacino play Michael Corleone in *Godfather, Part II*) perfect for his role of directing other people's lives. Like men and women who rule us in various fields, he knew how to use information, silence, secrecy, and half-compliments to keep those below him with whom he dealt in place. He already embodied the rationalized traits of the American ruling class. He was attractive, purposeful, seemingly humane, and liberal, but in achieving his purposes he would be as ruthless as his role demanded.

Something of his controlling role-character has already been suggested. When my foreman tried to punish me for refusing to work Saturdays and I yelled as I recounted the events to Ron, he coolly informed me that I would have to stop yelling if I wanted to talk to him. On my last day of work, as I was rushing to finish the job in seven hours instead of the usual ten, he called me to take an extra hopper someplace. When I said doing so would interrupt my routine and I would fall behind as a consequence, he insisted that nevertheless I was to do as he said. No doubt it would not normally have been necessary for him to be so assertive, except for my unusual reluctance to take on an added task on my last day. In the face of this assertion of authority, I complied.

Most revealing of how authority and power are exercised in tandem over workers, however, is another small episode that occurred with my superintendent after I had been laid off. At the close of my last day at work I looked for my foreman or superintendent in order to return the keys to the compactor, for which I had been responsible. Neither man was around, so I informed their secretary that I was putting the keys on my foreman's desk, where keys frequently had been left before. As I put the keys down, lawyer's intuition warned me to make sure I had a witness, so I said to an onlooking fellow worker, "Jack, you saw me putting these keys here." He nodded.

Several days later when I returned to the plant gate to sign a grievance I was perfunctorily filing through the union, I was informed at the gatehouse that my foreman wanted to talk to me. The guard called in, and, as my foreman wasn't available, I talked to my super on the phone. Ron said they hadn't been able to locate the compactor keys. Obviously suspecting me of forgetfulness, negligence, or worse, he then informed me that he had held up my final check because of the keys. I began to feel aggrieved and angry. I told him what had happened, that I had done the only thing with the keys

THE WORK PROCESS

that seemed reasonable and responsible since neither he nor Sam had been on hand the afternoon I was terminated.

Ron said, as if he had no alternative, that he would release my check when they found the keys. I blew my stack. Angrily and lawyerlike, I said I had done everything I could and that I had witnesses to that effect. Accusatorily, I declared, "First you lay me off and then you hold up my check for something that isn't my fault and over which I have no control." I hit the mark. For the first time in my experience with him my superintendent began to lose his own self-control, retorting in a threatening tone, "You're getting my dander up." I said I didn't give a damn, but then quickly tried to calm us both down. I suggested that he look again on my foreman's desk for the keys, which he did, to no avail. That was the last I spoke to him. Afterwards my foreman, who knew I was neither dishonest, forgetful, nor a saboteur, got on the phone. Sam said he hadn't known about my wages being held up, and indicated he would do what he could to release the check. He succeeded.

What is noteworthy about this minor incident is that it typifies how, when authority seems to fail, management quickly turns to its power over workers to try to discipline them. As far as I can tell, my superintendent was not being vindictive in holding up my wages. He was simply trying to maintain some leverage over me in case I had forgotten, lost, or stolen the keys. He was acting rationally, in accordance with his managerial role that was concerned almost exclusively with the interests of the company. Had I been an ordinary worker just laid off and expectably facing very hard times, his action, he must have known, would have delayed my getting the only check I would receive in the few weeks before Unemployment Insurance benefits could be paid to me.

On the job, workers are trained to be compliant to management's wishes. The man who only half-jokingly said that he'd decided after repeated trouble with his foreman during his first years on the job to "jump off the roof" if his foreman told him to because he was getting paid to obey, caught the spirit of the kind of cooperation expected by management of workers. Another man who refused to "cooperate" and complained during work time to his union safety committeeperson about a machine that had just injured him received a warning slip for doing so. He was told that, according to contract rules, he was required to get permission from his foreman before speaking to the safety person. Still another worker, who was trying without union support to get his wage grade raised since he often was assigned to do work not in his job category, which he believed was above his grade, was told by his foreman, "you got to do as you're told." To which the worker replied, "I know that. Any child knows that, but fair's fair."

There it is, still perhaps somewhat hidden from view. Workers are surrounded by rules and treated and disciplined as if they were schoolchildren. What is "fair" is not a matter of abstract justice, but a function of rules in the company-union contracts. To perform their jobs, to retain their self-respect and dignity and/or to protect themselves from being exploited too much, workers are regularly likely to break some of those many rules. But rule breaking in turn leaves them vulnerable and liable to being disciplined. The whole arrangement is psychologically and politically destructive of what little sense of self-respect and control of their own lives workers in our system are able to build up.

Moreover, in a society in which the search for approval from authority figures seems to be almost a way of life, at least for the better educated and for the characters on TV shows, workers have to live in a political work environment in which their authority figures rarely if ever show approval or appreciation for the job they do. Authority and power are normally exercised in the factory to organize and discipline, rather than to approve. So if factory workers also seek approval and appreciation, theirs is a deeply frustrating work life. Brought up to be such a seeker, I found my own need to be appreciated as a "good trashman" consistently unfulfilled, which often made me feel worthless and depressed. If, on the other hand, workers have learned from their experience not to seek or expect approval from workplace authority figures, their work, generally without inherent meaning, also largely is without extrinsic satisfaction. Either way, workers are made to feel not like valued men and women but like things to be manipulated and replaced if necessary for purposes of production.

THE WORK PROCESS

The appreciation workers most easily can earn is tailored to their own production: not personal approval for a job well done, but monetary return in the form of bonuses that seem to accrue automatically and impersonally when a worker produces above the standard set for his/her job by the time-study people. Earning such bonuses, however, often requires workers to manipulate reports of their output and foremen to implicitly tolerate this practice, because for bonuses to be effective as material incentives the rules and standards for their award almost demand that they be violated. In the process of "cheating," the worker's self-image is further demeaned, except insofar as s/he can take satisfaction in seeming to rip off the company.

The foreman's tolerance of and connivance in cheating, in addition, results in the worker's becoming further dependent upon the foreman, which is the name of the game. Compliance, as suggested above, is facilitated by workers feeling vulnerable to management's exercise of its broad discretionary power and authority. The feeling of being dependent on management figures and the feeling of being without meaningful alternatives is the foundation upon which management designs employee compliance.

As production is organized in American factories, workers are dependent upon management in a variety of ways. Production is organized according to a capitalist division of labor so as to fragment workers' experiences of production and so as to give them a sense that the organization of production is a mystery to which only managers hold the key. This mystification is one basis for managerial authority, the vision being that managers somehow "deserve" to control others' work because they understand how production is coordinated. The other side of that vision, which itself is only one of the ambivalent feelings workers have about managers, is that workers feel they are incapable of managing production themselves. Both feelings, about themselves and managers, serve to legitimate managerial power and facilitate worker dependence and compliance.

Beyond that, workers are dependent upon management both for decent equipment in order to produce and for safety measures to minimize the many risks in production. In these areas, ironically, management's lackluster performance only makes workers more dependent. For example, if equipment were maintained in excellent shape, the worker could do his/her job without the sense of having to rely repeatedly on management to coordinate repairs. And if the plants were safe places in which to work, which by and large they are not, concerned workers would not have to plead and bargain with management to get it to take even minimal steps to reduce safety risks.

In short, it is management's exclusive and nearly arbitrary control of the production process and of how workers are fitted into that process that at base keeps workers dependent upon managers. I did not control the immediate factors of production necessary for me to do a good job. I could not perform my work efficiently and responsibly unless management overhauled my normal fork or rented me a better one. Since I felt responsible willy nilly for doing my job well, I was in this sense at the mercy of my foreman. With such an orientation, I at times actually felt dependent to the point of helplessness. To the extent I learned to limit the scope of my sense of responsibility and to restrict my own initiative, however, I lessened my feeling of dependence upon management for doing my job. But in the process I also came to realize how much beyond my control doing a good job really was, which drastically reduced the satisfaction I took from the job.

Management, of course, has many methods for enforcing worker dependence. It has a wide variety of rewards and punishments it can dole out almost at will, from granting and withholding overtime, to issuing warnings that go on workers' records, to authorizing worker transfers and promotions, to firing and decreeing layoffs. In addition to all these more or less formal mechanisms for making workers compliant, managers in many small ways can informally make an employee's life immeasurably more or less bearable or unbearable and more or less secure.

Consider the matter of firings and layoffs. Workers I know believe that an employee who grieves too often against his foreman or in general is too assertive will eventually either be coopted into management or the union leadership or, more likely, be fired or forced into so intolerable a position that s/he will quit. Management of course has the option of choosing which way to deal with a particular

THE WORK PROCESS

worker. For example, workers believe that even the assertion of contractual rights is likely to be viewed by the company as making trouble. Whether this is the case (and from what I could see, it is), the repressive effect that these widely held beliefs have on all kinds of actions to redress grievances and improve the lot of workers is subtle but enormous.

When an old-time worker I often spoke to heard that another worker was suing the company, he said, "the company'll get rid of him, one way or another." When the union and company were negotiating a new contract and several of us at the plant wanted to get a bunch of workers we knew together to talk about the issues, nearly everyone we approached was hesitant to get together privately outside the plant even to discuss their own contract, because they feared losing their jobs. When I was trying to collect signatures from workers in my department on a petition to the union, I told a fellow worker I was willing to take the risk of bucking the union, that my job didn't mean everything in the world to me. His response was that I should never tell my co-workers that "I didn't care about losing my job," because so many of them fear losing theirs and fear doing anything that might put their jobs in jeopardy. When one man in my department, who apparently had been drinking during working hours on more than one occasion, was fired, his firing created an intensified atmosphere of intimidation within the department. After word of the firing had spread, another worker warned me that I had better go back to working Saturdays again or Sam would "get you."

Getting fired is a real disaster for a worker, particularly for one along in years and especially if the economy is in bad shape at the time. Getting fired for many terminates pension rights. The firing goes on one's employment record, making getting another job more difficult. And finally, being fired means that Unemployment Insurance coverage doesn't begin until five weeks after the effective date of job termination.

Getting laid off, though bad enough, does not carry these added disadvantages. But layoffs do perform an analogous function for the company beyond reducing total wage expenses. Layoffs further condition men and women to feel insecure and dependent upon the company. Workers know that who gets laid off and who gets re-placed in other jobs is not simply a function of invisible economic forces and seniority. They know that managers exercise discretion about who stays and who goes. And workers know that it is better to stay on the good side of those whose decisions so affect workers' futures.

Well short of firings and layoffs, management periodically asserts its formal authority and power by issuing warning slips, sometimes in bunches like bananas. On the day after I received my oral warning for "talking too much" (the comic in my department, who knew how much the man with whom I had been "talking" loved to talk, characterized my admonition as the only one ever given for "listening too much") at least three other men in the service department got oral warnings for not wearing safety glasses. These men had worked in the plant on the average for over 15 years. They understood the company didn't really care about plant safety, only about its insurance rates. They knew they were being slapped on the wrists like children. But after that they wore their glasses more regularly. And after my oral warning for talking, workers for a time were more cautious about chatting during working hours. Recognizing that management could in fact lay warnings on workers almost at will—since all workers make enough mistakes to provide management with many opportunities to discipline them—the same comic in my department claimed he actually went up to the foreman in anticipation and said "Sam, give me my warning slip now, 'cause I know I'll do something wrong."

Given the various ways management in our system has to discipline workers to accommodate them to the harsh demands of capitalist production, one of the most frequent complaints workers make is that superiors "don't treat us like human beings." Although no doubt some managers treat workers better than others, the way workers in general are treated cannot be understood in terms of the personalities of the individual managers. Nor can this treatment be ascribed simply to a lack of managerial concern for workers' lives, because the other side of the coin of this apparent mere lack of concern for workers is the intense concern managers have for production. Faced by a choice between workers' needs and the needs of

THE WORK PROCESS

production, managers—whatever their particular personalities—consistently must choose production. I saw the choice take its toll on managers, who are accountable to higher ups, as well as on workers.

One day I went to my foreman to report that the radiator cap on the 173 towmotor I was using was missing. In the course of a friendly discussion about the problem of keeping the fork in good working order, Sam said, "Production is up; repairs are up; and the pressure is up on everyone." Then, interrupting to answer the phone, he said to someone on the other end that the pressure had gotten to him too, which was why he recently had taken two days off. That was the only occasion in my seven months in the plant when I was able to observe tangible evidence of the toll production takes on managers. In the case of workers, the toll, particularly in terms of the fundamental inhumanity of their relations with managerial personnel, was almost daily in evidence.

One day I came late into the cafeteria for morning break to hear the tail end of an angry complaint by several workers about something that had happened with our superintendent. The two, who were the highest-grade blacks in our department and among the highest in the plant, had worked the preceding Sunday and had left before 2:00 P.M., instead of working through until 2:30. The gate guard apparently had reported that fact to Ron Merritt, who the next day bawled them out for leaving early. The workers claimed they had skipped their breaks and lunch half-hour so as to leave early. Both claimed they had told the superintendent off for treating them like that. In discussing the incident with Merritt, the issue of Sunday work itself seems to have come up, and they understood Ron to be telling them that when the company needed them "you got to work Sundays." To that one of the men had replied: "There's only two things that my grandpa in South Carolina told me I got to do. One is to be black and the other is to die." In fact, they both worked almost whenever they were asked/told, but they demanded the dignity of believing they were choosing for themselves whether to work.

At another morning break a month later, the men were talking about a verbal fight between our foreman and one of the workers, a

WORKPLACE AUTHORITARIANISM I

bull of a man who spoke with a stutter and usually seemed quite mild mannered. At some point in the argument Sam apparently had told the worker to "shut up." The worker responded furiously, telling the foreman off, apparently without stuttering, as some of the other workers who had witnessed the events were quick to point out. Everyone at the long table seemed angry about it, saying a foreman "shouldn't bring his own problems into work," and that "there ain't no boys around here" and "everyone should be talked to like a man." If the foreman was going to bawl someone out, even if the foreman was right, he shouldn't do it, they agreed, in front of everybody, but with the man alone. One worker, who always talked big, said he "don't have to take no shit from Sam. Working is enough shit." All visibly assented.

Such incidents, which happened frequently throughout the factory, may appear to be simply the result of disturbed personalities and other coincidental factors. They were not. In part, of course, they occured because of coincidental factors, like who the particular foreman was and how the foreman was feeling that day. But they would hardly have occurred at all were workers not considered and treated as means to the production end. The authority and power relations built into our system of production condition superiors as well as inferiors, making it almost inevitable that such behavior toward inferiors will regularly occur. That foremen, for example, rarely if ever tell their own superiors to "shut up" suggests how truly decisive the relations of authority and power are in facilitating such incidents with ordinary workers. Under our production system, the end of which is private profit, the human dignity of workers is and must be violated as a matter of routine.

As it is, workers' fragile, remnant sense of dignity and autonomy is something they protect vigorously. One man, for example, who had not worn the proper safety equipment for a job in a particular area, was threatened by his foreman with a warning slip and a ticket. The worker felt his foreman was pleased to have something over him and was playing with him. At some point the worker exploded at the foreman, saying "I ain't no dog or child" and "I either want the ticket or not, but I don't want to play no more." After some further plead-

THE WORK PROCESS

ing by his union representative with the foreman, the worker again said to the foreman, "Enough; do what you want to do, but do it." He later said to me, "I ain't needed no one over me since my mother had to be to drop me."

In the same vein was my own delayed reaction to the formal oral warning I received. I remember how, thinking about it a day later, I became angry. I wanted to protest to management about what I saw as an insult and an injustice. And the more I thought about the fact that I hadn't been behind in my job, had had my lunch half-hour interrupted, and had then gotten a warning, the more one-sided I thought it was. So the next day I stopped my super as he passed through the cafeteria and firmly but respectfully said I wanted supervision to know all the facts about what happened the day before. Not that I achieved any satisfaction. I might as well have been talking to the sphinx. Then, I mentioned it to my foreman, adding that "if we are treated like children, we will act like children." Sam didn't seem to really disagree and even seemed sympathetic. He simply said the other worker and I had been talking in too obvious a place, and the big brass saw too much of it. Still—shades of elementary school—the naked fact was that I had been warned for "talking too much." And I found such a warning in itself insulting and demeaning, particularly in the context of the day's events.

Sam's sympathetic explanation, though, somehow made it seem a little less insulting. But such explanations were hardly commonplace in the factory. There, as less crudely elsewhere in our system, those who ruled us did not explain themselves to us, except insofar as they were forced to do so or felt it served their own purposes. Information was understood as both a source and reflection of power and authority.

As indicated, the factory workers' subordination and related vulnerability is effected in part by the company's keeping from workers sufficient advance information about the factors of production and intentions of the company so likely to affect their lives. Perhaps the company is simply unconcerned with informing workers. To conceive of it as a lack of concern, however, is to miss the point. Keeping workers ignorant of such information is not merely convenient for

WORKPLACE AUTHORITARIANISM I

a management that has other, more pressing money-making concerns. Keeping workers ignorant also helps management control them. Ignorance, particularly in the face of economic instability, makes workers insecure, hanging for hard information upon company handouts that consistently come too late for a meaningful response. Management treats information as part of its private property and uses information to protect its own authoritarian rule.

Thus one day we were informed officially that effective the following day all overtime, a prized and widespread practice in the plant, had been cancelled. There was no time to adjust to such a cataclysm, which made inflation appear benign by comparison. Similarly in the case of layoffs, the company was singularly uninformative. Those laid off received only three days' notice. The postings of names of those people laid off in each shop gave notice to others still working there of what had happened. But, under the LIFO human inventory system of seniority in which the Last In (last hired) goes First Out onto the street, as workers with plantwide seniority were laid off their jobs, they "bumped back" to prior jobs in a seemingly unpredictable, crazy quilt pattern, displacing other, less senior workers in various parts of the plant.

Through it all workers felt increasingly insecure. Communication about these most vital matters was entirely by rumor. We questioned each other daily about what was happening, and, half disbelieving, passed on whatever we heard. Rumors bounced from one shop to another, filling the void created by the workers' dread and the company's secrecy. One day we heard that a major purchaser of our plant's products had cancelled yet another part of its mammoth order. Then that the purchasing company had cancelled its entire order. The next week that that company's work force was on strike, which was reassuring, suggesting that the order might merely be delayed until the strike was settled.

In the face of this, management was worse than uninformative. It was reassuring. Until layoffs actually began, the word spread informally by foremen—who themselves only get such information as those above them deem necessary and who cannot afford to contribute to worker demoralization since success in their job of directing workers is itself dependent upon workers' performance—was that there wouldn't be layoffs in our plant since we were so piled up with back orders.

In this context, workers, given their own lack of solidarity and a woefully ineffective union, waited, only half hopeful, like potential draftees during the Vietnam War, to be picked off individually. Company forthrightness on such crucial matters, by contrast, might well have provoked workers to mobilize to resist layoffs, which is precisely what the company and the union do not want. Better to let sleeping dogs lie.

This managerial attitude toward information, itself the joint product of management's lack of concern for workers' lives and concern for maintaining its own power and authority, is widespread and routinized in the factory and extends to a whole range of small matters. Thus, during the plant shutdown in my fourth week of work, when the compactor was shut down for more than a week so that concrete could be laid over the area where the container was set, my foreman made no effort to advise me when I would be able to get back on the job to begin to dump the mountains of trash that were piling up in the interim. Although I worried about getting to it and repeatedly asked him, until the day before I was to begin to dump again I learned nothing. On that day I told him that I had learned from the outside contractor that the rails to hold the container would be set in the concrete today. Sam indicated he already knew, whereupon I said that I was anxious about whether we could get the container delivered on the following day, a Friday, because the container service truck driver had told me that he had a lot of scheduled stops on Fridays, and I knew Blancs wasn't a scheduled stop, but a call-in. Sam again said he knew, and retorted that I should "let him do his job." I told him "that's fine with me, but I'm worried about doing my job." He responded that during shutdown there had been nothing else we could do and that he had been told by the outside contractor that no weight should be put on the concrete until noon Friday. Since I had not known day-to-day when I would resume my job as trashman, I would have appreciated being informed of that fact earlier.

WORKPLACE AUTHORITARIANISM I

This was not an isolated incident in my relations with my foreman. As recounted above, I was generally uninformed about matters as intimately related to my job as the future of my fork. What information I received was usually gleaned at my initiative rather than as a matter of course. Thus, one morning in mid-August, as I tried unsuccessfully to start the old 173, Sam walked over half-smiling and said, "No wonder; you don't know how to start it." Half-thinking he might be kidding, I replied straight, "Why don't you teach me." To which he sagely replied, "You'll have to learn yourself." By then I could see he was dead serious, and I retorted, "I hope you're kidding. Given the condition of this fork, you should be." He said he wasn't kidding, and then added shortly, "I've done all I can. I can't get you a new fork." I said, "I appreciate that, but this one is still lousy; it regularly stalls out, and getting it started is not a matter of learning how." Then fairly quietly, I heard Sam say something like, "Well, you won't have to put up with it much longer." At the time, still on probation, I had no firm idea of what he meant by that obscure remark. Was he planning to get rid of the fork or me?

I learned thereafter from another worker and then finally from my foreman himself that while Sam was criticizing me for not knowing how to start the towmotor, he was either seriously considering having its motor completely overhauled or had already decided to apply to have it done. A mechanic told me, when I asked if there was anything I could do to reduce the exhaust smoke from the fork, that there was nothing I could do; that its engine was shot; and that Sam was pricing a new engine. The meaning of Sam's remark about my not having "to put up with it much longer" only then became clear.

Soon after learning this, I was scalded by the fork's radiator erupting. From that moment I was determined to have something done about the fork. I spoke to Sam, who only then informed me about the recommendation for an overhaul having gone upstairs, where it had to be approved. When I asked how long approval might take, since I didn't want to be scalded again, he said about two weeks. More than two weeks later, without further word, I approached him again. I said I was willing to take advantage of Mr. Bradshaw's open door policy to tell him myself about the fork problem. Sam said,

"That ain't your job." To which I responded, "but it is my job to drive that fork, and it's unsafe." "Anytime you don't want to drive that fork, just say so," Sam answered angrily and authoritatively. What real choice did I have? I weakly repeated, "Sam, it's unsafe." In response, he began to explain to me that the cost for overhauling the fork was so high that it had to be approved by several levels of upper-level management, perhaps even including central headquarters in Pittsburgh. He also indicated that he had had some complaints from the union about the exhaust smoke. The union complaints obviously concerned him more than my safety or my convenience in doing my job, I realized.

Thereafter, as time passed with no apparent progress, I began to wonder whether anything really was being done to either fix the fork or get a replacement. I never found out for certain, because it was only after OSHA some time later formally prohibited further operation of the fork in the plant that I got a replacement. And it was three months after that that the 173 was returned, overhauled, just three days before I was laid off.

Perhaps I found the lack of information psychologically more difficult to tolerate than others in the factory. But others confronted the same problems. For example, the man who trained me for my job and who replaced me when I was laid off was kept in limbo for weeks after he had been bumped off his latest job without knowing what he would be doing. Even after I had received formal notice that I was to be laid off and had learned that Morton would be returning to his old job, it was several days more before management deigned to inform him.

In the face of the way management exercises its power and authority, it is hardly surprising that the majority of workers, laboring in purposeless jobs, have learned to "adjust" to their work context by generally avoiding responsibility and just "making do." Without having the authority and power necessary to do a good job, those who conscientiously attempt to do a good job become extremely frustrated. As a consequence, workers are socialized by our system to be less conscientious about their jobs and instead to simply give the impression of "doing the job." One man who drove a fork was delighted whenever his fork broke down and he couldn't work. As he saw such situations, it wasn't his time but company time that was being wasted. And he didn't particularly care whether his job got done so long as he got paid.

One day when I was trying to get to a hopper that was blocked by some rings in the aisle, I asked an older worker who was responsible if he could move the rings out of the way. He said his hand lift was broken, and that he couldn't even use it to do his own job. "But," he added, "if the company don't care, then neither do I. Fuck 'em."

Another related response by men and women who cannot control the factors necessary to do a good job is to deny responsibility for the effects that their trying to "make do" produces on others. When, for example, there was not enough room to stack rings out of the aisles and truckers therefore had to stack them in the aisles, often obstructing my hoppers, they almost consistently denied their responsibility.

Similarly, my foreman, who often tried to deny responsibility for equipment breakdowns and to shift the blame to workers, was simply trying to "make do" with the poor equipment with which he was provided. On the Saturday I was scalded, sustaining some third-degree burns, I went immediately down to Sam and said, "I have come to strangle you." "Why?" he half-nonchalantly asked. I told him that, like Morton before me, I had been scalded by the 173. I further told him he should get a new engine for the fork or get this one fixed once and for all. He shocked me by asking if I had had the radiator "blown out." Since that was the first I had ever heard about blowing out radiators, I said no. Morton, I told him, had never said anything about that. "Morton didn't tell you?" he asked with an almost incredulous tone. "No, and neither did you," I tartly responded, still in pain. "You have to blow it out about once a week or so," he said.

There I was, scalded by the company's deteriorating equipment, and Sam was telling me I hadn't maintained it properly, suggesting it wasn't his or the company's fault, but mine or Morton's. And there was some truth in what he said, for I later learned that blowing the accumulated dust out of the radiator grate allows better ventilation,

THE WORK PROCESS

thereby somewhat reducing the temperature of the water. But even clean, the fork ran too hot; the needle in its temperature gauge was frequently in the danger area. At bottom, my foreman sought to avoid responsibility for something over which he himself had only limited control.

There is still a third way in which responsibility is evaded. It is "kicking something upstairs." One pattern in dealing with work problems (though it risks angering foremen, who don't want to be burdened by workers' problems) is to take the problem to the foremen for them to make the decision. When a hopper broke and I was unable to fix it with the help of another worker, a third worker said, "Tell Sam and make it his problem." And on the first of many occasions on which my fork's horn ceased to function, a fellow worker advised me to notify Sam: "then he's responsible, not you, if something happens." Another agreed, saying as long as I told Sam, it would be "his ass, not yours."

Still another man, who had once been the company trashman, explained to me one day how he had done the job. He said he drove fast, beeping all the time, so people would learn to stay out of his way. "Let 'em think you're a bit crazy." When an onlooking foreman complained to him about the speed at which he drove he responded that he had to drive fast to get his routine done. When his own foreman told him to slow down, he did so. But then he didn't pick up all the trash. His main approach, too, was "to put the weight on the foreman."

A number of these patterned evasions seemed to converge one comical day in early October. My container had been full for a while and I was expecting the container service any time to empty it when an ancient janitor who dumped trash several times a day in the compactor suggested I look outside. Outside I saw there were hundreds of pounds of rocks piled up, blocking the container. The city contractor, who was repairing the road out back, had obviously left them there. I called Sam and told him we needed a payloader to move the rocks out. Just as I got off the phone the container serviceman came in. I asked him to wait a while, assuring him that my foreman was seeing to getting the rocks moved out of the way. The serviceman radioed in and waited, though he was about to go off duty. Nothing happened. Embarrassed, I went over to Sam's office. He said he would send two guys over with shovels. I said, "but Sam, it's like a thousand pounds of rocks." He replied that it wasn't that easy to get a payloader. When the two men came over carrying shovels and saw the piles, they cursed Sam out. One disappeared while the other and I began feebly to clear the rocks with shovels, which probably would have taken about three or four hours. Then the other man returned, with Sam following soon thereafter, having been informed again that shovels just would not do. Then it was Sam's turn. He cursed the city for leaving the rocks there, and then said he would go by the city field office to get it to clear the rocks away. But, apparently to put a face of reasonableness upon his earlier order, it seemed to us, he told us to clear by hand a smaller pile of rocks. Then he left. One of the men and I began to go at it with shovels, barely making a dent in it by the time the other guy returned with a worker we all knew from another department who was driving his payloader. There followed then some confusion as to who was going to authorize his moving the rocks with the payloader. I finally took the initiative, saying we all authorized it collectively. We laughed, and within 25 minutes the whole mess was cleared away. In this case, after a few false starts, workers actually assumed responsibility and authority to do a job that management had hestiated to assume. So evasion, although the general rule, was not the invariable response to difficulty.

In a context in which employees' negative attitudes toward the job are a response to the purposes for and ways in which management unilaterally exercises its power and authority over them, there is one redeeming feature. Unlike many areas of society where the allocation and exercise of power and authority is less distinct and crude, in the authoritarian atmosphere of the factory it is clear to nearly everybody not only that there is a "them" and an "us," but also who "they" are and who "we" are. Foremen mark the formal beginning of "them," and the highest-grade workers and some high union officials are seen as informally somewhere between "them" and "us." "We" do the dirty work. "They" command, punish and reward "us." No matter how friendly a foreman may be with his/her subordinates, every worker knows the basic fact of life. The foreman is the agent of the company and can't really be relied on as a friend. The foreman is one of "them."

II

Workers
and the Union

VI

Workplace Authoritarianism
Part II: The Union

LOCAL 1784 of the International Association of Machinists and Aerospace Workers (IAM) has a membership of approximately 1,550 members, who work at three Blancs plants in the Baltimore metropolitan area. Approximately 900 of its members work at the South Baltimore plant, where I worked, a majority employed on day shift. Of its 1,550 members, around 220 are women, nearly all in the South Baltimore plant. Numerically, the local is rather equally divided between blacks and whites. Its president in 1974–75 was white; its vice president black. Within the membership there are many divisions based on overlapping factors like sex, age, ethnicity, race, wage grade, skills, ability to earn production bonuses, seniority, and place of work. These divisions can be and are overcome at times, but they also can be and are exacerbated by management and by some union leaders to further reduce worker solidarity.

The relationship between the union and most of its leaders, on the one hand, and rank-and-file union members, on the other, is built upon two bases: first, upon workers' need for collective association and representation; and second, upon the exclusive power and authority to represent "organized" workers' interests to management accorded the union by the legal structure of the American political economy. Union monopoly means that the document that articulates and legitimates the regime of governance for production in the plant, the so-called collective bargaining agreement, must be negotiated by management with the recognized union. That contract, along with internal union rules, is the ostensible foundation for the relationship between individuals and their union. This relationship in a practical sense is embodied in two sorts of contacts, one sporadic and highly individualized, the other regular, formally periodic, and more collective.

An individual worker from time to time may deal with his/her union through the union shop steward or committeeperson for purposes either of filing a grievance against management or defending against managerial actions like the issuing of warning slips that affect the individual. Workers also can attend the regular, monthly union meetings at the union hall. Since this is the only formal institution in the union that provides the possibility for serious collective communication among workers and between workers and their union leaders, and since therefore it is a primary internal factor shaping union/member relations, these meetings merit further consideration.

As indicated earlier, the meetings were held once a month on Sunday mornings. Although there is no ideal time to hold union meetings since union members work three shifts and often six days a week, the choice of Sunday was hardly conducive to encouraging large attendance at meetings. Alternative times for meetings, on the other hand, were said to be precluded on the grounds that holding meetings at any time but Sunday would deprive workers on some shift of the freedom to choose to attend meetings. Given existing realities, however, this concern to formally assure all workers a freedom of choice seemed worse than misplaced. In practice the focus on protecting the formal freedom of choice operated to reduce the likelihood of its meaningful exercise. So few workers from any shift chose to attend Sunday meetings that regular meetings held at almost any other time, say late afternoon or evening, were likely to be enormously more convenient for and better attended by the vast majority of workers.

Be that as it may, Sunday morning had proven in practice to be a disastrous time. For those who worked six days a week—and during extended periods of high production hundreds of workers at my plant alone did—Sunday was their only day off each week. Understandably, they were less than eager to spend part of it at a union meeting talking about work. Moreover, for the many workers who were religious, Sunday morning meetings conflicted with church going. And for the countless workers who felt the need to "tie one on" each Saturday night, Sunday morning was the time to recuperate from hangovers.

At least partly because of when they were scheduled, then, the regular union meetings got turnouts that can only be characterized as abysmal. At the five I attended the average turnout was about seventy members, nearly half of whom appeared to be union officials of one sort or another. This meant, discounting for the moment the attendance of shop stewards, committeemen, higher union officers and the like, that approximately 3 percent of union members attended each regular union meeting. Since many of the rank-and-filers attending were repeaters, it seems fair to say that considerably fewer than 10 percent of the union membership attended more than one of the regular union business meetings a year.

This is extremely important for two reasons. It means, first, that for the overwhelming majority of workers contacts with their union were superficial, sporadic, and unsustained. Consequently, their level of information about the union was very low; their sense of collective will quite weak; and their meaningful input into so-called collective decision making within the union nearly nonexistent. Because one of the requirements for eligibility to union office was that a nominee have attended at least five meetings during the year preceding nominations in November, poor attendance also meant that probably fewer than 5 percent of the total membership in the local were even eligible to represent their union brothers and sisters. And approximately half of that 5 percent were incumbents and their hangers-on. Under these conditions union democracy is a sham.

As if this were not bad enough, two further factors make one wonder whether indeed the pressures discouraging active member participation in union affairs are not more than simply a product of "unavoidable circumstances." Until several years ago, our union meetings were held in a conveniently located hall that was rented from the Retail Clerks Union. When that union sought to raise its rental fees, the leadership of our local apparently balked and decided to buy its own hall. The place they chose, 3006 Hamilton Avenue, was about as inconvenient a choice in the area as they could have made. It was far from our work place and far from where the majority of the local's members lived.

Moreover, for any member who actually had made it one Sunday up to the Hamilton Avenue hall and sat through a regular union meeting, the incentive to return to sit through another can't have been very great. Union meetings, co-workers agreed, were so boring they couldn't take them. The meetings generally lasted for approximately two and one-half to three hours. They began with a mechanical salute to the flag. The salute was followed by nearly an hour of seemingly endless, often nonessential bureaucratic nonsense during which members were either "read to" or at best "talked at." Much of this time was taken up by the perfunctory and belabored reading of the minutes of the previous regular meetings and the minutes of all interim Executive Committee meetings, by the reading of disbursements to reimburse union officials for work time lost due to union business, and by the reading of various selected letters on an almost infinite variety of subjects that the local had received since the last meeting. Too much of the information was trivial. We learned that the local had contributed $20 to a county bullroast; that X had been reimbursed $25.17 for lost work time on such-and-such a day; and that Y had been reimbursed for travel expenses to some union-affiliated seminar, about which nothing was ever heard again. Most of the other information communicated that wasn't trivial was either communicated in such a superficial manner as to trivialize it, or was simply not amenable to oral communication. Thus we learned of the various motions and actions that were passed and taken at the last union and Executive Committee meetings. But we almost never learned what the issues were, what the arguments on each side were, and what the consequences of those actions might have been. Or we heard the periodic treasurer's report, which took perhaps five minutes to read to us and was so full of compressed and complex information that serious consideration of its contents was nearly impossible.

Obviously, most of the important information could be better put in the form of brief, written memos and posted in the plant on union bulletin boards, so that it could be seriously considered and so that people need not be mesmerized by its oral communication at union meetings. As it was, during this ritualistic hour or so that began each union meeting communication was a one-way street; next to nothing was seriously discussed. Nor was it made clear to attending members why we should have to waste part of Sunday listening to this ceremonial recitation. Approval of the minutes, like approval of nearly all actions taken by the Executive Committee, was more or less automatic. It was orchestrated by the local's shrewd president, Tank, who chaired the meetings, and tunefully played by various union hacks who on cue "so moved," "seconded," "called the question," and "moved to table."

The various committee reports that followed this exercise, although a decided improvement on what preceded them, were on the whole dull, disorganized, unintelligible, often without substantive content, and/or of interest to only a very small minority of members present. For the most part, the committee reports were made by union insiders, many of whom often seemed more interested in getting through the report than in educating members present concerning existing problems for purposes of organizing them to help alleviate those problems.

I still remember vividly one report given at an exceptionally large meeting during the contract negotiation process. In response to a rank-and-file member's question from the floor about what were the recommendations of a particular committee for the new contract, its chairman got up and read off something that went like this. Referring to our existing contract (few copies of which were in the hall at the time), he said, "on page twenty-four, paragraph twelve point one, we are deleting the words *xyz* and adding instead the words *abc*. And on page seventeen, paragraph five point six, we are changing the words *qrs* to *otv*." Having thus deepened our understanding of the issues before us, he sat down. Most committee reports were considerably better than that, and a few were excellent. But this one epitomizes the union leadership's capacity to render its members passive through the noncommunication of useful information and by restricting membership mobilization that leaders might not be able themselves to control.

With the end of the committee reports more than half the meeting had passed with only limited opportunity and encouragement for active participation by rank-and-file members. Some discussion of committee reports did occur, but generally within prescribed limits. Finally, though, if one had had the perseverence to suffer through what preceded, patience received its reward. Rank-and-file members were encouraged during a period called "For Good and Welfare" to take the mike to initiate discussion on whatever relevant matters they wished. The time was largely spent in members airing grievances against management, in protests against union action and/or inaction, and in educating the rest of us from workers' own personal experiences on such matters of common concern as health hazards and discrimination within the plant. This was the exciting part of the meeting, one of the times when the rank-and-file audience interacted most vigorously with the speakers, nodding, even shouting their approval or disapproval of what was being said. This was the time that a sense of worker collectivity emerged, even as grievances often were being aired individually. This was the time when much of the gobbledygook that served to separate the rank and file from its leaders and workers from any say in how the plant was run, was cut through, just for a moment, and workers talked about what they needed and deserved. This was a time for anger and joy, a time union leaders tolerated.

But then, why should they not have tolerated this release of pent-up frustration, given the current improbability that the necessary followup work could be done by the rank and file to push an issue through to an effective conclusion? Those of us who months later may have remembered, may have wondered what happened to a charge about the use of certain noxious chemicals in the Chrome Department? Why, we may have wondered, had the union Education Committee still not done something to communicate to us some of that information it gathered at those seminars we paid for its members to attend? Why hadn't our shop stewards and committeemen even bothered to educate us about our contractual rights? But we rarely found answers to such questions at subsequent union meetings. They got lost as we again got mesmerized, and as still other issues were raised by grievers.

So there are many reasons why attendance at union meetings is sparse and why union decisions therefore are made by a small leadership clique. But the fundamental reason why active participation in union activities is so low goes well beyond all the not insignificant circumstantial factors outlined above. That reason is simple and beyond question. Basically union members do not participate because they no longer expect much from their union, and, still worse, because they do not believe that their participation in union affairs can significantly alter the kept nature of the union.

During my first week on the job I cautiously began to ask around to find out what fellow workers thought of the union. This is what I learned. On the one hand, nearly everyone with whom I talked then and later agreed that "any union is better than no union at all." Some few specifically remembered back several decades to when the company had not had a union, when conditions for workers had been much worse. Notwithstanding this agreement, however, the current opinion about our local, and to a considerable extent about other unions with which employees previously had had extended contact, was not exactly positive. It can be summarized in two much-repeated remarks, first communicated independently to me in my earliest days on the job by several employees: "The union ain't worth a dime"; and "The union ain't worth a shit." These characterizations were echoed time after time in the actions and words of other employees. For example, one day in early December during our afternoon break, a middle-level machine repairman who had been with the company for years was complaining that he didn't have a high enough wage grade since he often had to train other employees with higher grades and show them how to do their jobs. In the course of his complaining, he said with a straight face that when he had joined the union, the union had given him an eight-ounce jar of Vaseline, "cause I was gonna get fucked by the company and by the union." Two other workers immediately chimed in, embellishing, "the union don't even give ya the Vaseline no more."

The man with whom I spoke most often about the union during my first weeks on the job was extremely negative about it. He said that when the union membership voted to strike in 1973 they had to do so over the recommendation of the union leadership to accept the contract. Blaming it on union acquiescence, he complained that the company didn't pay wages for sick days, and he complained that when he had been suspended for several days the union hadn't backed him up at all. Union meetings, which he rarely attended, he characterized as "bullshit." The union, he claimed, only cared about getting its dues checkoff every month. Three or four other workers the following day confirmed that the union was taken to be a company union, that the Safety Committee of the union, for example, did at best a mediocre job, frequently caving in to management arguments about "company convenience" rather than fighting for worker safety.

A minor incident with a union Safety Committeeperson may be considered illustrative. As I had been having trouble for some time clearing the countless stacks of rings piled all over the aisles, and since the situation seemed to be deteriorating still further, I reported the matter one day to my Safety Committeeman. I told him that there were rings in the main aisle on both sides in Building 2. He replied that this always was "the first issue raised at every Safety Committee meetings," and that the high-level company representative at the meetings repeatedly responded by pleading for "bearing with us" until a new storage area for finished rings was constructed. At each meeting the decision apparently had been made by our Safety Committee to "bear with the company," rather than to order a work halt in the overcrowded unsafe aisles. I reminded the Safety man that "if we asked the company to 'bear with us,' on something, you know what we'd get." He nodded. We exchanged complaints for a time. Then, at the end of our discussion, I asked, "So what am I supposed to do?" "Just drive right into the rings that are in the aisle," my Safety man nonchalantly and only half-jokingly said!

Such a response, of course, implied two things. First, that the Safety Committee couldn't/wouldn't do anything to rectify the situation. Second, that solutions for the problem had to be sought individually. Therefore, union abdication either meant the continuance of the unsatisfactory status quo, or alternatively the necessity for action on my part to rectify it. Such action would leave me vulnerable to direct company retaliation. In short, union abdication in areas over which it was supposed to exercise jurisdiction meant for all intents and purposes that anyone who sought to rectify unsatisfactory conditions must do so at his/her own risk. In such a case, the worker is nearly as well off without a union as with one.

The negative attitude about our union and how it functioned is widespread among employees. Another worker who had been with the company for more than five years, when asked by fellow workers to attend the next union meeting, made jokes to hide his own pessimism. He then put it this way: "The fuckin' union don't help nobody." Totally disgusted, he refused to attend any of its meetings. "Look," he shouted, "they didn't help X to get a higher pay grade. If it did something for me once in a while, I'd go to the meetings." The man claimed to have worked hard a few years ago, apparently along with the skilled-worker minority in the plant, to get rid of the current union. But the effort failed, and, he pointed out bitterly, "all the leaders of that movement were made bosses by the company."

As the process of negotiating a new contract in the fall of 1974 intensified, cynicism and antagonisms about the union increasingly came out into the open. On one afternoon an important official in our local, Marbles—a man who to his credit maintained much closer and more sustained relations with rank-and-file members than any of the other union officials—uncharacteristically came over to our side's cafeteria to join us at break time. I entered the informal bull session after it had begun, to hear the union official being cursed out as a "company man" and informer, being called a "Judas." Defending himself only slightly edgily and with wit and eclat, the savvy Marbles tried to turn the tables on his attackers, at which point I asked all those at the crowded table to take a hand vote on whether we thought the union was any good. Before we could drive the point home, Marbles, seeing defeat looming around the table, quickly replied, "They're all your friends," which they were not. At that point, a worker at the next table who stuttered and who seemed not to have been taking an active part in the heated verbal exchange at our table, quietly walked over to where Marbles was sitting and placed in front of him a picture he had sketched on a cafeteria napkin. On the napkin was the image of a snake. The point was made eloquently. There were cheers and jeers from all sides. The union official started complaining bitterly about "agitators" and "dissidents." But he like the rest of us knew what had happened. For a few brief moments all the despair and frustration that workers feel about their jobs, about the company and about the union had been released and transformed into anger, and that anger had focused on a target who had earned it, "doing the man's work."

On still another day, several middle-aged women from inspections confirmed what the men workers had earlier and repeatedly told me about the union. As I tried to persuade them to attend the next union meeting, one asked, "Why? It's a lousy union." I tried to convince her this was a very important meeting for the new contract. She ultimately agreed to come. But, just before we broke up, she looked over at me and asked, "Have you ever worked for a company where the union wasn't a company union?" Before I could try to fashion a reply, she interjected, "I never have."

After we had separated, I suddenly realized the irony of my prior misunderstanding of American unions and of how unions relate to the various economic systems in which they exist. Previously, when I had thought, for example, about the Soviet Union, where the state and the Communist Party are dominant, I understood that unions there had to be simply handmaidens to those institutions. On the other hand, when I thought about the United States, where government and political parties are not so dominant, I had more or less assumed, as a good liberal, that American unions therefore must be relatively autonomous. But now I could see clearly that in the American political economy, where the dominant forces are gigantic corporations, corporations dominate American unions. Unions in any society, I realized, cannot stand autonomous in any meaningful sense unless they embody the power of vigorous mass movements of workers. Otherwise, as in the United States and the Soviet Union today, they are the domesticated creatures of whatever institutions and classes are dominant.

WORKERS AND THE UNION

In such a context the union leader's role is a very subtle one. On the one hand, s/he must at least appear to represent certain of the interests of working men and women and must deliver at least often enough on certain of their demands to give some substance to the image. But, on the other, the entire production process and the determination of the relationship between the company and the unions is in fact dominated by the company. So union leaders must remain "sensitive to company needs" if they are to be able to deal on a daily basis with management. And they must accept management's definition of the nature and scope of the constrained struggle that unions may carry on with management.

By and large the various forms of company unions in the United States, which long ago accommodated themselves to management domination, remain as passive as their members allow. The reigning aphorism of most union officials, as my particularly cowardly shop steward said to me, is "don't rock the boat." Although in my local some officers undoubtedly had begun their careers of collaboration with motives of narrow self-interest, by now it is questionable whether such venal motives dominate their behavior. Abdication to company rule of the workplace today has become an article of faith. Workers' interests are wholly identified in union leaders' minds with the capitalist system. Union officials therefore believe, along with many rank-and-file members, that workers' interests are best served by the prosperity of the employing company, which in turn, leaders believe, requires the company's near-exclusive control of the conduct of its business. Thus there is only so much to be bargained about: wages, fringe benefits, and a host of limited issues whose resolution can indeed somewhat improve the workers' lot but cannot affect either the company's control, its ability to profit at workers' expense, or the purposelessness of most work.

Union collaboration at my particular company was so crass and so total that at times the local could barely perform its primary function of defusing and coopting discontent. For example, instead of taking the initiative during 1975 to press the company at least to spread the burden and risk of unemployment equitably by reducing the work week for all to, say, four days, or by rotating work weeks; instead of demanding that the company not hire trained workers off the street for skilled jobs while it was laying off workers who could have been trained quite quickly to fill those jobs, often at government expense; instead of trying to protect plant minorities like women and blacks, who inevitably suffer disproportionately under the LIFO human inventory system of seniority; in short, instead of at least confronting some vital but conflict-ridden issues, union leaders posted innocuous notices to "Buy American" and the like, notices that made it appear that no conflict exists between the class interest of workers and that of capitalists.

Although each union leader was somewhat different in his/her style, attitudes, and relations with the company and with union members, one man, Marbles, stood out above all others and may be taken to personify one type of union leader. Marbles, a committeeman and trustee of the union and a member of its important Grievance and Executive committees, was an older black, long ago retired from the armed forces, who was working out his final months until his retirement from Blancs, when he would get company retirement and Social Security as well. He was rumored to own several houses in Baltimore, though he regularly worked at Blancs as a janitor—that is, when he was not on union business. But whatever he was doing, before his retirement in January 1975, he always seemed to be around and available. He was a very clever, knowledgeable, and sharp-talking man, quick to employ rhetoric, quick to obfuscate, and protected from oversensitivity to criticism by the aplomb of the self-righteous. Appearing alternatively as a shuffler, even a clown, or a militant, he was alert to everything around him. He spent long periods of time with rank-and-file blacks and whites, not simply to help them with their problems (which he often did) but also to keep the union's ear close to the ground. He was at once appealing and repulsive, a man at once with certain faiths and seemingly wholly unprincipled, who simultaneously inspired trust and the recognition that he would betray it in his own, the union's, and the company's interests. Yet after he had retired, a fellow worker talking to me about a particular problem put it in a nutshell: "With Marbles gone I don't even know who to talk to about such problems." And that was the truth. Marbles was sorely missed by all of us. He was a man I deeply liked, respected, and despised.

WORKERS AND THE UNION

During the period that Marbles and I were on the job together I must have spent more than 30 hours listening, chatting, and arguing with him. As I became more openly active in the union, his views about me (I think) hardened, but he often seemed as interested in finding out what I was thinking as I was in his thoughts and motives. One day in late September we had a real argument, in which each of us revealed a lot about where we each stood. Among other things, we discussed the Vietnam War, Nixon, and Martin Luther King. We disagreed vehemently on all. Marbles backed the war and had only wanted it ended faster by annihilating "the enemy." He appreciated Nixon and not Martin Luther King. He seemed to recognize that the business of America was making money and, as with most things in his life, he did so unabashedly. With regard to me, he said he wished I "would listen to what the union leadership says and try to support them." But then he said he thought I was "one of those trying to dissolve the establishment." He didn't like dissenters and dissatisfied people and said he'd "send them all off in boats." He indicated he had noticed that I talked with others in the plant who expressed strong dissatisfaction with conditions there and had urged serious efforts to change conditions. He had us all pegged. He said he wanted Joanne Tower, a sharp employee we both respected and who had previously edited the union paper (which the union itself had closed down) to start it up again. But Marbles wanted the paper to come out again only under the total control of the union Executive Committee, which would pass on all articles before they could be published. "But, Marbles," I said, "that's un-American, prior censorship and all that." He hardly blinked, saying the union had to be protected from libel and had to control its own organs of information.

Marbles was beautiful to watch in action. To see him operating was to know him and to understand more about union-company collaboration and about the American way of life. One day at lunch he was taking some flak from several young workers who were complaining that another worker had been fired for petty theft and that the union had not stuck up for him. Marbles replied that the man had stolen company property and that "even stealing a roll of toilet paper was enough to get you fired." Furthermore, he said, the man had not wanted to file a grievance against the firing; he just wanted to forget it. And besides, Marbles added, the man "had other things on his record." But not content with that, he then went on briefly to lecture us. "There are two sides to every issue," our union representative told us, "and workers only hear the workers' side." "There are rules," he continued, "and we all have to obey them." And then, with great facility he added, "If somebody stole something from you, you'd be the first to complain." Getting a bit tired of what smacked too much of subtle propaganda, I retorted, "Suppose the rules ain't fair?" To which Marbles astutely responded, "Well, then you gotta contest the rules and try to change them."

For some reason, perhaps because of having been saturated with that alluring line, Marbles' remark made me realize something I had not understood about the nature of company-union collaboration under company domination and about the nature of political economy in general. There are, I belatedly recognized, two ways to dominate and exploit people. One is without rules, arbitrarily and capriciously. That way is crude and obvious, likely today to generate focused antagonism and not likely to be very efficient. We recognize that mode of oppression as a garden variety of dictatorship. But then there is another mode of oppression—with and through rules. That's the liberal-capitalist way. It is very efficient, and often after we have been screwed it is difficult to find someone to blame, other than ourselves. We call this "democracy" and "the rule of law." And if someone says, "but this rule isn't fair," the answer is, "Well, we have a democracy; we have due process; if you think it unfair it's up to you to change the rule through our established procedures."

Marbles always provoked me to see how the union and the society operated, like the time when he was angrily putting down a leaflet that several of us had secretly written and handed out. The leaflet attacked the union officers' lack of affirmative leadership in organizing support for a good new contract. Marbles was very angry about the leaflet, and when another worker who had read and agreed wholeheartedly with it challenged him with some of its assertions, Marbles finally in exasperation declared, "Just leave it to us leaders. We'll do it well."

Marbles' feeling that the inner circle should "benevolently" control everything was reflected in a related desire to keep all information about the plant and the union as closely held as possible. One day, for example, when a worker asked Marbles to look at a job index for a job other than the one he presently held, Marbles refused, saying the worker had no right to see it. At my urging, he said he'd show it to him, but Marbles felt it would be "like opening Pandora's box." I responded that I thought openness was the best policy. The union leadership almost to a person seemed to disagree.

If only because he was so accessible, Marbles began to get it from all sides as we entered the last few weeks before the contract issue was to be decided. When some workers from the Chrome Department were trying to find out "what the hell is going on in the negotiations," which were kept a total mystery from the rank and file until two days before we were to vote on the company offer, Marbles replied with his usual refrain: "Have faith in the Negotiating Committee—you elected them."

What, I wondered, could he have said if we had not "elected them"? What could he have said without what no doubt had been the union's usual peerless display of grass roots democracy in action? The man from Chrome, thinking in a slightly less philosophical vein, retorted, "You're the only one who has faith in them." A second man from Chrome chimed in that we needed strong leadership. Marbles, who knew everything that went on in the plant, sarcastically reminded the second guy that earlier he had been "thrown out as shop steward," to which the latter retorted that he had been "dropped" because he "wasn't willing to play ball or shut up."

Like all of us, Marbles of course was a very complex personality. Many of his actions—simply being there to hear and advise workers about their problems, and his clowning and wit, for example—endeared him to the rank and file. His advice, though consistently unmilitant as regarded the company, generally was the best available. When I had received my oral warning for excessive talking with another employee, for example, he later took me aside and told me how I should have handled it and how to deal with warnings in the future. First, he said, admit nothing. I had admitted my culpability. Second, only sign the warning notice under protest to protect your future position on the warning. The employee's signature is required but technically is supposed to merely indicate receipt. In fact signing the warning without protest is taken as evidence that at the time the employee acquiesced to its merit. I had not signed my warning under protest. Third, all warnings should be protested as a matter of course, Marbles added, since the front office checks out all protested warnings and foremen don't like to get too much attention of this sort from the front office.

When Marbles was advising the rank and file it was at times easy to forget where he stood, despite his frequently expressed sympathies for the company. At certain times he seemed almost to personify how a decent union might operate. But when he recounted some of his former exploits as a union heavy, he exposed himself and his fellow leaders.

One uncharacteristically lovely January day a notice went up on the union bulletin boards notifying members that monthly dues had gone up by fifty cents. I mentioned it at lunch to Marbles, who said it was now provided in our local's constitution that when the IAM Grand Lodge's per capita tax on local membership went up, our own dues paid to the local automatically went up by the same amount. Members of the union, he proudly pointed out, had absolutely no say in such raises any more. He was relieved, he said, that members no longer had any say, because "who would vote to raise their own dues?" Before the recently passed constitutional provision making the raises automatic, Marbles said, the union leadership had had trouble getting the raises approved by the membership. They had had to postpone consideration of the issue meeting after meeting until votes for outnumbered votes against. That wasn't easy, Marbles added, and he often had to move to table the issue for several meetings to get the raise passed. "But if members thought the union was doing anything substantial for them," I responded, "they would not be so opposed to paying reasonable raises in union dues. And, more than that, if they could understand why so much of our dues goes to the District and to the Grand Lodge and what we get in return for those funds, we might even support such raises."

Almost to a person, union members saw few or no substantial

benefits coming back to them in return for the huge sums of money their dues fed into the union bureaucracy. With the last raise, union dues for the lower grade employees became $9 a month. Assume that average dues paid were $10 per month. With over 1,500 members, that meant more than $15,000 a month went into our local's coffers. Of that monthly sum, I understood, approximately $3,000 went to the IAM District headquarters and about $7,500 to the Grand Lodge in Washington, D.C. On these crude estimates, the local kept $4,500 a month. That meant on a yearly basis the local retained about $54,000; the District, just from our local, got about $36,000; and the Grand Lodge got $90,000 from us alone.

For what? For subscriptions to the IAM's weekly, *The Machinist?* For lobbying? For assurances that if and when our local called a strike we would get strike benefits from the IAM? But our local had had only one strike since World War II, and that one, in 1973, lasted for only two weeks. From it members received not a penny in union strike benefits. And when I raised the issue of strike benefits at a union meeting in August 1974 (as it appeared we might well carry out another strike that November), a district representative informed us that we could receive strike benefits *only* if there was still any money left in the depleted strike fund. On that crucial matter he could give no assurances.

Of course, workers do not like paying out their monthly dues when many of them already are hard-pressed to make a living. The real sticking point, however, is that workers know they get so little in return for their enforced generosity. And that awareness is compounded by the fact that the whole issue has been taken out of their hands by leadership maneuvering that eliminates the opportunity for the union membership to discuss and vote up or down proposed raises.

You may have noticed there is a vicious-circle quality to much of what went on within the union. Circumstances, rules, machinations, and power and authority encouraged leadership authoritarianism and membership passivity and nonparticipation, which in turn served to perpetuate those very circumstances, rules, machinations, and that power and authority. For example, a friend who previously had been a member of a more effective union than ours had come to Blancs with the desire to become active in union affairs. Eager to get involved, after a time he became a shop steward. In that capacity he tried to help his fellow workers but found that his committeeman, his immediate superior in the union, repeatedly refused to back him up, for instance, refusing to countersign grievances that my friend thought clearly legitimate. Stymied, he quit his post as steward after several months. Later he shamefacedly admitted that even attending one meeting a month seemed to be more than he was willing to invest in the union.

For people like my friend, who wanted to work for our common betterment, there are three choices. Sell out to the dominant union factions and advance within the company union. Drop out completely in frustration from active participation. Or, most difficult, persevere; beat your head against the company-union wall to try to make step-by-step progress in raising the consciousness of fellow workers and taking back control of the union from the company and union leaders. Few members are willing to wage such a painful, time-consuming fight, and even a portion of those who are, unwittingly are infected by the disease they seek to combat and become little more than careerists in their own right.

Employees were at least partly aware of these sorts of vicious circles, which only increased their passivity. In a chance early encounter I had with a man who had been with the company for over 25 years, he spontaneously raised some of the problems that can be understood as vicious circles. As we talked about these problems, he unexpectedly said that the union needed more "militants," more fighters. But, he added, those who fought hard for the workers in the past were immediately smeared by the union as "radicals," "outside agitators," and "troublemakers." Some were then transferred or fired by the company. Others who proved not immune to company enticements were bought off by the company, promoted several grades, even made foremen.

In declaring, uncharacteristically, that the workers "needed more radicals" within their midst, the man supported that need by saying that employees at Blancs years ago used to have paid lunch half-hours, which the union apparently negotiated away in exchange for some benefit no one can recall. He talked of how for years union negotiators had supported contract raises on the order of three to five cents an hour, telling the assembled union members to vote to accept the contract offer because "it was the best the union could do." He spoke of the efforts several years earlier to oust the IAM, and of how bad organization and fear tactics had thwarted that effort. Just before the vote a false rumor had been spread that if the IAM were voted out NLRB rules required that there be no union at the company for a year, under which conditions the company allegedly then would have been free to fire employees.

Examples of vicious circles that discourage membership understanding of issues and activism abounded. Take the way the cost-of-living clause had been handled by the union. Cost-of-living protection is a primary concern of workers in a time of rapid inflation. The structure of benefits under the cost-of-living clause in our contract, however, was formulated in a manner that obscured its precise effect. In the contract automatic cost-of-living raises were tied to the Consumer Price Index (CPI). Quite aside from questions about the accuracy of that index in measuring the impact of inflation on workers' real wages, the practical significance of the formula used to compensate workers for losses in real wages due to inflation was extremely hard to grasp. For every point the CPI went up, a contractually fixed amount of money was periodically added to the employee's hourly wages, say one-quarter or one-half cent. Although such a formula obviously is much better than no cost-of-living protection at all, what this particular formula meant for a worker's wages when inflation went up, for example by 10 percent in one year, was unclear to nearly every worker in the plant. Does the formula provide for total protection against inflation, which in the hypothetical case of a 10 percent rise in inflation would require a 10 percent raise in money wages? Or does it provide only partial protection for real wages? And if only partial, what is the extent of that protection? Are workers under the formula compensated for 80 percent, 70 percent, or 50 percent of the inflationary rise? Few, if any members of the union knew the answers to such basic questions, and the leadership, if it knew, made no effort to explain the matter to workers. All efforts to have the issue clarified (and I was involved in a number of them), failed. Under the existing formula for cost-of-living protection even intelligent discussion of the issue was difficult, since the degree of protection was hard to pin down. Consequently, when the issue of cost of living arose in considering a new contract, the tendency within the framework of the existing formula—the type widely used in industry—was to try simply to improve the degree of existing protection by seeking in a new contract to have a higher wage raise per hour for every point rise in the CPI. But even that rule-of-thumb approach (as will be shown below) is a less reliable guide to actual progress than one might think because other factors affect the practical significance of cost-of-living adjustments.

Another vicious circle involves employee rights. By and large, when new employees were hired they were not informed of their rights by their union representatives. The company instead simply handed new employees copies of the 160-plus-page union constitution and of the 67-page union contract (1972) with the company. Until something actually happened to them, employees were likely to remain in the dark as to their rights and obligations. By then it might be too late. Worse than that, stewards and committeemen themselves often did not seem to understand the intricacies of the contract as it concerned the rights of their shop members; or worse still, they didn't really care.

One day, when a middle-aged woman came up to Marbles to complain that her foreman was threatening to give her a warning slip for a forthcoming absence for health reasons, Marbles advised her to talk to her own shop steward or comitteeman. But her shop, it turned out, had no shop steward, and she didn't know who her committeeman was. The woman herself, needless to say, was totally uninformed on how to proceed to defend herself. Marbles at least tried to be helpful.

When a young, black woman sought to charge racial discrimination in her department, she was given little help by her white committeewoman and short shrift by the union Grievance Committee—on which her committeewoman, Marbles, and the union president were nonelected members. The committee held that her complaint, as drafted, stated no legitimate grievance, and at a subsequent union meeting moved (in its usual motion after its usually unenlightening report) to have its report, including its determination to "withdraw" the woman's grievance, approved by the membership. Unusually, a floor fight was initiated by the woman and her friends, at the conclusion of which the rank and file voted to reject the committee's decision to withdraw the grievance. Nevertheless, some four months later when I was laid off, nothing positive had been done to resolve her grievance.

Events such as these show how our union operated, in repeated violation of the purposes for which unions were conceived by the American labor movement. Although unions are the one existing workplace institution where managerial power and authority might seriously be counterbalanced, unions themselves have subtly come to support managerial prerogatives. Through their own internal processes and procedural rules and under the guise of pseudo-democracy, unions have in addition contributed to increasing both authoritarianism and its converse, mass passivity, in workers' lives. The effect is twofold. First, despite unions, the individual worker is left in a number of areas feeling quite vulnerable to the exercise of managerial power and authority. Second, worker expectations for improvement in their working lives have been drastically reduced by the realization that management, generally with union acquiescence, largely and almost unilaterally determines what issues are open to negotiation.

The current collaborationism of unions is doubly important, because under the structures for collective bargaining set up by the federal government in the 1930s and 1940s unions in "organized" production units tend to "legally" monopolize the formal expression and articulation of worker demands and the efforts, such as they are, to meet them. In this respect alone unionized workers today may well be worse off with unions as presently constituted than they would be without them. Without unions it might be easier at least for workers to organize themselves for direct action to express grievances and to seek redress. Unions in America today primarily function as critical components of the apparatus of law and order to keep "the industrial peace," an apparatus that protects the regime of private ownership of the means of production, with all its necessary ramifications for workers' lives. Unions only secondarily, and almost universally within that capitalist law-and-order framework, struggle to realize the interests of workers. The union I had to join to work at Blancs, a closed shop, exemplified institutionalized collaboration.

WORKERS AND THE UNION

VII

The Union in Action and Inaction:
The Bargain

EXAMINING how the union operates, one sees that although it has contributed to raising the living standards and increasing the security of its members within the confines of the existing capitalist system, it also has contributed to the pacification, demoralization, and disorganization of its members as workers with a class interest. As such, the union effectively supports the continuation of the fundamental relationship between labor and capital in America.

This was evident in the way the local dealt with its most critical issues. The first, the new contract that would define worker/company relations for some time to come, arises periodically and is a bread-and-butter issue of substantial concern to the vast majority of union members. The second, the nomination and election of such middle-level union local officials as committeemen, trustees, and the like, occurs annually and elicits considerably less membership concern and involvement.

Both events involve the same interrelated aspects, one the external relation between workers and employer and the other the internal relation between the rank and file and their union leaders. In the case of the new contract the primary aspect is the external relation between workers and the company-employer. In this case the secondary aspect, the internal relation, though hardly unimportant, is decidedly subordinated in the workers' minds. By contrast, the internal relation between the rank and file and their leaders becomes primary in the local's elections, while the external relationship with the company becomes secondary. In each case awareness of the significance of the secondary aspect is quite limited, and the degree of worker participation therefore reflects concern with the primary aspect. What this means in practice is that workers do not sustain the higher level of involvement they feel for the contract issue during the union election process. Participation in the election process is extremely low. As a result, workers are caught in a vicious circle that defuses their main weapon, the union, when they deal with the company on matters of primary concern to them.

With the old contract slated to run out on October 30, 1974, the issue of the new contract began to be taken very seriously by workers during September. By early October it had become a preoccupation. By late October worker concern peaked, the culmination coming at the mass union meeting of November 3, which decided the issue. The election process, which took place in November and December, came as a decided anticlimax (see chap. 10).

By the time I began to work at Blancs in July, talk and concern about the new contract already had surfaced. There were numerous discussions about what workers needed from the new contract and various speculations about the possibility of a strike if the company was not forthcoming. The quality of these discussions and speculations quite naturally was strongly influenced by a variety of factors, ranging from workers' general feelings about the company, the union, and their individual jobs; to their appraisals of what effect the poor state of the national economy would have on the negotiations; to their senses of the past history of contract settlements at Blancs; to their more immediate appreciations of the previous year's strike.

That strike, about which there were differing interpretations and an enormous amount of confusion, seemed for several reasons to be especially important in shaping workers' outlooks on the upcoming negotiations. First, the fall 1973 negotiations provided the most recent and therefore presumably the best evidence of how the company again would approach negotiations. Second, since the only real alternative to accepting the company's final offer for a new contract is to strike, the previous year's strike was taken as strong evidence of whether a strike was likely to force the company to make a substantially better offer. It was seen as indicative of how effective a strike Blancs' workers were capable of mounting, and at what cost. The 1973 strike, the first at Blancs since WW2, thus was taken as a kind of ballpark cost-benefit analysis of the need and potential for another strike.

That earlier strike was viewed by the majority of workers as a failure. This contributed to a kind of fatalism about the strike as a feasible and effective weapon. Although some workers pointed out that the 1973 strike had achieved certain successes, primarily getting the company to pay fees for Blue Cross/Blue Shield coverage for retired workers over sixty-two, most felt that the benefits from the strike hardly justified its costs.

The costs were fundamental, and apparently for many workers unexpected. The strike, which lasted for two weeks, cost workers two full weeks' wages during the period preceding the Thanksgiving and Christmas holidays, when most people particularly need money. During that period not a penny in compensatory strike benefits was paid to workers by the union. Many workers claimed they had voted to strike in 1973 without fully understanding that the IAM, even if its strike benefits fund were sufficient to pay benefits from the beginning of a strike, does not pay benefits until the third week of a strike. As a consequence, a number of workers this year strongly opposed the notion of a short-term strike during which no assured income would be coming in. Likewise, since almost all workers recognized that Blancs was unlikely to make major concessions without being pressed very hard, many felt that an effective strike would have to be a long one.* This realistic vision of course escalated the probable costs of a future strike, making its probability still more unlikely.

The abstract right to strike, it is clear, in practice is so restricted by economic considerations that, even with strong leadership and support, it is likely to be exercised only when workers feel abused or feel themselves in extremis. What even a two-week strike means to

---

* In which case, after three weeks, benefits at the rate of $40 per week maximum would be paid until the strike was settled or the international's strike fund ran dry.

UNION ACTION AND INACTION

many union members is not easy to appreciate. One young white worker with a family said to me that the previous year, after two weeks without wages or benefits, he had been on the verge of caving in, though he claimed he could have held out a week or two longer with a bank loan.

And at Blancs the leadership necessary to carry out an effective strike had not emerged. Our current leadership was hardly what one could call bold in its defense of workers' interests. In 1973, as always, the leadership had supported accepting the company's final contract offer. It was only after Sid Ryan, the district business agent who presented the offer and announced the negotiating committee's support for it, was booed down and the membership voted to reject the offer that the leadership reluctantly came over to the majority's position. Thereafter, workers subsequently complained, as soon during the strike as the company made another substantial offer the leadership again supported accepting it, this time backed by the demoralized and disorganized membership who were not yet entitled to strike benefits.

As was the case again in 1974, during the entire process the leadership's efforts to shape workers in a solid front against the company were feeble. In 1973 the leaders made no preparations in advance for a strike, which took them by surprise. The lack of such preparations in turn minimized the likelihood of carrying on an effective strike, since members were not prepared to appreciate that they might require and were capable of such action. Nor were they organized to sustain it. Once the 1973 strike occurred, its organization was erratic and its level of mobilization low. No meetings were called to involve workers during the strike. The main source of internal communication among union members during this period was not meetings called by the leadership, nor even leadership directives, but rather a newspaper, *Like It Is*, begun by a group of independent reformers in the plant.

This year, during the period leading up to the vote on the new contract, the same pattern held. When in union meetings as early as August some of us asked for information about the extent of the union's strike benefit fund and about what preparations were being made in the event a strike became necessary, we were put off. One high union official bombastically responded, "We shouldn't be talking strike but negotiating hard." Despite not infrequent talk among workers, including conservative older workers, about the need to "walk if the company don't make us a good offer," the talk remained just that, because of a total lack of official and rank-and-file leadership in mobilizing the local to prepare. By August, the union newspaper—the sole effective channel for communicating with the membership outside of the regular monthly union meetings—had been closed down by the leadership. From then on there was between meetings no other official or semiofficial dissemination of information about contract issues and about possible preparations for a strike.

Yet workers knew they would have to fight hard to achieve anything beyond what the company was disposed to give them. One man who had been with the company for over 35 years characterized that disposition as, "The company never gave us nothing." In this context a strong minority, if not a majority, in advance of the contract negotiations adamantly opposed a strike. Another 30-year veteran worker epitomized this aspect of worker fatalism. He declared he had walked last year and gotten no benefits and he wasn't about to do it again. A young black woman summarized the lesson many had learned from the 1973 strike: "We never make up in a strike what we lose."

In retrospect, then, it appears that even though many of us may have thought and talked about a strike as an alternative to simply accepting the company's last offer, the notion of a strike was never made concrete to workers. Workers' anxieties, unless dispelled by some unexpected events or actions making them angry or conscious of their own potential power in solidarity, thus implied that their demands for the new contract would be drastically whittled down in negotiations. The practical issue then (it seems clear in hindsight) was not what workers could get if they united, but what they would settle for disunited, distracted, intimidated, and partly pacified. Contributing to this was the inchoate process of articulating demands, the content of the demands, the preexisting divisions within the work force, and the absence of positive leadership to unify workers.

Workers' needs/demands for the new contract covered the entire

UNION ACTION AND INACTION

142

gamut of workplace-, livelihood-, and leisure-related issues. But separate polls, earlier conducted by the newspaper *Like It Is* and by the vice president of the local, as well as informal soundings by myself and others, all confirmed that the main issues for responding workers were wages and fringe benefits. Workers were in closest agreement in wanting: (1) a substantial pay increase, on the order of at least fifty cents an hour; (2) better cost-of-living protection against inflation; and (3) effective provisions for sick pay. There were a host of other demands.

The relative importance of any demand for an individual worker varied tremendously, of course, depending upon the particular worker's situation at Blancs. For the large number of production workers, who relied very heavily in their earnings on incentive (bonus) payments, the issue of base hourly wage was considerably less important than for nonbonus workers. For people nearing retirement age, who had worked at Blancs for over 30 years, wage increases and cost-of-living protection for real wages were decidedly less important issues than increases in pension and retirement benefits. These last, in turn, were of little concern to the younger and newer workers who constituted a majority of the plant's workforce. For some, particularly those with large families, increased Blue Cross/Blue Shield coverage to include emergency room and dental and optical care, and prescriptions was very important. For others, increasing the number of holidays and the amount of vacation time, as well as protecting the worker's right to choose when to take his/her vacations by eliminating summer plant shutdown (a compulsory vacation for most workers) was a high-priority demand. Yet others were very concerned that overtime work be made more voluntary. One group thought it important that workers not be locked inflexibly into a long-term contract, and another felt that any new contract should run out in the spring instead of just before the winter holiday season, when, as the company knew, workers feel least able to afford a strike to achieve their demands and when cold weather can make walking a picket line very uncomfortable.

Out of all these disparate, overlapping demands a negotiating position and strong rank-and-file support for that position could and should have been produced. But in fact that never happened, in no small part because the leadership's negotiating position was never systematically articulated to the rank and file. No effort was made to unify the membership around an agreed-upon bargaining position. Instead, leaders were either silent or issued empty calls asking for blind faith in the Negotiating Committee.

Few contract issues were discussed in depth at the union meetings held in the months prior to the end of the old contract. And no effort was made by leaders to facilitate the rank and file in discussing and developing their own consensus on the issues. On the contrary, all negotiations were characterized by an exclusiveness and secrecy on the part of the local's leadership and the Negotiating Committee. As a consequence, workers neither had effective opportunities to be heard in the process, nor were they well prepared to evaluate the results of the process or to take effective action in the event those results were judged inadequate. In short, the workers came out of the negotiating process as divided among themselves as when they went in.

There is, to say the least, enough blame for this state of affairs to go around. Union leaders deserve a lion's share of the responsibility, both for their acts of omission and acts of commission. The company expectably played its cards in its own interest; none of us had anticipated its acting in our interests. The handful of activists in the plant, of whom I was one, were never able to act as an effective spearhead for building a workers' coalition. And finally, the rank and file never unified on their own around their common objective and against their common antagonist.

Instead, groups of workers often blamed other groups for their common plight, and not a few workers consistently badmouthed all workers. Not a few veteran male workers who were the primary support of their families blamed women workers for nonmilitancy on the grounds that women as "second earners" were less concerned than men with such issues as wages and fringe benefits. Some whites, especially middle-aged women, condemned some young blacks for their militant rhetoric at meetings and other black members for what they considered vulgarity and drunkenness at meetings. Many workers correctly blamed the leadership, remembering for instance that in the past, leaders as members of Negotiating Committees had consistently persuaded workers to take inadequate raises on the order of three to five cents an hour, arguing that was the best they could do. But, while recognizing the inadequacy of the local's leadership in representing workers' interests, few workers gave any indication they would persist in trying to change that leadership or even bother to attend meetings with any regularity. And finally some workers, and most leaders, blamed "agitators" and "troublemakers" for "stirring things up."

Through it all, divisions among groups of workers, based upon race, age, sex, and incentive pay differences, and still finer divisions based upon outright selfishness, were predominant. Some younger blacks, for example, who had both the savvy to contribute to raising workers' understanding and the consciousness of the issues and the support necessary to confront older leaders of the local, tended to be overprotective of their own political positions within the union and to be self-important.

All these factors came into play in the negotiating process, which can usefully be conceived of as taking place on at least three interrelated levels: the level of the Negotiating Committee, where company and union representatives worked in private to achieve an agreement acceptable to both sides; the level of the union meetings, where there was at least the formal opportunity for the rank and file to learn about what was going on and to express their opinions, support, and/or criticisms of the negotiations and where the company's offer is ultimately either accepted or rejected; and the level of informal exchanges and politicking related to the contract issues that daily and diffusely took place inside the plant. Although events at each level influenced those on other levels to some degree, the secret negotiations between company and union representatives lopsidedly dominated the entire process at all levels.

The most characteristic feature of the entire process was that the negotiations, for various reasons, were kept under the tight and self-interested control of a handful of people. The company delayed discussion of the critical wage and fringe-benefits issues until the final week of the negotiations. The union leadership acquiesced in this tactic and maintained secrecy about the progress and issues of the negotiations. And the rank and file tenuously but broadly accepted the alleged need for the Negotiating Committee to be discreet, even exclusive, in carrying on negotiations with the company. As a result, the membership played almost no active role in the process and the final decision. In the process many of the issues were rarely seriously discussed or fully understood. And the final decision by the rank and file was more a formal ratification of a take-it-or-leave-it company offer than an independent examination and evaluation of the offer and alternatives followed by a well-considered decision.

The negotiations dominated the entire process because until an agreement was achieved the negotiators were the only people directly involved in working out the "collective bargain" between the company and workers. They had the power and the authority. Equally important, they had a monopoly on information about what was going on. This secrecy hid the extent to which the company dominated the negotiations, though it was recognized generally that the company set the pace and defined the boundaries of what issues would be discussed and how. In acquiescing to this secrecy and domination, union representatives in the negotiations effectively strengthened the company's hand while at the same time they reinforced the pattern of mass noninvolvement in union activities. This in turn facilitated control of workers by the handful of union leaders. For both the union leadership and the company, rank-and-file politicization and mobilization posed the threat of loss of control. This was the basis for the essentially cooperative relationship between company and union leaders on company terms, the essence of "the bargain."

The nature of this unequal but symbiotic relationship was consistently manifested in the manner rank-and-file members were excluded from the process, both inside and outside of union meetings. The pattern at union meetings right up to the final meeting on November 3, at which the company's offer was presented, supported by the Negotiating Committee, and briefly discussed, was basically to avoid official reports on the substance and progress of the negotiations and to minimize discussion of the issues involved.

UNION ACTION AND INACTION

At the first meeting I attended, on August 11, all efforts to discuss the issues, to mobilize workers, to open communications, and to initiate preparations for a possible strike were parried by the leadership. The point of these initiatives, as I understood them, was not to prejudge the issue of whether we should strike, which properly was to be decided by workers only after seeing and evaluating the company's final offer. The point, rather, was to keep workers' options open: to try to assure that workers would have sufficient information and understanding of the contract issues and of developments in the negotiations, would be apprised of both the good and bad points of the company's final offer, and would be prepared in advance to implement a strike, so that if they determined to strike they could do so realistically.

At that August meeting several things happened that in retrospect suggest the union leadership did not intend to encourage, or even allow, any such developments. At the meeting it came out that the Language Committee, which initially works up the important demands other than wages and fringe benefits for the union's bargaining team, had not even been selected. A motion to elect a Strike Support Committee to make preparations for a strike was rejected by the president, on the ground that the appointment of such a committee according to the union's bylaws and/or constitution was the president's prerogative. And a request for information about the financial condition of the union's strike benefit fund was supported by the rank and file and thereafter ignored by the leadership.

If August seems early to be concerned about negotiations that had not yet begun on a contract that was to run until November 1, one thing should be remembered. Between that August meeting and the final meeting to decide whether to accept or reject the company offer, only two regular union meetings would be held. Consequently, if some issues were not thrashed out and some preparations not discussed and made well in advance, the likelihood was that whatever was done would be done without much contribution from the rank and file and without much encouragement for rank-and-filers to become active.

The next few meetings confirmed the pattern of leadership manipulation and obstruction that excluded rank-and-file participation. The September 8 union meeting was to be the first meeting of the negotiating process, a meeting at which the membership would vote on whether initially to authorize a strike. This strike sanction vote, as it is called, is important for two reasons. First, it is seen as a hammer in the hands of the union negotiators, warning the company that if necessary the members will vote to strike. Second, an affirmative vote authorizing a strike in advance is formally required both to give required notice to the IAM headquarters, making the local eligible for strike benefits, and as a precondition for any later decision by the members to reject the company's offer and actually call a strike.

Nevertheless, seemingly despite its importance, notice of the meeting still had not been posted by the union president by the Wednesday before the meeting. That afternoon, a young rank-and-file member put up his own notice of the meeting, angrily denouncing the leadership's tardiness in advising us about so important a meeting. His notice was quickly torn down. The following day the official notice was posted, thereby satisfying the inadequate bylaw requirement that members be notified forty-eight hours in advance of meetings.

In part, no doubt, because of the inadequate notice of the meeting, the turnout at the Sunday meeting was 60–70 votes short of the quorum requirement that 30 percent of the union membership attend the meeting at which the strike sanction vote is taken. For the nearly 400 workers who were present the meeting was run essentially as a holding action, carried on in embarrassment and the half-hope that if continued long enough a sufficient number of additional workers would drift in to satisfy the quorum requirement.

During the meeting, although the issues of the forthcoming negotiations were referred to, they were not systematically discussed. The meeting began as usual with the extended reading of the minutes of previous meetings, of letters received, and of disbursements for "comp time" to various union officials who had lost work time on union business. Because a quorum was not yet present, these readings were followed by several reports, a few of them relevant to the contract issue. But except for one report, given for the Language

Committee by Joanne Tower, the reports generally were ill-prepared, unenlightening, and hard to follow, at times to the point of being unintelligible. Even the Language Committee report—virtually the only serious report I heard at union meetings about contract issues that was delivered in a clear and comprehensible oral style to facilitate rank-and-file understanding—was so wide ranging that it was hard as a listener to zero in on the central issues. The report ranged from vacation time, to paid lunch hours, to overtime provisions, to the length of the contract term, to job training programs, to holidays. And although it raised a number of important demands, it did not organize them in a manner likely to facilitate building a rank-and-file consensus on shared minimal demands. Such a consensus had to be built, one can see in retrospect, if there was to be any alternative to accepting whatever the company finally offered.

After the reports there was strong rank-and-file criticism of the union leadership's delay in getting up notices of the meeting well in advance. The leadership was defended by several committeemen, one of whom in past years had been a leadership insider. He said that members knew union meetings were regularly scheduled for the second Sunday in every month, and that the notice had been put up sufficiently in advance to satisfy the formal notice requirements of the bylaws. The members, he charged, were to blame for the poor turnout, not the leadership. It was a typical leadership stance, ending with the charge that "those who didn't care enough to come don't deserve to be defended."

Following that, Bert, a young, white, radical activist no longer with Blancs, moved again to talk about a Strike Support Committee, but the local's president sidetracked his motion. The activist then asked the president to report to the membership on the wage and fringe-benefit demands that would constitute part of the negotiating committee's initial bargaining position. After declaring that he had already read off the demands at the previous meeting in August—at which the attendance was less than 20 percent of the attendance at the September meeting—the president was induced to read them off. Following that reading, there was little further discussion of the demands.

WORKERS AND THE UNION

Sitting there awaiting such discussion, I was surprised and appalled by its absence. Workers, I knew, were deeply concerned about wage increases and cost-of-living protection. Earlier, several had indicated privately that they intended to ask about these issues at the meeting. And yet it appeared that these issues would go undiscussed. Frustrated that one of our few opportunities to talk about them as a group might be missed, I decided to speak up myself.

I gave a short, impromptu speech on the need for full and clear cost-of-living protection in the new contract. I argued that the existing formula for figuring cost-of-living raises, based on rises in the CPI, was difficult for all of us to understand and inadequate as well. There was no reason why the cost-of-living coverage should be phrased in a formula that obscured rather than clarified the extent to which real wages actually were protected against inflation. Such obscurity, I added, could only benefit management, and continuing union leadership support for formulas that left us in doubt on so fundamental an issue was not in our interest. I concluded that whether we or the company should pay for inflation was one of the major issues for the new contract. From the applause and responses the next day at work, it appeared that most of the membership present at the meeting appreciated these issues being raised.

Between the September regular union meeting and the next regularly scheduled meeting on October 13, no special meeting was held to pass the strike authorization, although many of us had understood from the president that such a special meeting would indeed be called soon after the September meeting. At the regular October meeting, the last one scheduled before the contract was to run out, nearly 700 workers turned out to assure that the strike sanction would be passed. It was, by a vote of 528 to 27. But before the vote was taken nearly 150 workers had left the meeting, either because they knew they only had to sign in when they entered to count toward a quorum, because they got fed up with the meeting or were scared away by some of what actually happened, or because they had other commitments. In any event, although the advance authorization for a strike was given, several things occurred during the meeting that did not in any way enhance rank-and-file understanding of the contract

UNION ACTION AND INACTION

issues and, on the contrary, made it even less likely that Union members could unify around critical shared demands. The upshot was that, aside from the formality of the strike sanction vote, the last meeting before the contract was to run out made no positive contribution to the contract struggle and in fact tended to ignore contract issues altogether. It also furthered polarization among the rank and file along racial lines and on law-and-order issues.

The meeting was dominated by two unexpected events that, whatever the intentions of participants, distracted us from the contract issues. The first was a conflict over the young black woman's discrimination grievance against the company, referred to in chapter 6, which resulted both in airing many blacks' feelings that the company systematically discriminated against blacks and in inflaming racial tensions. The second was a speech by Bert that threatened to lead to a fistfight between Bert and Tank, president of the local. Though both diversions were I think unfortunate in terms of the immediate contract issue, the first may have been unavoidable under the circumstances. The second was wholly avoidable and not very productive in any sense, although responsibility for its climax lay at least as much with the local's president, who lost his cool, as with the white radical, who verbally flouted the president's authority.

As to the first, the conflict developed over the Grievance Committee's rejection of the grievance of a young black woman who had worked at the company for nine years. Normally a Grievance Committee motion to have its recommendations for the disposition of members' grievances approved is handled perfunctorily, like most motions at union meetings that affect individuals. But this time opposition to the motion developed on the part of the griever and several of her friends and allies, black and white, male and female. After an acerbic exchange, in which the leadership supported the actions of its creature, the Grievance Committee, and in which a number of the rank and file supported the griever, the members overturned the committee's decision and directed it to take action to support the intention and substance of the discrimination grievance.

In the process of successfully defending this grievance, which otherwise would have been dismissed, however, some rank-and-file members in the audience, black and white, apparently exchanged unpleasant or even threatening words. The issue of the contract was wholly lost.

The second distraction came with Bert's speech, a rambling one that among other things challenged Tank to show which side he was on. During the speech Tank several times ruled the speaker out of order, at some points correctly, many workers thought. But Bert continued. He appealed to the audience, with some support, for the opportunity to speak freely after the union leadership had had the mike turned off. One thing led to another and before anyone in the audience realized what was going on, the president leaped up, strode across the stage with gavel in hand to where Bert was standing, and began to lay hands on him. For a moment at least it appeared to many that a brawl might break out. It did not.

In both cases things could have been worse. But they also could have been much better. At best the October meeting was a lost opportunity. At worst it destroyed some of the very limited sense of rank-and-file unity that existed before the meeting. Although a substantial proportion of blacks seem to have felt that airing the discrimination issue was very important, the reaction to the meeting of the majority of workers I spoke to was fear of the potential for disorder arising from both events. Not a few women, some of whom I very much respected, indicated they might well stay away from subsequent meetings unless there were assurances trouble would not break out again.

As if in self-parody, the leadership's only effort at that meeting to communicate the sense of what was happening in the negotiations apparently occurred while the ballots for the strike sanction vote were being counted. By that time at least 90 percent of those still attending the meeting had dispersed, so the report, if indeed it was given at all as the leadership claims, was delivered to a nearly empty hall. Several of us who remained seated in the front rows talking during the entire time were not even aware that a report had been given.

Consequently, going into the final days of the contract negotiations the members were wholly uninformed, structurally uninvolved and excluded, and generally disorganized. As the last seven days of

UNION ACTION AND INACTION

October began, we did not even know when we would meet to vote on the contract. Since the current contract ran out at midnight Thursday, October 31, it was not clear whether the special meeting to decide whether to accept or reject the company's offer would be the Sunday before; the following Friday, November 1; or under some extension of the current contract on the following Sunday, November 3. The leadership, unwilling to call a union meeting to decide whether to extend the old contract, notified us on Friday, October 25, that it had decided to extend; that the meeting would be Sunday, November 3; and that it would "make every effort" to get the final contract proposal to the plant by Saturday, November 2, a day when the majority of the workers would not be at work.

Reaction, in particular to this last aspect of the notice, was immediate, angry, and widespread. Many workers well remembered that the year before written summaries of the contract proposal had been delivered to our plant too late on a Friday afternoon for most workers to see them before that year's contract meeting. Largely due to the efforts of one of the young, reformist blacks on the negotiating committee and his father (the vice president of the union), summaries at least of important wage and fringe-benefit provisions of the 1974 contract were available to workers after 4:30 P.M. on Friday, November 1.

On its face, the contract offer was neither very bad nor very good. Many workers, however, no doubt accurately, considered it "the best contract ever from Blancs." The offer was for a three-year contract with no "openers," which meant that all wage and fringe-benefit issues, along with "language" provisions, were fully determined in advance for the entire term. Given the level from which we started, the basic wage increases were low in absolute terms, though apparently not intolerably so: 35 cents an hour in the first year; and 20 cents an hour in each of the second and the third years, plus a skill increment of 2 cents in the first year and 1 cent each in the second and third years for each wage grade above 11. In my job, for example, the total raise was almost 11 percent in the first year (which however only brought me to a wage of $4 per hour), about 5.5 percent in the second year, and about 5 percent in the third year. The cost-of-living protection, on the other hand, seemed much better than under the previous contract, since it appeared to cover the entire contract term, and since the formula to figure cost-of-living adjustments was changed to provide a raise of 1 cent per hour for each 0.3-point rise in the Consumer Price Index, instead of 1 cent an hour for each 0.5-point rise in the CPI, as under the old contract.

Regarding holidays, the offer would add three more days to the Christmas/New Year's holidays, to provide, including weekends, a paid winter holiday shutdown from December 23 through January 2. As for pensions, the basic computation rate was increased from $8 per month paid for each year of service to $10 in the first year of the contract, $11 in the second year, and $12 in the third year. This meant that even during the contract's third year, a person who retired after thirty years at the plant would receive a basic gross of $360 a month from Blancs, hardly what one would call old-age security.

Blue Cross/Blue Shield benefits also were increased, with emergency room coverage in the first year, dental coverage in the third year, and a prescription plan in the third year. In addition, there were numerous other improvements in the "language" of the contract of various significances, one of the most popular of which was an experimental six-month plan to make overtime on Saturday and Sunday "completely voluntary" under the contract.

The union meeting that Sunday to decide whether to accept or reject the company's offer was attended by nearly 1,100 members. Contrary to widespread fears, the meeting was orderly and went quite smoothly. The leadership handled it well, keeping its cool and not getting overly picky about parliamentary procedure. But all the while it was in control, riding the crest of the wave of relief and support for the contract that increasingly dominated the meeting and made even discussing the contract issues, let alone opposing the contract, very difficult. On this, the only occasion that the terms offered could be discussed at length and seriously evaluated, a substantial proportion of union members, it seemed, no longer wanted to hear or to participate in such a process. Few people spoke against the contract, still

UNION ACTION AND INACTION

fewer coherently. Some who opposed it were drunk. The vote on the contract, which once the meeting had gotten underway was never in doubt, was 875 in favor and 219 opposed.

The dominant feature of the meeting was that the union leadership and (with one exception) all the members of the Negotiating Committee made no public effort to evaluate the contract. Rather, almost to a person, they explained the contract in order to sell it to the membership. With the partial exception of one young, black reformer on the Negotiating Committee, union leaders uniformly had only good things to say about the offer. The union district business agent, Sid Ryan, who had our main spokesman in the negotiations and who gave the union's presentation of the offer, did a reasonable job reading and explaining what the various provisions of the contract meant. At no time, however, did he on his own initiative discuss any shortcoming of the contract, refer to any continuing problems that the contract did not confront, or take steps to resolve or mention any respects in which the new offer was not an improvement on the old contract or was even a step backward. Given the poor state of the national economy and the fact that the contract offer was seen as a reasonable one, it seems probable that a majority of employees might well have voted to accept the offer no matter what. Nevertheless, the posture of the union leaders and the members of the Negotiating Committee undoubtedly significantly increased the momentum to accept and contributed to stifling open debate on the merits. The negotiating process, it turned out, had committed our own representatives to the company offer that emerged. Any movement to reject the offer would have had to be made in the face of the company's and the union leadership's efforts to manage its acceptance.

But the offer itself was not without serious, if in places barely noticeable faults. Since the leadership expectably had not even seen fit to refer to these shortcomings and since whatever rank-and-file opposition to the offer expressed at the meeting also expectably tended to focus on its most glaring inadequacy, the small hourly wage raise, I was prepared to speak about one of the other shortcomings. Because the company and the leadership of our union had made every effort to sell the contract to the members, I felt that the members at least should hear the other side before they decided whether to accept or reject the contract offer. This is what I said:

Sid has told us what's good about the new contract, and there is a lot that's good, but before we vote we must first of all be sure we understand the contract's important provisions.

In past years there frequently has been misunderstanding or insufficient consideration of some of these issues. Otherwise, how did we lose paid lunch hours? How did we lose the cost-of-living protection we used to have? This new contract is one of the most important and serious matters each of us will decide in the next three years. And I am afraid we might not fully understand all of it. Take, for example, the cost-of-living protection.

Obviously, with high inflation, cost-of-living protection is vital today. Cost-of-living protection under the new contract is better than it is now in one important respect. The penny an hour raise for every 0.3-point rise in the Consumer Price Index is much better than last year's penny raise for every 0.5-point rise. So, when we first look at the cost-of-living protection, it looks excellent.

But is that protection as good as it looks? I don't think so. In fact in another respect this new clause is a step backward from last year's, in that our adjustments are now made only every six months instead of every three months, as under the old contract. That is very important, because we never make up by the cost-of-living adjustment what we lose to inflation. And the longer between each adjustment, the more we lose. The periodic adjustment only stops us from falling further behind. For example, suppose prices go up a lot early in the period. You could be paying 80 cents a gallon for gas for five and a half months and 4–5 percent more for your food for several months before there would be any adjustment. So our losing the quarterly adjustment is a serious loss.

More than that, we are already at least three months behind in the cost of living under the old contract. And the new contract doesn't provide for catching us up on that. Notice, further, that the first cost-of-living adjustment in that contract is not until May 5, 1975. So we will be at least nine months behind on cost of living when the first adjustment is made. Nine months at a cost of living that has been rising at about 15 percent a year can mean a loss of over 10 percent in our real wages, which is most of the entire package we get during the first year of the new contract. In other words we may lose most of what we get under the new contract up to May 1975. And under the new contract our last cost-of-living adjustment is scheduled for May 2, 1977. So from May to October 2, 1977, when the contract runs out, for those five months we won't get cost-of-living protection. We will be falling behind again. If the next contract is anything like the last one and this

UNION ACTION AND INACTION

one, any new cost-of-living protection will not begin with an adjustment on the first day that contract is to take effect. So we will fall behind by a lot more then, too.

I think we should have done much better on cost-of-living protection. We should have received our first adjustment on the first day of the new contract period, like the wage increase. We should have had a final adjustment on the last day of the contract. And the adjustments should be made quarterly, not every six months. Our real wages are not protected by this contract.

The speech was reasonably well received. But neither that speech nor the efforts of any single individual or isolated small group of workers could have turned the tide on the contract issue. There was at that November meeting only one thing that might have resulted at least in serious consideration of the contract issues. That was if one of the two dynamic black reformers on the Negotiating Committee had broken ranks, spilled the beans on how the negotiations had been conducted, and tried to arouse the membership, particularly the young and the lower-grade workers, who benefited least from this contract, to realize that a substantially better contract had been achievable. But the members of the Negotiating Committee were under what amounted to an oath of silence. There was tremendous pressure on them from the leadership and from the majority of the committee not to break ranks. At one point, probably too late in the meeting, it appeared that one of the reformers might do so, whereupon he was warned by the local's president that he was bound not to divulge anything that went on in the negotiations. The negotiations and the minority opinions thus were kept secret from the rank and file during the negotiating process and even after the process had achieved an agreement. This conspiracy of silence left the rank and file deprived of the opinions of those closest to the issues.

Isolated even by his fellow reformer, the one member of the committee who seemed about to expose the process and its results couldn't quite get it together. He did manage to get up very late in the meeting to say he didn't think "the man at the bottom got much in this contract, the black guy who's a 10 or a 9 and has only been here a year or two." And he implied, I thought, that the Negotiating

Committee hadn't done all it might have to get a better offer. But he was understandably too intimidated to go any farther, and that far was nowhere. Consequently, the contract offer was accepted without much rank-and-file involvement in the official process, except for the formal up-or-down vote at the end, and without sustained collective discussion of the issues at union meetings.

UNION ACTION AND INACTION

VIII

On the Shop Floor:
What a Bargain!

DURING the entire period leading up to that final, relatively uninformed decision of November 3, there was of course another level to
the contract negotiations. That level, on which the rank and file were
extremely active, was decidedly subordinated to but separated from
the negotiations and meeting levels. Every day in the plant, workers
gathered in small groups, at break time, at lunch time, in the locker
room at the beginning and end of the day, and at various places
throughout the plant during work time to discuss and heatedly debate
their views. They discussed what was needed in the new contract,
what we might get, what our alternatives were, what was the state of
company preparedness for a strike and what was going on in the formal negotiations. As October, the final month of the old contract
term, began, workers' attention turned more and more to the formal
negotiations, where they knew the major decisions were being made.
Since no official information about the negotiations was provided to
us either by the company or the union, worker participation on the
day-to-day level increasingly was reduced to passing and debating
rumors. With our heightened concern over events that would directly
and materially affect our lives, all of us were forced by union secrecy
and exclusiveness to manifest that concern in this most alienated,
often trivialized form. We were collectively shut out from any form
of meaningful participation, powerless. So we did what was left to us.

In the absence of official statements on developments in the negotiations, it was inevitable that nearly all relevant communications among members would be rumors. No matter how good the source of the information might be, with no official or readily accessible way to verify information, as soon as information was passed by its recipient to another member it became, practically speaking, nearly unverifiable for the vast majority of the rank and file. Thus, if I learned privately from a member of the Negotiating Committee or from very reliable sources I knew to be close to members of the Negotiating Committee that, say, the company's first offer in late October on a wage raise was thirteen cents an hour in the first year and eight cents an hour in each of the second and third years, no matter how accurate that information might be, to third parties it could be nothing more than a rumor until it was unsystematically confirmed by what other workers might have heard from their separate sources. Reliable information was effectively indistinguishable from unreliable information. This further undermined meaningful discussion and planning of tactics and strategies for dealing with the company.

The rumors in October fundamentally concerned two things: developments in the formal negotiations and the company's degree of preparedness to undergo a strike if necessary to maintain its negotiating position. The latter sort focused primarily on "guesstimates" of the current supply and demand for the company's product and involved such considerations as the extent of company stockpiling of rings and the degree to which the company was ahead or behind on deliveries. In early October, for example, we heard at morning break from a Service Department worker, who in turn had heard it from a worker in the Shipping Department, that the company was already shipping out rings to meet orders not due for delivery until January. The company, he added, "is really prepared for a long strike, especially with all the overtime they've been giving us." But then in mid-October another veteran worker from elsewhere in the plant said he thought the company was way behind on orders. "Everything," he said, "is hot. They're all rush jobs." And he said he'd heard that the company was "breaking orders"—shipping out parts of orders just to minimally satisfy its customers.

A different kind of rumor about company preparedness was

spread, perhaps as a conscious tactic, on the last day of the old contract by one of the union committeemen. The committeeman, who that day had been observed talking to one of the company's chief executives in the plant, said he'd heard that the company was prepared to have police guarding the Shipping and Receiving departments in the event of a strike in order to assure the unobstructed passage of materials and products. Concerning the new contract, he added, "we'd better take what we can get."

Such rumors obviously were not always simply innocuous ways to pass the time. They had serious implications, intended or not, for how we evaluated our bargaining position relative to the company. When confronted by a group of us in the men's locker room with the charge that what he was saying constituted a scare tactic, the offending committeeman, who earlier had been telling workers that "Blancs is way ahead on orders," replied that he "just wanted people to be prepared." In response, members of the group said that to be prepared we should have more solid information on the state of company deliveries and that our committeemen should fight harder for us. The committeeman, as if to exculpate himself, conveniently blamed the lack of information on Tank.

However, most rumors that month concentrated on alleged progress or lack of it in the negotiations. The absence of hard information was total. Even a committeeman who once had been a leadership insider (as a former member of both the union's Executive Committee and the Negotiating Committee) frankly and with irritation admitted in mid-October that he had no idea what was going on in the negotiations this year. Now he agreed, as an outsider, that the process should be more open to the rank and file.

The negotiation rumors concerned various areas of workers' concerns and generally embodied at least implied outrage at what was rumored. One male worker in early October ridiculed what he had heard of the "successes" of the negotiations on "language." It had been agreed to change "he" and "his" to "they" and "their" to reduce sexist language in the contract. By mid-October it was rumored, apparently accurately, that the Negotiating Committee was still working on "language" and had not yet begun to deal with issues involving wages and fringe benefits. A few days later it was said that the company, which appeared to be delaying negotiations on the wage and fringe-benefit issues so close to working people's hearts, had asked for a three-day extension of the old contract. That rumor touched off several angry exchanges about whether, if true, the company should be granted such an extension even if benefits under the new contract were made retroactive to November 1.

The lack of substantive information about the negotiations was compounded by a continuing absence of procedural information regarding when the union meeting on the contract would be held. By the work week before the contract was to run out, the word all over the factory was that Tank would have to post some kind of notice to tell us if the meeting was not going to be that Sunday and to advise us whether there would be an extension authorizing us to work on Friday and Saturday, November 1 and 2.

By October 22 there was a rumor that the plant's foundry workers, who were in a small local of their own, had settled for themselves on a new contract. It was also rumored that the company wanted a three-year contract with no openers. And then, apparently before the actual negotiations on wages began, it was said that in the three-year contract without openers the company would offer a total of $1.05 in wage raises, which turned out in fact to be 40 percent higher than the offer we accepted. On October 24, it was rumored that the foundry workers, far from having settled, were going out that day or the next. In that case, during their strike and while our union's negotiations continued, we would have been able to collect Unemployment benefits, which are much better than strike benefits, as we would have been "locked out." On the following day I heard a rare rumor concerning how members of the Negotiating Committee had split on an issue, information that would have been very important to have had confirmed in order to make informed decisions on who to support and to vote for in the upcoming union elections. The rumor was that the committee had voted 10 to 2 to extend the contract, with only the two black reformers voting negative.

As the final four days under the old contract began, it was widely rumored that the negotiations were just beginning to take up the matter of wages and fringe benefits. Then I heard that the company was offering a total wage-and-fringe-benefit package of $1.50 on a three-year, no-openers contract, with the 13 cent and 8 cent wage raises referred to earlier. Only the two reformers, it was said, had opposed a long-term, closed contract. On Tuesday this wage offer was confirmed from an independent source. The reaction was mixed disbelief, anger, and an expressed determination to "walk" if it turned out to be the company's final offer, which of course it didn't. In the last two days of the negotiations there were various rumors about pensions, vacations, and cost-of-living coverage.

To say the least, the rumors were confusing and distracting. Passing rumors may have served as a vehicle for sublimating worker anxieties about the new contract and for discussing their needs. Beyond that, it does not appear to have served any very positive function, and rather appears to have contributed to worker passivity and divisiveness. For one thing, rumors often diverted us from considering what we might be doing to maximize our chances to get a good contract. For another, such rumors as the one about the company's very low first offer on wages may well have enhanced the attractiveness of the company's final offer. The first offer may itself have been made and even initially leaked, at least by some members of the Negotiating Committee, to do precisely that. Finally, workers tended to spread rumors about those provisions in the contract for which they individually had the greatest concern, thereby often reinforcing divisions among workers based upon such partialized concerns. In all, the erratic and piecemeal quality of the rumors hardly contributed to building a shared consensus on minimal demands.

Uninformed, ill informed, and misinformed until it was too late to do anything but vote to accept the company offer or to strike, workers were more vulnerable to day-to-day manipulation by the union leadership. Marbles was the union leader with whom I had the closest contact. I talked to him nearly every day at lunch. Notwithstanding his attractive and positive qualities, Marbles personified the leadership's tactics of delaying, distracting, confusing, scaring, and dividing.

Take again the cost-of-living issue, concerning which I repeatedly talked to him and other workers. In early September I asked Marbles whether the Language Committee, of which he was chairman, had decided anything about the cost-of-living escalator clause, and in particular whether they had taken a stand on my earlier suggestion that the new contract's cost-of-living clause should straightforwardly tie the percentage of wage adjustments to the percentage rise in inflation, thereby eliminating the complex formulas then in effect, which camouflaged the real extent of our protection against inflation. In response, I first understood Marbles to say that the committee had adopted the straight percentage idea. But when pressed he implied he still favored the kind of formula currently used. He also stated he wanted the committee to further investigate other formulas for the clause, like the one used at the local Bethlehem Steel plant, which he claimed to be examining. To that I doggedly responded that we certainly couldn't do better than a straight percentage formula, under which the amount of a worker's upward wage adjustments would be the exact product of his/her wages times the percentage rise in cost of living during the period. The company, which no doubt would not appreciate giving us full cost-of-living protection, on no account would agree to any formula that gave us adjustments beyond the rise in inflation. Marbles did not answer. Later that day I heard from another member of the Language Committee that his committee had not even discussed the cost-of-living issue. And some weeks later during the negotiating process, I learned that the cost-of-living issue was not within the jurisdiction of the Language Committee, since it was handled as a wage-and-fringe-benefit issue.

Then there was the day after the September union meeting, when Marbles said to me, "The employees loved your speech." I replied that "they love speeches that are clear and support what they know to be their own interest." Obviously impressed by the support for my position, Marbles seemed either to be trying to win me to his position or to consult with me. He said frankly that the company would never agree simultaneously to give us a big raise and also make up for the loss in our real wages incurred due to the inflation since the last cost-of-living adjustment the past spring. That should be a matter to negotiate out, I replied. The leadership should try to get us

164

a big raise and full cost-of-living protection for the future. Marbles said they were shooting for an immediate 25 percent raise, which would effectively include the adjustment for past cost-of-living rises, and for complete protection in the future under the straight percentage approach. In fact, in the new contract we received an average wage raise of 7 percent a year over three years, and a still inadequate cost-of-living protection, based on the same confusing formulas. In all probability the percentage approach to cost-of-living protection never was seriously considered or proposed by the union negotiators.

On another issue, in mid-September I asked Marbles when the special meeting we were supposed to have for the strike sanction vote would be. He said it would be announced when the president returned. While our contract was running out and union organization for the negotiations was in total disarray, the president and vice president of the union, we learned, were away for a week in Wisconsin, attending a seminar course on collective bargaining. Marbles said there was no rush to have the meeting. The next regular meeting would be October 12, and, he added, we wouldn't necessarily have a meeting before that. We didn't.

After lunch one day in mid-October, when I returned to the cafeteria to dump the trash, I saw Marbles taking flak from some workers from the Chrome Department who were clearly dissatisfied with the lack of information about developments in the negotiations. Marbles did his usual bit about having faith in the Negotiating Committee, which culminated with his conversation-ending "you elected them." But somehow the conversation did not end with that rhetorical genuflection to liberal democracy. One of the Chrome workers instead retorted, "You're the only one who has faith in them." Another demanded, "We need some leadership."

Of course we were already getting a certain brand of leadership, personified in Marbles. That brand was epitomized by how the union officers handled the extension issue. The problem, as indicated, was that our contract would run out in the middle of the work week. Therefore we either had to extend the old contract to authorize working for the remainder of the week, call a meeting to vote on the company's offer on the next work day after the contract ran out, or call the meeting for the Sunday before the contract ran out. Given the way the company was delaying making its offer on wages and fringe benefits, the last choice seemed out of the question. So that left two choices. Marbles, discussing the matter as if primarily concerned with what the employees wanted, said he had advised Tank to opt for an extension. He said some members would be mad at Tank either way, but that production people would be madder still if they had to lose a day of wages and bonuses to attend a meeting. With that, he recounted in support of his position certain past events during which, on a prior Christmas Eve when the heating in the plant had broken down, production workers given the choice of going home early or continuing to work in the cold allegedly had chosen to continue on for the money. But, I replied, the contract issue involves money, too, and employees might very well be willing to stop work on November 1 to discuss the company offer at length. "Why don't you call a special meeting to decide whether to extend the contract?" I asked. To that, Marbles replied that if the union called a special meeting to consider the extension, people would "cause trouble," by which he seemed to mean in part that they might very well vote against an extension. Later in the week, referring again to the idea of holding a special meeting to enable the membership to decide whether to extend, Marbles said, "We can't afford to have a meeting"; we "can't risk it." This was the standard leadership stance, reflecting its ultimate distrust of the membership.

At other times during October, Marbles would scare people in a variety of ways. He talked of banks failing and not getting full return on deposits. He said he thought the IAM strike benefit fund was probably depleted, so we wouldn't even be able to get the maximum benefits of $40 a week if we struck. And of course he talked about the danger of a minority of workers arousing the majority, which is why the leadership decidedly did not want to call any more meetings than it had to. Marbles was a disorganizer par excellence. He was, as an old black who had worked for the company for years put it, "smart in the wrong direction."

He was not unique in that. Another very high officer of the local, in response to the challenge to the leadership at the October

THE SHOP FLOOR

meeting, had told a veteran worker who still remembered vividly what it had been like at Blancs before the union, that "some people were out to overthrow the union." This tactic, similar to Marbles's repeated cries of "outside agitator" and "troublemaker," was not very far from the red scare tactics so effectively plied in the late 1940s and 1950s and still retained in the union's armory. A different union official on the Friday after the negotiations had ended, when the union leadership side by side with company management were going through the plant among the rank and file actively trying to sell the contract, put the contract offer to workers this way: "Can you live with it?" Not, "Can we and should we do better?" But, "Can you live with it?" This was the perfect defeatist line, aimed at persuading workers that the offer was not so bad as to make a strike worthwhile.

That's how the union leadership led us on the shop floor during the negotiations. What a bargain!

IX

Activists and Organizing

WHILE all this was taking place, a handful of workers in the plant, myself included, consciously tried to inform themselves on the issues and processes involved in the contract negotiations, to arouse other workers to greater awareness of those issues and processes, and to prepare themselves and others to defend our common interests as workers. Snatching free moments during work and at breaks, we talked individually with other workers. After work we put out leaflets, spoke up at union meetings, and tried to convene a broader group of workers to exchange information and opinions and to plan tactics and strategies.

But we were never able to function effectively as a responsible group of activists, in no small part because of the rift between two New Left, self-styled Communist organizations, with one or the other of which most of the activists appear to have been affiliated. Our own incapacity to organize ourselves seriously reduced our ability to mobilize others around a shared understanding and plan for action. And that, combined with the nearly total absence of emerging rank-and-file leadership, meant that there was in the plant no sustained alternative to the sort of leadership provided by union officials. The two black reformers, who might have provided such an alternative, had already been largely coopted into the formal negotiating process and therefore did not function consistently and openly as alternative rank-and-file leaders. The activists never were able to take up the slack.

In my efforts to "organize," which began after having been on the job for about a month, I related to three groups in the plant: rank-and-file members, with whom I spent the most time and from whom I learned the most; union officials; and other activists. From union officials I primarily sought information. From rank-and-file workers I sought information, a sense of their perceived needs, and their cooperation. And with activists, in addition to seeking information and insights, I tried to stimulate cooperative action aimed both at clarifying our own and other workers' perceptions of the shared conflictual relation with the company, specifically as it was embodied in the negotiation process, and at galvanizing more active worker participation in that process. These aims, needless to say, were extremely difficult to achieve. The negotiations, which dominated workers' awareness from Labor Day to November 3, were structured to give the appearance of fundamental harmony of interests between the company and workers while rendering workers passive and excluding them from active participation.

That first day after the August union meeting, when I began to do what I came to see as organizing, I felt my way as I went. At the time, with two exceptions, I had no idea who the activists in the plant were, or with which ones I might share the minimal political consensus necessary to enable us to cooperate. I also was barely beginning to develop a sense of various rank-and-file concerns and problems and to get better acquainted with my fellow workers in the Service Department. During my first week organizing I intuitively chose to speak to members of all three groups, and what I heard was portentous.

On the first day I spoke with Sarah, a young black woman, who complained about how the company had treated her. She declared almost fatalistically that the "old ladies" in her department were not about to work for a better union, but indicated that a number of the black workers in the Service Department might be movable. After our talk, I spoke with five to ten of my fellow workers, reporting that the union meeting the day before (which they had not attended) had been useful once the bureaucratic claptrap was out of the way. I encouraged them to attend the next meeting, speaking concretely to several who had expressed concern that the new contract should provide "dirty money"—added compensation for doing particularly dirty tasks. I advised them that their demand had not been one of those referred to at the meeting and strongly suggested that if they wanted it included they had better keep after Marbles and his Language Committee, which otherwise wasn't likely to show particular concern for their needs. They recognized that they would have to fight for whatever they'd get.

Several days later I talked with Marbles, whom I had been warned by many fellow workers and an activist not to trust. He felt me out on whether I had liked that Sunday's union meeting. I replied, "Yes and no." In response to his asking how so, I said I thought the formalities were a waste of time but that it got good when the employees spoke out. He seemed surprised, and said we had to get the minutes read and approved. I disagreed. Then we began for the first time to talk about the cost-of-living escalator. I asked him what was to become my standard question about using percentages. He responded, typically, that certain wage-raise formulas were used, and that we could do better by improving the wage-raise/point-rise ratio in the formula. He acted as if using such formulas clearly was best for us. The important thing, he said, first, was to get cost-of-living coverage into the new contract and, second, to get a better wage-raise/point-rise ratio. Still unable to understand why we should use such formulas at all, I pressed him. He finally conceded that my suggestion, which would ensure an average cost-of-living wage raise exactly equal to actual inflation,* "would never be bought by the company." He concluded (half-heartedly I thought) that we should nevertheless negotiate for complete coverage.

Before the week ended I completed the circuit, speaking for the first time to Barbara, a worker I had just learned was an activist. We agreed on the need to organize for a possible strike, but she expressed serious reservations about cooperating with those other activists in the plant who were affiliated with the Revolutionary Union (RU), which

---

* This assumes unjustifiably the accuracy of the index that is used to measure inflation.

ACTIVISTS AND ORGANIZING

was engaged in a struggle with the October League (OL), with which she apparently had sympathies.* On the basis of past experience, she felt that members of the RU sought to organize narrow groups they could dominate. She believed that the RU followed an adventurist line, repeatedly isolating itself from broad segments of workers and often turning them off with militant-sounding rhetoric. Pete, the worker I talked to later that afternoon who was a member of the RU, denied the charges. He said he recognized the need to play down such explicit rhetoric while organizing for a potential strike. But he also claimed that, shorn of such rhetoric, the reality of class struggle should and could be communicated to and is understood by workers. He indicated he wanted to cooperate with all activists in the plant. Such were my first glimmerings of what seemed to me a largely counterproductive, sectarian struggle involving most members of the very small group of activists in the plant—people who ironically had come there not only to work but to organize.

In that first week the lines that had been drawn were faintly observable: the activists, who talked of organizing the rank and file but threatened to decline to organize their own ranks; the rank and file, who often talked angrily about "fighting" for what they needed but appeared to be too respectful, weary, intimidated, or pacified to persist in putting pressure on union leaders to represent workers' interests; and the union officials, who fast-talked about getting workers what they needed in the new contract but in practice at best sought only to make a bad situation slightly more bearable and were unwilling or unable to say and do things that might seriously jeopardize their own positions with the company.

In the weeks that followed these intimations were confirmed. When I next spoke to Barbara I said I thought we had to put out some kind of plant newspaper to take the place of the one the union leadership had closed down, allegedly under company threats to sue for libel. She agreed that a newspaper was needed, but countered that workers weren't interested in one at the moment, and that we should wait until after the next union meeting. We did wait. In fact we were

* The Revolutionary Union later became the Revolutionary Communist Party. The October League later became the Communist Party (Marxist-Leninist).

WORKERS AND THE UNION

still waiting by the time I was laid off in February of the following year. On the issue of cost of living, she disagreed with my tentative support for straight percentage protection. She argued cogently that in raising everybody's wages by the percent inflation drove prices up the absolute amount of the periodic adjustment would be higher for workers in higher grades. Under the present formulation, by contrast, every worker got the same absolute amount in the adjustment. This was fair, she declared, since inflation hits the poor relatively harder than the better-off. There is no reason, therefore, to give workers in higher wage grades more money in the adjustment than those in the lower grades.

I could see her point and was unclear about which approach to take on this important and complex issue. On the one hand, I believed that the main issue was who should pay for inflation. The best way to deal with that issue, I thought, would be to eliminate the mystifying formulas that disguise the reality that workers under existing contracts largely pay for it. The most effective way to make this unalterably clear, I thought, would be simply to put the burden for whatever rise in inflation occurred on the company. In that way all workers' real wages would be protected. By contrast, under the existing formula, not only was it unclear who ultimately paid for inflation, but also workers at different wage grades almost inevitably got differential protection of their real wages, since with the adjustment amount constant for all wage grades, the adjustment as a percentage of the wages was different for different grades.

When I again discussed the issue with Barbara after first discussing it with other workers, I suggested a compromise formula that basically adhered to the percentage approach but gave some recognition to the egalitarian principle she supported. I also said that I didn't think we should seek to upgrade lower-paid workers or change the unequal wage structure primarily by means of the cost-of-living clause. If existing inadequacies and inequalities deserved to be attacked, they should be attacked directly, I felt.

In the ensuing discussion we seemed to be having difficulty communicating. She countered that we had to find an index that was more accurate than the Consumer Price Index in reflecting inflation.

ACTIVISTS AND ORGANIZING

I agreed but said that was a separate issue, since whatever the index used to measure inflation, the question of which formula to apply to that index to calculate the amount of the wage adjustment remained. As we talked, it became increasingly clear that—whether because of principled commitment, a realistic recognition that neither the company nor the union leadership would accept the percentage approach, and/or simply because she was too close to the union framework—Barbara, like Marbles, had accepted the wage-raise/point-rise framework and was focusing her attention on getting the most favorable ratio into the contract demands. I continued to believe that the percentage approach was sounder for many reasons. Demands formulated in that way, it seemed to me, were clearer for purposes of political education; were more likely to provide a basis for unity in the event of a strike; and were most materially beneficial to workers, if they could be achieved. On the other hand, I recognized a conflict between desirable principles and strategies: the one aimed at exposing the conflicting class interests of workers and capitalists and the other aimed at upgrading the least-well-off workers and reducing wage differentials slightly. I believed that clarifying who was paying for inflation and clearly putting as much of the burden as possible on the company was most important. I told Barbara that I thought she was too caught up in the union's vision of the escalator clause. Once within that framework, confusion about who actually would be paying for inflation was inevitable, I argued, because in the actual negotiations the union probably would fall back from whatever ratio it had decided constituted full coverage, and consequently when we voted on the offer none of us would understand the extent of our coverage. She countered by asking what the fallback proposal on my percentage approach would be. Anything that maintains the clarity of who is paying for inflation, I answered—for example, a wage raise of 80 percent of the rise indicated by the CPI during the period.

During the entire discussion I was sensitive to the fact that at no time did Barbara, whom I respected, indicate she was willing to work with me or with most of the other activists in the plant. At one point when I asked her if she was a "loner," she seemed to respond in the affirmative, while simultaneously affirming the bankruptcy of such a stance. With regard to working with me, she quite accurately said that we didn't know each other well enough to establish a "basis for mutual trust." Beyond that, she also seemed to indicate that my eagerness to organize around the contract/strike issue was something she didn't quite share. She saw the new contract as only one event in a complex, longer-term process. Undeniable as that point was in the abstract, it suggested a different evaluation of the stakes involved in the contract/strike issue and therefore a potentially different commitment to organizing around it. This, I realized much later, was a very important difference in politics between us, a difference that was manifest all along the line in terms of how much and what sort of effort she and I were to put into organizing on this issue. I began to wonder, as Barbara and I talked over the weeks, whether she also might be protecting a certain image of respectability she had built up in the plant for working within the union, and whether Barbara's primary strategy might not be simply to get the best she could for workers within the structure and concepts laid down by the union and the company. A "progressive trade unionist," she had been derisively called by Pete, a member of the rival RU.

Whatever, two days after that first lengthy talk with Barbara I again spoke to Sarah, who came farther out of the closet as an activist. Sarah was suffering from the chronic malady of activists; she was discouraged. She said she sometimes "despaired about workers getting it together with all the ethnic divisions and individualism among Americans." She said she really didn't know how many she could trust among her fellow workers. And she asked angrily, partly reflecting her own sense of isolation, "Why have I been able to get my head together while most of the others have not?" These were unanswerable fears and questions. I just told her I thought we activists should get ourselves organized first, that we should have a get-together before the next union meeting to discuss what contract issues most concerned workers and to discuss the best organizing tactics. Later that day, I learned from an RU activist, Sarah suggested to several activists that they get together at her house Saturday night. I wasn't asked, so I didn't go. The get-together apparently never was held. And the September union meeting came and went with the activists in a continuing state of disarray.

With several major exceptions, our activist work from mid-September until the company's offer was approved in early November was carried on exclusively through the countless individual discussions each of us had with fellow workers; the leaflets several of us wrote, edited, and arranged to be printed and handed out; and the public talks we gave at union meetings. Although during that time I met on several occasions after work with Sarah and Barbara, both of whom tended toward OL, and often discussed matters at length with Pete of RU, at no time did all the activists ever get together to try to coordinate their efforts. Efforts by me to set up such a meeting all failed. As a member of neither organization, I wanted us to all work together if possible, and therefore tended to shuttle unsuccessfully back and forth between the two factions.

On the day after the September union meeting at which we failed to achieve a quorum for the strike sanction vote, about twenty of my rank-and-file co-workers, men and women, whites and blacks, progressives and conservatives, came up to compliment me on my first cost-of-living speech and to talk about related matters. Most expressed appreciation for my attack on the leadership. Others primarily approved of my getting involved in the union and said we could change it if we worked at it. One said, "The company don't want to hear the kind of shit you was throwing at them," and predicted Blancs would either try to buy me off or get rid of me. Some suggested specifically that I should run for a union office. One worker in my department expressed a kind of pride that "our trash man" could lay it out like that. Almost all showed that they understood the objective situation and that they appreciated my "telling it like it is," which included seeing the company as our main antagonist and our own leadership as weak and unreliable at best and collaborationist at worst. This waterfall of appreciation confirmed my general belief that the contract/strike issue was an extremely important one, and that it should be utilized to mobilize rank-and-file interest, consciousness, anger, and activity—all required to win a good contract, to win back the union, and to give workers some renewed sense of their own power.

That belief, which on balance I still think is correct, committed me to trying to play an active role in the process. One of my first opportunities came several days after the September meeting, when Pete handed me a draft of a leaflet to comment upon. I didn't much like the draft, I told him; it was too vague and too stylized in its rhetoric. I suggested some leading questions be included; some were. For the most part, however, that first leaflet, as it came out on Friday, September 13, was very similar to the original draft. It said:

DOES THE UNION LEADERSHIP WANT US TO WIN A GOOD CONTRACT?

Last Sunday about 350 Blancs workers came to a meeting to vote to sanction a strike if we don't agree to a contract by the 1st of November. These workers came with very short notice (2 days at most) and just about all had a serious attitude towards what we were supposed to do.

However, we did not have enough people at the meeting to have the vote. This fact gives us a black eye in the view of the company. Blancs can look and say, "These workers can't hurt us—they can't even get their own stuff together."

WHY WAS THIS SO?

Tank said the reason why nobody else came was that nobody cares and the people are too ignorant. Figures this old sell-out he would try to turn stuff around on the people instead of dealing where he and his small group of buddies are at.

Why did the union officials put the signs up about the meeting too late for people to make arrangements to come?

Why can't people get a straight answer as to how much money we are asking for?

Why is the Strike Committee only 6 people when it is supposed to be at least 15?

Even though this Sunday set us back some, it won't be hard to turn it around. Those of us who were there came out mad and when the next meeting happens we'll push our co-workers to attend. But we won't stop there.

We're tired of our union leadership's foot-dragging, wrecking ways. We're going to light a fire that will either burn them up or make them jump.

CONCERNED BLANCS WORKERS
Labor Donated

Perhaps because it was handed out at the end of the work week—the following day was my first Saturday off since shutdown—I never did get much of a reading on rank-and-file reactions to this

ACTIVISTS AND ORGANIZING

leaflet. Those days I spent most of my free time talking and thinking about how to help unite the various groups within the factory into a coalition supporting certain minimal contract demands. From discussions with other workers it was clear that the fragile coalition, which spontaneously came into being just long enough in 1973 to reject the company's offer and to vote to strike and then proceeded to disintegrate, had formed around a variety of demands. This year, to form a stronger coalition, a strategy had to be worked out to appeal to older, middle-aged, and younger workers, all at the same time. And related to this, I felt, the activists had to try to form an expanded group of workers to discuss and plan these matters, whose members themselves would represent such a coalition. Such members, then, would simultaneously improve our understanding of the issues from various perspectives and enhance our capacity to reach out to the larger groupings within the factory to which they belonged.

I talked with Barbara about some of these matters. We discussed several prospects for inclusion into the group. In the course of the discussion, several new points of disagreement came out. First, she opposed attacking the union leadership, arguing that this was a time we had to unite against the company. I disagreed in large part, conceding that attacks on leadership should not be frivolous but should be developed around serious disagreements on important issues and arguing that such attacks could be useful not only to clarify the issues but also to mobilize the anger toward the leadership that so many employees individually felt. Barbara was concerned that I sided with RU on this matter, and in fact I was closer to their position on this issue. She stated, in addition, that she didn't think she could work with members of RU, which eliminated nearly half the activists in the factory and made me wonder again whether she was willing to cooperate with me.

Since Barbara was hardly forthcoming, I wound up cooperating mostly with Pete in getting out the next leaflet. I did show an initial draft of that leaflet to Barbara and Sarah, however. Sarah said she thought it was good. Barbara said she thought it was too long and lacked zip, but more important, she felt it primarily reached out to those already disaffected and not to those afraid to strike. That may well have been so, but none of us knew how to reach and mobilize the intimidated.

Mistakenly, I relied on Pete to get the leaflet printed and distributed. Although it came out essentially as I had redrafted it, it took more than two weeks to get it out. In the interim I worried and talked. I worried that my hand in the leaflet would be recognized by union leaders, especially in the references to cost-of-living protection. I talked with Marbles, who kept claiming that it was "the officers who run the union, and what's wrong with the union is the people in it." I talked with Morton, who correctly charged that the union leaders give us the contract stuff all in a package at the last minute so "the people can't understand it." I talked with Pete, who was supposed to be getting the leaflet out, criticizing him for dragging his feet. He said he'd been sick, and I wondered how well organized RU was if it couldn't even get a one-page flier out in ten days.

On Tuesday, October 8, the leaflet finally was distributed outside the gates after work. It read:

WELCOME HOME TANK
We hope you had a wonderful time in Wisconsin at our expense, while we were working and waiting for you to call that strike sanction vote meeting you promised to call.

You shouldn't have gone to Wisconsin to study collective bargaining at a time when our contract is running out, when we failed to get the strike sanction vote, when the most important negotiations with the company in 3 years are about to begin, and when preparations must be made here in case we have to strike.

FIGHT FOR US
Your main problem is not that you don't understand collective bargaining. You union leaders know how to negotiate with Blancs but you don't fight for the needs of union members. And no seminars in Wisconsin on collective bargaining will help with that.

We favor union unity in our struggle with the company. But we support only a unity based on fighting hard for the employee's needs. We oppose unity based on surrender to the company.

NO CRUMBS FOR US
We will continue to speak out to build a unity that responds to the needs of workers here. We will continue to speak out on the bread-and-butter issues the union leadership hardly ever discusses at our union meetings.

ACTIVISTS AND ORGANIZING

We think you should know that the workers at Blancs are not going to take crumbs from the company table again this year. If you try to ram that kind of contract down our throats another time, we will spit it out all over the company and you union bosses.

WE DEMAND

For starters we demand:

1) at least a 75¢ an hour wage increase for the first year and a similar increase for any further period covered by the contract.

2) a cost-of-living clause that really does fully protect us and one that is clear to all of us. We are fed up with those confusing formulas that try to hide the fact you union leaders haven't fully protected our wages from inflation. 14¢ an hour for our last cost-of-living adjustment! Are you kidding?

3) 25-year retirement, also protected by a cost-of-living clause, so the retirement benefit is worth something when we retire.

AND THAT AIN'T ALL! THERE ARE MANY OTHER NEEDS TO BE MET. WE WON'T SURRENDER ON THE IMPORTANT ONES. SO THIS YEAR YOU'LL HAVE TO DO MORE THAN TAKE WHAT THE COMPANY OFFERS. YOU'LL HAVE TO FIGHT FOR US AND WIN!

CONCERNED BLANCS WORKERS
Labor Donated

The next day, rank-and-file reactions to the flier varied; most I heard were favorable. An older white woman who worked in the Inspections Department and was as far from being an activist as one could get asked me what I thought about it. I asked her what she thought. She said she thought it good and said she also liked the paper being sold outside last evening that accused unions generally of siding with the companies. She concluded almost desperately, "it's really tough around here, isn't it?" When I asked if she was coming to the union meeting that next Sunday, she said she would if she could get someone to take care of an invalid family member while she was out. Another woman who was very strong and progressive said she thought the flier was "beautiful." One veteran worker felt it was "all right" but apparently hadn't paid much attention to all the details. Another extremely conservative male worker predictably thought it was "out in left field." Several others I asked had not seen it at all. Barbara said the only feedback she had gotten was favorable, but correctly added that whether people liked it or not wasn't necessarily the most important issue. *The* issue, she said, was the results it would bring. The workers, she asserted, need leadership. I certainly didn't disagree but was unsure what that meant concretely. The passivity of workers, I responded, had to be overcome for them to support and develop their own leadership. One way to stimulate them to overcome their passivity was to help them mobilize and direct their anger.

With the critical October union meeting coming up that Sunday, I had prepared another flier for immediate distribution while waiting for the last one to come out. In doing so, I substantially rewrote the draft Pete had earlier given me and circulated the new draft to Sarah and Barbara. Again, Sarah thought it very good. Barbara still disagreed with the tactic of continuing to attack Tank and the union bosses, which she said contributed to polarization and made other lower-level union officials feel they were being attacked too. She said that in her experience attacking the company and the union simultaneously usually fails, since the union is all the workers have. Although I agreed with the final point, I continued, on balance, to disagree with her tactics. In response to her criticism, however, I did redraft the flier to target almost exclusively on named top leadership. We also talked about the possibility of getting together on Saturday. I said I thought it was politically irresponsible for the activists not to get together. Barbara repeated still more firmly her refusal to work with the RU members, though they appeared willing to work in a coalition with her.

The Friday before the union meeting of October 13 the latest leaflet came out. It read:

WE WON'T SETTLE FOR A SELL OUT
Come to the union meeting this Sunday morning at 10 at Edmondson High and vote to authorize a strike. We must authorize a strike in advance to be eligible for the union's strike benefits in case we do vote at the end of October to actually strike. More important, the more people come to the meeting and vote strike, the more seriously the company is going to have to deal with our demands.

TURNING POINT
These next few weeks can be a turning point for us in protecting and improving our standard of living and in getting this union straightened out.

We know two important facts. First, Blancs never gives us anything we don't fight hard for, and more, Blancs is making record profits and sure can afford to pay us a lot more money.

Second, inflation this year is cutting our wages by 15–20%. There is every reason to believe it will be at least as bad next year. That means that unless our wages are adjusted upward in line with inflation, if, for example, you now earn $3.50 an hour, you will need a raise of from $.52 to .70 an hour just to stay even!

WHO PAYS FOR INFLATION

So the main struggle between us and the company will be over WHO PAYS THE COST OF INFLATION. We must fight to protect our real wages and make sure the company pays for inflation. We must get a cost-of-living clause in the new contract that fully protects our livelihood.

UNITE TO FIGHT!

We know it won't be easy. The top union leadership doesn't want us to strike even if a strike becomes necessary. The union bosses are in bed with the company, and they don't want us to disturb their comfort.

That means Tank, Sid Ryan, etc. will continue to try to delay, confuse, and scare us. As we move closer to an actual strike vote, we can expect our sellout leadership to tell us the company is prepared for a long strike, that it's producing and shipping ahead of schedule. They'll tell us whatever they think will discourage us, split us, and keep us down.

BUT WE CAN BEAT THE COMPANY AND OUR TURNCOAT UNION LEADERS IF WE UNITE TO FIGHT THEM. WE HAVE A LONG WAY TO GO AND A LOT TO AC-COMPLISH. LET'S MAKE THIS MEETING OUR FIRST STEP.

STRIKE VOTE MEETING — 10 AM SUNDAY — EDMONDSON HIGH SCHOOL

CONCERNED BLANCS WORKERS
Labor Donated

The leaflets were distributed outside the plant gate by RU people before and after the day shift. I first knew they had been distributed when I spotted one tacked up on a main bulletin board, with another union leader's name written in as an additional target next to Tank's and Sid's. Although I didn't see many being carried into the plant, an older white man in the Shaft Seal Department asked me approvingly if I knew who had done it. I said no. A middle-aged black man in my department said he thought the flier was good, but that he still wouldn't go to any union meeting held by this union. A skilled, middle-aged white worker in my department, who had been a union committeeman elsewhere and had been active in our union during his ten-plus years at Blancs but who in recent years had largely dropped out of union work, was delighted with the flier. It was, he said, "spreading like a disease all over the plant."

His opinion was particularly important, because he was some-one we hoped to recruit to work with us. His politics ranged from re-formist to his bumper-sticker credo, "America, Love It Or Leave It." He was a useful prospect because his own experience and intelligence had led him to think like an organizer. As we stood and discussed the leaflet and the general situation in the plant, he said, "We got to find out what the workers want and give it to them. Then they'll come to us." He added, "You just got to get 'em rollin' at the meeting."

Not all the reactions, of course, were positive. I overheard two white men discussing the leaflets. The younger was talking about the previous leaflet, saying that he thought the demand for a 75 cent raise was too high, but agreed that cost of living was a real concern. The middle-aged man, who obviously totally disapproved of all the leaflets, said he had discounted the first flier, but that this one might "be trouble, since it will get the stupid ninnies who work in the plant to vote for strike," which he clearly did not want. He continued bad-mouthing his fellow workers, adding the leaflet was "too professional to have been done by any of the ninnies in the plant, so it was proba-bly done by hippies." For them, he hoped "it gets cold tonight and they all freeze to death."

With the leaflet out, the next thing was to get together with the activitists to try to prepare for Sunday's meeting. When I spoke to Barbara, she refused categorically to meet with anyone from RU. She also accused me of trying to get her to agree with policies of which she didn't approve. I, on my side, was feeling my own frustrations. I told her I was tired of trying to chase her down to get her to cooper-ate. She indicated, in partial response, that she would be willing to meet with me and Sarah alone, though again she said she thought my politics in attacking the union leadership were like RU's. I con-ceded I agreed with RU on that issue, but added that I had criticized the main RU activist for seeming to attack unions in general and for encouraging or at least allowing radical newspapers with which he was associated to be passed out simultaneously with the Blancs' fliers.

I left saying that if she wanted a meeting it would be up to her to arrange it. Angry, I went to talk with Sarah, who was sympathetic, but backed her friend Barbara in refusing to meet with RU members. Sarah repeated that in her experiences with RU in the plant it consistently effectively isolated the left. As we talked the lunch half-hour away, Barbara came by and we all talked together, in the process agreeing to meet ourselves the next day after work. We agreed that the main approach to organizing had to be to win over the middle forces in the factory, but we disagreed on the correct tactics to do that. I said I thought attacking the leadership on issues could contribute to that, since nearly everyone knew how bad they were. Sarah was very pessimistic, in any event, about prospects for organizing for a strike. I said I thought that prospects depended on what the company offered, how the union leadership responded, and what impact we could have.

As we talked, Barbara and I tried to straighten out our political/personal relationship. I repeated that I very much wanted us to work together and said, "If the radicals in the plant can't cooperate, how can we ever expect to win?" After we broke up, I advised Pete that Sarah, Barbara, and I would be meeting the next day but that they were unwilling to meet with him. He was less than pleased. "What about the other people I invited?" he asked. "What others?" I countered incredulously. "You had no right to ask anyone else." I was sorry, I said, that the two women were unwilling to work with him. But I felt I should meet with them. We left it at that.

At the following day's meeting in a White Coffee Pot restaurant near my home, Barbara did most of the talking. It was informative. We also made some decisions. We decided to press the leadership to assure us we would all have the company's final offer in hand at least two days before any vote. We agreed that the Negotiating Committee should be asked at this meeting to give a report on progress to date in the negotiations. And finally Barbara said that to combat defeatist rumors she planned to present to the union president some hard evidence that Blancs was not in good shape in production and shipping and to ask him to inform the membership.

WORKERS AND THE UNION

These were sensible ideas, but to the best of my knowledge only one of them ever was implemented and its purposes achieved; and that occurred well after the October meeting. At the meeting, the Negotiating Committee did not give a report while the members were present. There was no action to ensure we would have the final offer at least two days before the vote on the contract. And no mention was made by the leadership, then or thereafter, of Blancs' production schedules. In fact, the union meeting, not without some responsibility on our parts, was largely distracted from immediate contract issues by the discrimination grievance. It was not a meeting that made me proud of my own behavior or made me feel I could rely on the initiative and leadership of my fellow activists, either.

The day after the union meeting we three met at Barbara's house to evaluate it and discuss what we should be doing in the coming weeks. We disagreed in our evaluation of the discrimination grievance being aired the day before. I alone saw it primarily as a distraction from the immediate contract issues. We agreed that Bert, who spoke at the meeting, had contributed to the physical confrontation with Tank. We discussed putting out a leaflet restating minimum demands for a good contract. But while I also wanted to include something in the leaflet to put pressure on the leadership and on the Negotiating Committee, Barbara wanted to softsoap attacks on leadership. We agreed she should do a first draft soon and pass it around.

In the plant, after the near-confrontation at the meeting, there was discussion and anxiety about violence at union meetings. As we moved into the last two weeks under the current contract, the additional uncertainty concerning what was going on in the negotiations and what kinds of results the negotiations were likely to produce also contributed to roller-coaster feelings in the factory. One day, perhaps because of one rumor, people were optimistic and up; the next day, pessimistic and down.

By the end of the week I was wondering what had happened to the draft of the leaflet Barbara had said she would compose. She called Thursday night to say she had been sick and unable to do the draft. In discussing what should be included in the leaflet in addition

ACTIVISTS AND ORGANIZING

184

to the minimum demands, I suggested at least we should point out that we had heard nothing so far about the negotiations and that we were entitled to regular reports from the Negotiating Committee instead of rumors. Before we hung up, she informed me she had heard from a friend that there was talk among officials about trying to get Bert thrown out of the union, and that one middle-level union official had said he wanted me "looked into," too. That scared the hell out of me, but I continued to think we should put pressure on the leadership in anything we did.

During those important days, because of my organizing activities, I became aware, as if for the first time, of the widespread existence in the factory of fear: Many workers' fears of violence at union meetings. My fear of being found out and fired. Another black woman's fears of becoming the center of controversy and being isolated and fired. That fear, the fear of losing one's job, was most pervasive and deep-seated. Related to it was the fear of being branded as a radical or a troublemaker. These two fears operated in combination to keep the lid on politics in the factory. Fear in the factory was an overwhelming, though not always obvious, political fact.

The RU members, I realized, operated as if they were less afraid of losing their jobs than the rest of us. That fear differential had its good and bad aspects. On the good side, it meant they were more willing to take chances with their jobs, were seemingly more courageous in their attacks on the company and union leadership. On the bad side, though, given the profound fears other workers had of losing their own jobs, it meant that RU members in the eyes of the vast majority of workers often appeared adventurist. They said things and took risks that other workers were unwilling to support. By contrast, those sympathetic to OL seem to have had a longer-term concern for keeping their jobs and therefore appeared to be more afraid of losing them. The greater fear, again, had good and bad sides. On the good side, it brought their conduct more in line with the majority of workers with whom they shared this fear. On the bad side, it made them less likely to take the lead in attacking the company or the union leadership. The trick, I realized, was to walk the fine line between being intimidated and being foolhardy. But to be able to do that one needed first to appreciate how fear dominated politics within the factory.

The appreciation was drilled into my head during the next week, when I primarily tried to do two things: first, to get out another leaflet; and second, to pull together a small meeting of older, middle-aged, and young, and black and white, and male and female rank-and-file workers with the three activists to prepare for the contract vote.

The first task simply meant working with Barbara to get a draft out and then taking it to the printer. After reading her first draft I indicated I didn't think it was strong enough. I felt she was not responding to the strong feelings in the plant on how the leadership was handling the extension issue and on the lack of information regarding the negotiations. She agreed, and said she didn't know how to write a stronger draft. I did.

After revising the draft and gathering reactions to it from several workers, we took it over to a local movement printer's house, where the two of us discussed tactics and strategy as we waited for the printer. While waiting we decided to try to organize a meeting of about ten people for the following week, probably on Wednesday, the next-to-the-last day under the contract. We decided to meet the Monday before to see how we were doing and to prepare a tentative agenda for the Wednesday meeting, which, given the fears of the rank and file, we decided should be held in the privacy of someone's house rather than in a bar.

That Friday, before the final week under the old contract and only hours before the union leadership advised us when the special meeting would be and that we would be working the following Friday under a contract extension, I got to work at 6:00 A.M. as usual, carrying about 500 leaflets into the plant hidden under my jacket. Since my fork had a flat, a godsend for a change, I was able to spend most of the next two hours distributing fliers around the plant, taping them up in public places, leaving small piles of them in locker rooms, and passing them out to workers I knew. At first I was extremely nervous and tried to distribute them as stealthily as possible, but I increasingly relaxed about it. As I distributed them, I worked out a routine for fast

ACTIVISTS AND ORGANIZING

unobtrusive delivery, folding some up and placing them in various pockets so I could get them out quickly when I had to. I tried to avoid obvious "company people," like Marbles, but since it was neither a particularly militant nor radical leaflet I became somewhat more open about its distribution. In the process, I got a lot of good reactions. Some workers asked for more copies, so they could distribute them. In the cafeteria, I saw a fellow worker encouraging others to read the leaflet. Another worker, upon reading one, said, "There's something in here for everybody," which of course was the idea. Marbles, on the other hand, was going around taking the leaflets down off the walls. We each proceeded on our respective rounds, more than half-conscious of what the other was doing.

By and large the reaction to the leaflet among rank-and-file workers was excellent. On the other hand, one committeewoman, I heard, was very distressed by our leaflet, which was fine with me. The chief negotiator for Blancs, I learned several days later, came into the negotiations that day waving our leaflet, "Good Contract or Strike," and demanding to know who was negotiating for the union, anyway—as if to say, "Can't you keep your rank and file under control?"

This is how the leaflet read:

GOOD CONTRACT OR STRIKE
WE NEED:

I. *To Know What's Going On:* That means the rumors, official silence and secrecy must end. The negotiating committee should be giving us reports telling us what's happening. And it means we must know well in advance when the meeting for the contract vote will be.

II. *The Chance To Take Part in Important Decisions Affecting Us:* That means if the negotiating committee wants to recommend extending the present contract beyond Oct. 31, it should call a union meeting so we can decide whether to extend. And it also means that we must have the company's final proposal in writing several days before any vote on the contract so we can discuss the offer among ourselves first.

III. *A Good Contract:* Which means these rock-bottom demands must be met:

1. A *wage increase* of at least 75¢ an hour, which is not out of line. Retail clerks got 60¢. Even the IAM's paper, *The Machinist*, recommends a 15% increase, which comes to 60¢ on a $4.00 base.

2. A *cost-of-living escalator* clause providing full protection from inflation, with quarterly adjustments. The negotiating committee is asking for a quarterly raise of 1¢ an hour for every .2 rise in the Consumer Price Index, which is only a little better than auto and steel workers already get.

3. A *pension increase* to $12 a month per year of service, which means $360 a month before taxes for a 30-year person. Full retirement should be possible after 25 years. The pension should have a cost-of-living escalator. And Blue Cross/Blue Shield must be fully paid for by the company.

4. Better *Blue Cross/Blue Shield benefits*, with emergency room coverage, a dental and eye-care plan and a prescription plan.

5. Five *leave days* for sick or personal leave. Also Sickness and Accident Insurance increased to $100 a week, to begin after 3 days out.

6. *More vacation* time. Two weeks after 1 year; three weeks after 5 years; and an additional week for every additional 5 years.

7. An *end to discrimination* and favoritism in promotion and training, with training programs to give those in deadend jobs, blacks, and women a fair chance to advance.

8. An *18-month contract*, ending in April 1976, so we can get away from the negotiations ending in winter before the holidays.

ALL OF THESE DEMANDS HAVE BEEN WON BY OTHER UNION WORKERS IN BALTIMORE. WE'VE GOT TO STICK TOGETHER TO FIGHT FOR ALL OF THEM — BLACK AND WHITE, OLD AND YOUNG, MEN AND WOMEN —ALL TOGETHER, AND THEN WE'LL ALL BENEFIT. AND IF WE DON'T GET A GOOD CONTRACT, THEN WE'VE GOT TO STICK TOGETHER WHEN WE GO OUT.

COMMITTEE FOR A GOOD CONTRACT
(Union labor donated)

With the leaflet out and some positive reactions in, I decided to spend what time I could find during the rest of the day trying to commit the group of rank-and-file workers Barbara and I had agreed upon for the Wednesday meeting. I first approached a white man who was very dissatisfied with his work. In his response, without quite saying straight out that he was afraid to meet because of job insecurity, he all but said it. He said he didn't want to meet because, being near retirement, he had "too much to lose." And then he said, anyway, "It don't do no good." Felt fear and a sense of futility, a lethal combination in opposition to activating workers to work together in their own interests. Slightly taken aback, I asked him to think some more about his decision, to think about whether he was willing to concede to himself that he was not free to meet with fellow workers outside the plant to discuss plant problems. I said I'd get back to him early the next week. Later that day I caught up with my friend with the good sense of organizing and asked him. His response was more elusive, but the message essentially was the same. He said, "They'd call us radicals" and "Now isn't the time to meet." All the while he denied he was afraid to meet. But, then, how could he admit to himself his fear of meeting to discuss such legitimate issues in the free America he so militantly advised others on his bumper to love or leave? Finally, before the day was over, a young black worker who really moved around the plant did commit himself to come.

That Saturday I asked a progressive woman I respected to join us. She said she would if she could get a babysitter for her child, since her husband was likely to be on a different shift than she next week. I asked a young white man, who was a Viet vet and had a certain flair for verbally shooting from the hip at the leadership. He assented. And finally I asked two middle-aged black men in my department, one of whom said yes and the other of whom did not say no. So far, so good, I thought. The only two seeming refusals had come from the two middle-aged white men.

The following Monday I checked back with people to set a time and to try further to firm them up. The young white woman seemed to want to come, but felt she was going to have sitter problems. So it looked like she was out. The young white man was firm. The young black man was firm. The two middle-aged black men were solid. But the white man near retirement was definite about not coming, notwithstanding approaches by me and by Barbara. The other middle-aged white man, when I caught up with him at the end of the day, remained evasive, saying he would let me know definitely on Wednesday. He tried to make excuses about being busy, and about not having a ride. I said I'd give him a ride. He was impressed when I told him we might have a member of the Negotiating Committee there. But not so impressed as to commit himself.

When I talked to Barbara after work that day, we filled each other in on what we'd heard about the day's negotiations. She had asked a middle-aged black woman we both respected to come to the Wednesday meeting. The woman had agreed to do so. We talked about an agenda for the meeting, and about how we should prepare for the Sunday union meeting. For instance, we weren't even sure what kind of a quorum and/or vote was required for a strike vote. Barbara said she would check the union bylaws and constitution. We talked about the importance on Sunday of getting the minority on the Negotiating Committee to air their opinions to the membership. It was a good discussion, but I felt a growing apprehension that my activist friend was not making a maximum effort to organize for either the Wednesday or the Sunday meeting.

The next day, Tuesday, anger was growing in the plant at the reports of the company's first wage offer. Mild-mannered, generally intimidated workers I knew were talking strike if this was to be the company's final offer. The company, I assumed, was too smart for that. It occurred to me that it had consciously made such a low offer to begin with in order to make any subsequent better offers appear good by comparison. That first offer was reported to be so low that Marbles disbelieved the report. Anyway, he said, based on his experience, such an early offer (three days before the contract was to run out!) didn't matter much. We wouldn't really know what was going on, he said, until Wednesday evening or Thursday noon. He agreed the company's main strategy was to delay until late so we'd be confused, and agreed that twice the company's alleged initial offer of 13 cents an hour "wasn't nothin'."

Wednesday came and with it my increasing realization that Barbara hadn't done much for the afternoon's meeting. She had contacted only one person to come, and had decided not to try to contact any people she knew in our local from Blancs' other plants. During the day the middle-aged black woman she had contacted said regretfully she might not be able to make it, because she might have to go to the hospital. One of the middle-aged black men in my department, having known about the meeting for more than four days, late in the day informed me that he had to give someone a lift home and consequently either might be late or might not be able to make the meeting. The other middle-aged white man declined to come. Sarah was out sick.

After work, apprehensive that we wouldn't even have a meeting,

I drove over to one of the worker's apartments with the other black man from my department. I was feeling impatient, frustrated, and angry. Once we got there, we had to wait another 20 minutes before Barbara arrived. That only increased my depression. As a result I more or less suffered through the meeting of the four of us, a meeting that added little to our preparedness or our strength. We agreed that "several" of us, no doubt Barbara and I, would try to get a summary of the final company offer out on the morning of November 1 in order to ensure that the membership would get the information before the union meeting, as well as to show up the union leadership, which had not assured us it would get the offer to the plant before Saturday. When at 6:15, during the meeting, a member of the Negotiating Committee called to ask who was there and said, when he heard, that he'd come by in about fifteen minutes, I petulantly decided I wasn't willing to wait any longer. Two of us left before he arrived.

Intellectually I knew that political organizers could not afford to be immature, but my reaction to the events was nonetheless emotionally and politically immature. It was as if I at times believed I could turn around a political situation that had been deteriorating for decades. Patience, realism, and consistency, I came to realize, are as important in organizing as analysis and surface courage and militancy.

I talked, somewhat guardedly, with my fellow worker about some of these problems as I drove him home, and by the next day felt somewhat better. When I was bringing in my first hopper on that last day of the old contract, the black woman who hadn't been able to make it to the meeting waved me down and apologized for missing it. She had indeed had to go to the hospital with her husband. She said we needed more meetings among workers. And recognizing the problems of getting workers together, she said it would be best to walk out from work together with them so that they couldn't scatter, and then to meet some place nearby. She said, "We are 90 percent of the company as soon as we realize it." Talking to her made me feel better and more hopeful.

Later that day I had a good talk with Barbara. I told her I was let down and angry because she had done so little and had come so late. She said she had waited to pick up the black activist, who hadn't shown, and also had waited for the woman who had had to go to the hospital. I suggested she organize her own schedule better next time.

We agreed to meet that night, after midnight, to get together a summary of the company proposals with some questions and criticisms of them and some suggestions about the upcoming union meeting. We planned to do it between 2:00 and 5:30 A.M. The printer had agreed to get up to help us out. I said I'd call her that night. We also talked about workers' fears—how seemingly they were afraid even to admit they were afraid; that, for example, they avoided saying outright that they wouldn't come to the meeting and then at the last minute either found an excuse or just didn't show.

As if to confirm the pressure workers are under, the young woman who had been unable to come because she hadn't found a sitter said some of the more pacified older women in her department had been watching her. One, having seen us talking together, had said something to her about my being an "agitator." That label in a fear-filled environment amounted to the kiss of death.

That night Barbara and I spoke to each other several times on the phone. When she learned the details of the smart company offer she said she didn't really want to try to put a leaflet out before morning. I, of course, was not eager to stay up all night either, and therefore didn't push strongly to do it. The union leadership now was said to be trying to get the offer out to the membership by noon Friday. We both knew that whether it did or not, the offer itself was not the sort to make a strike likely. So we let a chance for political education slip by. What that meant, I see in retrospect, was that the next day it was primarily union officials and those others committed to supporting the offer who communicated it to the rank and file. Nothing offset the momentum built up to accept the offer.

In the plant that next day the general reaction to the offer was mostly favorable, though much of it was expressed in narrowly self-interested terms. No one I spoke to thought the basic wage raise was even decent, but for those who were in high wage grades the skill increment substantially sweetened the pot. For a grade 4 worker, for example, it meant fourteen cents an hour more than the basic raise. Most employees, of course, were grades 8, 9, and 10. So when one high-grade worker in my department was crowing about his raise, he irritated most of the rest of us, and we told him so.

All day the union officials, along with company executives, were selling the contract. Various reservations about certain of its provisions were submerged in the way the entire issue was presented to us—take it or leave it. And the union leadership's defeatist line was politically effective. Most employees at least felt the offer was not so bad that they couldn't "live with it." That was the attitude and mass momentum they carried into the contract meeting on Sunday. At that meeting Barbara said not a word. The company offer, as indicated in chapter 7, was accepted.

During the period before November 1, we had tried to organize workers to put pressure on the Negotiating Committee and the union leadership to get us a better contract, to involve the rank and file more in the process, and, alternatively, to seriously prepare for a strike. We had not done a very effective job. But throughout we were nearly the only ones who consistently tried. Not a single information sheet came out from the leadership during that time. No one in the plant but us produced and distributed leaflets. No one, to the best of my knowledge, tried to get workers together outside to discuss these matters and to organize for the union meetings.

With our own deficiencies, and given all we were up against, we simply couldn't turn the situation around. What we were up against, some of which has been indicated, was nothing less than a barely visible, integrated liberal dictatorship. What that meant concretely became still clearer in the context of the upcoming union elections.

WORKERS AND THE UNION

X

Union Elections:
The Democratic Formalities

IF the union left too much to be desired concerning both the manner in which it represented its members externally to the company and the manner in which it communicated the contract negotiations to its members, how well did it function regarding what primarily were internal matters?

The second most important event of the year in the union, the nomination and election of the local's middle-level officers, can be taken as illustrative. This election process in our liberal democratic society is the declared source of union legitimacy, and the main means within the system to influence union policy and affect its leadership. As such, and particularly given the high level of dissatisfaction among members with the union, one might expect that the election process would involve most of the union's members. It did not. To most members the nomination and election process was largely a nonevent. Like an increasingly high number of their fellow citizens, in federal, state and local elections, they chose not to be involved.*

By contrast, I was involved in the process in three ways, none typical of the general membership. In ascending order, reflecting the intensity of involvement in the process, I voted; I was interested to

---

* In national elections the percentage of eligible voters that vote still is substantially higher than in the union elections, but winning candidates nonetheless are elected by only a minority of the eligible electorate. In 1976, for example, 26 percent elected Jimmy Carter President.

more than a passing degree in the nomination and election of certain candidates, for whom I did a limited amount of informal campaigning; and I made an effort to run for the post of committeeman of my shop. The overwhelming majority of union members, who doubtless had already learned what it took direct involvement to teach me, did none of these.

My decision to run for committeeman was made in late October, after seeing how the top union leadership and my own representatives operated during the contract negotiations. In making the decision, I recognized that if successful, I would be obligated to serve a full year's term, which I committed myself to do. That meant remaining in the factory beyond my year's sabbatical leave from the university.

Whether the decision to seek union office was a correct one, taken primarily in the real interests of co-workers rather than in service to an aggrandized vision of what I might be able to contribute, I am not sure. At the time I felt it was the right thing to do. In any event, correct or incorrect, the decision involved me more deeply in a process that may shed further light on how the union operated and the effect of that method of operation on workers.

Although my final decision to run for union office was not made until after the present leadership had increasingly exposed itself, specific events going back as far as early September concretely contributed to the decision. The day after my first cost-of-living speech at the September 8 union meeting, for example, co-workers' response to the speech first put the idea of running in my head. That day, Fred, a middle-aged white electrician in the Service Department, complimented me on the speech and said, "It's important you get involved in the union." A middle-aged black man I barely knew, from another department (who I later learned was the numbers runner in the plant), said, "That was a good speech. I want you to run for something." And a young black man in shipping said, "In five months or so you could be a shop steward." A young black woman with whom I had not previously spoken at any length and who herself had not even attended the meeting came up and said she heard I "spoke real nice at the meeting yesterday. Everyone is talking about it." That day, I remember, I first began to think about becoming a committeeman or shop steward.

As I tried to put in perspective the spontaneous expression of appreciation and need communicated to me by fellow workers, I took tentative steps that Monday to find out what I could about union posts. First, I learned from members of the Service Department that our current steward, Tommie Saunders, was slated to "move up" to committeeman when Marbles retired in January 1975. Tommie, I was told, like all shop stewards in the plant, had been appointed by his committeeman, not elected by the rank and file. Although Tommie almost universally was regarded as a first-rate electrician, there were strong early indications that he was neither respected as a union representative nor popular with the men in the shop. A number of employees in the department, for example, were angry that he had not even attended the union meeting the day before, as Tommie chose instead to work Sunday to earn double-time. Tommie, subsequent events confirmed, indeed, was seen by the vast majority of workers in the shop as a self-serving "company man." Yet there he was, representing us to the company as our shop steward and, unless opposed and defeated in the December election, likely to move up to the still more important post of committeeman. He was a man I increasingly came to feel should be opposed.

In trying to learn how to go about developing an opposition candidate to Tommie, I spoke with my main source on union rules, the man who had appointed Tommie, Marbles. He confirmed my understanding that shop stewards are appointed and comitteemen elected by their departments and advised me of an eligibility requirement for all offices. Employees, he said, have to be members of the union for a year before they are eligible to hold office, "so outsiders can't come in and take over the union."

Talking several days later with Fred, the knowledgeable, veteran rank-and-filer in the department, I tried to find out more about Tommie Saunders, about possible alternative candidates, and about eligibility requirements. During the course of our brief discussion I appealed to Fred to run himself against Tommie. He firmly declined, saying he wanted no part of union office and indicating that Tommie was unlikely to be opposed by anyone in the election for committeeman. No one else, it appeared, wanted the office; and in any event, Fred doubted whether anyone else in the department could satisfy a second eligibility requirement for office. I then learned a member also has to have attended at least five regular union meetings during the year preceding nominations to be eligible for office.

As we continued to talk about the posts of committeeman and steward, Fred urged that we work to get better people in office. "Tommie," he said, "could be on his way out, and he knows it. We have to organize. Then many of the colored employees will back us up." If he was correct, as subsequent events repeatedly indicated, then, even though many members opposed Tommie's election and few affirmatively supported it, as things stood Tommie would be elected by default. Under those conditions, I increasingly came to see my own candidacy as a solution to our shop's problem of inadequate leadership. For better and for worse, I became the opposition candidate I had been looking for, which meant that with regard to the elections I often was in the uncomfortable position of "organizing" for my own candidacy.

When I next discussed the matter with Marbles, about a week later, I hinted at my interest in the position of committeeman. Marbles, foxy as ever, did not take the bait. He simply confirmed the time and meeting requirements, and added that shop stewards nominated by elected committeemen must be approved by the local's Executive Committee, of which he was a member. Although he suggested that the eligibility requirements might be waived by the committee in "special cases," he ended the conversation asserting that Tommie Saunders would be the department's next committeeman.

As September passed, I talked to other workers about the posts of committeeman and steward. No one else, in fact, was willing to run for comitteeman or to serve as steward. And it was unclear whether anyone else in fact was eligible, based upon the five-meeting requirement, which in theory sounds quite reasonable but in practice is not.

That requirement effectively contributed to maintaining in office the current leadership, which, if nothing else, generally maintained its attendance record. For others to satisfy the requirement demanded a prior level of commitment to attending meetings that with few exceptions was rarely found among the rank and file. The exceptions were of two sorts: (1) the small number of personally ambitious men and women who wanted to "make it" in the union; and (2) the small group of reformers willing to persist through all the union claptrap in an effort to make the union at least somewhat better for its members. The vast majority of workers, whether they had worked in the plant for five or twenty-five years, were ineligible for union office.

It was when I again spoke to Marbles about the matter, that he expressed the leadership's typical managerial attitudes toward plant politics. It was then he said he didn't like dissenters and dissatisfied people and would "send them all off in boats," told me that he saw the people with whom I talked most in the plant, and then proceeded to name off almost every activist and reformer in the plant with whom I had ever had any association. He said he wanted the union newspaper to start up again and wanted Joanne Tower, the reformer who previously had edited it, to edit it again, but only under total Executive Committee supervision and censorship, which Joanne refused to accept. Marbles wanted the union paper to be a house organ for the leadership, just as he wanted all "comers" in the union to stand with the leadership clique.

When I said I thought that Joanne and a black woman reformer would make good shop stewards but that their committeewoman refused to appoint them to existing vacancies in their department, Marbles coolly parried that they were eligible to run this year for committeewoman against the incumbent, as both had satisfied the time and meeting requirements. The Executive Committee, he added, was unlikely to waive those requirements in my case, despite the fact that the election in my department otherwise would be uncontested.

As I continued to probe in the following weeks to find out how the rank and file felt about elections and the union leadership, I learned there were two polar opinions among union members. One, which appeared predominant among middle-aged whites and focused on the top leadership, was not so much supportive of the present

UNION ELECTIONS

leadership as it was specifically fearful that if Tank were not reelected president the following year a black, like the current vice president, might be elected instead. The other, which tended to be held by younger workers, particularly blacks, was willing and even eager to turn the whole lot of leaders out. Reflecting a situation similar to that in the Service Department, a young black in shipping said his committeeman "ain't worth shit, but no one else wants the job, so he's elected without opposition."

In part because this was such a widespread problem, I decided to press my own candidacy in the Service Department against Tommie Saunders, notwithstanding the likelihood of being ruled ineligible. In late October a fellow worker in the department advised me to try to deal with the eligibility problem by presenting a petition to the Executive Committee signed by members of the department who supported my request for a waiver of the eligibility requirements.

My main problem regarding eligibility was that by the time of nominations, the second Sunday in November, I would have been in the union for only three months instead of the required year. In addition, although I had attended every regular and special union meeting since becoming a union member, by the date of nominations I still would be one meeting short of the required five regular meetings. To compound the eligibility problem, the outside possibility of a strike vote at the coming November 3 meeting made it imperative, if I was to resort to a petition, that the petition be drafted and signed before that meeting. Otherwise, if the membership did vote to strike it might thereafter be very difficult logistically to collect signatures.

Consequently, on the next-to-the-last day of the current contract, I asked Fred (with whom I was on good personal terms) if he would nominate me for committeeman. He was delighted at the idea and also agreed without hesitation to pass around the petition. With his advice I drafted the petition, which said: "We, the undersigned members of the Service Department (South Baltimore Plant), call upon the Executive Committee of our Local #1784 to waive the time and meeting requirements for eligibility for nomination to the post of shop commiteeman for the Service Department South Baltimore Plant for Ric Pfeffer, Badge #52365, so he can compete in the December election."

WORKERS AND THE UNION

A short time after the petition was ready, however, Fred returned to say that Marbles had told him the Executive Committee couldn't waive both requirements, only one. In the telling, Marbles apparently also had suggested that Fred himself run for the office, instead, but Fred remained unwilling to run. As we talked, Fred seemed to be backing away slightly from the idea of passing the petition around. We discussed it some more, and he agreed to try it out. We both felt the Executive Committee probably could manage to do whatever it really wanted to. As a threshold matter, however, we had to get the eligibility rules straight.

To do so, I sought out Marbles, who though biased, remained the most accessible and knowledgeable union official I knew. Again, I understood Marbles to say the Executive Committee could waive the requirements, but that it probably wouldn't. I explained to him that by the election date in December I would have five regular meetings in, though I'd only have four by the November nominations. What I really needed, I said, was a waiver of the time requirement. Marbles said he didn't remember waivers of time requirements in the past. The waivers he knew of involved the meeting requirement: for example, in a shop where no employee had put in the necessary number of meetings, the Executive Commitee in its discretion had waived that requirement. In the usual case, I realized, waivers would be needed only for the meeting requirement, which so many veteran workers failed to satisfy.

About my candidacy Marbles at best remained noncommittal. He said he would nominate Tommie Saunders. To my assertion that it would be good for the union to have a contested election, like the two-party system, he vaguely responded, "Well, maybe someone else will run." And then, politic as ever, he added, "You might be appointed steward." He said he'd mention it to Tommie to consider me.

Meanwhile, Fred had been taking the petition around and was beginning to have more serious second thoughts. Organizing efforts in the plant frequently are frustrating, but Fred had had more than the usual problems. He had taken the petition first to his fellow skilled workers, with most of whom I had had the least personal contact. The two troubleshooters among the electricians, very conservative whites, had refused to sign and branded me a "radical." A third electrician wouldn't sign, and the two white millwrights, whom I knew better, also declined. In addition, Tommie, also an electrician, appeared to be highly offended at what his fellow electrician was doing. He asked Fred why he was campaigning for me: "What did he promise you?"

On the brighter side, in one morning Fred had signed up a very conservative, middle-aged, white plumber, the two middle-aged white carpenters, and about 12 other members of the 52-person department. About half who signed up were white, though more than half the department was black. Among blacks, with whom I worked more closely, I had stronger support, I knew. By midday, however, Fred had lost his sense of humor and was determined to drop the matter. He had taken flak, largely from members of his own group of electricians, who were among the most privileged members of our entire department.

Fred gave several reasons why he wanted to stop taking the petition around. Marbles again had assured him there was no chance at all that the Executive Committee would waive the requirements. Tommie, he also said, would get him somehow if he continued to actively support me. And anyway, he added, I should have waited a year, since, as I later confirmed, several of the workers who initially refused to sign the petition simply felt I "hadn't put in the time," which was undeniable.

I understood Fred's position. He had much more to lose than I, and I said so. But I did want him to recognize that in part he was afraid to press on. The most he would concede was that, after all, he didn't know me that well, and that he wasn't going to "stick my neck out for someone who has only been here for a few months and might leave anytime."

As we talked, Fred's fear of appearing to be too closely associated with someone branded as "radical" came out. In his mind Jimmie Hoffa and the Teamsters are "Communists"—a label that for Fred seemed to cover a multitude of evils—so I could imagine his anxieties about continuing to pass the petition for me around. I thanked him for his help. During the rest of the day I noticed him making subtle overtures to Tommie, as if to make up.

WORKERS AND THE UNION

By the end of the day I was trying to find someone else to take the petition around for signatures. In a talk with Jerry, a black friend in the department, I asked for his advice. He said that I already had fifteen names from the department on the petition, which showed some strength. He said personally he'd also be glad to sign it. But I had hoped Jerry would volunteer to pass it around. Since he hadn't, I indicated I didn't feel I could take it around myself and asked if he would be willing to do so for me, saying I wouldn't be at all offended if he said no. Jerry said OK, without enthusiasm, and we talked about who else might be likely to sign up. I was aiming for 30 signatures, about 60 percent of the department, and hoped Jerry could get about 10 more signatures.

In seeking support, I knew I had several problems. First, my position as a fighter for the rank and file and against the leadership had made me some enemies, as well as friends, among the rank and file. Second, the fact that I was on a one-year sabbatical leave from the university made me impatient to move early to try to get a union post. My haste, I knew, meant some workers who otherwise respected me would feel I hadn't "put in the time" and they would not support my nomination. But I simply was not willing to stay in the factory as a trashman after the summer of 1975 unless I had something else going for me at work. Therefore I was unwilling to wait patiently to run until the following year's (1976) union elections.

On the other hand, I also had several advantages. I was well known within my department, on good terms with the vast majority of its members, and had strong support from the men I knew best, the black workers and the carpenters. Tommie, by contrast, had practically no support within the department, except among the small group of electricians. If I were allowed to run, it seemed very probable I could win. Marbles put it more emphatically. Tommie, he said, had run for committeeman before against him and had received very few votes. I would, "swamp Tommie in a contest," Marbles said.

So, first and foremost, my problem was one of eligibility. This in turn meant that to the extent the union leadership had any discretion regarding the issue I was dependent upon their good will and/or their deference to my rank-and-file support within the department. Since I clearly could not count on the former, I was determined to make a show of the latter. In the final analysis, however, the rank and file have no effective means in such cases to impose their opinions on the Executive Committee.

With the approval of the new contract on November 3, attention focused briefly on the upcoming nominations and elections. On November 4 Marbles caught me at work to inform me that the Executive Committee had no authority to waive the time requirement because it was part of the international union's constitution and therefore could not be waived by the local. He conceded that he might not have gotten it quite right before. The meetings requirement, he added, had been waived previously for stewards but not for elected officials.

I told Marbles I could not understand why there should be stricter standards for elected than for appointed positions. To check the rules myself, I asked to see Marbles' copy of the most recent bylaws, which had been amended more than six months earlier but still were unavailable to the membership in amended form. At first Marbles denied he had a copy, which I knew to be untrue. Then he said he didn't have time to get it. Then he said it was his personal working copy and not for others' use. Annoyed, I said, "Look, you're my committeeman, and I want to see my local's bylaws." He hemmed and hawed, and produced a stream of thin excuses. The amended bylaws, he said, would be available at the next union meeting. I had heard that before.

In that vacuum of information all I had going for me, it seemed, was the petition. Jerry, however, had been cautious in moving it. In several days he had gotten only another four signatures. Fred had not even been signed up. Others likely to support my candidacy had not yet been approached. Disappointed, I uneasily decided to try moving the petition myself. In the two hours left before quitting time eight more people signed up. One elderly black man refused to sign because he was afraid: "I'd rather not sign that. The Service Department don't want me here anyway. They hit at me from so many ways now."

At the end of the day I checked the constitution of the international, which, sure enough, required one year in the local lodge.

The local's bylaws did indeed require five meetings, I learned. So it seemed that to run I would have to get a waiver of the meeting requirement from the local's Executive Committee and a waiver of the time requirement from the international headquarters. Formally, I was stymied. Stubbornly, I continued moving the support petition nevertheless. Several people who previously had hesitated to sign signed up as the list grew and I talked with them. One signed up on the unsolicited assurances of his brother-in-law in another department with whom I often ate lunch. By the end of the week I had 60 percent of the department signed up—a much higher percentage than actually voted in any of the local's elections.

As the week wore on, however, I became concerned about who might nominate me at the Sunday meeting. I wanted to ask someone to do it, but I wasn't sure that anyone from the department would even attend the meeting. I hesitated to ask people to give up a Sunday morning for my candidacy. In checking around, it seemed most of the department expectably was not going, though several of the blacks who supported my candidacy said they would spread the word.

While I was thinking about Sunday's meeting, Fred suggested that I try talking to Tommie in an effort to convince him to make me his shop steward in return for my withdrawal from the committeeman race. I was quite agreeable to that, given the improbability I would be declared eligible for the nomination. But of course Tommie knew that too, so I didn't have much bargaining power to get the appointment. Fred had spoken to Tommie about such a compromise and recommended me to Tommie as the best man for the post of steward. In response, Tommie apparently had been very evasive, saying he wanted to check to see what the other guys wanted. Fred still thought I should speak to Tommie personally.

That day I waited to speak to Tommie in his workroom after hours. When I put the offer to him, he again refused to commit himself. Tommie said I was the only person who wanted the job so far, but he pretended to want to see how the other guys felt. On its face, that was fair enough, so I showed him the petition that indicated that I had the affirmative support of 60 percent of our fellow workers. Tommie still wouldn't commit himself. Knowing I would be declared ineligible, he was immovable, and said instead that I should run for committeeman if I wanted to. Then with more than a trace of bitterness in his voice Tommie added that he had "been here for 25 years"; that he hadn't "just come." I tried to avoid a confrontation, saying I thought we could complement each other well: "You have experience and technical knowledge and I argue well for the guys." Tommie again declined to join the issue, saying there was "no glory in being a steward or committeeman, just work and very little money. There are more important things in my life. I don't even know if I will get nominated myself on Sunday." And in any event, "I will not campaign for the job," he concluded.

That was disingenuous. He must have known Marbles had been planning for months to nominate him. There would be no need to campaign for the job if, as seemed almost certain, there was no opposition. Moreover, although Tommie was evasive with me, several workers advised me that Tommie already had offered the job of steward to others in the department, to Fred for one; and for another, to one of the less well respected whites in the department. So with the meeting for nominations only two days away my candidacy was in bad shape. I had not yet found someone to nominate me. If nominated, I would almost certainly be declared ineligible. And the man most likely to be our next committeeman was quite unlikely to agree to appoint me as his steward.

Before leaving work that Friday, I decided to try one other possible course. I called the federal Department of Labor and spoke to a compliance officer about the legality of eligibility requirements. The issue, he said, was whether they are "reasonable." Whether they are considered reasonable in turn depends upon their practical effect on the eligibility of members. So far so good. But, then, he also said that to be entitled to appeal the union eligibility regulations to the Department, I first had to be nominated and then had to make all the allowable appeals within the union before I could bring a complaint to the Department of Labor. Such a regulation, requiring what is known as the "exhaustion of local remedies," meant that I had to go through what promised to be a futile bureaucratic procedure within the union before I was entitled to go through a similar procedure within the federal government.

As in my case, the requirement to exhaust local remedies, whatever its rationalizations, in practice drastically reduces the number of complaints brought by workers to the federal government. Unless, say, one plans in advance to bring the complaint as a test case, a worker has little or no reason to go through internal union procedures that are so unlikely to bear fruit. Thus the whole system contributes to the maintenance of the status quo, which is precisely what was maintained at the following Sunday's union meeting.

The nominations meeting turned out to be a farce. It was attended by perhaps 75 employees, most of whom were union officials and friends whom they had brought along to nominate them. Tommie Saunders, away at some training course to further upgrade his already considerable electrical skills, did not even bother to attend. From my department, there were in fact only three in attendance: Marbles, me, and a black lead-man who had signed my petition but could not be depended upon for anything. I nonetheless asked him while the meeting was in progress if he would nominate me. He assented, but when the nominations were called somehow managed to be in back, chatting, and said nothing. As a consequence, I ambivalently nominated myself, a practice I had seen several other members do just before me.

In most departments there had been only a single nomination, in several by the incumbent for himself. One or two departments did not even put forth a nomination. In our department Marbles nominated the absent Tommie, and I nominated myself. Out of eight departments, in only two others, where members of the young, reform faction within the union had been nominated against incumbents, was the election to be contested. Reformers also were nominated for the at-large positions of trustee and "conductor" (sergeant at arms), who inexplicably sits on the Executive Committee of the union.

Thus nominations were made at a meeting attended by approximately 5 percent of the local's membership. There it was determined that for most of the offices to be filled there would be no contest. The elections the following month, I thought then, might well involve more extensive rank-and-file participation, but the only people who would be on the ballot would be those previously nominated at a meeting that tangibly reflected the extreme noninvolvement of workers in their own union. For example, unless I unexpectedly was declared eligible, Tommie would be nominated and elected by the casting of one nominating vote, Marbles'.

As I waited for the notice of ineligibility, which allegedly was supposed to be given within five days after the nominations, I realized that, like other union members, I knew nothing about how to appeal the expectable declaration of my ineligibility. I also realized that the appeals process would be time consuming and was unlikely in the extreme to produce anything positive. I was not likely to get much help from my shop steward, Tommie, or from my committeeman, Marbles. Before I had heard anything formally from the Executive Committee, the word was out informally through one of the other committeemen that the union leadership had decided not to allow me to run. When I approached Tank the following Tuesday, still hoping that some arrangement might be made, his response squelched whatever hope remained. I indicated to him I expected that I might be ruled ineligible and that I intended to appeal that ruling. He reaffirmed that the local lodge could not waive the one-year requirement of the Grand Lodge, and that I therefore would have to appeal to the Grand Lodge in Washington, D.C., for such a waiver. Half-bluffing, I indicated that if my appeal were denied, I would challenge the legality of the eligibility rules themselves. Tank expectably was monumentally unconcerned at the prospect. Undoubtedly aware of the investment of time and energy required for such a challenge, and of the improbability of its success, he offhandedly replied, "It's your privilege."

Still, I thought I would follow through on the appeal and was considering how to frame it. The five-meeting requirement at least was quite vulnerable to attack, since in practice it excluded the vast majority of union members from eligibility for office. Combined with the fact that the union hall was located so far from where we worked and from where most members lived, it effectively restricted the significance of members' votes for their officers.

While I thought about these matters, a number of other related, contradictory things were happening on the floor. On the one hand, several workers in other departments asked me with concern how my candidacy was going. A group of older, white rank-and-file members renewed their talk of running me for union president at a subsequent election. Several other workers, on the other hand, independently hassled me about my politics. A white security guard at the front gate accused me of being a "big agitator," saying I'd only been at the plant for a short time. And a hip-looking, young white worker said he'd heard from an older white that I was a Communist and that I would be leaving now that the workers had approved the new contract and rejected the possibility of a strike. He was suspicious of me also, he added, because I was "too intelligent to be a trashman." I agreed, and said I was about to request a promotion, but wanted first to get my job performance review so I would have a record on which to base my request.

By Monday of the following week I still had not been formally advised of my ineligibility. It seemed to me such notification was a necessary basis upon which to ground an appeal. I began to wonder whether the leadership was simply inefficient or was trying to delay me. By Wednesday I still had not heard. Increasingly I felt worn down and considered simply accepting the expected decision without challenging it. But that morning something happened to momentarily galvanize me again. A middle-aged black woman whom I very much respected said she had a compliment for me. She said a not particularly progressive woman in her department had said to her yesterday that "we got no one to run against Tank for president except the new guy on trash." She added that she herself felt I seemed to "have it together, to know when to go and when to stop." I deeply appreciated being appreciated and said so. I indicated, however, that the election for president was two years away and that I had to learn much more about the union by being a steward or committeeman. She agreed and said, "Hang in there with the union, 'cause we need you." I decided to keep trying.

Shortly thereafter I found Tank in the cafeteria and asked about my eligibility and the notice. He said I'd hear by letter later in the week, and that I would be ruled ineligible under both the time and meeting requirements. As each day passed, it became increasingly

UNION ELECTIONS

unlikely that even a successful appeal would enable me to be voted upon in the December 8 elections. Consequently, the delay in notification, whatever its causes, was eroding my commitment to challenge the union rules.

By Tuesday, November 26, I still had not received any notification. When the carpenters in my department that morning asked me what was going on about the committeeman post, I said I didn't know, but that I wasn't optimistic. I said I was pretty sure Tommie would be the next committeeman. One of them responded that he had talked to Tommie, again supporting my being made his steward. The following day I told Tank I still hadn't received any notification. He said he'd get me a copy of the letter, which had been sent certified mail. He had a copy hand delivered to me at noon, and when I returned home in the evening I found the certified letter there.

Several days later at work I learned that one of the women reformers who had been nominated for office also had received a letter declaring her ineligible for having failed to satisfy the meeting requirement. I asked if she planned to fight the ruling, hoping to be able to cooperate with her in an appeal. If we were going to challenge the ineligibility rulings, I knew, we had to act immediately to appeal within the union to lay the basis for a subsequent outside appeal to the Department of Labor. Among people with whom I regularly spoke, however, there was no strong support for an appeal. By Thursday, December 5, I decided simply to accept the decision. I was learning realism and resignation.

People I spoke to understandably were more concerned with the two upcoming contests between reformers and conservative incumbent committeepersons. It seemed the crucial factor in both contests would be how many supporters of the reformers would actually come to the meeting to vote. Marbles predicted the incumbents would win both elections, though he acknowledged that at least in the case of the contest between Joanne and the incumbent in the Inspections Department Joanne would probably win if the election were held in the plant with all the workers present. However, he predicted that "her people ain't coming to the meeting." The union leadership clique, by contrast, like other political machines, excelled at getting itself voted into office.

WORKERS AND THE UNION

As anticipated, the elections that Sunday were poorly attended. One reformer, running for committeeman from a shop of approximately 300 workers, lost by 20 to 7. The union-wide election for sergeant-at-arms was decided by a vote of only 99 to 45, with the son of the local's recording secretary—a young toady of few other noticeable qualifications—also beating the reform candidate. Joanne lost 23 to 11, in an election she subsequently unsuccessfully challenged.

The results confirmed two conclusions suggested earlier. First, it is very difficult to beat the established leadership at the polls. Second, the elections are of little interest to the overwhelming majority of union members. Only 5 percent of the membership turned out to participate in the nominations and barely more than 10 percent voted. A big vote-getter received the perfunctory support of 7–8 percent of the membership. So much for electoral legitimacy.

With the elections over, the only post left to be filled was shop steward. Still, no one else besides myself seemed eager or even willing to serve. Since Tommie, our committeeman-elect, was not to be installed in his new office until January, he had said he would not pick his steward until then. I could hardly be optimistic about my own prospects. As Marbles conceded, Tommie was even more of a company man than Marbles himself. He was the sort of man, said the black lead-worker in our department (who ironically was appointed by Tommie as his shop steward after I had been laid off), who would "snitch on his own mother." He was skilled and sympathetic enough to the company to have been made a foreman long ago. Word had it, though, that the company had passed him over several times for outside people because he "couldn't handle men well." Such was our new committeeman. And, although I wanted to be shop steward, I had no particular desire to work under Tommie.

When I asked Marbles for advice, he indicated he had told Tommie that he should "above all appoint someone you can work with." Translated, I felt sure that meant, appoint someone who doesn't have any independent base of support with the workers and who isn't likely to act independently. In short, appoint someone like Marbles' own stewards—Tommie and the steward in the Research and Development Lab—people who are "dependable" and pliable. Marbles said he thought Tommie was "afraid of me." He suggested I try to reassure him that I would "cooperate." If Tommie did actually appoint me, Marbles added to my surprise, his impression was that the Executive Committee would not oppose my being made steward. Anyway, Marbles concluded, even if Tommie doesn't appoint you, "you'll be committeeman next year. The men already respect you. They shout hello across the road." That made me feel good, but it didn't get me any closer to the stewardship. I would just have to wait until Tommie was ready to move.

By mid-January, despite denials to the contrary, it appeared he was making his move. One day without notice a likeable but unrespected middle-aged white worker in our department, who frequently had been the butt of friendly jokes, appeared in the cafeteria wearing the shop steward's badge. Workers were astounded at the apparent choice. One of the carpenters told Tommie he was a "fucking idiot." Even the usually loyal electricians communicated their dissatisfaction to him. The lead-man who subsequently became steward said he would "get a petition up; I won't accept being defended by those two dummies." And a black friend of mine told the man wearing the badge that he liked him personally but would "rather have Ric as steward."

Against my more prudent judgment and with pent-up emotion, I approached Tommie directly and asked whether he had in fact appointed the man as steward. Expectably, he was evasive. First he said it was a joke, that the man had wanted to wear the badge for a day, so he had let him. Then he shifted his ground, saying, "You know it takes a week or two to get approval of appointments."

"So, you have appointed him," I virtually charged, and added, "A lot of us around here, including myself, don't find it very funny."

The other men in the department almost unanimously opposed the appointment, though most couldn't believe it really had been made. My own reading of the situation was that Tommie was floating the idea of the appointment to see if he could get away with it. A man of little courage, Tommie, I felt, wanted on the one hand to appoint someone he could control, but on the other to avoid creating any furor by the appointment. In talking with fellow workers I tried to press them to take the appointment seriously enough to express strong opposition to it to Tommie. Otherwise, they might wind up with the man as their next shop steward, as Tommie predictably would ride out the initial opposition, wait until it blew over, and then announce the man's appointment.

The next day, confronted by several of the men, the appointee flatly denied the whole affair had been a joke. Tommie, he said, had offered the post to him several times, asking him to take it, though the man didn't want it. When Marbles found out about the incident, he couldn't believe it. He said the man would be "a catastrophe" as a shop steward and probably couldn't get the approval of the Executive Committee. But who else, I asked, can Tommie appoint? Who else is reliable? Marbles named the electricians and the carpenters, but I knew Tommie already had asked several of the most promising candidates among them and had been turned down by all. If Tommie obviously didn't want me, he still needed someone to fill the post. "He can't beat someone with no one," I thought at the time.

During these events workers in the shop continued to approach Tommie to repeatedly suggest he appoint me. A millwright said, flatly, "Why don't you give it to the only man who really wants it?" To which Tommie had shot back, "I'm the one who chooses, not Ric." Tommie had been waiting for this chance for a long time, and he wasn't about to be pressured into anything. After talking to Marbles and several of the electricians, I decided to again try to reassure him. When I found him on the way to lunch, I said I understood that "I am not your first choice for steward, and that is your business." I said I was "still interested" in the post and implied, quite dishonestly, that I would cooperate with him. My appointment, I added, would be "a popular choice among the men." Tommie listened to it all, poker faced.

During the following week I continued to talk to various workers in the department. One, a very sharp electrician whom I had not known very well in my first few months on the job and who earlier had refused to sign my petition, said Tommie was afraid "you will rock the boat." The electrician said he would put in a "good word" for me.

To complicate matters, while I awaited Tommie's decision I depended upon him in another respect as my union representative. I felt I needed my long-overdue job performance review before I could apply for promotion to another job, and Tommie was the only union representative I could go to to help me pry it out of management. I mentioned the matter to him one day in late January. He said he'd take it up directly with Ron, the super, bypassing my foreman. In fact (I learned later), he went only to the secretary, who later mentioned it to me. The following morning, however, Tommie told me at breaktime as if he had spoken directly with a management official, that I had "no right to a merit review," that "it isn't in the contract." He asked me if I had read the contract. I said I hadn't. Merit reviews, he then incorrectly declared, are "given at the convenience of management." Besides, he added, merely repeating what the secretary had said to me the day before, "If you don't hear any complaints, you're better off just keeping quiet." Incredible! That was the all-too-typical advice from our union representative.

The whole episode struck me as not quite right. This was the first I had heard from anyone that merit reviews were given only at the "convenience of management." So later in the break I went over to where Tommie was sitting with some other workers and raised the issue of merit reviews. After some discussion, Tommie began to hem and haw and finally reversing himself, volunteered to go in with me to speak to Sam, my foreman. As the break ended and he began to leave alone, I asked if he was going to find Sam. "Yes," he said. After he had left several workers at the table urged me to accompany him to make sure he did. I joined him, and we waited for the absent Sam for ten minutes, while Ron was on the phone. After a while Tommie said we should return that afternoon, but just then Ron got off the phone and Sam appeared. Tommie led me over to Sam, muttering something to me about getting permission to do union business. But then he simply asked Sam if there was any rule requiring merit reviews at particular intervals. I was dumbfounded—a union official, while allegedly representing a worker, asking the involved company agent what the rules entitled the worker to! Sam of course said, "No, there is no rule." Tommie then said I was concerned about getting my merit review. Sam replied he was overloaded with work, but he promised to do the review over the weekend, at which point Tommie turned to me in front of Sam and said, "Well, you can't ask any more than that."

WORKERS AND THE UNION

Not content with apparent progress on one front, after we had left Sam I put the matter of the stewardship to Tommie. I said I'd like to know straight out whether he was going to appoint me. He tried to evade the issue, not wishing to say directly that he would not appoint me. In his long line of excuses and hinting, he did say again that he didn't appreciate "some people coming in off the streets who want to make it fast." He said he hadn't known me very long, and he claimed he had a "moral obligation" to the man to whom he had first given the steward's badge, as the only one who had supported him at the Union Hall. Exasperated, I replied that that man had signed the original petition for me, that he had not even gone to the union meeting in question, and that he had told me he didn't want the post and had turned the badge back to Tommie. Thereupon Tommie repeated he had been waiting for twenty-five years and that he didn't like all the pressure on him to appoint a steward when technically he didn't have to appoint one at all. He was angry at the criticism and suspicion directed at him. That was in the nature of the job, I said. But, Tommie countered, it hadn't been like that before. And then it came out: he was insulted and angry that I had challenged him for the committeeman post. He seemed to feel I had besmirched his victory, saying no one before had challenged the quality of an uncontested election. I responded that "times are changing" and asked him again to tell me if he refused to appoint me. Again he refused to refuse, but he spoke vaguely of "people stirring the men up." "Do you mean me?" I asked. And in his most courageous moment, he responded, "Well, haven't you?" I responded that the men were angry and frustrated in their jobs and hardly needed stirring up, a half-truth. As we talked further, I realized that Tommie, like many American politicians, saw his office as his private property. He said he knew he had to take flak from the management people in the office, but not from the men. I said he was "elected by the men to represent them, and that gave them the right to criticize." Marbles, I pointed out, got criticized all the time but had known how to take it. Tommie increasingly was trying to break away. In a final, futile effort to reassure him I would cooperate I said that if he appointed me I would offer to resign after six months if he was dissatisfied with the job I had done. Not that gullible and unpersuaded, he continued to avoid committing himself, saying he wanted to decide for himself. I suggested then that he let me know by a certain day. Unexpectedly, he assented and agreed to tell me his decision by the following Friday.

I left Tommie disgusted with myself for trying to make myself appear acceptable to such a gutless, evasive, deceitful sycophant. The following Tuesday at noon I got my favorable merit review from Sam. Three hours later, I was notified by the same Sam I would be laid off on that Friday. On Wednesday Tommie came by and said, "I want you to know I didn't know about the layoff list when we talked last week." "That may be true, Tommie," I answered with bitterness, "but I don't know it for a fact. And, like the rest of the men, I have very little reason to believe what you say. We're all suspicious of you, because you don't tell us the truth; because you suck around Ron all the time; and because you're afraid to stand up." Tommie didn't even bother to deny the charges. Instead, he characteristically, accurately, and tellingly responded: "I learned a long time ago that the first guy that rocks the boat is the first guy to get axed." Of course, Tommie survives, individually.

So much for my aborted effort to achieve union office and for the union election process, which is not conducive to producing union officers likely to fight for workers' interests. Even in a unit of such manageable size and community of interest as local 1784, liberal democracy repeatedly proved itself primarily to be a means for preserving the status quo rather than for even mild reform. Without appearing to do so, seemingly "democratic" institutions contribute to the defense of the power and authority of the union establishment.

The union remains today as entrenched and stolid as ever, simultaneously the object of widespread cynicism that borders for the time being on fatalism and yet somehow the embodiment of the legitimacy of workers' needs and hopes. The very processes that appear to contribute to that legitimacy, however, seem also to operate to demoralize and frustrate workers rather than galvanize them to seek to develop control of their work and life environment.

For me an end had come to the factory version of liberal authoritarianism. For the rest of the men and women at the plant, work and life goes on as before to this very moment.

WORKERS AND THE UNION

Conclusion to Parts I and II:
Liberalism and Dictatorship

"Gino's gives you freedom of choice."—BICENTENNIAL SLOGAN FOR GINO'S
FAST-FOOD RESTAURANT CHAIN.
"You may say I ain't free but it don't worry me.—NASHVILLE. *

PREVAILING reality in American factories, as exemplified
by Blancs, is not good for human beings. We like to conceive of life
in the United States as fundamentally humane and "liberal." But reality in the factory is neither humane nor "liberal," at least not in any
sense in which the word "liberal" normally has been understood.†
Rather, work life is inhumane, and it is "liberal" only in another
sense in which liberalism must come to be understood, as one side of
the capitalist coin whose other side is dictatorship.

The ideology and mythology of American society, which apply
in variations to its central institutions where men and women work,
are liberal. Liberal ideology is founded on individualism, competition, private ownership of the means of production, formal economic
and political freedoms, procedural due process, constitutional rights,
legal equality of opportunity, and formal democracy. Liberal ideology

---

* "It Don't Worry Me," by Keith Carradine. Copyright © 1975, American Broadcasting
Music, Inc./Lion's Gate/Easy Music. Used by permission only. All rights reserved.

† Although the term "liberal" often is employed today in the United States to distinguish
certain people and/or policies from others described either as "conservative" or "moderate," in
its broadest sense the word "liberal" includes the full range of what currently is considered
mainstream American politics. So-called conservatives by and large are simply liberals of the
nineteenth-century variety. So-called liberals are indeed also liberals, of the twentieth-century,
welfare-state variety. And so-called moderates are liberals who mix the two varieties. For an excellent, liberal discussion of American politics in this sense, see Louis Hartz, *The Liberal
Tradition in America* (Cambridge, Mass.: Harvard University Press, 1955).

demands a commitment to and justification for these ideals as among the highest human goods. In its mythology American liberalism asserts that these ideals are being practiced in our society and that that practice in fact contributes to social and individual well-being.

The reality is quite different from ideology and myth. Within the context of capitalism, which necessarily has nurtured liberalism,* liberal concepts today serve to legitimate a social system that, despite some positive aspects, is on the whole quite destructive to social and individual well-being and poorly serves the majority of its members. This reality, like the ideology and mythology, exists in variations throughout the society, but it is most easily comprehended in such institutions as factories. There, liberalism is daily exposed as a thinly veiled class dictatorship, which, often in subtle ways, dominates all areas of life in the United States. In the factories liberalism and its most cherished institutions can be seen as insidious weapons in the hands of the few, which operate and are used to split up, confuse, demoralize, delay and pacify the many. Liberalism, then, is not simply a set of interrelated ideals that our society in practice fails to achieve. As the main content with which Americans are socialized, liberal ideology and mythology are tools for indoctrinating American workers to accept the political economy of capitalism. And liberal institutions operate as mechanisms for keeping the American working class, as a class, in its place.

If it seems strange to describe liberal America as a dictatorship, albeit the most sophisticated form of dictatorship in world history, that in itself is related to the influence of liberalism on us. We tend to think of only two forms of dictatorship: individual dictators, who openly exercise something approximating absolute power in an arbitrary and unpredictable manner that can approach capriciousness; and monolithic single-party "totalitarian" dictatorships. With these limited self-serving conceptions of dictatorship, liberal America in all its constitutional glory can hardly be conceived of as a dictatorship. On the contrary, in our written history and accompanying mythology it has been conceived as the very antithesis to dictatorship. Under a

---

* The relationship between liberalism and early capitalism is brilliantly brought out in C. B. MacPherson, *The Political Theory of Possessive Individualism* (London: Oxford University Press, 1962).

WORKERS AND THE UNION

formal political system involving checks and balances, elections, constitutional rights, the rule of law and the like, the power of our top public officials cannot be exercised in the absolute and arbitrary manner of sterotypical dictators.

But three things further need to be said. First, our vision of dictatorship tends, as one might expect from a liberal vision, to focus one-sidedly on so-called "public," "political" leaders and institutions and to ignore "private" economic leaders and institutions that generally have a greater impact on people's daily lives. Second, the stereotype of traditional and modern dictators exercising absolute power in purely arbitrary ways is grossly and conveniently exaggerated to enhance, by contrast, America's image as a society ruled predictably by law, not men. Real dictators, for all practical purposes, have never had the powers over society as a whole we have ascribed to them. Although in terms of particular decisions, say, about a certain subject's life, their power may have been nearly absolute (and heinous), the powers of dictators always have been circumscribed—if not by statutory law and constitutions, then by a variety of other, not necessarily less effective, factors, including custom, countervailing power, societal notions of right and wrong, and prevailing technological limits on the exercise of power. And third, from the vantage point of the vast majority of people who have been subjected to dictatorships, their most fundamental characteristic is not absoluteness, arbitrariness, unpredictability, or personalization of power, but rather the essential exclusion of people from control over their own lives. Under dictatorships the people are basically powerless within the system to change the main directions and conditions of their lives. These are "dictated" to them, not simply by nature and history, but by certain other people.

Understood in this way, a dictatorship need not be embodied in a single individual nor in a handful of people who rule crudely and overtly from a central place. Dictatorship can be exercised instead, as it in fact has been throughout most of recorded history, by a much broader group of people in the society—for example, by one class over another. It can be exercised through complex institutions and much more diffusely and subtly than our conventional versions of dictatorship would allow. As societies have become more complex and "rational," so too the forms of dictatorship have had to become more complex and "rational." Unpredictability has had to be reduced. Often the reality of dictatorship has had to be disguised and moderated by formal institutions that appear to give to the majority of the people the power to determine their lives. But this is, after all, mostly just an appearance. Particularly in the realm most critical to capitalism, the realm of social production for private profit, capitalist dictatorship remains severe and observable, if only one can open one's mind to it.

As in the past, liberal ideology and mythology today play roles in maintaining the system, the significance of which are difficult to overestimate. In the final analysis liberalism does much more than legitimate existing institutions and politically socialize people to accept them. Beyond that, it establishes capitalism in its material and nonmaterial aspects as effectively inevitable, as the only thinkable system for us. At bottom, liberalism inculcates in us a vision of the world and of human nature that strongly discourages us from believing any decent alternative to bourgeois-democracy-cum-capitalism can exist. After all—so the argument always goes—men are what we see them to be and as such they are ill-suited to life in cooperative, participatory, and egalitarian societies. To believe otherwise, it is said, is naive. As further proof of this proposition, societies that profess to be socialist are made to appear as the "real dictatorships," places where the rights and freedoms we enjoy in America are denied to their citizens. The dream of an alternative form of society, then, is concretized and transformed into a nightmare. This reinforces the minimalistic, Churchillian world outlook to which we have been subjected repeatedly: that if our society is not actually the best of all worlds, certainly it is the least bad and therefore the best possible.

The illusions perpetrated on us by liberalism thus function in a variety of complex ways to sustain its capitalist foundation. For example, the illusion of meaningful freedom of choice in the face of its commonly trivialized reality does double duty.* On the one hand,

---

* E.g., in automobiles we choose between a Pinto and a Nova, but we cannot buy any single car that is inexpensive, safe, durable, comfortable, reliable and economical; or in jobs we choose between one bad one and another.

WORKERS AND THE UNION

the illusion reduces the feeling of being locked into a losing game in which there is no significant hope of achieving much human satisfaction and respect, or even surcease. While we still believe we have meaningful free choices, we believe that we can make a better life for ourselves. On the other hand, combined with the closely related attachment to individualism even in its trivialized, often faddish reality, the illusion of choice produces feelings of self-blame in the vast majority of workers for whom "making it" is barely a dim hope. For if we are free to choose and if the responsibility is individual, then failure means we have only ourselves to blame. The social system, which puts a premium on success, appears by contrast to have generously provided us with the opportunity to succeed and therefore cannot be fundamentally faulted.

The reality for most Americans is so different from these illusions that their persistence is striking testimony to the depth of impact social indoctrination can have on human beings. For most of the tens of millions of unskilled and so-called semiskilled blue- and white-collar workers—the majority of all American workers—their lifetime job choices are quite limited even by conventional standards. And if to these conventional criteria are added such concerns as potential for human growth on the job, capacity for meaningful participation in deciding major, work-related issues that affect workers' job and home lives, and potential for achieving through the job a sense of purpose in life greater than material aggrandizement, then the nature of free choice in practice exposes the continuing liberal commitment to it as at best self-deception. Even in good times the poor, the unskilled, and the semiskilled have little or no meaningful choice. In hard times the illusion of free choice itself is seriously subverted, as men and women mostly just try to hold on to what they have. Those with skills and seniority on the job, for different reasons, also generally do not in bad or normal times have much choice. They have too much invested in staying with a particular company to be able to afford to choose an alternative position, which in any event is unlikely to be substantially better than their current job. It is a fact that most workers do not and cannot after a period relatively early in their working lives progress to jobs that are qualitatively more rewarding. And a majority never even approach obtaining the sorts of jobs most of us see as rewarding.

However, so long as the illusions of individual free choice are maintained, the individual worker is likely to be still hopeful for conventional advancement, escapist (addicted for example to alcohol, TV, religion, and/or consumerism), and/or resigned to failure and self-blaming. In any case s/he has been rendered, for the time being at least, ineffective as a force for changing the system. While some illusions persist and there is hope within the system, the worker need not feel so locked in and therefore need not become acutely aware of his/her life dependence upon the employing company. The worker can always verbally assert his/her independence and say, as one did recently to me, "I don't need this job. I got along for thirty-five years without it and I can do it again." However, protestations do not change facts. Even in the best of times the alternative for most workers to "this job" is unlikely to be much better. And in any event, the very availability of choice is limited over time for most workers, because a worker can not effectively exercise such a choice too often without paying a high penalty. The more often an average worker moves from one job to another, even if the move is voluntary, the less likely is it that s/he will be moving to a better or even to an equivalent job. Employers by and large do not want "unreliable" workers in better jobs. They want "stable" men and women they can depend upon.

These often are men and women who recognize at some level of consciousness the power the employing company has over their lives and who effectively respond by making themselves malleable to their employer's requirements, even as they may proclaim their own independence. At times, when they are not so consciously defending their integrity, however, workers give eloquent testimony to feeling a lack of meaningful choice. When encouraged to say how they feel about their jobs, they often say "it's a job" or give the impression they are just "doin' time." With such a realistic assessment of their current work and their real choices, they, of course, have little incentive in most instances to face the dislocations and troubles connected with exercising their largely illusory freedom of choice.

WORKERS AND THE UNION

The semiconscious realization that there is no alternative livelihood to one's present work life is related to the broader, still less articulated vision that there is no realistic alternative to the social system
that determines that life. With this false consciousness, workers para-
doxically may at times even describe themselves as "satisfied" in their
work. Satisfaction is relative, and workers who at present see no available alternatives that would be more satisfying may verbally describe
themselves as "satisfied," even as they respond practically to their
working life predominantly with the mixture of passivity and es-
capism described earlier that expresses their deep dissatisfaction.

This mixture, if not actually conspiratorily concocted and sustained by the American ruling class, could hardly have been more effectively formulated to its benefit. The passive response to worklife
entails the de facto acceptance of a regime of production with its at-
tendant antagonisms and frustrations that most workers despise. Such
an acceptance, like the life itself, is humiliating. The extreme dislike
of work combined with that humiliation drives most workers to try to
dissociate themselves from their work lives to the extent possible. The
goal of most workers, therefore, is "to get out of the goddamned factory," or warehouse, or office as fast as possible once they have put in
the overtime needed to make enough money to live. Wanting to have
as little as possible to do with the workplace and wanting, if possible,
not even to think about the workplace after they leave it, workers
unwittingly but eagerly abdicate in the one area in America where
they have the potential for power.

Furthermore, while on the job most workers act as if they are
uninterested in and/or fearful of exercising many of the very freedoms
and rights that liberalism allegedly cherishes, nourishes, and protects.
Their dominant and accurate feeling is that their jobs are not very
secure and that therefore they must be compliant most of the time in
areas of particular concern to employers. Combined with their persisting liberal illusions, this can produce what on the surface appear
to be curious results. Workers, for example, struggle for the opportunity to make overtime contractually voluntary, as if to reassure themselves that with legal guarantees they will have the freedom to choose
whether to put in overtime. But then, both because of financial need

LIBERALISM AND DICTATORSHIP

and because of the need to please their employers, given the opportunity, workers overwhelmingly tend to continue to work overtime, even though the decision to do so is effectively coerced by their total circumstances. *Such is the essential nature of liberal freedom. It tends to be theoretical and formal, its significance dwarfed by the coercive quality of practical existence.*

So it is with freedom of speech, freedom of association, and freedom to strike. A worker technically is free to say whatever s/he wishes. And in fact a worker can talk fairly freely with workers s/he knows are trustworthy. But as soon as s/he talks to a larger group s/he risks being subjected to harassment and retaliation at the hands of union leaders and the company. As soon, that is to say, as s/he tries to be politically effective in using speech to achieve such subversive goals as creating a union that is controlled by the rank and file and independent of the company, so soon are the risks incurred. Strong dissent, even of the liberal variety, is perceived as likely to make the dissenter a target for company retaliation. For example, workers at Blancs do not want to be seen handing out leaflets, and many do not even want to be seen reading them. This obviously makes any organizing for change very difficult.

The company does not have to act very unambiguously or very often to communicate to the rank and file that they are expected to stay in line and keep their mouths shut. Most of the activists referred to in earlier chapters have been terminated for one declared reason or another. Whatever the stated reasons, the message was communicated.

Take the case of my own layoff. Although the circumstances attending it may well have been the result of a series of coincidences that delayed my being "bumped" from the trashman's job long enough for the company to fill all other entry-level positions so I could not be re-placed in another job, many workers I talked to did not see it as simply coincidental. In one way or another, they suggested they thought it to be retaliation for my outspokenness. My shop steward reminded me that "the first guy to rock the boat is the first guy to get axed." A high union official said he thought the company was "trying to get rid of me" and revealed that the union president had opposed his supporting my grievance about the layoff. A number of the rank and file in an extended discussion at one afternoon break could not understand how I could be bumped off my job by a worker who had seniority rights to a higher-level job that he voluntarily declined to exercise.

Speech that is not protected from a high risk of penalties obviously cannot be free. That the penalties are imposed by "private" rather than "public" agencies does not fundamentally alter that fact. As indicated in the discussions above of the contract negotiations and the union elections, the same holds true of association. Fear of association in the plant was and doubtless remains very strong. At times fellow workers I talked with even were questioned by other workers and foremen about their association with me and with other activists. One activist in particular was informally advised by her foreman with whom she should associate. Friendly workers in the plant were afraid to meet even in private for fear they would be branded as radicals and/or troublemakers and suffer accordingly. I too was afraid for a time to be seen with a worker who it seemed to me was clearly slated for oblivion. That fear in the plant layered upon itself, the net result being the felt need to appear respectable, which is to say to not get too far out of line in public. Those who did get too far out of line risked being fired, or at least labeled in ways that played upon the fears of other workers, thereby impeding association.

In three other central areas—elections, due process, and the twentieth-century version of the "free contract," the collectively bargained contract—liberalism in the factory is more insidious than its opposite, illiberalism.* With regard to the first, as indicated in chapter 10, democracy, responsiveness, and accountability have been reduced largely to electoral formalities. As for due process, although it doubtless serves some positive functions, on the whole it acts as a barrier to, rather than a guarantor of, substantive justice. Concerning

* In saying this, I do not imply that fascism is preferable. On the contrary, fascism in most respects is far worse than liberalism. Fascist repression, however, is manifest to a liberal consciousness.

LIBERALISM AND DICTATORSHIP

collective bargaining, despite its seemingly benign appearance, it operates as a most sophisticated form of imposing "law and order" on the workplace under a consensual guise.

First, take due process. The purpose of rules requiring that certain procedures be followed and providing institutional means for protecting specified interests of workers presumably is to maximize as "rights" the likelihood that those interests will be vindicated. And no doubt, in not a few cases these procedures do safeguard individual workers against particular violations of their recognized interests. But the cost paid for such protection is extremely high—so high, I am convinced, that workers as a class under a liberal system stressing individual redress of grievances through elaborate procedures appear to be less able to protect their own interests than under a less proceduralized regime.

The primary functions and effects of requiring elaborate procedures in our system for asserting and protecting workers' individual rights are multiple, related, and mutually reinforcing. The emphasis on liberal due process individuates workers' grievances, thereby discouraging the pursuance of grievances by putting the burden and initiative on a single individual; it also defuses grievances, and delays their settlement. *The major cumulative result of this proceduralization of substantive conflict is pacification,* which is achieved in several ways. Workers, vaguely advised that grievance procedures are available but frustrated in using them to the point that most often are unwilling to make the effort, therefore see themselves as "choosing" not to press their "rights." Having made that individual "choice," they have less reason to blame anyone but themselves for their continuing oppression. They have made their bed. Now they must lie in it.

And their bed is a solitary one. Where once in the face of an arbitrary or unjust act by management against a worker, workers might well have taken immediate direct, collective steps through a job action, a walkout, or even a sitdown, today liberal proceduralization directs the aggrieved individual worker into drawn-out formal grievance procedures. Liberal alternatives provided obscure the class conflict between oppressors and oppressed in a procedural maze and a language of "rights," while simultaneously atomizing workers into individual grievers, who too easily forget that the source of their rights is power and the source of their power is unity with other workers. Liberal rights and procedures function, in short, to accustom workers to not acting together and, like liberal history, to draw a curtain between them and the consciousness of their class struggles that are responsible for the benefits they enjoy today.

An example of how some of these mechanisms operate on workers is provided by the woman who filed a grievance on grounds of racial discrimination, a case referred to briefly in chapters 6, 7, and 9. The nature of that complaint expectably assured it of widespread support among a large number of blacks and some whites once it was brought to their attention. Thus, you will recall, when the union leadership at a meeting tried to dispose of the case, objections by the griever and others were supported by the majority of workers at a well-attended meeting. To that extent collective action was taken to support the proceduralized, individualized grievance, a rare case in itself.

But as soon as the public meeting was over, the grievance once more dropped out of sight, lost in committees and procedures. Discussions the day after the meeting with certain unsympathetic white workers further revealed how the procedural element complicated their understanding of the case. They argued that since the griever had not filed the grievance in a way that clearly alleged discrimination, the grievance had properly been rejected by the Grievance Committee. When I tried to explain that justice required that the real issues involved be faced even if the grieving woman had not complied with procedures, and suggested also that the grievance could simply be amended, they were unimpressed.

The following day, Marbles, under pressure of rank-and-file support for the griever, said the Grievance Committee would act to amend the grievance. Five weeks later when I spoke to him about it again, he assured me the grievance indeed would be taken to the next stage in the grievance procedure, pre-arbitration. But, he hastened to add, it would have to go to "pre-arb" as originally drafted, not as amended into an explicit complaint about racial discrimination. The union Grievance Committee, it turned out, had been "unable" to meet since the October union meeting at which support for the grievance was expressed. So there had been no opportunity to amend the grievance. As an unamended grievance, of course it was bound to lose.

The virtue of the way it would lose is that the loss would pass totally unnoticed. Over the weeks the anger of those who supported the grievance at the October union meeting would in any event have abated. If an effort were made at the next meeting to object again to its disposition by the pre-arb committee, to again forcibly bring it to workers' attention, it would be difficult to rekindle that fire, particularly with the additional procedural snag—the failure of the Grievance Committee to meet. As grievances drag out and are proceduralized, it becomes increasingly difficult to identify and mobilize support on the substantive issues. Where procedural technicalities are advanced as reasons for particular dispositions, the significance of the underlying substantive concerns becomes obscured. Commitment to and concern for justice becomes debased, as grievances, like defendants in our criminal process, are silently administered through mazes into obscurity.

The practical meaning of liberal proceduralization as a guarantor of the existing domination of workers as a class, even as it appears to be the guarantor of their individual rights against their dominators, is evident also in the manner in which effective appeals beyond union processes are drastically limited by the law. Take the case of the union eligibility requirements for nomination to union office. In the case of my local the requirements are not on their face unreasonable, though they effectively exclude perhaps 95 percent of the union membership from eligibility. But no matter how unreasonable in practice the eligibility requirements may be, the limitations on appeals beyond the union as the judge of its own rules are the same. The operative rule of American labor law, referred to in chapter 10, states that before one may appeal such internal union rules to an outside body, one must first carry the appeal through all the relevant appeal procedures within the union.

From the perspective of the ACLU that requirement may be

manageable. The ACLU can decide in advance to appeal a certain case all the way to the Labor Board or the courts if necessary, and its staff can devote the necessary time and energy to the appeal, notwithstanding an awareness that the internal union appeals are unlikely in the extreme to produce desired results. Local officials, it is obvious, are unlikely to issue rulings liberalizing requirements that serve to keep them in power. But for the rank-and-file worker without even the limited resources of the ACLU, the requirement that s/he "exhaust local remedies" within the union to become eligible to appeal to the Labor Department is itself too exhausting. The overwhelming fact that most workers are not willing to expend their time on such matters makes the "right" to an outside appeal a farce for those who most need protection.

The more procedures that are required of the average worker to vindicate an interest, the less likely is that interest to be protected. A worker should not have to be a fanatic to achieve reasonable protection of his/her rights. But at present that is what generally is required. Neither I nor another nominee for union office, for example, was willing in the event to challenge the union rules and carry an appeal through the union to the Labor Department. So union elections stay as before. And in a vicious circle, due process, that darling of liberalism, becomes its own mockery even in an institution like my local that might be small and cohesive enough to approximate the liberal town-meeting democratic ideal.

The hypocrisy of liberalism is clear, too, in the collective bargaining process and contract. Collective bargaining was developed ostensibly to redress the gross inequalities in bargaining positions between the burgeoning corporate employers and their individual employees. Confronted by the crudely coercive economic reality behind the abstracted ideal of individual freedom of contract and by tremendous labor unrest in the 1930s, welfare-state liberals formally adopted collective bargaining as the means to equalize the bargaining power between employees, taken as a collectivity, and employer.

That hardly has been the result of collective bargaining. Nor could it be, for the basis of inequality lies in the class nature of American society, which is untouched by collective bargaining. Although collectively bargained contracts not infrequently have advanced the material and nonmaterial well-being of workers, they have done so at high costs to workers' direct involvement in determining their own working conditions and to workers' capacity to otherwise enforce their demands upon their employer.

The collectively bargained contract effectively sets the rules for the workplace, rules that American courts will enforce as law if necessary. Aside from federal and state statutes relating to certain aspects of many jobs, like minimum wages (pegged scandalously low) and minimum health standards (infamously incomplete and barely enforced), the contract provides the exclusive, operative standard on the job for defining justice. A worker's rights are limited to what the contract says they are. When workers accept that contract they in effect consent, for the sake of any benefits they may achieve through it, to the entire regime of production that is implied. And most workers see their act of consent that way. Thus, within days after the new contract was signed in my plant, much less anger and struggle was evident among workers. The issues of what constitutes a "just wage," a "just pension," etc., were for the time being practically closed once again, as the slightly revised ground rules for employment had been ratified by the workforce.

Notwithstanding their exclusion from all but formalistic participation in the collective bargaining process, and even with a "company union" representing them in their bargaining with the company, workers' "free" consent to the contract offer legitimated in their eyes their continued exploitation. That the company dominated both sides of the negotiations was more or less recognized, but not taken to vitiate the validity of the agreement. The acceptance of the contract thus reaffirmed industrial peace, on terms that left ultimate control and power in the hands of the company but effectively implicated workers in its affirmation. How much more effective, as liberal capitalism has learned, is the rule of a dictatorship that is assented to!

Assenting to that dictatorship increasingly means workers are expected to surrender their main weapon in their struggle with employers. By contract they nearly always give up their right to strike during the contract period. And the contract period, if capitalists have their way, will get longer and longer. Without the legal right to strike over work issues, workers if they wish to strike are forced to wildcat. That in turn means they will be without union strike benefits and will have to face the coercive power of courts, as striking UMW coal workers once again saw to their dismay in September 1975. If the next stage in the advance of workers' rights under American capitalism is the imposition of binding arbitration upon contract disputes, including disputes arising from failures to achieve agreement on a new contract, then the incorporation of labor unions and the disarming and pacification of workers will appear nearly complete.

A recently issued postage stamp commemorating collective bargaining aptly says on it, "From conflict . . . accord." It does not of course say, "From class conflict." Nor does it say, "Imposed accord." But that is the main historical purpose and reality behind collective bargaining and other liberal institutions: to produce from class conflict a consensus on terms most favorable to capitalists. Liberal institutions in our society are an important means by which certain classes rule over other classes, legitimate their rule, and minimize the likelihood that the ruled classes can unite together in class action to take power in their own interests. That the dictatorship is embedded and disguised in ideas and institutions that purport to value freedom, individual rights, and equality of opportunity is one of the strengths of liberalism.

III

Work and the Capitalist System: Six Books Considered

XI

The Books and the Problem
of Understanding: A Reintroduction

IN previous chapters I have tried to show how in one factory capitalism victimizes and manipulates the producers of its wealth. I have argued, too, that liberal ideology and sophisticated liberal institutions, despite outward appearances, work hand in glove with the cruder institutions of material production. The equality and protections offered by liberal society, I have suggested, while not simply a sham, are basically class determined and class serving. Thus, as Anatole France wrote in the nineteenth century, "The law forbids the rich as well as the poor to sleep under bridges, to beg in the streets, and to steal bread." This essential truth remains.

Still, you may remain fundamentally unpersuaded. Reasonable and vital questions remain to be answered. Is it really true, you may ask, that work in America is basically as I have described it? And if so, is capitalism, as I have analyzed it, indeed primarily to blame?

Concerning the description of work, I believe I can prove beyond a reasonable doubt that the answer is yes. This proof is relatively easy, in part because its truth is hardly in dispute, and in part because much of your own work and life experiences conform to and confirm my descriptions.

Concerning the analysis, however, the task of persuasion/education is significantly more difficult. Our socialization, our dominant institutions and values, and even our very mode of conceptualizing life interfere with understanding capitalism as the source of so many of our problems. Adequate consideration of this matter therefore demands that an alternative mode of understanding, which I am myself only just beginning to develop, be used. Appreciating and developing that mode requires time, study, and practical struggle from each of us. No mere argument and no amount of evidence can substitute for that protracted learning process, which in its fullness is nothing less than the revolutionary transformation of our lives. Consequently, no single book can finally persuade in realms where "persuasion" integrally implies the rejection of so much of what we have been taught to be and see.

Nevertheless, in our struggle to understand and change our lives books can be of considerable help. Books, in combination with our experience, can at crucial times contribute to redirecting our vision as we grapple with our unquestioned and unfounded assumptions about American society and human nature in confrontation with the realities of our and others' lives. This is what reading Marx and certain Marxian writers did for me as I sought especially to understand my experiences working at Blancs.

These writings, I found, are far more complex and flexible, and far more useful for understanding our world than we have been led to believe. Whatever you may have heard or felt about Marx, you can learn much from his powerful analysis if you can for a time suspend your disbelief in and profound suspicion of it. The book you are reading in some sense is an invitation to do just that. It is an effort to show you that the basic Marxian orientation of my descriptions and analyses, which places capitalism at the center of our societal problems, makes sense. And it is an effort to communicate that sense not simply to academics but to members of all the classes, groups, and strata within our society that truly "need to know."

The effort itself, of course, is problematic precisely because of the underlying nature of our capitalist existence, which severely restricts its chances of success. The societal problems, which are reflected in the problematic quality of the effort, ultimately can only be solved by us collectively as we make our own future history. But if I cannot hope to communicate directly to many members of the working class or to transform your understanding and your behavior, I

SIX BOOKS CONSIDERED

may at least hope to provoke you to consider the probability that you have been trained to misunderstand our world.

My task in this narrower sense I take to be twofold. First, I must convince you that my *descriptions* of work in one factory are applicable more or less throughout the society. To do this, I will show you that my descriptions generally are confirmed by the experiences and reports of others, elsewhere. And second, I must convince you that my mode of *analysis* is at least useful, and perhaps even necessary, for understanding. To do this, I will show you two things: the poverty of the prevailing, non-Marxian analyses of why work in the United States is the way it is, and the richness of the Marxian analysis.

My approach to this still ambitious task is, I think, a modest one. It reflects an awareness of the limits on my own understanding of the subtle inner relationships among the various aspects of our sophisticated capitalist system, as well as a realistic recognition of the difficulties in moving people to re-view their world. The approach aims, on the one hand, at maintaining wherever possible the concreteness of the Blancs case study and, on the other, at minimizing the use of any abstracted analysis that is not implicit in the structure of the shared daily life we all experience but somehow do not yet "know."

In following this approach, I focus intensively on six of the most useful recent books about work in America, most of them rich in the details of daily life. I use these books by way of quotation, summary, and/or comment to confirm and enrich my descriptions and analyses and to indicate aspects of the capitalist mode of production that can be understood only through a Marxian mode of analysis. I rely on Marx's and Marxian theory and refrain from presenting my own wholly articulated theory of capitalism or capitalist work, which would require a knowledge and understanding of technology, labor history, and political economy that exceeds my achievements. Thus my presentation is suggestive rather than definitive. The direction and emphasis of the analysis is set; the particular explanations of various interconnections are not.

In the current literature on work there is, I believe, general agreement that the quality of work life and the kinds of problems most workers have to face on their jobs are as I have indicated. The broad consensus breaks down over the issue of *why* work is the way we all agree it is and over the related issue of *what to do* about it. The pattern of the breakdown of consensus on these issues is not random. The breakdown, rather, lies along intertwined intellectual and political lines that form a continuum whose poles are two very different understandings of why work is as it is and what to do about it. The various books about work in America are spaced along this continuum.

At one pole are the mainstream liberal books that in our capitalist society dominate the literature about work. The authors of these books either ignore the "why" issue altogether or, in discussing it, stubbornly refuse to seriously consider that the primary source of commonly recognized workplace problems might be capitalism itself. At the other pole are Marxian books, whose authors understand capitalism in Marxian terms and take capitalism as the fundamental source of work problems. With differing understandings of the sources of the problems, recommendations concerning what to do about the problems expectably are different. The liberal authors recommend reform within capitalism to solve problems they do not see as necessarily generated by the capitalist system; the Marxian socialists ultimately favor overthrowing the system they take to be the source of the problems. In between are books that are harder to classify.

Of the six books I refer to at some length below in support of my argument about capitalist work, two are unadulteratedly mainstream liberal; one is unquestionably Marxian-socialist; and the other three are harder to classify. Each of the six is among the best known of recent books on work and is, at least on its own terms, excellent.

The two conventionally liberal books, Richard Balzer's *Clockwork** and the Report to the U.S. Department of Health, Education and Welfare (HEW) entitled *Work in America*,† deplore existing working conditions but predictably seek and find only explanations and reforms that would leave the capitalist system intact. As in most

---

* New York: Doubleday, 1976.   † Cambridge: MIT Press, 1973.

SIX BOOKS CONSIDERED

liberal writings, capitalism is either not even mentioned or not seriously discussed: for example, the term "capitalism" never appears in the eight-page index to *Work in America!*

At the other end of the political-intellectual spectrum is Harry Braverman's superb *Labor and Monopoly Capital*,* which probably is the most enlightening, clearest analysis to date of the pattern of development since the nineteenth century in both the work process and the structure of the working class under American capitalism.

In between are three books that are not easy to classify. They range from Studs Terkel's damning *Working*,† a series of interviews with more than 100 workers, who in their own words describe and analyze their different jobs and lives; to Richard Sennett's and Jonathan Cobb's provocative *The Hidden Injuries of Class*,‡ a libertarian, anticapitalist, psychocultural analysis of working class people; to Barbara Garson's rich *All the Livelong Day*,§ an attractively concrete description and criticism of the demeaning effects on work and workers of the capitalist division of labor and capitalist unions. Of these three books, Terkel's appears closest to the liberal pole, Garson's to the Marxian pole.

Thus the six books examined bridge the two basic political-intellectual categories that reflect and enhance the division of the modern world: the liberal category, whose authors in effect appear to favor a kind of "capitalism without pain" and would therefore treat the symptoms of capitalism's cancer with aspirin-like reforms; and the Marxian-socialist category, whose author fully understands that capitalism is the main source of a pain that cannot be ended without a socialist revolution to eliminate the source. The three authors in the residual area appear to hold few illusions about capitalism but, with the partial exception of Garson, and Cobb in his separate Afterword, they do not engage in full-blown Marxian analysis of capitalism.

Five of these six books focus on work itself. The implications of work are explored somewhat differently in each. In *Clockwork*, for example, which is the liberal counterpart to my book, Balzer develops the sense of work life through an account of his own experience

---

* New York: Monthly Review Press, 1975.   † New York: Pantheon, 1974.
‡ New York: Alfred A. Knopf, 1972.   § New York: Doubleday, 1975.

PROBLEM OF UNDERSTANDING

working in one factory. In *Working,* on the other hand, Terkel builds up the sense of work life from the grinding accumulation of accounts of very different jobs at widely separated workplaces, whose sole relationship to each other implicitly is simply that they are all part of a single capitalist political economy. Garson's *All the Livelong Day,* relying on experiences and interviews at each of a handful of workplaces, develops the sense of capitalist work through a combination of the two approaches. Her approach is simultaneously more extensive than Balzer's and more intensive than Terkel's. These books share a common, dominant feature with the work you hold in your hands: they directly depend upon their authors' work experience and/or upon accounts of others' work experiences obtained through personal interviews with workers.

By contrast, *Work in America* and Braverman's *Labor and Monopoly Capital* depend on other sources and approaches. *Work in America* combines an interpretive summary of conventional social science data and understandings of the quality and the societal implications of work with a related argument for reform. Braverman's book is a complex Marxian overview of how the forces of capitalist accumulation, especially as they are embodied in the capitalist division of labor and capitalist technology, historically have shaped our jobs and our working class.

Somewhat different from the other five is Sennett's and Cobb's *The Hidden Injuries of Class.* The main focus of this book is not so much work itself as the non-work lives of the working class. What is being exposed here is how being working class—a reality ultimately defined by one's relationship to the means of production—negatively affects its members in their relations to their inner selves and in all their social relations, at home and in their communities.

Together, these six books very tangibly bring out how work and class shape each other, and how the lives of working class men and women at and away from work are decisively and adversely affected by what are only two aspects of one capitalist reality—their work and their class. All six are quite clear on how crucial work is to societal life, on what work is like, and on what it does to workers in the United States. And it isn't pretty.

SIX BOOKS CONSIDERED

XII

What Work Is Like

TO illustrate these points about the quality and the centrality of work life, I refer to Barbara Garson's skillfully balanced and eloquently outraged *All the Livelong Day*, to Studs Terkel's best-selling *Working*, and to the informative, unimpeachably mainstream social science HEW report, *Work in America*.

Garson's general picture of capitalist work and workers' lives is consistently, if not uniformly, dismal. Typical reactions by workers to their work are just what a reader by now might expect. Aside from moments of interviews in which workers often characterize their jobs as "not so bad"—a phrase that usually seems to mean the workers interviewed can neither envision a better job they might actually have a chance of getting (which makes theirs relatively "not so bad") nor think of any spectacular atrocity to effectively communicate just how *un*spectacularly bad their jobs really are—aside from this, workers' descriptions of their various jobs are remarkably similar and routinely negative.

The white-collar clerk with the typically trivialized, fragmented job of checking one column on a form against another, who is not trained to do or "supposed to understand" anything else, resists at first pointing out to a superior an error she has found that is not part of her job, saying, "If they're gonna give me a robot's job to do, I'm gonna do it like a robot!" (p. 171). A spirited woman who has worked for years in a ping-pong equipment factory describes the plant as a "dungeon." Another woman in the same plant, when asked how the factory might be run differently, responds at first that it would be smoother if a particular forelady were off "our back." But when asked why that forelady is on workers' backs, she responds dejectedly, "Ah, I don't know. All bosses is the same. All jobs is the same."

A young woman worker new to a tuna fish cannery, when asked what she thinks of her work, answers: "I don't think about it. . . . I just do it. I try not to look at the clock so the time will pass more quickly." To help the time pass she plays head games and has sexual fantasies about the dark tuna meat, which at least in the early weeks on the job took her mind off how "dull and boring" the job is.

At a cosmetics factory, workers on the "Herbescence line," reacting at first in disbelief upon learning that Garson wanted to write a book "About these jobs?" (p. 58), then instructed her to write about "how hard we work," about "How boring" the work is, about how hot it is on the line during the summer and how management had air conditioned the upstairs where lipsticks are made, not because they cared about the workers, but "just 'cause the lipsticks might melt." Workers told Garson to write about "how fast the lines are now"— "They keep getting faster"—and about "the new supervisors": "Why should they treat you like dirt just because you work in a factory?"

At the notorious Vega automobile plant in Lordstown, Ohio (which in the early 1970s achieved fame as the classic example of the trend to speeded-up, subdivided tasks and of workers' increased hostility to that trend), workers expressed their feelings about their jobs. "It pays good . . . , but it's driving me crazy," says one (p. 87). Another, whose father worked for 35 years in similar but less sophisticated auto factories, says that when his father came home, "he never talked about the job. What's there to say," he adds, shifting to speaking about his own job: "A car comes, I weld it; a car comes, I weld it; a car comes, I weld it. One hundred and one times an hour" (p. 88). In that context, most workers seek whatever diversions from the job they can find or fabricate—a surreptitious cigarette, fantasies, water fights: "Anything so you don't feel like a machine." For some, like one veteran worker, it seems almost too late: "I don't do anything any more. . . . I think the time passes fastest if you let your mind just phase out and blend in with the speed of the line" (p. 88).

It is not the seeming domination by machines alone that alienates workers. At the tuna cannery a woman worker who had been there for four years describes how the "line ladies," veteran workers who act as junior supervisors, make their production line quotas: they figure out which workers they can effectively push—"the ones who really need the job" (p. 38). She complains of the petty, callous, and arbitrary treatment and demeaningly childish punishments handed out to workers. And then she says, "you feel bitter. Why should you put out for them? Why should I care about a line lady who's rushing around saying she wants her fish by three-twelve? Why should you put out when you're nothing to them as soon as you stop skinning fish?" (p. 39).

Similarly, several workers at the Lordstown Vega plant describe working for GM as "like the Army. . . . Supposedly you have a contract so there's some things they just can't make you do. Except, if the foreman gives you a direct order, you do it, or you're out. . . . fired or else they give you a DLO—disciplinary layoff. Which means you're out without pay for however long they say" (p. 90).

Tight discipline, it appears, must be maintained in the factory because, given the extreme degree of dehumanization of the work process, material incentives alone are insufficient to keep humans working at the level of productivity the company demands. Of course, if you think you're being taken advantage of, say by a speedup, you can always put in a grievance, like

"this boob Larry. . . . Guy next to me. . . . he calls the [union] committeeman and files a seventy-eight [a grievance claiming that the job can't be done in the allotted time]. I walk up to him afterwards and say, 'Look at you! Now you're smiling and you're doing the goddamn job. You can wipe your ass with that grievance.' Two months later he's still doing the job just like GM wants him to. The union is saying, 'Hang on fellah, we'll help you,' and he's still on the line like a fucking machine" (p. 91).

Sabotage under these circumstances is partly an act of vengeance and partly "just a way of letting off steam," a diversion. A worker on night shift recounts,

"Last week I watched a guy light a glove and lock it in the trunk. We all waited to see how far down the line they'd discover it. If you just miss a car they call that sabotage. They expect the sixty-second minute. Even a ma-

WHAT WORK IS LIKE

chine has to sneeze. Look how they call us in weekends, hold us extra, send us home early, give us layoffs. You'd think we were machines the way they turn us on and off" (p. 93).

Alienated from their jobs, from the company, from themselves and from the product, workers at Lordstown typically say, "General Motors—all they care about is money. Not the worker, not the car, just the goddamn money" (p. 94). A young worker who hates his job but has become dependent on the higher wages auto plants pay and does not see any real alternative, recognizes he is effectively locked in: "If I'm gonna do some dumb job for the rest of my life, I might as well do one that pays" (p. 92). Another, overhearing his mother express the hope that maybe he will quit "when he gets his car paid off," shouts from outside the room, "Ha! . . . They got those cars planned so they fall apart the day you make the last payment" (p. 96). A third young worker concurs: "Cars are your real trap. . . . You need the car to keep the job and you need the job to keep the car. And don't think they don't know it. They give you just enough work to keep up the payments. They got it planned exactly, so you can't quit" (p. 91). So much for "freedom of choice," which only further demeans workers by making them feel as if they are really the individual authors of their despised class fate.

The story of what the capitalist division of labor has done to the auto industry is in essence the same for other "rationalized" industries. Two industries Garson visited in the Pacific Northwest, mink fleshing and medical lab analysis, have been "rationalized" along similar lines. As the industries were "redesigned," so too were the "daily lives of their employees." Their jobs were made "lighter, . . . more repetitious and monotonous than before" (p. 127). Thus, Garson writes,

Under the more extreme division of labor each person feels further and further removed from actually running a [lab] test or fleshing a mink. . . . The checks and counts and incentive bonuses reflect the bosses' recognition that, under the new system, workers need rewards and punishments. There's less in the work itself that brings satisfaction or suggests a compelling need to keep going.

On the books Pacific Fur Foods and UML [United Medical Laboratories] are successful operations. Of course, they have no way to measure their . . . [success] except in money. [What is lost in the "rationalization"—] Lifetime friends, good conversation, a chance to move about and admire a fine pelt, these don't enter into . . . [the boss's] calculations. Meanwhile, . . . a chance to learn all the operations, the pride that makes you finish up in the lab the way you would in your own kitchen, these are being rationalized out at UML (p. 139).

What is true of so-called blue-collar work is true as well of so-called white-collar work, and for the same reasons. With respect to white-collar jobs, the "rationalization" effected by the capitalist division of labor has created similarly fragmented, simplified, repetitive, and boring jobs. Thus, ironically but inevitably, the "industrialization of office work" increasingly is enlarging that huge body of workers whose class boundaries cut across traditional blue- and white-collar distinctions. That single working class is joined objectively, if not yet in the consciousness of its members, by a set of common problems, among them the work problems that produce in its members a shared sense of intense alienation from and antagonism to their jobs.

The quality of "rationalized" work at the Fair Plan Insurance Company, for example, is both representative of much white-collar work and familiar to those aware of the quality of blue-collar work. There, hundreds of women work processing insurance forms. Various sections do

subdivided parts of the paper work . . . like coding, checks, filing, and endorsement typing. . . . The women . . . sat at steel desks like mine, each working separately on a stack of forms or cards. Every section had a supervisor who counted and checked the work. She recorded the number of pieces we completed, and the number of errors we made, on our individual production sheets. These production sheets were the basis for our periodic merit raises. . . . Aside from counting and checking, the supervisors also tried to curtail talking and eating at the desks (p. 157).

The way the jobs are set up, women don't really work with each other:

our work certainly didn't facilitate personal contact. As a matter of fact it required a contrivance for me to ask [another worker whose child was in the hospital] how her son was . . . , [because] a clerk can't just saunter across the room [and ask such questions]. . . .

Even if we had been allowed to talk, the job would not have encouraged closeness. Though our desks were as close together as they could be, we worked far apart from each other; each woman stapling, stamping, sorting, or figuring over her own pile, vaguely competing for a better production sheet.

Even the worker whose son was very sick could continue to produce effectively in her reduced job. Despite being distracted, "she could fulfill her function for Fair Plan. The bosses didn't have to notice her distress until she actually cracked up. And then they could replace her in one day with someone who would pick up her speed in less than a week. The job was deliberately designed that way" (p. 158).

The work at *Reader's Digest*, where about two thousand workers process complaints, subscriptions, and sales promotions, also is characterized by "the same extreme division of labor, the same close supervision with the same production sheets and merit raises" (p. 159).

At the *Digest*, workers are organized, moved around, and effectively made to do whatever is required by the system of production for profit. Although, for example, many of the workers interviewed disliked doing overtime because it seriously interfered with their nonwork lives, they generally did it when "asked." One worker, who originally took the *Digest* job because of its nearness to her home and because by getting off at four she could be home early for her children, says, "But they asked for so much overtime and they marked you down if you said no. I needed the job too bad to refuse. So I never knew when I was really leaving by four. I had to pull my kid out of the Cub Scouts because I couldn't do my part in the car pool" (p. 174).

Another, in resignation, says,

"When I first came here I used to cry . . . because of all the things I couldn't do any more. I was . . . young . . . then. I wanted to take sewing classes and I wanted to go out dancing. But you never know when you can make Saturday classes and doing the same thing over and over all day, you get too tired to go dancing. By now it doesn't bother me any more. They give you sick days, they give you holidays, they give you time off for funerals, and at this stage of my life that's all that comes up anyway" (p. 174).

SIX BOOKS CONSIDERED

So, human beings, like their jobs, are shaped and divided up. Off the job, life generally is reduced to what the demands of and rewards from the job permit. On the job, workers are deprived of the sense of purposiveness, inventiveness, and achievement that can energize aspects of all work.

Many simple and grand human works have been constructed from such energy. Others, like the pyramids, have been built by slaves who had no say in the outcome, and no vision of the fruits of their labor. Without that vision, that internal energy, a great deal of external force had to be applied to keep the hands and feet moving.
Today most of us toil like the pyramid builders. . . . typists [in large offices] are given no say in the overall use of their labor and allowed little vision of where even their own single stones, their few finished pages, will be piled. Under such circumstances, every motion is a great effort. . . . Consciously [doing such work] . . . soon becomes exhausting or, at best, in a work situation . . . hypnotic (pp. 210–11).

"For workers," Garson concludes,

it's a dilemma. . . . Real work is a human need, perhaps right after the need for food and the need for love. It feels good to work well. But it feels bad to be used. . . . As long as control over the means of production stays in the hands of owners, managers, or pharaohs, we will be forced to make goods that we don't necessarily need and to work in ways that are debilitating and humiliating. . . . (p. 219).

Just how destructive our jobs are and how they affect our social relations is evident also from Studs Terkel's immensely varied interviews with workers of every stripe. Most men and women, it is clear, take little satisfaction from their work and feel, in their work- and non-work lives, quite helpless and powerless. Only a minority achieve satisfaction and a sense of self from work they feel is of some worth and over which they feel some control.

This is especially obvious in the series of interviews with an airline stewardess, an airline reservationist, a model, an executive secretary, and a hooker. Unconscious of the underlying problem and in self-doubt, they, like the rest of us, search to make themselves feel more valuable as human beings. To enrich themselves they often seek glamor, money, power, and relations with important people. But, as their interviews reveal, generally it doesn't work.

WHAT WORK IS LIKE

246

Their interviews individually add to our understanding of how capitalism affects each of them. Collectively and juxtaposed to each other in what Terkel calls "A Pecking Order," the interviews also confirm the essential emptiness of that part of the American dream which holds out the promise of glamorous, interesting jobs. Equally important, the interviews expose how a typically capitalist obsession with commodities infects human relations. Workers are not only treated on the job like things to be bought and sold. They, in turn, in their relationships with their own selves and others ambivalently tend too often to act, and be treated, not as human beings but as commodities with a market value.

When Terkel interviewed her, Terry Mason had been an airline stewardess for six years. Like the majority of stewardesses, she is from a small town. In fact, Terry took the job to get out of Broken Bow, Nebraska. From there, being a stewardess looked glamorous. She was the youngest and only one of six daughters in her family not to get married right after high school and settle down in Broken Bow. The rest of her family is proud of her. They see only the image, stewardess, and think it's fantastic that a member of their family is getting out and "seeing the world."

In harsh reality, however, stewardesses are part of what airlines sell when they sell a seat on a plane. Stewardesses, therefore, are merchandised, like any other commodity. They are packaged by the company to serve prevailing company demands and standards of what "the customer" wants. Stewardesses are told what to wear, how to do their hair, how to smile, how to move, how to look into men's eyes, and how much to weigh. At stewardess school, for example, Terry was taught how to be "womanly" or "sexy" when lighting a male passenger's cigarette: "The idea is not to be too obvious about it. They don't want you to look too forward. That's the whole thing, being a lady but still giving out that womanly appeal, like the body movement and the lips and the eyes" (p. 42).

A kind of conformity, which the company believes will help sell its product, is enforced. As fashions change year by year, so does the desired model for stewardesses. When Terry was at "stew" school, all the stewardesses were made to look alike: "they wouldn't let you say how *you'd* like your hair cut, they wouldn't let you have your own personality, *your* makeup, *your* clothes" (p. 44). Stew schools are more permissive now, as airlines recognize that variety sells seats and drinks too. All wigs used to be forbidden; now they're allowed. But styles still are enforced: "Our airline picks the girl-next-door type. At one time they wouldn't let us wear false eyelashes and false fingernails. Now it's required that you wear false eyelashes, and if you do not have the right length nails, you wear false nails" (p. 42).

Stewardesses are not supposed to be human beings. The rule is,

"the passenger is right. When a passenger says something mean, we're supposed to smile and say, 'I understand.' We're supposed to *really* smile. . . . Even when they pinch us or say dirty things, we're supposed to smile at them. . . . That's the main thing, smile. When I first went to [stewardess] class, they told me I had a crooked smile. [The teacher] . . . showed me how to smile. . . . Even if we're sad, we're supposed to have a smile on our face (p. 46).

"They call us professional people, but they talk to us as very young, childishly. They check us all the time on appearance. They check our weight every month. Even though you've been flying twenty years, they check you and say that's a no-no. If you're not spreading yourself around passengers enough, that's a no-no" (p. 47).

Terry is no longer proud she's a stewardess. As a single woman, she has learned to hide her profession. For many, being a stewardess never was their first choice: "A lot of stewardesses," Terry says, "wanted to be models. . . . A stewardess [job] is what they could get" (p. 48).

Beryl Simpson was an airline reservationist for twelve years. Her job was "very routine, computerized," and she "hated it with a passion." She would get "sick in the morning, going to work feeling, Oh, my God! I've got to go to work" (p. 49). The last years on the job in particular were

"horrible. The computer [Saber] had arrived. . . . Sabre was so expensive, everything [and everyone] was geared to it. Sabre's down, Sabre's up. Sabre's this and that. Everything was Sabre. . . . It was almost like a production line. We adjusted to the machine. The casualness, the informality that had been there previously was no longer there. . . ."

WHAT WORK IS LIKE

And again, it wasn't just the technology that made the job intolerable:

"They monitored you and listened to your conversations. If you were a minute late for work, it went into your file. I had a horrible attendance record—ten letters in my file for lateness, a total of ten minutes. You took thirty minutes for your lunch, not thirty-one."

Happily, Beryl's work life has improved since she left the airlines to become an employment counselor:

"When I was with the airlines, I was taking eight tranquilizers a day. I came into this business, which is supposed to be one of the most hectic, and I'm down to three a day. Even my doctor remarked, "Your ulcer is healed, it's going away." With the airline I had no free will. I was just part of that stupid computer" (pp. 49–50).

Now, of course, Beryl is free to take only three tranquilizers a day to get through the job. She's making more money now and likes her job better, but she's lost the "status" she used to have working for the airlines. Her boyfriends, she finds, like women with "status" jobs. One "never dates Judy, he never dates Joan. He dates a stewardess or a model. He picks girls for the glamor of their jobs" (p. 50). Our capitalist culture has so succeeded in selling these jobs that men, even in their private lives, wish to be associated with women who hold them. All the men Beryl dated while she was an airline reservationist had been deluded: "I knew I had a dumb, stupid, ridiculous, boring job, and these people were glamorizing it" (p. 50).

By comparison, Jill Torrance really does have a "glamorous" job. She's a successful, fifty-dollar-an-hour, high-fashion model, whose face is seen in magazine ads and on TV commercials. She models for "whatever kind of products anyone wants." Her job is to help sell products. To get the opportunity, she first has to sell herself, by conforming to the reigning fashion: "Now the natural look is in. Jumping up and down or staring out there. . . . What's natural about looking into space? They want you natural but posed. . . . How can you feel natural with three pounds of make-up, in some ridiculous costume, standing there and looking pretty?" (p. 51).

Her first reaction when the phone rings in the morning and she gets a job call is "Oh, crap" (p. 52). "I'd like to say I'm sick and can't make it, but I seldom turn something down unless I think it's really awful. . . . When you're working for one agency, they expect you to be on call" (p. 51).

Jill got into modeling because she couldn't afford to go to college. While she was working as a receptionist during high school in her hometown (South Dakota) beauty shop, someone suggested she try modeling. Jill went to New York City at the age of eighteen, and, like a "lot of girls who go into modeling. . . . from very poor families. . . . from Ohio or Indiana or some place like that. . . . [she was] very vulnerable. . . . [and didn't] know what [she was] . . . doing" (p. 53). She did the cocktail party rounds to meet advertising people and she caught on and began making "all this money for smiling and pinning a flower on a guy" (p. 53). But "It didn't turn out to be that simple":

"Usually you're competing with anywhere from thirty to sixty girls. They're cattle calls. Sometimes they take you in ten at a time. You wait from forty-five minutes to an hour before you're called. . . . It's like going out on a job interview every day. Everybody is very insecure. . . .

"There's no training needed, no kind of background. . . . You learn while you're working. I didn't think it was funny the first few years because I was so nervous. After you relax, you see how absurd it all is. . . . You never really feel at ease and you force yourself to do things not natural to you. It's always something that you really aren't, that someone else wants you to be.

"You feel like you're someone's clothes hanger. One day someone will say you're great. In the next studio, they'll say you're terrible. It changes from minute to minute: acceptance, rejection. Suddenly it doesn't mean anything. Why should you base your whole day on how you look in the morning?" (pp. 53–54).

Jill doesn't like her job. What she likes about the job is the free time away from it and the money it provides her. Still, she finds most other work available to women in the United States, like being a secretary, even "more degrading than modeling," as well as decidedly lower paying. She feels she

"should do something else, but there is nothing I can do really well. I'm established and make a steady living, so it becomes pretty easy. It's not very

WHAT WORK IS LIKE

fulfilling. . . . You stop thinking when you're working. . . . Most models, after one or two years, can't be very interested in it. But they got involved with the money, so it's difficult for them to quit. And there's always the possibility of [still more money, the dream of] the commercial that's going to make you twenty thousand dollars at one crack" (p. 54).

Models, too, need their work fantasies because their work lives, like the work lives of factory and office workers, are so empty. Models, extremely dependent on pleasing others and without even the compensating, relatively stable companionship that exists in the factory and large offices, are very isolated. When she works, Jill goes "off into my own world most of the time. It's difficult for me to talk with the others. . . . we sort of talk about everyday gossip. You end up smiling and being nice to everybody. You can't afford not to be" (p. 55).

So much for the glamor of modeling.

Anne Bogan, by contrast, is happy in her work. She is the exception that proves the rule. She likes to serve—particularly men, and particularly important men. Her job, as private secretary to the president of a corporation with headquarters on the thirty-second floor of a skyscraper, affords her the opportunity to mix with male executive types. Anne appreciates the good treatment she gets, especially compared to how she was treated on former jobs: "They treat me more as . . . on the executive level" (p. 55). She's interested in her work, career minded, and "perfectly happy in my status" (p. 56). She likes the dinners with businessmen, the background music in the restaurants, and "the caliber of people . . . you . . . run into. People who have made it" (p. 56). She believes she's been successful with businessmen, "because I'm a good listener and interested in their world. I enjoy it, I don't become bored with it. They tell me about their personal life too. . . ."

She believes it is important that wives of executives should be "interested in their work" and, not surprisingly, that "the wife of an executive would be a better wife had she been a secretary first," because "As a secretary you learn to adjust to the boss's moods" (p. 56). Anne Bogan, in short, is the perfect female subordinate for a male chauvinist boss. In a job where she is accorded some degree of respect for her service and where she can feel close to "the action," she finds work enriching.

Happily, most of us are not satisfied with such personal subordination. Unhappily, not many of us in our society can hold jobs that provide even these objectively demeaning satisfactions. Most of us, in fact, have jobs that resemble Roberta Victor's former job as a hooker more than we would care to admit. That "job" provided her with an unadorned, piercing perspective on the rest of us. Although she may not be fully conscious of all its implications, Roberta understands how capitalism, and relatedly sexism capitalist style, shapes jobs and life.

Focusing exclusively on women, Roberta suggests how capitalism has transformed heterosexual relations in general into subtly disguised "transactions":

"A hustler is any woman in American society. I was the kind of hustler who received money for favors granted rather than the type of hustler who signs a lifetime contract for her trick. Or the kind of hustler who carefully reads women's magazines and learns what it is proper to give for each date, depending on how much money her date or trick spends on her" (p. 57).

The cash connection is simply more blatant in the case of a prostitute. Her tricks pay her in exchange for whatever it is they are seeking, not always sex.

She didn't have to learn her trade, "because my training had been in how to be a hustler anyway":

"I learned it from the society around me, just as a woman. We're taught how to hustle, how to attract, hold a man, and give sexual favors in return. The language that you hear all the time, "Don't sell yourself cheap." "Hold out for the highest bidder." . . . [Kissing] may not be proper on the first date, but if he takes you out to dinner on the second date, it's proper. If he brings you a bottle of perfume on the third date, you should let him touch you above the waist. And go on from there. It's a market place transaction" (p. 58).

As a young call girl, Roberta catered to the wealthy and the respectable. For this class of men, Roberta learned the appropriate ways to present herself and the proper social rituals to perform:

WHAT WORK IS LIKE

"The understanding is: it doesn't get conducted as a business transaction. The myth is that it's a social occasion.

You're expected to be well dressed, well made up, appear glad to see the man. . . .

There's a given way of dressing in that league . . . well, but not ostentatiously. . . . You have to look as if you belong in those buildings on Park Avenue or Central Park West. You're expected not to look cheap, not to look hard. Youth is the premium. . . ."

Although in the very beginning Roberta found the job exciting, to continue as a prostitute she had to "turn myself off." Not unlike the factory or office worker, "I had to disassociate who I was from what I was doing. It's a process of numbing yourself. . . . I found I couldn't turn myself back on when I finished working" (p. 60).

As she got hooked on drugs, she dropped in class from call-girl work to streetwalker work. And of course as she dropped in class, so did her customers, so did her "performance," and so did her entire life. Her rapid decline is like a condensed practical lesson in class analysis and in the entitlements of each class.

"As a call girl, some of my tricks were upper echelon cops, not patrolmen. Priests, financiers, garment industry folks, bigtimers. On the street, they ranged from *junior* executive types, blue-collar workers, upwardly striving postal workers, college kids, suburban white collars who were in the city for their big night, restaurant workers. . . ." (p. 62).

As a streetwalker, she was subjected to all kinds of risks and injuries from which her previous upper class work style and clients had protected her. She was robbed, threatened, hit, entrapped, arrested, and sent to prison. There were, however, a few redeeming features to Roberta's fall:

"As a streetwalker, I didn't have to act. I let myself show the contempt I felt for the tricks. They weren't paying enough to make it worth performing for them. . . .

"It was strictly a transaction. No conversation, no acting, no myth around it, no romanticism. It was purely a business transaction. You always asked for your money in front. If you could get away without undressing totally, you did that" (p. 62).

Okay! Okay! you may be thinking. We all know that being a hooker means you have to sell part of yourself. But what does that have to do with most jobs in America? Roberta answers, as she contrasts being a call girl with being a streetwalker:

"It's not too different than the distinction between an executive secretary and somebody in the typing pool. As an executive secretary you really identify with your boss. When you're part of the typing pool, you're a body, you're hired labor, a set of hands on the typewriter. You have nothing to do with whoever is passing the work down to you. You do it as quickly as you can" (p. 62).

Looking back on her life as a prostitute, Roberta reveals as she talks personally how much she understands about what work and our society are like:

"As a call girl I got satisfaction, an unbelievable joy—perhaps perverted—in knowing what these reputable folks were really like. . . . I was in *control* with every one of those relationships. . . . I called it. . . . It was a tremendous sense of power.

"What I did was no different from what ninety-nine percent of American women are taught to do. I took the money from under the lamp instead of in Arpège. . . ."

But, she continues, trouble is,

"You become your job. I became what I did. I became a hustler. I became cold, I became hard. I became turned off, I became numb. Even when I wasn't hustling, I was a hustler. I don't think it's terribly different from somebody who works on the assembly line forty hours a week and comes home cut off, numb, dehumanized. People aren't built to switch on and off like water faucets. . . ."

With a life experience of "field work" behind her, Roberta concludes in the best tradition of sociology:

"The overt hustling society is the microcosm of the rest of the society. The power relationships are the same and the games are the same. Only this one I was in control of. . . . I knew I was playing a role. Most women are taught to become what they act. All I did was act out the reality of American womanhood" (pp. 64–65).

But, then, what of the reality of American manhood? If men are subjected to one less layer of subjugation, are they really more in control, more satisfied in their work? Apparently not. The typical patterns revealed in Terkel's interviews with both men and women work-

WHAT WORK IS LIKE

ers are summarized in his moving introduction. Let Terkel answer at some length for himself:

This book, being about work, is, by its very nature, about violence—to the spirit as well as to the body. It is about ulcers as well as accidents, about shouting matches as well as fistfights, about nervous breakdowns as well as kicking the dog around. It is, above all (or beneath all), about daily humiliations. To survive the day is triumph enough for the walking wounded among the great many of us.

The scars, psychic as well as physical, brought home to the supper table and the TV set, may have touched, malignantly, the soul of our society. . . .

[This book] is about a search, too, for daily meaning as well as daily bread, for recognition as well as cash, for astonishment rather than torpor; in short, for a sort of life rather than a Monday through Friday sort of dying. . . .

There are, of course, the happy few who find a savor in their daily job: the Indiana stonemason, who looks upon his work and sees that it is good; the Chicago piano tuner, who seeks and finds the sound that delights; the bookbinder, who saves a piece of history; the Brooklyn fireman, who saves a piece of life. . . . there is a common attribute here: a meaning to their work well over and beyond the reward of the paycheck.

For the many, there is a hardly concealed discontent. The blue-collar blues is no more bitterly sung than the white-collar moan. "I'm a machine," says the spot-welder. "I'm caged," says the bank teller, and echoes the hotel clerk. "I'm a mule," says the steelworker. "A monkey can do what I do," says the receptionist. "I'm less than a farm implement," says the migrant worker. "I'm an object," says the high-fashion model. . . .

Communiques from the assembly line are frequent and alarming: absenteeism. On the evening bus, the tense, pinched faces of young file clerks and elderly secretaries tell us more than we care to know. On the expressways, middle management men pose without grace behind their wheels as they flee city and job. . . .

In all instances, there is felt more than a slight ache. In all instances, there dangles the impertinent question: Ought not there be an increment, earned though not yet received, from one's daily work—an acknowledgement of man's *being?* . . .

The drones are no longer invisible nor mute. Nor are they exclusively of one class. . . . They're in the office as well as the warehouse; at the manager's desk as well as the assembly line; at some estranged company's computer as well as some estranged woman's kitchen floor. . . .

Reflecting back on his interviews, Terkel continues:

As people talked of their jobs, it was as though it had little to do with their felt lives. It was an alien matter. . . .

To maintain a sense of self, these heroes and heroines [of daily life] play occasional games [on the job]. . . . "just to break the monotony. You want quittin' time so bad."

The waitress, who moves by the tables with the grace of a ballerina, pretends she's forever on stage. . . . The interstate truckdriver, bearing down the expressway with a load of seventy-three thousand pounds, battling pollution, noise, an ulcer, and kidneys that act up, "fantasizes something tremendous." They all, in some manner, perform astonishingly to survive the day. These are not yet automata. . . .

Perhaps [it is the fear of being laid off, fired, and unemployed] that most haunts working men and women: the planned obsolescence of people that is of a piece with the planned obsolescence of the things they make. Or sell. It is perhaps this fear of no longer being needed in a world of needless things that most clearly spells out the unnaturalness . . . of much that is called work today. . . .

That "unnaturalness," of course, is hidden from us in our roles as purchasers and consumers. The terrible labors that go into producing the commodities we unthinkingly purchase and consume are lost in their commodity form. All we see is the final, packaged product. A UAW local officer sees more: "Every time I see an automobile going down the street, I wonder whether the person driving it realizes the kind of human sacrifice that has to go in the building of that car. . . ." The problem is, as one worker said, "Most of us, like the assembly line worker, have jobs that are too small for our spirit. Jobs are not big enough for people" (pp. xi–xxiv).

Most of us, the authors of *Work in America* certainly would agree, are confined in small jobs. The meaninglessness of work causes not only human frustration but human devastation. This becomes clear because the authors of the task force report, in line with their charge from then-Secretary of HEW Elliott Richardson, examine not only work itself, but also "health, education and welfare problems from the perspective of . . . work" (p. xi). In consequence they not only confirm the existence of the brutal reality that constitutes working for capitalism—though they do not blame capitalism as such. They also make clear that this reality has wide-ranging, very destructive effects on society at large.

WHAT WORK IS LIKE

The facts of the profound impact of work on life apparently startled even Secretary Richardson, who, after reading the report, wrote: "one cannot help but feel that however deeply we have cared in the past, we never really understood the importance, the meaning, and the reach of work" (p. vii). The institution of work, the authors do understand, can be employed like a searchlight to illuminate the quality of and interrelationships among other parts of daily life. We are reminded, for example, that work can enhance or demean life. Work can contribute "to identity and self-esteem" and can be useful "in bringing order and meaning to life. Work [can offer] . . . economic self-sufficiency, status, family stability, and an opportunity to interact with others in one of the most basic activities of society" (p. xv).

But precisely because of its centrality, the authors continue,

if the opportunity to work is absent or if the nature of work is dissatisfying (or worse), severe repercussions are likely to be experienced in other parts of the social system (p. xv). . . .

as work problems increase, there may be a consequent decline in physical and mental health, family stability, community participation and cohesiveness, and "balanced" sociopolitical attitudes, while there is an increase in drug and alcohol addiction, aggression, and delinquency (p. xvi).

In fact, *Work in America* shows, our work variously disables and literally kills us. And, expectably in our capitalist system, "workers and society are bearing . . . costs that have their genesis in the workplace" (p. xvii). Attention increasingly has been directed to these costs, in large part because of the many overt expressions by workers in the late 1960s and the early 1970s of discontent with their jobs and lives. During these years, notwithstanding the ballyhooed material well-being of the hypothetical "average worker," flesh-and-blood workers by the millions repeatedly demonstrated their dissatisfactions in a flood of strikes, absenteeism, sabotage, and higher turnover rates. In the face of all this, people wanted to know what is wrong.

The HEW report's answer is that the primary source of the problem lies in what our jobs have become—reduced in content and scope. This low "intrinsic" quality of jobs means that their performance cannot afford workers a sense of challenge, responsibility, and accomplishment. "Intrinsic" factors, the authors conclude, are the primary causes of worker discontent; so-called "extrinsic" factors, like wages, are secondary.

In support of this conclusion the report cites the results of a study of over 1,500 American workers at all occupational levels in which workers were asked to rank 25 aspects of work in order of importance to them. Workers, as one might expect from my Blancs case study, ranked their most important conscious concerns as follows:

1. Interesting work
2. Enough help and equipment to get the job done
3. Enough information to get the job done
4. Enough authority to get the job done
5. Good pay
6. Opportunity to develop special abilities
7. Job security
8. Seeing the results of one's work (p. 13).

Summarizing the findings of that study, the HEW task force reports:

What workers want most, as more than 100 studies in the past 20 years show, is to become masters of their immediate environments and to feel that their work and they themselves are important. . . . the most oppressive features of work are felt to be avoidable: constant supervision and coercion, lack of variety, monotony, meaningless tasks, and isolation (p. 13).

As it is, the "boring, dehumanized and authoritarian work" that workers are disciplined to perform is done at "some cost to their psychological well-being." That cost can be very high: "Anger that does not erupt may be frozen into schizoid depressed characters who escape into general alienation, drugs, and fantasies" (p. 22). The "alienation," so widespread today among our workers, is characterized by feelings of

1) powerlessness (regarding ownership of the enterprise, general management policies, employment conditions and the immediate work process); 2) meaninglessness (with respect to the character of the product . . . or the production process); 3) isolation (the social aspect of work); and 4) self-estrangement (p. 22).

WHAT WORK IS LIKE

Such feelings, as Karl Marx recognized more than a century ago,* actually reflect what capitalist relations of production have done to work and workers. Workers feel powerless because under capitalism they are alienated from the ownership of the means of production and therefore do not have control over the basic decisions that shape their lives. Their jobs, they understandably feel, are meaningless, because most have been designed to achieve meaning almost exclusively in capitalist not human terms—a meaning that can be expressed fully in corporate income statements and balance sheets. Workers feel isolated because they are made to compete and because technology has not been designed to emphasize cooperation. And they feel estranged from themselves in no small part because they are not allowed to express themselves in their work.

If these are the problems, how widespread are they? According to *Work in America*, extremely. In addition to the relatively small number of what the task force calls the "classically alienating jobs," like assembly-line jobs "that allow the worker no control . . . and seriously affect his mental and physical functioning off the job," most of the remaining 98 percent of jobs in the United States also appear to be very "alienating" (p. 13). Regarding them, the task force estimates by one quite sophisticated measure that a substantial majority of all white-collar workers are dissatisfied, as are three out of four of all blue-collar workers (p. 15).

What condemning the majority of our workers to very unsatisfying jobs for a lifetime means in human terms is forcefully brought out in the task force's discussion of work and health. The discussion shows that our work is unhealthy for human beings. The general argument is that the quality of public health is closely and directly related to the quality of work.

Too often, the authors write, we have oversimplified issues of public health: "health and medical care are not synonymous. . . . Improvements in work hold out opportunities for *avoiding* physical and mental illness. . . ." (p. 76). The truth of this general argument

* Karl Marx, *Economic and Philosophic Manuscripts of 1844*, in Robert C. Tucker, ed., *The Marx-Engels Reader* (New York: Norton, 1972), pp. 56–67; and see Bertell Ollman, *Alienation* (Cambridge, England: Cambridge University Press, 1971).

SIX BOOKS CONSIDERED

becomes undeniable in face of the overwhelming array of evidence the task force marshals to support the propositions that unsatisfying work substantially contributes to poor public health and, conversely, satisfying work substantially contributes to good public health. Job satisfaction, the authors indicate, is

one of the best ways of extending the length of life [because]. . . . work role [and] work conditions. . . . [affect our feelings, and] feelings are the primary . . . [determinants] of behavior and a major influence in health and sickness (p. 79). . . .

In an impressive 15-year study of aging, the strongest predictor of longevity was work satisfaction (p. 77).

More specifically, heart disease and poor mental health often are related to job problems. Much of the risk of heart disease—the cause of about half of all deaths in the United States—is accounted for by socio-psychological factors. Prominent among the factors associated with a high risk of heart disease are "job dissatisfaction," "occupational stress," "excessively rapid and continous change in employment," "certain personality characteristics" that can be affected by jobs, "low self-esteem," and "lack of stability, security, and support in the job environment" (pp. 79–81). In addition, "a variety of mental health problems have been related to the absence of job satisfaction. . . . workers in low-skilled and unskilled jobs," for example, "have poorer mental health than do workers in skilled jobs." Workers in low-level jobs "adapt by limiting their aspirations and their expectations . . . [which in turn leads to] a lack of involvement in the job and, consequently, a lack of self-fulfillment" (p. 82).

From a classic, 25-year-old study of industrial workers, Arthur Kornhauser is cited as having made the following important findings, which subsequent experience and research have broadly confirmed:

Work was the most central measurable instituion in the lives of workers, above family, leisure, and social activities, but only 25 percent of the workers would choose the same kind of job if they had to do it again.

Feelings of helplessness, withdrawl, alienation and pessimism were widespread. . . .

Workers with lowest mental health and job satisfaction scores were often escapist or passive in their non-work activities: they watched television; did not vote; and did not participate in community organizations (p. 83).

WHAT WORK IS LIKE

From all this evidence, the authors of *Work in America* correctly conclude that workers who have not adjusted to their work environments may well be healthier mentally than those who have:

Where mobility is blocked, where jobs are dehumanized, where rewards are slight, failing to strive hard at the job can hardly be a criterion of mental illness. Madness may lie in adjusting to the pathologies of organizations. A person who becomes a automaton in an automated factory or office may have adjusted perfectly, but he hardly enjoys good mental health (p. 84).

To illustrate, they continue,

In . . . [a] study of women employed by the Bell Telephone Company, those who were considered to be "healthy," by such measures as compliance with job demands, days absent from work, and the ratings of company psychiatrists, were often unmarried, lived routine, dull, and withdrawn existences, and refused to get involved with other people (p. 85).

The words and routine on-the-job conduct of workers who have thus "adjusted" and may therefore describe themselves as "satisfied" with their unchallenging, mindless, trivial, and monotonous work cannot be taken at face value. Their very adjustment and declaration of satisfaction must be appreciated as part of a destructive circularity, in which people who cannot get what they need as human beings are ground down and socialized to consciously want only what they can get. Such adjustments are poignant evidence of unremitting societal failure.* For, as Kornhauser penetratingly wrote, "The unsatisfactory mental health of working people consists in no small measure of their dwarfed desires and deadened initiative, reduction of their goals, and restriction of their efforts to a point where life is [at best] relatively empty and only half meaningful" (quoted at p. 85).

Of course, workers do have a choice. They need not adjust to capitalist work; they can instead freely choose not to adjust. But what does choice itself mean if, as the task force recognizes, most workers have only these "two options: to maintain high expectations from

---

* These "adjustments" are also very fragile. For a moving discussion and dramatic example of the error of taking what may appear to be working class apathy at face value, see André Gorz, "Workers' Control Is More Than Just That," in Gerry Hunnius et al., eds., *Workers' Control: A Reader on Labor and Social Change* (New York: Vintage Paperbacks, 1973), pp. 325–43.

SIX BOOKS CONSIDERED

work, and thereby suffer constant frustration, or to limit their expectations, which produces a drab existence" (p. 85). Such choice is not meaningful. It is a choice between destructive alternatives. Either way, workers lose.

WHAT WORK IS LIKE

XIII

The Whys of Work and What To Do about It

BY now it should be as unnecessary as it is easy to accumulate further evidence that this is what work in the United States generally is like. There really is not much serious disagreement on the matter. The crucial question is *why* most work is so dehumanized, authoritarian, boring, etc. On the answer to this question, by contrast, there is serious disagreement. Garson puts the blame squarely on capitalism; Terkel is difficult to pin down; and the authors of *Work in America* primarily blame a particular form of business management called Taylorism (see chap. 14).

Garson's analysis is quite summary and straightforward. The main cause of worker dissatisfaction is the capitalist division of labor, which for three basic capitalist reasons has been extended beyond all human reason. Capitalism needs: to control workers in production; to replace skilled workers with unskilled in order to reduce labor costs; and to create workers likely to be docile because they are aware of their easy replaceability and therefore of their deep dependence.

As a consequence of this inhuman division of labor, a vicious circle has been built into capitalist production. Because the purpose of production is to produce profits for the few, jobs for the many are designed primarily to achieve that goal. Because the resulting quality of work life alienates workers, a variety of devices are needed and developed to facilitate supervision and control. These devices, which include an extreme division of labor (of which the Vega plant is only one example) further alienate workers and require in turn either additional supervisory mechanisms or a more human redesign of jobs. Additional supervision, however, only compounds the problem. And the scope for a meaningful redesign of the job is extremely limited, since the purpose of production remains the production of profit for the few.

The limits on job redesign are set, to put it another way, by the irreducible and strong, if usually muted, element of *class conflict* within the workplace:

The sociologists may not believe in it, the labor unions may not believe in it, and the workers may not believe in it either. But large corporations know that they are there to squeeze as much as they can out of workers for as little as possible. They assume that the worker, in return, would like to give the company as little as possible (pp. 142–43).

The underlying assumption, firmly grounded in reality, upon which jobs are designed, therefore, is "class war."

Reforms in the quality of work under capitalism generally occur only when workers compel them, either through positive struggle or through a kind of negative resistance to the extreme division of labor, which persuades the company that certain reforms will protect or improve its profits. Regarding the potential of typical liberal reform, Garson is appropriately skeptical:

At the point where the costs of absenteeism, errors, sabotage, industrial accidents, and crack-ups exceed the benefit of streamlining, at that point, large companies start making small plans for job enrichment.

The purpose is not to make jobs pleasant but merely to roll back to the stage where they are do-able. . . . When the company plans it people always suspect that they are being used—which they are. Almost every experiment with enrichment succeeds at first because of the novelty, the change of pace. But eventually the new pace becomes the mandatory norm. The workers begin to feel that it's just another gimmick to increase productivity—which it always is.

The ultimate goal is still profit, and the job is still as narrowly defined, as rationalized as the company can profitably make it (pp. 143–44).

So workers are used and must be abused by our system. But management, Garson concludes, also is caught long-term in a serious bind.

THE WHYS OF WORK

The problem for management is that they must simultaneously suppress and yet rely upon human judgment. They need human beings and yet they fear human beings. They respond to that fear with an intensified division of labor and increasingly costly supervision. In the end they create jobs that are [still] far too complex for robots, but, on the other hand, far too regimented for chimpanzees. So they are stuck using human beings. That's always a danger. For . . . [capitalism] there is no final solution, only more and more costly controls. Eternal vigilance is the price of taking away other people's liberty (p. 219).

Whether Terkel would agree basically with Garson's analysis is almost impossible to say with any surety from his book. Although he effectively transmits the words of people "not often heard from" describing what work is like, he does little to provide more than elusive and at times seemingly contradictory hints as to why he believes it to be so. This failure to explain, coming from one as sympathetic and thoughtful as Terkel, is especially glaring because the more moving are the book's dismal accounts of worklife, the more the question of "why" cries out in the concerned reader's mind. On this important question Terkel's introduction—the only place in his 600-plus-page volume where he overtly provides his own insights into work—is a study in indirection.

According to one reading, Terkel seems to ascribe the main sources of the workers' lot to a variety of factors other than capitalism itself. Thus it may be that most work "by its very nature" does violence to body and spirit (p. xi). Or the culprit may be "the automated pace" of our technology, which produces a workplace that is "impersonal in nature" (p. xxiii) and wipes out "name and face . . . and . . . feeling" (p. xii), or the "perverted 'work ethic' " (p. xxiii), which makes us feel that "No matter how demeaning the task, no matter how it dulls the senses and breaks the spirit, one *must* work" (p. xii). Or is it simply the "smug respectability" and "obtuseness" in " 're-spectable' quarters" to the "wretched truth of . . . [the workers'] lot" (p. xiii) that is responsible? Or perhaps the absence of a sense of purpose on the part of workers in most jobs, which thereby denies workers their "secure place in a portion of reality, in the human community" (p. xvi)? Or the fear of being "unemployed" (p. xvii); or of being "no longer needed" (p. xviii)?

SIX BOOKS CONSIDERED

But if it is any or all of these factors, we must ask Terkel why these factors exist, and how they relate to each other. Why has our work ethic been "perverted"? Why the pace that makes our jobs "impersonal"? Why are tasks so demeaning? Why are "the respectable" "obtuse"? *Are* they "obtuse"? Or are they basically possessed of conflicting interests, which mold their experience and world view? And so on. On these matters Terkel seems to be of little systematic help.

Yet following another reading, we may interpret Terkel's Introduction at least as indirectly pointing, clue by clue, toward capitalism as the primary source of these and other work- and life-related problems. The demeaning emphasis in production on quantity rather than quality he says, is part of the emphasis on "Gross National Product" (p. xii), which may be Terkel's euphemism for "profits." The "wretched truth of . . . [the workers' present] lot" still leaves for the future some vague and unnamed "possibilities of another way, discerned by only a few before . . . , thought of—if only for a brief moment . . .—by many today" (p. xiii). Could that be socialism? Regarding his own former job reading otherwise worthless radio scripts, it took Terkel's exposure to "The sales charts of [the program's sponsors] Proctor & Gamble and General Mills . . . [to finally make it] quite clear" to him that what he was doing "really [was] work" (p. xvi). Work, so understood, is capitalist work: it is an activity that is not satisfying, is otherwise purposeless, and is done for someone else's profit, in return only for wages.

Workers are haunted by the "specter" of unemployment. This "planned obsolescence of people," Terkel reminds us, is "of a piece with the planned obsolescence of the things they make. . . . Or sell." And the "fear of no longer being needed" exists "in a world of needless things that most clearly spells out the unnaturalness . . . of much that is called work today" (p. xviii). Hence, dehumanized work, the production of worthless things, and the treating of workers like commodities to be bought, sold, and phased out as the system requires are all interrelated. And if Terkel does not tell us what that "system" is, he does seem to agree "the system stinks" (p. xxii). He recognizes, too, that a worker's "respectability" in our society has no necessary relation to the social worth of the jobs he performs (p. xvii),

THE WHYS OF WORK

perhaps a hint of the class nature of job "respectability." Terkel is aware as well not only that "the system" is basically at fault, but also that it is hard to get at—"Who you gonna sock?" (p. xxiii). He knows too that the feelings generated in workers of helplessness and purposelessness are an integral part of the system's aggressive defense mechanisms: "Thus the 'dumbness' (or numbness or tiredness) of both [the working and middle] classes is encouraged and exploited in a society more conspicuously manipulative than Orwell's [totalitarian vision]" (p. xxiii).

But, on any reading, that is as far as Terkel goes. In the end we must be satisfied with his evocative, elusive points, because in the final analysis Terkel refuses to make a final analysis. Refuses, I say, because it is hard to believe he does not know that capitalism *is* the problem.

If he does know, and if Americans, as I believe, desperately need to understand that capitalism is their problem, then Terkel's decision not to pursue the connection has serious political implications. The issue is how best to facilitate understanding in an American public that for decade upon decade has been propagandized and indoctrinated by a system that self-protectively has sought to prevent understanding. In this historical context indirection will not do. Most of Terkel's readers, I fear, will not conclude, as he might wish, that what they are reading about is capitalist work. Instead, they are more likely to think they are reading about work as it must be, or work under a "perverted work ethic," or work diminished by the "impersonality" and "pace" of modern technology and modern organization.

In that case, what Terkel primarily has done is to provide in easily accessible form some immensely important raw material about work. Persuading Americans how that material must be understood and beginning to demonstrate that what our daily lives reflect is a many-faced but single, integrated, and oppressive capitalist system are tasks left to others.

These tasks, needless to say, are not the ones the authors of *Work in America* have taken up. On the contrary, although they seem to recognize much of the reality that today constitutes working

SIX BOOKS CONSIDERED

for capitalism, the report's authors overtly disassociate the objective factors allegedly causing that reality from the abiding nature of capitalism itself. More than that, they treat these very factors as having become counterproductive in capitalist terms. Consequently, according to them, not only *can* our workplaces be meaningfully reformed; they *must* be so reformed. Reform is necessary, of course, to make work more humane, but also, conveniently, to eliminate practices that, if they once admittedly contributed to the capitalist drive for higher profits, now are said to interfere with that core pursuit. The authors of the report thus present us with the standard liberal argument—*that meaningful reform can and must be carried out, and that it will benefit everyone, workers and capitalists alike.*

To accomplish the initial disassociation of capitalism from the causes of workplace problems, the report primarily attributes the objective causes of the oppressive quality of work life to two interrelated developments: the dominant school of "scientific management" known as Taylorism, which has dehumanized jobs; and the so-called "industrial efficiency model" of measuring business success. These developments are treated by the task force as somehow not intrinsic, or any longer necessary to the preservation of capitalism. The source of the objective problem therefore is not capitalism as such, but these practices, which indisputably were developed as central aspects of the capitalist system but allegedly now can be reformed away to produce a "humanistic capitalism" (p. 23).

If objectively worker dissatisfaction is a byproduct of the effects on jobs and work life caused by Taylorism and the industrial efficiency model, subjectively dissatisfaction is a result of the rising, unrealized expectations of workers for fulfillment at work and of workers' frustrations with the failure of the traditional American Dream of independence. Hoping to become their own masters, workers have found themselves instead in fragmented, extremely dependent work situations. And the problem is getting worse, not better: "Taylorism and a misplaced conception of efficiency is . . . [no longer] restricted to assembly-lines or [even] . . . to the manufacturing sector. . . . The service sector [, which now is the main source of jobs in the United States, also] is not exempt" (p. 19).

THE WHYS OF WORK

In most service businesses the spurt in employment has occurred in lower-level jobs, which have been streamlined to neither demand nor allow for the development or exercise of much autonomy or skill. While this may result in greater "efficiency" in the immediate narrowest sense, it also "increases routinization, and opens the door to job dissatisfaction for a new generation of highly educated workers" (p. 19).

As fewer and fewer people are self-employed and more and more jobs in our country have come under the "domination of large corporations and government" (p. 21), workers increasingly have been subjected to the demands of Taylorism and the industrial efficiency model. These demands have been reinforced by the concurrent demands of large-scale bureaucratic organization—which, like Taylorism, industrial efficiency, and machine technology, is understood by the task force wholly independently from capitalism:

large corporations and bureaucracies . . . typically organize work in such a way as to minimize the independence of . . . workers and maximize control and predictability for the organization. Characterologically, the hierarchical organization requires workers to follow orders, which calls for submissive traits [in workers], while the selection of managers calls for authoritarian and controlling traits.

With the shift from manufacturing to services [as the major employer of workers]. . . . the tyranny of the machine is perhaps being replaced by the tyranny of the bureaucracy (pp. 21–22).

This degeneration of work need not continue, the report's authors declare. For them, all things seem possible within the capitalist system. Jobs can be redesigned to be satisfying; enough jobs can be provided to put our people to work; and in the process other societal needs can thereby be met. Capitalism does not require bad jobs, authoritarianism, unemployment, or a poorly served public. Quite the opposite. Meaningfully redesigned jobs can improve workers' lives fundamentally and

give, for the first time, a voice to many workers in an important decision-making process [within the workplace, from which they are presently excluded]. Citizen participation in . . . [that] arena where the individual's voice directly affects his immediate environment [in turn] may do much to reduce political alienation in America (p. xviii).

SIX BOOKS CONSIDERED

And happily a "vigorous job creation policy"—necessary because "the first . . . element in job satisfaction is to have a job"—can be planned so as to accomplish "the many things that patently need doing in our society, but [for some unexplained reason] are not being done" (pp. xviii–xix).

But if our work-related problems are so widespread and destructive, have been recognized for decades, and are curable through reform, why have we allowed them to persist and even worsen? The task force's lame answer is that the current, allegedly outdated quality of Taylorism is of recent vintage. Before that Taylorism served capitalists' interests very effectively, whatever its costs to workers. It

propagated a view of efficiency which, until recently, was markedly successful—so long as "success" was measured [exclusively] in terms of [a firm's] unit costs and output. Under . . . [Taylor's] tutelage, work tasks were greatly simplified, fragmented, compartmentalized, and placed under continuous supervision. The worker's rewards depended on doing as he was told and increasing his output. Taylor's advice resulted in major, sometimes spectacular, increases in productivity (pp. 17–18).

Fortunately for all concerned, Taylorism today has outlasted its utility because of the rising quality of the workforce, which is said to be better educated, less traditionally deferential to authority, and more demanding of job satisfaction than before. Taylorism therefore must be discarded. Efforts over the decades to humanize Taylorism, the authors recognize, have not dealt with the heart of the problem. The task force concludes, therefore, that it "is necessary to consider both the social needs of the workers and the task to be performed" (pp. 18–19). This perspective, its authors declare, "challenges much of what passes as efficiency in our industrial society" (p. 19). Perhaps.

The challenge has two quite different aspects. In its first aspect the "challenge" is wholly consonant with capitalism's "industrial efficiency model." In this respect the challenge merely emphasizes that the human damage and disaffection caused by dissatisfying jobs involves real dollar costs for capitalists: "As the costs of absenteeism, wildcat strikes, turnover, and industrial sabotage became an increasingly significant part of the cost of doing business, it is becoming clear that the current concept of industrial efficiency . . . mistakenly

THE WHYS OF WORK

ignores the social half of the equation" (p. 19). Dissatisfied workers, moreover, do not work up to their potential, so "the human element in productivity" is not being effectively exploited. Workers who are more productive can make more money for capitalists.

In its second aspect, however, the challenge is grounded more clearly in human, not capitalist, terms. For example, the authors point to the high human toll caused by worker alienation. Still, on the face of it, capitalism does not appear to be in conflict with human needs, because capitalism does not seem to be the source of the alienation. Rather, "alienation is inherent in pyramidal, bureaucratic management patterns and in the advanced Taylorized technology, which divides and subdivides work into minute, monotonous elements" (p. 22). And yet, when the task force comes to the matter of "What Can Be Done" (p. 23), it does seem to be talking at least obliquely about capitalism. What it proposes to improve job quality suggests that unreformed capitalism, at least, does conflict with human needs. But, thankfully, capitalism is reformable.

The proposal generally is to make capitalists more responsible for the effects of their supposedly "private" business behavior—in the jargon of the report, to incorporate social efficiency standards increasingly into the industrial efficiency model. The supporting argument is as follows. Since work, health, welfare, family stability, and education are interrelated and "mutually influential," and since work itself plays such "a dominant role" in society, improving the quality of, say, public health in part requires improving the quality of work. Work, therefore, should no longer be so single-mindedly shaped by the pursuit of profits. Other societal concerns increasingly have to be taken into account, and often given precedence. Hence, "the responsibilities of employers . . . have to be greatly changed." The existing, predominantly "narrow interest of producing goods and services" must be subordinated to "the broader interest of relating that production to other social concerns" (p. 23).

What we are talking about (the authors obscure by indirection, the use of euphemisms, and the use of such terminology as "industrial efficiency," "social efficiency," "externalities," "diseconomies," and the like) *is capitalism*. The effective focus is social production under private ownership for private profit. The task force, arguing that we must increasingly emphasize concern for social efficiency, judiciously describes the alternatives this way:

"Industrial efficiency" is . . . defined in its usual economic sense: the goal of an enterprise is to obtain the maximum output at a given level of costs (or a given level of output at a minimum cost). In optimizing costs and outputs, all substitutions ("trade-offs") are internal to the operation of the enterprise. Labor and capital . . . are substituted for one another to achieve efficiency for the firm, without regard to [so-called] external effects.

"Social efficiency" draws on the economic notion of "externalities," which recognizes that the production of goods or services by a firm may result in costs or benefits that occur in society and which are not accounted for in the internal audit of any firm or all firms together. If the externalities are "diseconomies," the firm may be industrially efficient but socially inefficient. If the externalities result in social "economies," the firm may not be industrially efficient even though it is socially efficient. The social efficiency concept includes a variety of [economic and] non-economic costs, such as the costs of social and political alienation (p. 24).

Behind this protective jargon and distinction lies a potentially vital point, because the difference between "industrial efficiency" and "social efficiency," if I am correct, ultimately is related to the difference between capitalism and socialism. Although under capitalism the matter of social needs and social efficiency cannot totally be ignored and under socialism the matter of industrial efficiency also is of concern, priorities in the two systems tend to be radically different. Under capitalism industrial efficiency standards are dominant and ideologically presumed, incorrectly, to best serve social needs. These standards in fact have been adjusted in the direction of satisfying real social needs only in the face of social conflict, which gave capitalists little choice. Under socialism, by contrast, the dominant standard is satisfying social needs, and industrial efficiency standards increasingly are to be subordinated to that task.

In suggesting greater emphasis on social efficiency in business accounting, the task force, of course, does not intend a revolutionary change in our social system. Rather its members seem to be proposing only another step away from crude capitalism toward "welfare" capitalism. But then it remains to be seen whether, aside from tem-

THE WHYS OF WORK

porarily appeasing workers, such movement toward "responsible capitalism" would fundamentally improve the quality of work life. I doubt it. And it also remains to be seen whether in any event capitalists would be willing to so move.

In this regard, the authors hope to achieve a meaningfully increased "sense of corporate responsibility" through the "internalization" of societal costs and benefits in corporate accounting and decisionmaking. But they recognize that the progress in this direction that has been achieved to date has been utterly inadequate. In the area of occupational health and safety, for example, the money paid out by employers in insurance premiums for Workman's Compensation coverage for employees "represents some 'internalization' of the social disadvantages of hazardous employment but only a small portion . . . , obviously, not enough" (p. 26). The gross inadequacy of the sense of corporate responsibility in this area is reflected, the authors continue,

not only . . . in the small amount of compensation relative to earning capacity, but also in the increasing injury-frequency rate, the rising average days of disability per case, and the increasing severity rate, which has been the lot of a majority of occupations. . . .

If the social diseconomies of hazardous employment were fully internalized by industry, one would expect the injury and disease rates to decline, on the assumption that it would be worthwhile [in capitalist terms] to reduce the contribution of this factor to industrial inefficiency (p. 26).

Of course, if I am correct, with the full "internalization" of such human and societal costs, we no longer would have capitalism. The industrial efficiency model would then have fully incorporated social efficiency standards. Capitalists historically, we know, have fiercely resisted just such "internalization." Their so-called "failure" to adequately protect workers and the rest of society is hardly the product of inadvertence. It pays capitalists handsomely, by holding down their own costs, even as that "failure" also "results in deaths, ruined lives, medical costs, public assistance, and other costs borne by individuals and society, not by industry" (p. 26). The point is that capitalists in their role as capitalists are not concerned with broader questions of humanity.

SIX BOOKS CONSIDERED

Therefore, if one does not wish to challenge the destructive system itself, one must convince its ruling class that reform will pay. To make their proposals more palatable and attractive to the capitalists who decide such matters, the task force provides examples of progressive capitalists and businesses that have seen the light and are profiting in its illumination. These are the exemplary few.

The centerpiece of the task force's reform proposal is job redesign, which boils down to redesigning the technology of jobs to make them more challenging, less fragmented, and more various; increasing the collective identification and "autonomy" of workers organized in production groups; rationalizing job classifications; minimizing status differences among classifications; and reducing supervisory control, while increasing "facilitative leadership." Redesign entails increasing worker participation in a limited but not insignificant range of decisions that obviously and immediately affect their jobs—decisions concerning a working group's specific production methods, internal distribution of tasks, work hours, leadership, and the like.

In support of their proposal, the authors predictably argue its feasibility from a mere handful of experiments in work redesign, nearly all of which have been "confined . . . to small work groups" (p. 96) rather than extended to entire plants or corporations. These few, limited experiments are taken by the task force to show that "not only can work be redesigned to make it more satisfying but . . . significant increases in productivity can also be obtained. In other words, workers can be healthier, happier in their work, and better contributors to family and community life than they are now, without a loss of goods and services and without inflating prices" (p. 94). How reassuring! Our glaring work problems do not involve conflicting and ultimately irreconcilable class interests. On the contrary, capitalists and workers, with some help from the government, need merely be educated concerning their real interests to enable reform to set things right.

Only one small, nagging doubt remains. It is a doubt the report's authors candidly recognize, but do not and cannot resolve:

If the advantages of redesigning work are as compelling [for all concerned parties] as the examples used here suggest, what need is there to advocate it

THE WHYS OF WORK

or, for that matter, write about it? Why not simply get out of the way to avoid being crushed in the stampede? The answer is, of course, "it isn't as easy as it looks" (p. 111).

Some such answer, "of course," is demanded, because the fact is that, to say the least, "job redesign techniques . . . have not been used on a wide scale" (p. 91). According to quoted statistics, only "some 3,000 American workers [in total ever] have been involved in [the sorts of apparently meaningful] *extensive* redesign efforts" the authors propose (p. 103). This means, even if one assumes that all 3,000 still were involved at the time in the efforts, that less than .01 percent of our workforce was enjoying the fruits of what the authors propose for most of the rest. Indeed, such job redesign under capitalism must not be quite "as easy as it looks."

Why, then, in the eyes of the task force, has job redesign been so rare? Why has there been what the authors in a monumental understatement characterize as a "reluctance of employers to move swiftly" (p. 111) in this direction? The task force's direct answers to this crucial question are so transparently superficial and unsatisfactory that rather than convincing the reader, the answers only raise doubts about the nature of the report's analysis.

First, the task force says, there have been all those "personnel theories, administrative panaceas . . . , and consultants" that have failed. These failures and "the bad experiences of employers in the past have led them to ask: whom can I trust?" Poor GM! Poor U.S. Steel! Poor Exxon! Poor big business, which has striven so mightily to make jobs satisfying only to meet with repeated frustration and a consequent loss of faith. Second: "Some employers . . . simply do not know how . . . to redesign work themselves" (p. 111). But haven't employers generally managed somehow to learn what they wanted to learn in other realms to achieve their own purposes? Why not here? Third and related, some employers lack "experimental information" concerning firms similar to their own and hesitate to redesign jobs before having "directly applicable information." But, again, if capitalists truly believed job redesign would enhance profits, why would they not collectively and individually generate the neces-

SIX BOOKS CONSIDERED

sary information and take the needed risks? Or why would they not at least influence their government to do it for them—as they have in so many other areas? Fourth: "Some employers may be willing . . . [to redesign jobs] but lack risk capital for transitional costs. . . . [which], In the short-run, . . . may not be trivial" (p. 111). Doubtless so, but businessmen historically have been willing to risk capital when and where they believed it would pay them. That they have not done so for job redesign presumably reflects their continuing determination that it is not worth the risk. And finally: "In some industries there is opposition from trade unions to the notion of job redesign" (p. 111–12). Yes; but why? Why should trade unions so frequently oppose or soft-soap transformations that promise to make jobs more satisfying and workers more active? To ask the question is to answer it. Generally, unions, like capitalists, do not want to encourage higher levels of meaningful worker involvement and participation.

If the reader is not persuaded by the task force's explanation, neither it seems is the task force itself. For, after having more or less perfunctorily recited these reasons for business' and unions' opposition to job redesign, the task force then gets to "the bottom line." "The bottom line" is capitalism:

we recognize, in the final analysis, that the reluctance of employers to act will never be overcome by arguments based simply on improving the welfare of workers. Employers for the most part see their responsibility in terms of profits. . . . It is imperative, then, that employers be made aware of the fact that thorough efforts to redesign work . . . have resulted in increases in productivity (p. 112; certain emphasis deleted).

Consequently, the primary task of these reformers of capitalism is the usual one: to convince capitalists that reform pays. This is the only way to move capitalists to adopt substantial reforms not already effectively demanded by organized workers, even when such reform is necessary and fundamental for the public good. Job redesign, the task force argues, indeed is fundamental to our very democratic way of life. Increases in worker participation will give workers the feeling of being able "to control the aspects of work intimately affecting their lives" and thereby will help resolve a largely unexplored "contra-

THE WHYS OF WORK

diction in our Nation—between democracy in society and authoritarianism in the workplace" (p. 104). To expand "democracy," however, we must first convince our capitalists it will be profitable.

But even if it were true that job redesign would prove to be profitable, to what sort of a resolution of this "contradiction . . . between democracy . . . and authoritarianism" might its implementation lead? And if we now know something of the nature of "authoritarianism in the workplace," what in fact is the nature of "democracy in society"? Without pausing to consider this latter question, the task force does indicate by understatement its answer to the former. Its sought-after reduction of authoritarianism in the workplace would hardly produce "democracy" in the sense of majority control: "Not all of a company's decisions, of course, are turned over to the workers when they participate in management. Upper-level managers continue to run the company" (p. 104).

With such "democratization" of the workplace, the suspicion arises that, though the forms might be changed, the essence of capitalist dictatorship would be maintained. One suspects, further, that the "contradiction" the authors conceive is not really between dictatorship and democracy but rather between what I would call two forms of dictatorship—liberal and illiberal. Their proposal is only to further liberalize the workplace, which certainly would help to bring the form of workplace governance more into line with the form of societal governance. In both realms liberal institutions then would not only moderate and somewhat defuse, but also legitimate and disguise a marvelously complex class dictatorship.

Liberal reform does not and cannot alter the essence of the capitalist class dictatorship. It can only "liberalize" it. Whatever reformers intend, the objective foundation of liberal reform is the acceptance of capitalism. And capitalism sets severe limits on what we are and what we can become. We therefore must come to understand what capitalism is and the limits on reform it imposes.

SIX BOOKS CONSIDERED

XIV

Work and Advanced Capitalism:
The Objective World

TO fully appreciate American capitalism today, we must understand its essential history. Capitalism *is* what it has become as a matured, if still dynamic, "mode of production." To understand its essential history, we must use a framework of analysis capable of exposing that history—a framework radically different from those that prevail within our capitalist system. For our system, like all social systems, seeks to hide, not expose, its essence. The framework I have found most useful is Marxian.

But one cannot simply pick up Marxian analysis and begin to use it as one might pick up a shovel and begin to shovel. It has taken us years to learn, consciously and unconsciously, how to exist and think in a liberal-capitalist society, and it will require considerable time and effort for us to learn to use, apply, and develop a Marxian alternative appropriate to our particular circumstances. Alternative frameworks involve ways of thinking, theories, language usages, and terms that of necessity are as strange to us as are their world views. Our lifetime socialization into our present mode of being and thinking means that a radically different mode will appear at the outset to the uninitiated as alien, even confused and confusing. We must try to make sense of it, as we try to make sense of our own experience.

There is, unfortunately, no easy place to begin this struggle to understand. Understanding every aspect of the alternative framework presupposes understanding the whole, just as understanding the whole presupposes understanding its aspects. Forgetting this, all too often we may apply our own mode of understanding to Marxian language and theory, which conveniently makes of them non-sense.

Take, for example, the term "mode of production." To us that phrase might be understood to refer to the characteristic ways things are physically produced in a society—say, in its factories. The capitalist "mode of production," then, would refer to the distinctly capitalist ways in which things are produced in capitalist units of production. This, surely, is a reasonable interpretation, but it is too narrow, nonetheless. In Marxian analysis the term "mode of production" also generally refers more broadly to the entire interlocking social system of organized production, distribution, and consumption and to its necessary social relations and states of consciousness. The capitalist mode of production, then, involves everything in our society necessary to maintain and reproduce capitalism, which probably includes the sorts of families we live in, the kinds of mass media, education, and government we are subjected to, as well as the kinds of production units we work in.* The narrower interpretation of the single term makes Marx into an economic determinist and a mechanical materialist, which he is not; the correct interpretation allows him to be what he is—a historical materialist who understands the world dialectically.

Some appreciation of these difficulties in approaching Marxian analysis is vital for reading this chapter, which is based on the first half of Harry Braverman's marvelous book, *Labor and Monopoly Capital*. Braverman goes to the heart of capitalism by focusing upon the development of the crucial and distinctively capitalist relationship in production—the relationship between capitalists and wage workers—and upon its effects on the labor process and on our working class. The essence of this relationship, the purchase and sale of human labor, is the means by which the capitalist system achieves its basic purposes, the generation of profit for the owners of the means of production.

Although the purchase and sale of labor predate the develop-

* With regard to education see Samuel Bowles and Herbert Gintis, *Schooling in Capitalist America* (New York: Basic Books, 1976).

SIX BOOKS CONSIDERED

ment of capitalism, wage workers did not become a "numerically significant [class] until the rise of industrial capitalism." And they did not constitute the "numerically dominant form" of labor in any country until well into the nineteenth century. In the United States, for example, wage workers constituted no more than one-fifth of the population as late as the early nineteenth century; by 1870 they had increased to about two-thirds; by 1940 to about four-fifths; by 1970 wage workers constituted approximately nine-tenths of the population (Braverman, pp. 52–53). Wage labor, in short, became the dominant form of production relationship as industrial capitalism became the dominant form of production, and "The rapidity with which [that relationship] . . . won supremacy . . . emphasizes the extraordinary power of the tendency of capitalist economies to convert all other forms of labor into hired labor" (p. 53).

In the capitalist context, workers increasingly became wage workers because they effectively had no other way to make a living. Capitalists, on the other side, increasingly hired workers with part of their capital because they had no other way than through the labor process to generate the surplus that is the basis for profit and to thereby enlarge their capital.

Since the power to labor is an inalienable part of all humans, the capitalist buys not that capacity itself, nor even "an agreed amount of labor, but the power to labor over an agreed period of time" (emphasis deleted). As the owner of the use of that labor power, the capitalist is as well the owner of labor's products (p. 54). The value of these products can and normally does exceed the necessary cost of hiring the worker, because humans can produce by their labor more than they need to be paid for purposes of maintaining and reproducing themselves.

As the capitalist seeks through a variety of means to enlarge and extract the surplus from others' labor, the adaptability and indeterminacy of human labor power confronts the capitalist as a crucial dilemma:

in purchasing labor power that can do much, he is at the same time purchasing an undefined quality and quantity. What he buys is infinite in *potential*, but in its *realization* it is limited by the subjective state of the work-

WORK AND ADVANCED CAPITALISM

ers, by their previous history. . . . and [by] many other factors, including the organization of the [labor] process and the forms of supervision over it. . . . Having been forced to sell their labor power to another, the workers also surrender their interest in the labor process, which has now been "alienated." . . . In this setting of antagonistic relations of production, the problem of realizing the "full usefulness" of the labor power he has bought becomes exacerbated by the opposing interests of those for whose purposes the labor process is carried on, and those who, on the other side, carry it on (p. 57).

Consequently, it "becomes essential for the capitalist that control over the labor process pass from the hands of the worker into his own. This transition presents itself in history as the *progressive alienation of the process of production* from the worker; to the capitalist, it presents itself as the problem of *management*" (p. 58).

The origins of modern management lie in capitalists's growing need to control workers in ways unachievable through precapitalist forms of control over producers. To satisfy this need, capitalists had to create forms of control suited to their peculiar purposes. These forms are incorporated in the production and social relations that increasingly have come to characterize the developing capitalist mode of production.

In the beginning of industrial capitalism, capitalists primarily had to manage with the means of production and of control inherited from the prior epoch. In their early workshops capitalists basically took labor as it came to them, without significantly altering traditional methods of production. The labor process "thus remained under the immediate control of the producers in whom was embodied the traditional knowledge and skills of their crafts" (p. 59).

In this early period of industrial capitalism capitalists sought to treat labor like any other raw material. They tried to buy labor "as a definite quantity of work, completed and embodied in the product" (pp. 60–61). To accomplish this they employed various subcontracting and putting-out systems, under which materials were distributed on a piecework basis through intermediaries to workers for manufacture in their own homes. These were transitional forms of management, but they prevailed well into the nineteenth century. Only then did capitalists gradually begin to assume "the essential

SIX BOOKS CONSIDERED

function of management in industrial capitalism, control over the labor process" (p. 63). Hence, "the specifically capitalist mode of management and thus of production did not become generalized until relatively recent times, that is, within the last hundred years" (p. 61).

Transitional management forms had been beset by irregularity and slowness of production. But most critically these forms suffered from "their inability to [facilitate a dramatic] change [in] the processes of production" (p. 63):

Based . . . upon a rudimentary division of labor, the [putting-out] system [for example] prevented the further development of the division of labor. . . . [Although] the attempt to purchase finished labor, instead of assuming direct control over labor power, relieved the capitalist of the uncertainties of the latter system by fixing a definite unit cost, at the same time it placed beyond the reach of the capitalist much of the potential of human labor that may be made available by fixed hours, systematic control, and the reorganization of the labor process (pp. 63–64).

To realize this potential, capitalists had to learn new methods of control. "Under the special and new relations of capitalism, which presupposed a 'free labor contract,' they had to extract from their employees that daily conduct which would best serve their interests, to impose their will upon their workers while operating a labor process on a voluntary contractual basis" (p. 67).

The new, antagonistic, developing relations that shaped production demanded distinctive forms of managerial control, even as they made possible the imposition of such control. The development of management was based on the evolution of a capitalist division of labor, which simultaneously reduced labor and workers to fragments and divided conceptualization from execution, locating conceptualization in a separate body of people called managers.

The division of labor, of course, is not unique to capitalism. All societies have carried out what Marx has called the "general" or "social division of labor," whereby the body of workers are divided along craft or occupational lines. But "no society before capitalism systematically subdivided the work of each productive specialty into limited operations" (p. 70). This "detailed division of labor" within the various labor processes is qualitatively different from the social division of labor: the latter

divides society among occupations, each adequate to a branch of production; [but] the detailed division of labor destroys [these] occupations. . . , and renders the worker inadequate to carry through any complete production process. . . . While the social division of labor divides *society*, the detailed division of labor subdivides *humans*, and while the subdivision of society may enhance the individual and the species, the subdivision of the individual, when carried on without regard to human capabilities and needs, is a crime against the person and against humanity (pp. 72–73).

Capitalist management is indelibly implicated in this continuing crime. For the detailed division of labor that constitutes the crime reflects "the marriage of technique with the special needs of capital" (p. 75).

There are two aspects to the detailed division of labor in production. The first is the separation of the labor process into its constituent elements. That separation does not in itself create the detail worker. At Blancs, for example, I often voluntarily organized my labor process to separate out and aggregate similar elements in the repetitive task of picking up, dumping, and returning hoppers to their sites. Thus, instead of performing the entire task continuously on each hopper, frequently I would pick up three or four hoppers, line them up somewhere convenient for dumping, and then dump them all one after another. No matter how I analyzed and reorganized my labor process according to its elements, however, I continued to perform all the elements of the complex task. I was not a detail worker.

What creates a detail worker is the allocation of the separated constituent elements of the work process by the capitalist to different workers. This "detailization" hurts workers and helps capitalists. It not only increases productivity and management control but also, as Charles Babbage long ago recognized in his famous *On the Economy of Machinery and Manufactures* (1832), cheapens the cost of labor to the capitalist.

Fragmented and allocated among different workers, the various elements of a complex task, which otherwise would have to be performed by a single worker with sufficient skills and strength to execute all, can now be performed by different workers, no one of whom requires the level of skill and training of the predetail craft worker. Detailization thus simultaneously reduces the time the most skilled of workers must devote to job elements that do not require skill and re-creates those elements as detail jobs for the unskilled. With sufficient scale of production the total labor power required to perform the entire process can be bought more cheaply as dissociated fragments than as a capacity integrated in each of a number of workers. This is Babbage's great principle, which "is fundamental to the evolution of the division of labor in capitalist society" and "eventually becomes the underlying force governing all forms of work in capitalist society" (pp. 81–82).

In accordance with Babbage's principle, those who purchase labor power as a commodity have a "special and permanent interest" in cheapening this commodity. As a consequence,

Every step in the labor process is divorced, so far as possible, from special knowledge and training and reduced to simple labor. Meanwhile, the relatively few persons for whom special knowledge and training are reserved are freed so far as possible from the obligations of simple labor.

In this way, a structure is given to all labor processes that at its extremes polarizes those whose time is infinitely valuable and those whose time is worth almost nothing. This might even be called the general law of the capitalist division of labor. . . . It shapes not only work, but populations as well, because over the long run through its effects on the social division of labor it creates that mass of simple labor which is the primary feature of populations in developed capitalist countries (pp. 82–83).

The creation of this deprived mass necessarily was accompanied by the creation of an increasingly sophisticated capitalist management, which required for its development its own "management experts." With the beginnings in the last half of the nineteenth century of advanced capitalism—large-scale industry, oligopolistic organization, and "the purposive and systematic application of science to production" (p. 85)—the stage was set for the related development of a theory and practice of management capable of capturing and furthering the essence of such capitalist production. That theory and practice came out of the scientific management movement and its synthesizing genius, Frederic Winslow Taylor.

WORK AND ADVANCED CAPITALISM

Taylorism, expectably, is not a theory and practice of management applicable to all modes of production. Contrary to the belief of the authors of *Work in America*, it is "nothing less than the explicit verbalization of the capitalist mode of production" (p. 86). Adaptable and useful for capitalist purposes, Taylorism today dominates the world of production.

As a relatively undisguised example of capitalist social science, Taylorism is blatantly utilized to study and shape work "on behalf of those who manage it rather than those who perform it" (p. 88).

It starts, despite occasional protestations to the contrary, not from the human point of view but from the capitalist point of view, from the point of view of the management of a refractory work force in a setting of antagonistic social relations. It does not attempt to discover and confront the cause of this condition, but accepts it as an inexorable given, a "natural" condition. It investigates not labor in general, but the adaptation of labor to the needs of capital (p. 86).

Although the development of various methods of control is of the essence of management and preceded Taylor's contributions, with Taylor and scientific management the concept of control "assumed unprecedented dimensions":

Taylor raised the concept of control to an entirely new plane when he asserted as an *absolute necessity for adequate management the dictation to the worker of the precise manner in which work is to be performed.* . . . Management, he insisted, could be only a limited and frustrated undertaking so long as it left to the worker any decision about the work. His "system" was simply a means for management to achieve control of the actual mode of performance of every labor activity, from the simplest to the most complicated. To this end, he pioneered a far greater revolution in the division of labor than any that had gone before (pp. 90–91).

Since Taylor understood that workers, uncoerced, would tend to produce no more than they believed was "fair," and since he correctly concluded that capitalist management therefore could not rely on workers' own initiative to achieve the maximum it sought, Taylor argued that management had to increase its control over workers' labor. As a theorist for bosses, Taylor took the vague notion of "a fair day's work" to mean "all the work a worker can do without injury to his health, at a pace that can be sustained throughout a working life-time" (p. 97). Thus Taylor's entire approach was shaped to extract the maximum physiologically feasible surplus from workers.

Under then-existing forms of management, Taylor pointed out, workers effectively had substantial informal power over their production because collectively they, not management, possessed much of the knowledge of how production is carried out. In such circumstances, management could not even independently determine how much output workers were capable of producing, let alone extract a maximum. To remedy this situation Taylor advocated and demonstrated in practical experiments with workers that management had to divest labor of its knowledge and power and, in turn, itself come to control and dictate every aspect of the labor process.

What Taylor decades ago so baldly and publicly advocated is embraced by management in our more sophisticated, image-conscious times only as "now-unacknowledged . . . assumptions" (p. 92). Beneath current managerial cosmetics, however, the body of Taylorism lives in all its ugliness. Therefore, it is vital for us to understand Taylor's core principles and methods and to recognize that Taylorism is the essence of advanced capitalist management. For these purposes Braverman's summary of Taylor's three basic principles and their implications is unparalleled.

The first principle is *"the dissociation of the labor process from the skills of the workers"* (p. 113). To accomplish this, Taylor argued that managers must "assume . . . the burden of gathering together all of the traditional knowledge which in the past has been possessed by the workmen and then of classifying, tabulating, and reducing this knowledge to rules, laws and formulae." Achieving this will enable "management to discover and enforce those speedier methods and shortcuts which workers themselves, in the practice of their trades or tasks, learn or improvise, and use at their own discretion only." The effort is to render the labor process "independent of craft, tradition, and the workers' knowledge. Henceforth . . . [the process] is to depend not at all upon the abilities of workers, but entirely upon the practices of management" (pp. 112–13).

The second principle is *"the separation of conception from execu-*

286

tion" (p. 114). This is "the key to scientific management" and means that "All possible brain work should be removed from the shop and centered [instead] in the planning or laying-out department" (quoted on p. 113). Since, however, the capacity for men and women to conceive of and execute the task to be done is an essential and distinctive feature of human labor, divorcing conception from execution amounts to

dehumanization of the labor process, in which workers are reduced almost to the level of labor in its animal form. . . . [Such dehumanization,] while purposeless and unthinkable in the case of the self-organized and self-motivated social labor of a community of producers, becomes crucial for the management of purchased labor (p. 113).

This separation, as today's white-collar workers know all too well, is not restricted to manual labor: "mental labor is first separated from manual labor and . . . is then itself subdivided rigorously according to the same rule" (p. 114).

What this monumental transformation of human labor implies for our social structure and our very consciousness becomes clear only as Braverman lucidly draws out its implications:

The first implication of this principle is that Taylor's "science of work" is never to be developed by the worker, always by management. This notion, apparently so "natural" and undebatable today, was in fact vigorously discussed in Taylor's day, a fact which shows . . . how completely Taylor's hotly contested assumptions have entered into the conventional outlook within a short space of time (p. 114).

In line with the Babbage principle, this separation of conception and execution, cheapens "the worker by decreasing his [required] training and enlarging his output" (p. 118). Taylor, typically, is crudely explicit on this point. The full potential of his system, he writes, "will not have been realized until almost all of the machines in the shop are run by men who are of smaller calibre and attainments, and who are therefore cheaper than those required under the old system" (quoted on p. 118).

The separation of conception and execution and their allocation to management and workers respectively is therefore necessary both in order to ensure management control and to cheapen the worker . . . , and for this purpose the study of work processes must be reserved to management and kept from the workers, to whom its results are communicated only in the form of simplified job tasks governed by simplified instructions which it is thenceforth their duty to follow unthinkingly and without comprehension of the underlying . . . reasoning (p. 118).

The third basic principle of Taylorism "is the *use of this monopoly over knowledge to control each step of the labor process and its mode of execution*" (p. 119). Under Taylorism workers' jobs are conceived of by management as tasks composed of elements, the execution of which is planned out and calculated in advance by management. Hence, the labor process "no longer exists as a process in the imagination of the worker but only as a process in the imagination of a special management staff" (p. 119).

Although conventional analysts would have us believe that this form of division of labor is simply a function of the increasing bureaucratization and scale of production and distribution, Braverman with his historic insights appreciates that such controls are "better understood as the specific product of the capitalist organization of work, and reflects not primarily scale but social antagonisms" (p. 120n).

Modern management, based on Taylor's three principles,

arose as theoretical construct and as systematic practice . . . in the very period during which the transformation of labor from processes based on skill to processes based upon science was attaining its most rapid tempo. . . . [Modern management's] role was to render conscious and systematic, the formerly unconscious tendency of capitalist production. It was to ensure that as craft declined, the worker would sink to the level of general and undifferentiated labor power, adaptable to a large range of simple tasks, while as science grew, it would be concentrated in the hands of management (pp. 120–21).

This wrenching transformation in the relations of production continues today to be recapitulated in the development of new occupations as they are created, routinized, and brought under management control. Even at this moment history is being reenacted within such large segments of our increasingly homogenized modern working class as retail sales, clerical, and secretarial workers (see Braverman, chapters 15–17).

WORK AND ADVANCED CAPITALISM

In the main, at the outset of each of the constantly renewed wrenching adaptations of workers to increasingly dehumanized capitalist work, the "adjustment" is accomplished not so much by cultural and ideological persuasion as by overwhelming socioeconomic force. Take the exemplary case history of the transformation of automobile manufacturing and auto workers by the Ford Motor Company in the early 1900s.

At the beginning of the century when the company was established, skilled, all-around craftsmen built the autos. By 1914 labor had been reorganized with the utilization of "the endless conveyor chain upon which car assemblies were carried past fixed stations where men performed simple operations as they passed" (p. 147). This innovation greatly increased productivity, almost immediately cutting assembly time for a car by nine-tenths.

Accelerated production was the result not only of this reorganization of labor but also of "the control which management, at a single stroke, attained over the pace of assembly, so that it could now double and triple the rate at which operations had to be performed and thus subject its workers to an extraordinary intensity of labor" (p. 148). With enlarged control, Ford moved to cut costs further by eliminating incentive pay and replacing incentives with more effective supervision. Thus "Craftsmanship gave way to a repeated detail operation, and wage rates were standardized at uniform levels" (p. 148). New conditions of employment, which increasingly became characteristic of the auto and other industries, were being established.

The imposition of these conditions was not accomplished, however, without serious and prolonged struggle. Workers began to rebel and to desert Ford. Ford faced its worst labor crisis: in 1913 the turnover rate of workers was 380 percent! As long as workers could find better jobs elsewhere, they did.

The capitalist response to the crisis was on two levels: the first was individual, but over time became generalized practice; the second was systemic. On the individual level, Ford responded to the flight of workers and the related threat of unionization by dramatically increasing wages well above prevailing area rates to $5 a day. This pay raise made Ford jobs monetarily attractive, whatever the

conditions of work and speedup. Under the conditions of intensification and increased exploitation of labor that preceded and accompanied the wage raise, it is no wonder Henry Ford later referred to
the raise as "one of the finest cost-cutting moves we ever made"
(quoted on p. 150). Such moves thereafter were generalized as one
characteristic way for big business to attract workers to and hold them
in despised and increasingly exploitative jobs.

The systemic response to the crisis is still more revealing in two
respects. It shows why the strong "natural revulsion" of workers to the
new assembly line work initially occurred and how it eventually was
contained and dissipated. What produced worker revulsion and made
it so apparent, Braverman writes,

is the fact that Ford, as a pioneer in the new [form of the] mode of production, was competing with prior [forms] . . . of the organization of labor
which still characterized the rest of the automobile industry and other industries in the area. . . . As Ford, by the competitive advantage which he
gained, forced the assembly line upon the rest of the automobile industry, in
the same degree workers were forced to submit to it by the disappearance of
other forms of work in that industry. . . . In this microcosm, there is an
illustration of the rule that the working class is progressively subjected to the
capitalist mode of production, and to the successive forms which it takes,
only as the capitalist mode of production conquers and destroys all other
forms of the organization of labor, and with them, all alternatives for the
working population. . . . (p. 149)

[A]s in all of the functionings of the capitalist system, manipulation is
primary and coercion is held in reserve—. . . manipulation is the product
of powerful economic forces, major corporate employment and bargaining
policies, and the inner workings and evolution of the system of capitalism itself. . . . The apparent acclimatization of the worker to the new [forms of
the capitalist mode] . . . of production grows out of the destruction of all
other ways of living, the striking of wage bargains that permit a certain en-
largement of the customary bounds of subsistence for the working class, the
weaving of the net of modern capitalist life that finally makes all other
modes of living impossible. But beneath this apparent habituation, the hostility of workers to the degenerated forms of work which are forced upon
them continues as a subterranean stream that makes its way to the surface
when employment conditions permit, or when the capitalist drive for a
greater intensity of labor oversteps the bounds of physical and mental capacity. It renews itself in new generations, expresses itself in the unbounded

WORK AND ADVANCED CAPITALISM

cynicism and revulsion which large numbers of workers feel about their work, and comes to the fore repeatedly as a social issue demanding solution (pp. 150–51).

In all this we can see the capitalist tendency to reduce workers to mere *objective* instruments (factors) of production that are subordinated to the *subjective* determinations of management, as well as the repeated, if sporadic, appearance of profound worker resistance to that tendency. The tendency itself is the product not simply of technology and mechanization as such but of capitalist management. For scientific management both conceptualizes and actually seeks *"to treat . . . workers . . . as machines"* (p. 173).

Taylor, for example, urged management that, in striving to gain control over the job to extract greater production from workers, it should measure the "elapsed time for each component operation of a work process" (p. 173). To his time study was later added motion study, "the investigation and classification of the basic motions of the body" that comprise "the building blocks of every work activity" (p. 173). In the resulting time and motion studies, motions are visualized in machine terms, and a necessary time for its performance is attributed to each motion. With the analysis and collection of appropriate data, all routine jobs by these methods can be broken down into elemental motions and allocated times. Workers then can be required to approximate the performance of machines in the labor process.

This mechanical conceptualization of work and its enforcement on workers is not incidental to, but rather typical of how capitalism appreciates and affects labor:

Since management is not interested in the person of the worker, but in the worker as he or she is used . . . , this view is from the management point of view not only eminently rational but the basis of all calculation. The human being is . . . regarded as a mechanism articulated by hinges, ball and socket joints, etc. . . . In this we see not merely the terms of a machine analogy used for experimental purposes, nor merely a teaching metaphor . . . , but in the context of the capitalist mode of production the operating theory by which people of one class set in motion people of another class. It is the reductive formula that expresses both how capital employs labor and what it makes of humanity (p. 179).

SIX BOOKS CONSIDERED

Happily, humanity refuses to accept its transformation into a mere object in the labor process. Refusing to perform as living machines but nonetheless constrained by a system that seeks such performance, *workers produce as part of "a struggle, whether organized or not"* (p. 180n; emphasis added).

In this unending struggle, management seeks through a variety of means and with uneven success to achieve its ends. The particular development of machinery within capitalist society has been part of that effort. Machinery was introduced and developed not only (as conventionally understood) to directly increase productivity, but also to increase managerial control over the labor process and to cheapen labor. So if on one level the history of mechanization may be understood simply as "an increase in human control over the action of tools [and]. . . . over labor processes by means of machines and machine systems" (pp. 192, 193), on another level the abstraction of "increased *human* control" turns out concretely to mean an increase in control by a minority over, and at the expense of the majority.

On this point Braverman is brilliant and moving:

In thus acquiring concrete form, the control of humans over the labor process turns into its opposite and becomes the control of the labor process over the mass of humans. Machinery comes into the world not as the servant of "humanity," but as the instrument of those to whom the accumulation of capital gives the *ownership* of the machines. The capacity of humans to control the labor process through machinery is seized upon by management from the beginning of capitalism as the *prime means whereby production may be controlled not by the direct producer but by the owners and representatives of capital.* Thus, in addition to its technical function of increasing the productivity of labor—which would be the mark of machinery under any social system—machinery also has in the capitalist system the function of divesting the mass of workers of their control over their own labor. . . .

[I]t is in the nature of machinery, and a corollary of technical development, that the control over the machine need no longer be vested in its immediate operator. This possibility is seized upon by the capitalist mode of production and utilized to the fullest extent. What was mere *technical possibility* has become, since the Industrial Revolution, . . . [a capitalist] *inevitability* that devastates with the force of natural calamity, although there is nothing more "natural" about it than any other form of the organization of labor. Before the human capacity to control machinery can be transformed

WORK AND ADVANCED CAPITALISM

into its opposite, a series of special conditions must be met which have nothing to do with the physical character of the machine. The machine must be the property not of the producer, nor of the associated producers, but of an alien power. The interests of the two must be antagonistic. The manner in which labor is deployed around the machinery—from the labor required to design, build, repair, and control it to the labor required to feed and operate it—must be dictated not by the human needs of the producers but by the special needs of those who own both the machine and the labor power, and whose interest it is to bring these two together in a special way. Along with these conditions, a social evolution must take place which parallels the physical evolution of machinery: a step-by-step creation of a "labor force" in place of self-directed human labor; that is to say, a working population conforming to the needs of this social organization of labor, in which knowledge of the machine becomes a specialized and segregated trait, while among the mass of the working population there grows only ignorance, incapacity, and thus a fitness for machine servitude. In this way the remarkable development of machinery becomes, for most of the working population, the source not of freedom but of enslavement, not of mastery but of helplessness, and not of the broadening of the horizon of labor but of the confinement of the worker within a blind round of servile duties in which the machine appears as the embodiment of science and the worker as little or nothing (pp. 193–95).

Capitalist technological development thus further separates conceptualization from execution and by means of the continuing destruction of craft and its remnants generally reduces execution to "operating." Thereby, through socio-technological history, a new sort of worker has been created: the ubiquitous and low-priced "operator":

The design which will enable the operation to be broken down among cheaper operators is the design which is sought by management and engineers who have so internalized this value that it appears to have the force of natural law or scientific necessity. . . . Here we see once more the Babbage principle, but now in a setting of technical revolution. The process has become more complex, but this is lost to the workers, who do not rise with the process but sink beneath it. Each of these workers is required to know and understand not *more* than did the single worker of before, but much *less* (p. 200).

This material development of capitalist technology that has contributed so to subordinating workers to a labor process controlled by others has been paralleled and reinforced by the development of a fa-

SIX BOOKS CONSIDERED

talist and apologist capitalist ideology. This ideology conveniently attributes such subordination, with all its human implications, not to capitalism but to a kind of technological inevitability:

It has become fashionable . . . to attribute to machinery the powers over humanity which arise in fact from social relations. Society, in this view, is nothing but an extrapolation of science and technology, and the machine itself is the enemy. The machine, the mere product of human labor and ingenuity, designed and constructed by humans and alterable by them at will, is viewed as an independent participant in human social arrangements. It is given life, enters into "relations" with . . . workers, relations fixed by its own nature, is endowed with the power to shape the life of mankind, and is sometimes even invested with designs upon the human race. This is the reification of a social relation; it is . . . nothing but a *fetishism*, in Marx's sense of the term. "In order . . . to find an analogy, we must have recourse to the mist-enveloped regions of the religious world. In that world the productions of the human brain appear as independent beings endowed with life, and entering into relation both with one another and the human race. So it is in the world of commodities with the products of men's hands. This I call . . . Fetishism. . . ." This fetishism achieves its greatest force when it attaches to those products of men's hands which, in the form of machinery, become capital. Acting for the master in a way which he plans with inexhaustible care and precision, they seem in human eyes to act *for themselves and out of their own inner necessities* (pp. 229–30).

Machines—and the capitalist relations of production and division of labor that machines reflect, embody, and enhance—were not ordained on some technological Olympus. Rather, all these phenomena were developed in history by a particular ruling class as it struggled to realize its own nature and interests. During the past hundred years, for example, the capitalist division of labor has been crucially shaped by the growth of a class of oligopoly capitalists. As capital was concentrated and centralized, the capitalist division of labor was personified anew and in more advanced form in a radically different structure of occupations and labor processes—which is to say, in a radically changed working class.

Through integrally related changes in the structure of occupations and labor processes, capitalist technology and management have played a dynamic role in producing today's working class. The changes have been dramatic. Along with agricultural mechanization

WORK AND ADVANCED CAPITALISM

and the well-known shift from farm to nonfarm work, there has been since the 1920s within the nonfarm sector itself a decline in a proportion of workers engaged in the vital goods-producing industries like manufacturing and mining. And within these industries themselves there has been a similar decline in the proportion of those directly engaged in production. As all possible conceptualizing was removed from the point of production, "a shadow replica of the entire process of production in paper form" (p. 239) was created, which fueled the growing demand for and proportion of nonproduction employees in goods producing industries. Among these nonproduction employees, real technical expertise again was concentrated in a relatively small group of conceptualizers: engineers, scientists, and the like. And as this grouping itself emerged into occupations, its members in turn were subjected to some of the same constraints imposed on less illustrious mass occupations. In engineering, for example, management replaced

engineers and draftsmen with data-entry clerks and machine operators, and further [intensified] the concentration of conceptual and design knowledge. Thus the very process which brought into being a mass engineering profession is being applied to that profession itself (p. 245).

Meanwhile, among the much larger body of "lower-grade, routinized technical or unskilled [nonproduction] . . . jobs" (p. 256), the number of clerical workers in particular has expanded tremendously: "Since management now carries on the production process from its desktops, conducting on paper a parallel process that follows and anticipates everything that happens in production itself, an enormous mass of recordkeeping and calculation comes into being" (p. 246).

As the modern corporation has grown, capitalist management also of necessity has expanded, and itself become a labor process comparable to others, even as high-level corporate figures have come to exercise awesome influence over our world. The development of these realities, Braverman shows, can be appreciated in terms of the necessary creation of corporate marketing organizations, the necessary changes in corporate management structure, and the increased significance of corporate coordination for capitalist society.

SIX BOOKS CONSIDERED

Corporations developed marketing apparatuses for the same reason they developed other sorts of administrative controls: to minimize uncertainty:

Since markets must remain the prime area of uncertainty, the effort of the corporation is therefore to reduce the *autonomous character* of the demand for its products and to increase its *induced* character. For this purpose, the marketing organization becomes second in size only to the production organization in manufacturing corporations. . . .

These marketing organizations take as their responsibility what Veblen called "a quantity-production of customers. . . . the fabrication of customers . . . [is] carried on as a routine operation, quite in the spirit of the mechnical industries and with much the same degree of assurance" (pp. 265–66).

The goal is to shape consumers to the needs of production rather than the reverse.

In response to the development of such specialized corporate functions as marketing, and to the related growth in the scale of operations, the structure of corporate management also has been drastically altered. Whereas formerly the enterprises's owner-manager usually had exercised all the functions of management directly, today these functions have been subdivided among a complex of specialized departments:

The particular management function is exercised not just by a manager, nor even by a staff of managers, but by an *organization of workers under the control of managers, assistant managers, . . . etc. Thus the relations of purchase and sale of labor power, and hence of alienated labor, have become part of the management apparatus itself. . . .* Management has become *administration, which is [itself] a labor process conducted for the purpose of control within the corporation* and conducted moreover as a labor process exactly analogous to the process of production, although it produces no product other than the operation and coordination of the corporation. From this point on, to examine management means also to examine this labor process, which contains the same antagonistic relations as are contained in the process of production (p. 267).

With the octopuslike growth of the modern corporation as the main organizational form of advanced capitalism and its increasing domination of people's lives, the capitalist mode of production begins to realize its own totalitarian potential—capitalism becomes co-exten-

WORK AND ADVANCED CAPITALISM

sive with societal life. For the first time in human history capitalism *"takes over the totality of individual, family and social needs and, in subordinating them to the market, also reshapes them to serve the needs of capital. It is impossible to understand . . . the modern working class . . . without understanding . . . [h]ow capitalism transformed all of society into a gigantic marketplace"* (p. 271; emphasis added).

The interrelated phases of this total takeover are superbly analyzed by Braverman in his shocking chapter "The Universal Market." It shocks first because Braverman sheds a radically revealing light on something we assume we already know quite intimately—our own daily lives—and second because Braverman thereby helps us to understand something we are not supposed to know at all: how the capitalist mode of production literally has "determined" the nature of our existence. Beyond this, Braverman's analysis of how "capitalism transformed all of society into a gigantic marketplace" suggests how totally we have come to accept as natural the torturous transformations capitalism, especially in the last seventy or eighty years, has produced in our lives. And it suggests also by its very richness how terribly impoverished alternate explanations based upon technological determinism really are.

The first step in the complex transformation process was to penetrate the family to subvert its relative self-sufficiency as a unit that essentially consumed what it produced without significant recourse to the market. It was, in short, to turn food and then clothing, shelter, and other necessities into commodities to be bought and sold in the market, where capitalists could realize a profit from employing wage labor to produce them. To accomplish this the family had to be displaced as a production unit. This was achieved in part by "the tighter packing of urbanization," which made it impossible for the family to continue its "former self-provisioning practices" (p. 275).

This process of "extending the commodity form" into previously untouched areas of life

eventually leads to the dependence of all social life, and indeed of all the interrelatedness of humankind, upon the marketplace. The population of cities, more or less completely cut off from a natural environment by the division between town and country, becomes totally dependent upon social artifice for its every need. But social artifice has been destroyed in all but its marketable forms. Thus the population no longer relies upon social organization in the form of family, friends, neighbors, community, elders, children, but with few exceptions must go to market and only to market, not only for food, clothing and shelter, but also for recreation, amusement, security, for the care of the young, the old, the sick, the handicapped. In time, not only the material and service needs but even the emotional patterns of life are channeled through the market.

It thereby comes to pass that while population is packed . . . together in the urban environment, the atomization of social life proceeds apace. In its most fundamental aspect, this often noticed phenomenon can be explained only by the development of market relations as the substitute for individual and community relations. The social structure, built upon the market, is such that relations between individuals and social groups do not take place directly, as cooperative human encounters, but through the market as relations of purchase and sale (pp. 276–77).

This process further weakens family and community, which calls into being new branches of production "to fill the gap," which in turn further weakens social and family life, which then requires "new services and commodities [to] provide substitutes for human relations in the form of market relations" (p. 277). The trend culminates in "the conversion into a commodity of every product of human labor, so that goods-producing labor is carried on in none but its capitalist form" (p. 278).

In these and other ways we are

enmeshed in a web made up of commodity goods and commodity services from which there is little possibility of escape except through partial or total abstention from social life as it now exists. This is reinforced from the other side by a development . . . analogous to that which proceeds in the worker's work: the atrophy of competence. In the end, the population finds itself willy-nilly in the position of being able to do little or nothing itself as easily as it can be hired done in the market place. . . . (p. 281).

Of this universal market that is our society, Braverman concludes:

[It] is widely celebrated as a bountiful "service economy," and praised for its "convenience," "cultural opportunities," "modern facilities for care of the handicapped," etc. We need not emphasize how badly this . . . civilization works and how much misery it embraces. . . . Just as in the factory it is not the machines that are at fault but the conditions of the capitalist mode of production under which they are used, so here it is not the necessary provision of social services that is at fault, but the effects of an all-powerful marketplace which, governed by capital and its profitable investment, is both chaotic and profoundly hostile to all feelings of community (pp. 281–82).

Thus has advanced capitalism made us dependent in almost every aspect of our lives on the class that, among other things, pays us wages for our labor, controls production of the items we produce and consume, and organizes to its benefit our consumption and even our social services.

SIX BOOKS CONSIDERED

XV

Liberalism and the Destructive Shaping of Our Consciousness: The Subjective World

WITH Braverman's help, we can better understand that capitalism in its obsession for profits has shaped our work and infiltrated our material being. But to apprepiate how capitalism has been able to do so, we must know more about the ways capitalism has shaped our very consciousness and "needs."

Richard Sennett's and Jonathan Cobb's *The Hidden Injuries of Class*, by examining how workers feel about their lives, enables us to see that the American capitalist class structure and its intimately related culture in combination degrade, distract, and disarm most Americans. In the confining context of a class structure that in fact does not allow broad and meaningful opportunity for social mobility and for gaining a sense of individual achievement, our capitalist culture stresses the values of individualism, freedom, equal opportunity, and competition. This combination atomizes and disables the working class, leaving workers and many of the rest of us frustrated, resentful, and if not quite pacified, at least for the time being properly demeaned and usually in place. Class domination and class conflict, we come to understand, take place on another, hitherto-unthought-of level. The more observable forms of class domination and conflict that occur externally in our workplaces are complemented by a closely related form, which, tragically, is internalized and occurs in our homes and within our very selves.

300

Understanding this form of class domination and conflict, Sennett and Cobb properly argue, is vital to understanding how our capitalist system has maintained itself. Why, they want to know, hasn't the oppressed majority in our system overturned it? Raw power (of which Sennett and Cobb say all too little), to be sure, has been used against workers time and time again to keep them in place when they have rebelled. In addition, many workers for the time being have been "bought off." But to the extent our rulers have succeeded, workers, more profoundly, have been gutted from within.

The values, processes, and institutions responsible for this subtle, system-maintaining kind of human devastation are (although Sennett and Cobb do not say as much) *at the center of liberalism.* Liberalism, in this sense, infects us from childhood, well before we get to the workplace. And it continues to warp our consciousness and to demean us throughout our lives under capitalism.

Sennett and Cobb initially pose the issues in a series of brief case studies. First, there is Frank Rissarro, who

worked his way up from being a shoeshine boy at the age of nine [through being a meat cutter, finally] to classifying loan applications in a bank. He makes $10,000 a year, owns a suburban home. . . . He is a man who at first glance appears satisfied . . . and yet he is also a man who feels defensive about his honor, fearing that people secretly do not respect him (pp. 18–19).

Frank had hoped in his life to achieve a position in which, like the middle-class, especially educated people of his visions, he would not simply be a creature of circumstance. But, after making it into white-collar status and achieving "the outward signs of material respectability . . . he still feels defenseless." His conclusion is "something must be wrong with *him*; his unhappiness seems to him a sign that he simply cannot become the kind of person other people can respect" (pp. 25–26).

Then there is Carl Dorian, a young apprentice electrician, who feels somehow deeply dissatisfied but cannot pinpoint any particular problem:

"I can't say as I'm really content. There's no problems at work because I just do what the boss says . . . he's not a tyrant or anything. . . . I like doing electrical work. . . . I feel like I'm taking shit even when, actually, even when there's nothing wrong. . . . I feel like I'm being held back, like I'm not on top of things . . . maybe sort of powerless. . . . not being in control of things. . . ." (pp. 34–35).

Carl, of course, is quite right. He is not in control of things. The owners and managers of things are in control of workers as well as things. Yet being right doesn't protect Carl from blaming himself for the class-imposed condition he does not really understand.

Nor does it help to deliver Ricca Kartides, a first-generation immigrant to America, from the bind he is in. In Greece, his "less advanced" home country, Kartides held a teacher's degree. When he came to the United States twelve years ago, he was without money and had no knowledge of English. As a result, Ricca was channeled, temporarily he hoped, into unskilled labor. Once doing it, he "found himself stuck . . . having to work long hours to provide for himself and his family, . . . [with] neither the time, the money, nor the energy to return to school for the credentials that would get him into a white-collar job in America" (p. 47). He became a janitor. However, that was not the worst of it. People began treating him like he was worth less as a human being.

As a maintenance man who lived in the apartment house for whose upkeep he was responsible, Kartides was told to "use the back door" and to "never let his children play on the empty lawn surrounding the building." He responded

by making heroic efforts of time, work and personal sacrifice so that he could own a home of his own. His hope was that by freeing himself from other people's interferences, he could feel more confident about himself. It was not to own . . . that he worked so hard for a private house; it was to gain a sanctuary, . . . where . . . he would not find his place in society thrown in his face over the smallest matters. The home is . . . [where] "my children can play without nobody telling them what to do" (p. 48).

But, expectably, things have not worked out that way for Ricca Kartides:

He . . . bought property in a nearby suburb . . . in order to be free, yet must work fourteen hours a day at two jobs in order to pay for his "freedom," leaving him scant time to enjoy his home. He bought property in order to create an independent sphere of living for himself and his family, yet, in the very process, finds himself sacrificing his social life to pay for this privilege. . . . Since his house, like many residences in or near American cities, lacks access to good public transportation, he must buy a car, and that, too, takes money. And more money, for a man who cleans or paints houses or sells shoes, comes only from longer hours spent on the job and away from home.

He understands the trap in which he is caught. He knows that the actions he has taken are not yielding the promised rewards, yet to do nothing, to be just "Ricca the janitor" who uses the back door and yells at his kids when they set foot on the apartment house grass, is unbearable (pp. 48–49).

But what, the authors rhetorically ask, have Ricca Kartides and the others done wrong? The answer, of course, is nothing. That answer only leads to another harsher question: Why do so many people like Ricca "feel their dignity is on the line?" Why do workers "take their class position so personally?" (p. 29). Put another way, what is it about our society that has led workers who have been "reared in a class where men [in fact] have severe limits imposed on their individual freedom to choose" and who nevertheless have struggled "to establish more freedom in order to gain dignity," to still feel that their struggle, "while successful on the surface, is eroding their confidence in themselves"? How, to put it most bluntly, is "the class structure in America . . . organized so that *the tools of freedom become the sources of indignity*" (p. 30)?

The answer, one hastens to add, is not the fashionable one gleefully offered by our system's various apologists—that men like Frank Rissarro were made insecure by their relative success in "moving up" within American society. That cannot be an adequate answer, because "the same issues of dignity and self-respect appear in the lives of people who remain manual laborers. These issues concern the everyday experiences of working-class survival as well as the exceptional . . . [experiences] of success" (p. 31).

The search for dignity, Sennett and Cobb believe, is a human one. All men and women want to be treated with respect. Different societies, however, establish different standards for awarding respect. In caste society, for example, the matter is simple and definitive: only the few are held to deserve the respect they inherit by birth rather than earn by deeds. In American society, by contrast, all men and women in principle are said to deserve respect as human beings. In practice, however, respect in the United States must be earned.

To achieve respect here a person must prove s/he is a "self-reliant individual," someone who "can take care of himself" (p. 55). This standard of individual self-reliance developed in our history when most white, male Americans, at least, appeared to be independent as self-employed small farmers and businessmen. But today, when only 5 percent of our population is self-employed, such a standard for respect obviously flies in the face of fundamental reality. Despite that, "independence" still matters greatly to people. Why?

The answer, Sennett and Cobb argue, involves the "hidden dimensions of individualism in a corporate society" (p. 58). Individualism in the United States requires that a person to earn respect show through the expression of his/her individual abilities s/he stands out from the masses of people. Individual worth is established and measured by ability exhibited in various performances, and the "calculations of ability create an image of a few individuals standing out from the mass" (p. 62). When people feel their self-worth is purely a function of their ability to perform and they build their own sense of self-respect on the basis of "badges of ability" pinned on them by those who evaluate their various performances, "an enormous weight [is put] on how well . . . [the individual] can perform; [and] if the performance doesn't earn respect, then who is at fault? . . . the person involved [is threatened] with a feeling of inadequacy" (pp. 66–67).

As people strive to become among "the few," there remain "the many" who cannot. What of them? They are not generally described by testers, teachers, or personnel supervisors as "stupid, untalented, or empty" but rather as "Average, adequate, ordinary: it is a language wherein personal recognition of the few is balanced by impersonal toleration of the many; it is a matter of good versus neutral." The masses become "invisible" people. Thus our sort of competitive, individualistic "search for dignity . . . requires an image of social inequality. . . ." One rises out of the "lesser" mass as an individual who outperforms most others in the struggle of life.

LIBERALISM AND OUR CONSCIOUSNESS

The rationalization for this harsh capitalist reality, according to Andrew Carnegie, is that merit receives its just deserts: "The justice of industrial capitalism in America . . . is that society *here* will not fail to reward a man of talent. If a man is worthy of escaping poverty's terrors, he can do so. [Conversely, for the many, if they do not] . . . have the ability to "make it," by what right [do they] . . . complain?" (p. 72). The many have no right. They allegedly had their chance and failed to show enough ability to earn distinction. For our many, despite certain material improvements in their lives, to remain in the working class is to feel "inadequate." The jobs they perform are the sort "where people do not feel they express enough that is unique in themselves to win others' respect as individuals"—which only confirms their fear that they may not deserve better. In this "morality of shaming and self-doubt," the seeming freedom to better oneself is for most "an accursed freedom" (p. 74).

Everyone in our society, from whatever class, is cursed with this scheme of values, but for members of the working class the burden is still heavier:

The plumber has a radically different experience of these phenomena than the professor because of where he stands in the society and what he does. [His closer] . . . association . . . with [the] . . . . masses suggests that he will have a harder time asserting himself at all because other people—people higher up and even, perhaps, people like himself—think he doesn't have as much ability to start with as does a professor (pp. 75–76).

Class prejudice, in short, compounds the real objective problems members of the working class face in trying to "earn respect." And class prejudice cannot easily be wiped out, because "it serves a purpose, as does this whole scheme of individuals recognized and respected by virtue of ability. This purpose is to continue the inequities of the world of nineteenth-century . . . capitalism—on new terrain" (p. 76).

Class rule, then, involves much more than simply imposing the power of the few upon the many through the ruling class's control of certain resources the many vitally need. If class rule were only a matter of power, the many could simply have overthrown the few long ago. But throughout history it obviously has been extremely "hard for

SIX BOOKS CONSIDERED

the oppressed to revolt against injustice" (p. 77). Why? Because every successful class society creates its own "values . . . to legitimize the right of some to control the lives of many, convincing the worker that he *ought* to submit his labor to the will of others. . . . [Of course,] the more . . . the many . . . surrender their own freedom to the few, the less chance they have of respecting themselves as people with any countervailing rights" (pp. 77–78).

Hence, although workers today may feel our society has restricted their freedom to develop into valuable human beings, "they are not rebellious in the ordinary sense of the word; they are both angry and ambivalent about their right to be angry" (p. 79).

This ambivalence has its origins much earlier in life. How legitimized authority in the United States creates human problems of freedom and dignity is especially obvious in the institutional life at the working-class Josiah Watson Grammar School. There, the liberal authoritarianism employed by teachers helps to inculcate a debilitating sense of self-blame before authority figures in the masses of young people whose hands will perform the blue-collar and lower-white-collar jobs of the future.

Watson teachers believe that strict authority is necessary to "make this school work" and expect that the many cannot perform well. In acting out these expectations, they transform them into reality. Teachers quickly single out a few children and communicate to all that the few are different. The result is that the few do perform better, and the many come to realize that teachers react with less enthusiasm to their performances and are discouraged. By the time the children in this school reach fifth or sixth grade, "the split between the many and the few who are expected to 'make something of themselves' is out in the open; the aloofness [shown by the many toward the few] . . . in the second grade has become open hostility by the sixth" (p. 82).

The privileged few are treated by the many as goodie-goodies and "suck-ups." The results are tragic in their familiarity. The many direct "their anger at their schoolmates who are rewarded as individuals rather than at the institution which is withholding recognition of them" (p. 83).

LIBERALISM AND OUR CONSCIOUSNESS

In response to rejection by the teacher, the "ordinary" working class boys—the many—develop a "counterculture of dignity" that sets them off from the few and gives them a sense of broad solidarity among themselves.

What most cements them as a group . . . is the breaking of rules—smoking, drinking, or taking drugs together, cutting classes. Breaking the rules is an act "nobodies" can share with each other. This counterculture . . . is . . . an attempt to create among themselves badges of dignity that those in authority can't destroy (pp. 83–84).

The very counterculture patterns, however, are taken by parents and teachers as confirmation that the many don't deserve the respect reserved for the few. Those who simply seem to "hang around" are seen as lacking in potential to do more. So, achieving some dignity within the counterculture "exacts a toll by the standards of the outer world" (pp. 83–84).

This division of young human beings into "groups with a shared sense of loyalty and individuals alone but 'getting somewhere,' characterizes many levels of education. . . . Ability will make . . . [the few] into individuals, and as individuals they . . . [may] rise in social class" (p. 84). The masses, of course, are condemned simultaneously to live an undignified life and to question whether they deserve better. Can you imagine a more effective way to minimize the need for force in maintaining the existing class structure?

Those caught up in the situation normally do not rebel because each blames him/herself for failure: "The system must work, for the child can see that a few are chosen—but not he. Could he have paid more attention, worked harder?" (p. 88).

The situation is analogous for adult workers. Take the case of George Corona, a senior foreman in a factory in the aerospace industry. Like teachers, he feels himself confronted by a mass without real talent. He feels powerless, responsible to his superiors but dependent on the workers he commands to do the job. He is afraid of failing and of falling back into the mass from which he earlier emerged. At work he feels "at once harsh and inadequate." He feels he doesn't have "any real independence." His sense of inadequacy is increased by his belief

SIX BOOKS CONSIDERED

that, if he really had the drive and the ability, he ought to have become a scientist out from under, neither responsible for the drones nor to his superiors. . . . here is a man, fully cognizant of how much the corporation has defined his role for him, beyond his control, still feeling this same sense of personal responsibility. . . . He is at once, in his own mind, in control and powerless, someone who has succeeded in and someone who is alienated from the corporation because of the hidden dimensions of individuality, ability and unequal worth (pp. 92–93).

Although the workers under Corona feel somewhat differently about themselves, a common sense of emptiness marks Corona, the many in school, and the ordinary workers. All feel that the classday or workday, when they have to perform, is "not the 'real time' in their lives." The many in school think real life will start when they get a job;

then they would come alive. Adults who move into the institution of work, however, react to its demands for performance the same way the children did to the demands of school: they think about the meaningful time in their lives as the time spent outside the institution. Corona, for example, feels that "the job's just cash to live; the things that matter every day to me are at home." . . . Carl Dorian, the angry young electrician, also feels absent at work. When he was in school, he says, he always thought of work as an activity in which he could "stop daydreaming"; now he daydreams at work—but what the next kind of real time is, he has trouble imagining.

Corona feels "absent" at work because he feels compromised there. Carl and other workers who have not acquired even the symbolic independence of a foreman, feel this way for somewhat different reasons. When you are just taking orders, you are not really alive, you almost cease to exist in the present, you blot it out (pp. 93–94).

The paradox, as a worker pointed out, is that "The more a person is on the receiving end of orders, . . . the more the person's got to think he or she is really somewhere else . . . to keep up self-respect. And yet it's at work that you're supposed to 'make something' of yourself. . . ." (p. 94).

Workers hold themselves responsible for their feelings of absence at work and blame themselves for not making more of themselves. They blame themselves for being in the position of having to take orders. What occurs amounts to a

LIBERALISM AND OUR CONSCIOUSNESS

self-accusation, . . . a sense that the 'lower' a man [is defined by others and] defines himself in society in relation to other people, the more it seems his fault. . . . in secret he feels ashamed for who he is. Class is his personal responsibility, despite the fact he never had a chance (pp. 96–97).

This is truly a form of class domination—legitimated, disguised, internalized, and felt as personalized failure.

Class domination is also internalized in another related form, as class conflict. In the elementary school described above, for example, students, like workers in factories, face a choice that ultimately must be understood in such class terms. Both have to choose between seeking to impress superiors and maintaining a sense of camaraderie with peers. If Frank Rissarro chooses to develop and show his full abilities in the hopes of "making it" with superiors, in success he separates himself from the many. If, on the other hand, he chooses to side with the many, he cannot establish himself as a capable individual, and career success becomes unlikely.

Often in the face of such unhappy polar choices students and workers seek a balance. They may try to develop and show some, but not too many, of their abilities. Or they may try to remain in solidarity with their comrades, so long as it is not at too great a cost to their "careers." Performing such daily balancing acts, however, does not liberate individuals from the class-imposed bind, for successful balancing involves compromising both standards. The balancer is neither just another member of the mass nor a full-blown "individual" performing at peak capacity. Frustration, guilt, and self-doubts are built into such a situation.

Class-imposed, internalized conflicts exist as well in the community and within the family itself, just as they do in the schools and workplaces. In a society where individual achievement in self-reliance is taken as the highest badge of worthiness, participating in more traditional extended families, for example, is now taken as "a source of personal humiliation rather than of collective strength" (p. 107). So, in search of an American Dream of freedom and dignity built upon the illusion of individual independence, Americans are choosing to leave their remaining precapitalist, extended families, even as they experience a sense of loss at the family's breakup. The system-serving irony of this choice of "independence" is that by free-

SIX BOOKS CONSIDERED

ing themselves from the complex interdependencies of the traditional family, Americans simultaneously are atomizing themselves more (as separated individuals and as nuclear families) and are becoming less able to sustain themselves within the new family unit.

Consequently, the individuated search for independence, to the extent it achieves success in its own terms, reduces the support Americans formerly enjoyed as members of broader family collectives and thereby frequently results in its opposite: *the creation of a profound but different sort of dependence, an impersonalized dependence—this time, on the faceless, universal, labor, service, money and goods market.* If, for instance, an individual recently "liberated" from an extended family can no longer rely with assurance on that family to see him/her through hard times, s/he can always make an application for a loan at his/her "friendly neighborhood bank." If s/he is not too poor, s/he may even be able to freely choose which bank to pay through the nose for the needed money.

How convenient it all is! In our consciousness, capitalism and liberalism, if they stand for nothing else, stand for increased freedom and independence. In reality what seems to be happening is something more like a change in the kind of dependence—a shift to a formal, almost nominal, marketplace freedom that is ballyhooed as "independence."

This sort of increased "freedom" and "independence" is, of course, nothing new under capitalism. It should not be taken at face value. In historical perspective it is one aspect of a much grander, long-term process rooted in the origins and evolution of capitalism. That process in essence frees people from more traditional, face-to-face relations of dependence in order to bind them into more depersonalized relations of dependence upon capitalists and capitalist institutions. Through this same process, peasants centuries ago were freed of their traditional relationships with feudal landowners, from which they had derived their livelihood. Dispossessed, they were effectively forced to earn their bread by "freely" selling their labor to rising capitalists.* Independence from the older, less productive, and more obvious kind of bondage then as now left people vulnerable to the new

* For a very detailed, often marvelous account of this process, see E. P. Thompson's classic *The Making of the English Working Class* (new ed.; New York: Penguin Books, 1968).

kind of bondage, which came to be conceived as "freedom." Thus capitalism, from its earliest periods, has created, and today continues to create, new forms of diffuse, impersonalized relations of dependency, ideologically disguised as "freedom" and "independence."

Given this reality of a dependence that is at once profound, depersonalized, and disguised as its opposite, the vast majority of Americans who are indoctrinated in liberal values can hardly as individuals feel otherwise than "powerless" and "inadequate." Efforts to reduce these feelings generally prove unsuccessful, even futile, because the efforts themselves so consistently are founded upon the same illusions and false values that have given rise to the feelings of powerlessness and inadequacy in the first place.

Take the widespread effort to achieve dignity by "sacrificing for the children." Many workers who are constrained in their own lives, resolve "to shape the actions open to them so that, in their own minds, they [feel] . . . as though they . . . [act] from choice rather than necessity. . . . The dignity . . . [they hope] to wrest from their circumstances . . . [is] expressed . . . in a paradoxical morality of personal sacrifice" (p. 121).

John Bertin paints equipment for a large factory and feels "people treat him like nothing." He feels, too, that his life on the whole "has in itself no power to gain his children's respect." However, he does have one claim on them, "the fact that he is sacrificing himself, his time, his effort, for them. . . . Having been so repeatedly denied by the social order outside himself, now he will usurp the initiative, he will do the denying, the sacrifice of himself will become a voluntary act" (p. 122).

Although sacrifice for the children is seen by American families of most classes as redeeming the struggles of adult life, sacrifice is experienced quite differently from class to class.

To devote . . . one's life to the children has an obvious set of class limits: you must have something to give them. A destitute worker, perennially out of a job, can't feel that his sacrifices give meaning to his family life. . . . A wage-worker [by comparison] is attempting to perform the most difficult of balancing acts: on the one hand, he wishes to be with his children, to play with and show concern for them; on the other hand, he knows that the only way he can provide decently for . . . [them], and give his life some greater meaning, is by working longer hours, and thus spending much free time away from his family. . . .

Sacrifice, as an attempt to redeem the traumas in a person's life, becomes divided into unequal classes of experience. . . . [A] working-class person has less chance than a middle-class person of sacrificing successfully; class definitions intrude to derail him from a sense that he has made an effective gift of his own struggle to someone else (pp. 124–25).

This lower chance of success in sacrifice for working-class people is not simply because as parents they have fewer resources they can sacrifice or because children of workers have still less opportunity than children of middle-class families to achieve "dignity" in life. Another dimension is involved as well. Sadly, even if the working-class child "succeeds," the sacrifice is not likely to enhance the dignity of parents who have come to blame themselves for their class position, because at the core of their sacrifice is a sense of "self-contempt, the plea that the children not become the same as . . . [the parents]" (p. 122).

The search for dignity through sacrifice is not only generally futile; it also serves to maintain the system.

If you are a working-class person, if you have had to spend year after year being treated by people of a higher class as though there probably is little unusual or special about you to catch their attention, if you resent this treatment, and yet feel also that it reflects something accurate about your own [lack of] self-development, [you may turn to self-denial in the hope of achieving dignity. In doing so, the sacrificers do not think]. . . . about doing away with the class structure. They, too, are individualists, concerned with their right to be exempted *personally* from shaming and indignity. In turning people against [themselves and] each other, the class system of authority and judgment-making goes itself into hiding; the system is left unchallenged as people enthralled by the enigmas of its power battle one another for respect (pp. 147–48, 150).

But if the heart of the problem is simply that most of us have a "false consciousness"—that we have been deceived into believing dignity can be achieved through these destructive contests for individual recognition—then an adequate solution would appear to entail no more than education to change people's minds. This unthreatening

LIBERALISM AND OUR CONSCIOUSNESS

"solution" appears especially plausible if the problem of false consciousness is presented, as it too often is in *Hidden Injuries*, in a manner so abstracted from the essence of American capitalism that it is unclear why and how capitalism in fact is its source.

Nonetheless, Sennett and Cobb do recognize that American society systematically teaches people to strive to validate the self through distinctive merit. Workers appear to act as if under "some compulsion . . . from the larger society" (p. 152).

But why is this demand that individuals demonstrate their abilities to achieve a sense of human dignity socially imposed? The answer, the authors suspect, lies in a kind of "devil's utilitarianism," which "assumes that American society [or, more accurately, a certain class within it] 'benefits' when it makes people feel anxious, defeated, and self-reproachful for an imperfect ability to command the respect of others" (p. 153). Our class society "is a society of . . . resources unfairly distributed because some have arbitrary power. . . . [In this context,] the psychological dimensions of class serve a purpose in legitimating deprivation, unfair allocation of resources, and paltry rewards" (p. 159).

Thus *American society*

injures human dignity in order to weaken people's ability to fight against the limits class imposes on their freedom. . . . the use of badges of ability or of sacrifices is to divert men from challenging the limits on their freedom by convincing them that they must *first* become legitimate, must achieve dignity on a class society's terms, in order to have the right to challenge the terms themselves (p. 153; certain emphasis added).

In addition, self-doubt stimulates patterns of spending in our system that are necessary to sustain our political economy. In incisive passages, Sennett and Cobb finally link these "hidden injuries of class" to contemporary capitalist production, distribution and, consumption. These interrelated aspects of economic life

cannot [meaningfully] be separated. . . . [The capitalist] system of economic life that produces an aggregate affluence of goods and services actually demands that the goods and services be distributed unequally.

Affluence, [as]. . . . Marxist economists Paul Baran and Paul . . . Sweezy maintain, is a matter of constantly expanding production through the making and remaking of standards of comfort. Once everyone, or at least the great majority, has enough to eat, a place to sleep, and other necessities of survival, the factories can stay open . . . only by allotting goods and services unequally to a few, who appear more comfortable than the rest. Since these goods and services are purchasable, the people below work to consume more in an effort to narrow the margin of inequality in enjoyment of comforts; the factories then produce for mass demand. As a result, however, those at the top get still more goods and services, or new ones and the cycle begins again. The survival of . . . [today's capitalist] industrial production system thus depends on the unequal allocation of affluent resources; to redistribute the flow, you would have to change the nature of the source (pp. 161–62).

But why do Americans in fact play these destructive capitalist "games"? Surely the "man who goes into debt to buy a second car doesn't do so thinking it is his obligation to keep the capitalist ruling class in power. To say that he is envious doesn't explain why he is so. . . . To say advertising or public-relations propaganda tricks him into thinking he needs more and more . . . doesn't account for his receptivity" (p. 162). What ultimately makes us susceptible to capitalist manipulation is the imposed sense of injured dignity that is the subject of Sennett's and Cobb's book:

Whatever plateau of material circumstance a person achieves seems to him inadequate by comparison to the comforts of people who stand higher; he wants to be like them, and so he moves on to consume more and more. The vision of an inadequacy in one's "standard of living" suggests that . . . class psychology . . . [is] at work here. The constructions of class and personal worth . . . serve a purpose in motivating people to consume through destructive replacement. . . .

Sacrifice turns a man toward the future. In the future, people he loves [expectably] will be different from him, they will have different needs and desires; he becomes vulnerable, say, to sales pitches for encyclopedias a salesman has told him his children will need "someday." Moreover, . . . [w]hen through the process of economic expansion new symbols of comfort among the well-to-do replace old ones—two cars instead of one, a speedboat . . .—he is hard put to resist the admonitions to buy, because all these objects may be necessary for someone to live a "really" respectable life, and he isn't at that point. . . . The dream of the future, enacted in one's own life as self-sacrifice, thus makes a man yield to rather than resist the productive order putting him in vulnerable position in the first place (pp. 163–65).

LIBERALISM AND OUR CONSCIOUSNESS

People buy on the universal market under a compulsion to achieve self-dignity—another aspect of the fetishism of commodities.

Although this compulsion to "sacrifice for an unknown future, . . . this erosion of pleasure through consumerism stretches across all social classes in [our] society . . . ," workers are particularly vulnerable to its effects. The main reason is the "insecurity in the way blue-collar income accrues" (p. 166). The dreams of and sacrifices for homeownership and for the children's education require workers to save conscientiously. "These dreams can become realities *only* if . . . [they] can routinely put away money. . . . [But even in prosperous times there are] striking fluctuations in . . . [the] incomes. . . . of wage earners . . ., depending on how much work and overtime . . . [they can] get" (p. 167). With a steadily increasing, seemingly self-generated need for more income in the face of fluctuating amounts of income, a worker may complain about corporate and government action and inaction, but the practical problem of saving to achieve his/her goals is experienced more as a personal problem:

even when times are good, the pressure is on him; his income, now touching the margin of existence, now offering him a goodly surplus, becomes a perpetual burden. . . . "Sure . . . let's see with a little overtime and stuff on the side I make $12,000, which is okay, well actually I was only making about seven thousand a few years ago, but I just can't control the outgo, . . . the more I earn the farther behind I seem to be, money's . . . just out of my hands to control." . . .

Consumerism oriented to the future thus increases the sense of uncertainty about the self's present needs. Earning money gives a person little sense of immediate gratification . . . and little reinforcement year after year to his belief in his own power to cope. Money may [in some elusive] someday make a man feel he has accomplished what he wants; but "someday" does not make him feel stronger now (p. 168).

Thus, in the quoted words of Herbert Marcuse, are "the needs and satisfactions" of capitalism's "underlying population" shaped to "serve the preservation of the Establishment" (p. 169). As such, the hidden injuries of class in America are an integral and necessary part of our capitalist system of production, distribution, and consumption and of its integrated class structure and culture. In the United States

SIX BOOKS CONSIDERED

the activities which keep people . . . [striving after] more money, more pos-
sessions, higher-status jobs, do not originate in a materialistic desire, or even
sensuous appreciation, of things, but out of an attempt to restore a
psychological deprivation that the class structure has effected in their
lives. . . .

What happens . . . is that manifold acts of personal restoration added
one to another, family to family, city to city, become transformed into a
[cumulative] force that keeps the wounding society powerful.

Class [in capitalist] society takes away from all the people within it the
feeling of secure dignity in the eyes of others and . . . [in their own eyes].
It does so in two ways: first, by the images it projects of why people belong to
high or low classes—class presented as the ultimate outcome of personal
ability; second, by the definition the society makes of the actions to be taken
by people of any class to validate their dignity—legitimations of self which
do not, cannot work and so reinforce the original anxiety (pp. 170–72).

This same sort of vicious circle, through which the very efforts
of individuals to restore injured dignity keep "the wounding society
powerful," operates with some variations within the so-called new
working class of white-collar workers. Although most white-collar
work has become as unskilled and routinized as most blue-collar
work, and is done at pay scales that often are lower, employers nevertheless require high educational credentials of successful applicants
for these relatively mindless jobs. The gap between the level of skills
demanded by the job and the level of "certified knowledge" demanded by employers to get the job serves its own devil's functions.
For one thing, it generally allows only those with the proper educational credentials to move up into the white-collar world, which at its
summit is quite different from the blue-collar one. Therefore, factory
workers cannot easily move into this world. The existence of the gap,
in turn, creates the illusion of fundamental difference, which induces
the children of blue-collar workers to strive to enter the seemingly
higher-class world of white-collar work. By such means, "the productive order is creating a new mass of people who do routine tasks" (p.
178). Like many of their parents before them, these sons and daughters of blue-collar workers who have achieved white-collar status have
found that crossing the latest barrier does not in fact yield "the promised emotional gratification." They have found, instead, "the same

emotional frustration" their parents found in the promised land of increased economic security and increased affluence. And once again the frustrations from being "caught up in this historical shift" are experienced

as a problem of their own . . . inadequate ability to cope. . . . [Consequently,] although certification of mind for these low-level white-collar jobs has little to do with job performance, it . . . . is . . . a necessity to keep class inequality alive in a changing set of productive relations. . . . by making people feel a disparity between what they ought to be as persons as a result of being educated and what they experience directly in their new work, such certification persuades them that the onus rests on themselves. . . .

[In sum,] Calling people's dignity into question is a means by which a class society can create [seemingly] new classes of limited freedom as the old classes disappear. The [ostensible] change of class is portrayed in the society as a matter of improvement, of success, of upward mobility; the frustration and resentment threatened by the gap between promised reward and continued constraint of freedom is diverted into a problem of the self, so that . . . anger at the "system" is undercut because inwardly . . . [workers blame themselves] for not making something of . . . [their] opportunities (pp. 178–83).

Thus do liberal culture, ideology, and capitalist class institutions effectively impose class domination. Thus are problems of class domination disguised, felt, and responded to as problems of personal worth.

XVI

Unions:
Policemen for the Bosses

COMPLEMENTING the impact of our liberal-capitalist society in warping our consciousness and rendering us weaker and more vulnerable to manipulation, specific liberal-capitalist institutions in the workplace like unions primarily function day to day to enforce the status quo.* Even as unions offer certain limited benefits to the minority of so-called organized workers, they repress and disorganize them so they cannot collectively pursue real alternatives and distract and domesticate them so they will despair of the very possibility. The composite picture of unions that emerges from Barbara Garson's *All the Livelong Day* essentially confirms, even as it enriches by its variety, my analysis and description of how the union at Blancs functioned and what it did to workers.

The Table Top Sports Corporation's Ping-Pong equipment factory, the Bumble Bee tuna fish cannery, and the Helena Rubenstein cosmetics factory, the foci for Garson's discussion of unions, represent respectively a "standard nonunion shop," "an unfortunately typi-

* This chapter, as its title reflects, emphasizes what I take to be the dominant institutionalized reality of American unions. Generally subordinated to and in sharp contradiction with that dominant reality is another, very different one, in which unions are an expression of and a locus for intense working class struggle and resistance. The course of development of the historic United Mine Workers strike of 1977–78 exemplifies the interplay between these contradictory realities. For those who wish to learn more about this other side of unions, I strongly recommend two quite dissimilar popular labor histories: Jeremy Brecher's anarchistic *Strike* (Greenwich, Conn.: Straight Arrow Press, 1974), and Richard O. Boyer's and Herbert M. Morais's Old Left *Labor's Untold Story* (New York: Cameron Associates, 1955).

cal union," and a "model union local." In the "unorganized" Ping-Pong equipment factory, overall conditions are much worse than those at union-shop Blancs. The work itself is not noticeably worse in the Ping-Pong equipment factory than at my piston ring factory, at the tuna fish cannery, or at the cosmetics plant. Workers there, as elsewhere, are isolated from one another by the extreme fragmentation of jobs and by the "isolation . . . built into the architecture and the organization of most factories" (p. 19).

But the minimally redeeming features that obtain elsewhere do not exist in the Ping-Pong equipment factory. Standard wages, then about $2.25 an hour, are terrible, if common then throughout the unorganized shops where most of America's workers labor. Physical working conditions are bad: "It's a terrible greasy dirty place" (p. 6). Jobs tend to be dead ends: "When they assign you a place that's it" (p. 6). Without union protection, workers are yelled at, warned, and even fired for doing things like sitting down while working, talking, and going to the bathroom. Fringe benefits are practically nonexistent: "At this place you're only paid for what you work. No holidays, no sick pay, no nothing" (p. 18). And workers are simultaneously afraid of and indifferent to the idea of organizing a union.

By contrast, at the tuna fish cannery working conditions, wages, and protections for workers are measurably better, doubtless because Bumble Bee, like Blancs, is unionized. But the union at Bumble Bee calls to mind the union at Blancs in more ways than this. Bumble Bee's union does not really fight for its members' interests either. Thus, although cannery workers at the end of the day stink of fish from their jobs, "clean-up time" is unpaid. As a result, the company need not provide enough sinks for workers, who crowd the few troughlike sinks before leaving for home: "Clean-up time is another thing we didn't win in our contract," one worker says. "If they had to pay you to clean up they'd put in more sinks," another adds. "Aw no," a third interjects, "If it was on *their* time, they'd invent a hose to spray you down as you walked out the door. Spritz, spritz, spritz" (pp. 28–29).

The point may seem a small one, particularly to readers who do not get dirty on their jobs, but it is indicative of how the union, the company, and the workers relate, and its effect on workers' attitude toward themselves, co-workers, their union, and their jobs is not insignificant: "There's still no wash-up time. It's like pigs at a trough. You get shoved around, water poured down your dress, poked in the eye" (p. 30). The executives' bathroom, we know, will be quite different.

The behavior of this cannery union on more basic bread-and-butter issues is considerably more telling and again remarkably like the behavior of Blancs' union. The main struggle between cannery workers and the company has been over so-called "casual workers," temporary seasonal workers who earn less and enjoy fewer benefits than permanent workers. The "casual workers clause," allowing the company to hire these cheaper workers, was inserted into the cannery contract during the 1971 contract negotiations by the packers' association to cut costs. It was accepted at the time by union negotiators and passed by rank-and-file permanent members without much protest. Conveniently for management and union officials, contracts are negotiated and accepted during months when seasonal workers are not around to defend themselves.

During the summer after the 1971 negotiations the tuna fish cannery was crowded with the cheaper casual workers. Shorter hours prevailed for permanent workers during the year following, because, many felt, so much tuna had been canned in the preceding summer by seasonal workers. Consequently, at the next contract negotiations, hostility to the casual workers clause led to a six-week strike that was "settled" by the union with something less than victory for the workers.

Mary Hyrske, a veteran worker and former union steward and member of the local's executive committee, who herself opposed the clause because she felt that equal work should yield equal pay, describes how acceptance of the clause was managed. Typically, the top company negotiator explained to the union's negotiating committee that Bumble Bee needed casual workers to remain competitive. Typically, the representative from the union's own international headquarters employed easily recognizable divide-and-rule tactics against his own constituency, explaining to union leaders how older workers would benefit from retaining the casual workers clause. The international's rep, in a move that on the face of it appears unimpeachably democratic, then recommended that the executive committee "should vote for it . . . so we could present it to the members and let them discuss it." But, again typically, the subsequent membership meeting turned out to be the kind of union meeting where discussion is not encouraged: "It was a meeting," in Mary Hyrske's words, "where the different members of the negotiating committee got up to speak about why it was a good contract" (p. 36). At that meeting, Mary, who all along had opposed the clause and did not understand how the international's rep even "could bring up a casual workers clause and not speak against it himself," nevertheless did not feel free herself to speak against the clause because "I wasn't on the negotiating committee" (p. 36).

Lorett, a rank-and-file worker, was furious about what had happened: "Bumble Bee didn't lose a thing in that strike. . . . They gave [the casual workers] . . . a raise, but they kept the casual workers. They call 'em something else" (p. 30). Nan Cappy, another scrappy rank-and-filer, says, "A lot of us feel the company has bought the union" (p. 41). She lays the blame for the casual workers clause on the union and explains how union and management together manipulated the workers:

Now some of those [older] women think, "Why should a kid get what I've worked for?" And . . . [management] plays upon that. And the others, they just believe the company and the union. It's like banging your head against the wall. That's when I really want to quit. . . .

The union has done it to these women so many times. So many times. . . .

They finally got themselves together to strike. A six-week strike. (Leave it to our union to have a contract that expires before the season so you can strike for a month without hurting the company.) But those women struck for six weeks. And the union comes back with this probationary worker thing. They get thirty cents an hour less until four hundred and eighty hours. But we won, they say. There's no more casual workers.

I could have told the women to hold out. That the company could still fill the place up with as many casual workers as they wanted. But what's the use? Why should they keep on striking when no matter what they do the union will still sell them out?

SIX BOOKS CONSIDERED

I feel it's useless. Every contract time we'd have to fight the company *and* the union. That's when I feel like quitting (p. 42).

Workers like Nan have learned from their experiences that when they call on the union they are likely to be frustrated. Yet they habitually call on the union, which is all they feel they have. On one of the infrequent occasions, for example, when a group of workers at Bumble Bee stood together against an effective pay decrease, they called the union and were told they "were right but 'go ahead and work the job.' " (p. 40). And when, after work, 22 of them went down to the union office, the union business agent, Stella, told them to "write it up" as a grievance and arranged a meeting with a top management official. "We'll hear his point of view," Stella said, "and we'll have another chance to answer" (p. 40). In the event, workers were not given a chance to talk. Another meeting with management followed, "and again we were not supposed to talk. They did all the talking and it dragged on for weeks," until finally Stella simply surrendered, saying, "It's in the contract but the company won't give in. But we're here to take up any other cause" (p. 41).

Thinking back on the role the union played in these events, Nan Cappy says, "Well, if we hadn't gone to the union in the first place . . . [and instead] all twenty-two of us went into the [company's] office as angry as we were . . . but, when the women have a grievance they call the union" (p. 41).

Stella, of course, is an elected union official, but "no one ever runs against her." Once when a man was set to run against her, "out of the blue, a week before the election the company offered him a better job. . . . So Stella was elected again with no one running against her." Nan herself considered opposing Stella at the last minute but couldn't because "It turns out there's a rule that you have to have attended a majority of union meetings throughout the year. And you have to be nominated a month before and this was only a week before" (pp. 41–42).

In the face of this familiar reality at Bumble Bee, is it any wonder that Mary Hyrske, the former union steward who would like "everyone . . . [to] be involved and come to the meetings so they

UNIONS: POLICEMEN FOR THE BOSSES

could understand and fight for their rights," inevitably is disappointed because "they don't come and then after the negotiations they feel the union pulled the wool over their eyes" (p. 35)?

The unions at Bumble Bee and Blancs are typical unions. The union at Helena Rubenstein, by contrast, is reputed to be "one of the best union locals in the country." Local 8-149, Oil, Chemical and Atomic Workers International Union (OCAW) truly has done a lot for its members. They get the highest pay in the industry; they have relatively good fringe benefits; they have "the right to rotate positions on the assembly line. . . . every two hours. . . . 'Not that one job is so much different from another,' " according to the local's president (p. 62). At its best, the OCAW local also has been "militant" and "democratic" and "has never given up the daily struggle on the shop floor" (p. 64).

The trouble is, its major victories were won and the original tone of the local was set in a series of struggles that took place a generation ago. Those struggles involved meetings that, according to the local's former president, "were really union meetings. Everything was hammered out in the open in front of everyone" (p. 65). Workers were actively involved and stood together. Union officials led the fight.

Today, by contrast, and despite conscious efforts by dedicated union leaders, severe and telltale signs of degeneration are apparent. The degeneration is part of what American unions become once they begin to enter into contractual agreements with companies. Becoming a party to such an agreement means that between contract negotiations, which is to say day after day in the factory, the union is turned into one of the main enforcers of the contract. Thus, writes Garson, "For all its militancy the . . . [OCAW local] has accepted a contractual and moral obligation to help maintain certain standards of production. In this sense they help management to keep the workers working" (p. 67). Under these circumstances, it is hardly surprising that the function of union stewards in circulating around the plant "hearing grievances and interpreting the contract" is transformed into a weapon for management: "In most cases that [function requires] . . . explaining why the workers haven't got any rights or why now is not the time to act" (p. 74).

SIX BOOKS CONSIDERED

Understanding this fundamental reality, members willy nilly become increasingly separated from the union that no longer actively leads them in what objectively remains a class struggle. Some workers who might, for example, make good shop stewards refuse to serve because they do not feel the kind of solidarity that would encourage them to accept the responsibilities of union office (p. 64). Other, older workers, who "know what work would be like without a union . . . . [nonetheless] grumble about the union now, and few come to meetings" (p. 64). To younger workers, who have not experienced the earlier struggles that united workers with their union, the union most tangibly appears simply "as a payroll deduction." Officers, too, are separated. The local's full-time president, an activist in the earlier struggles who remains an unusually committed, decent trade unionist and who, by choice, earns the same salary as an officer he'd be earning by working in the plant, now works at a union office outside the plant. However, officers are not as alienated from the union as workers, who, over the objections of union leaders, voted to hold union meetings every other month instead of every month.

For members, going to meetings has become a chore. The sense of common struggle has been drained away as part of the same process of institutionalization, which, the local's president himself complains, enables the local to "win everything too automatically these days." Discrete negotiations, not mass struggles, are the tools for achieving the kinds of victories the union today by and large seeks. For Local 8–149 this has come to mean total reliance by workers on the negotiating skills of the local's president. Thus the very solidarity and mass involvement that enabled workers earlier to win major victories has been eroded. "Of course," says the local's president ambivalently, "the whole purpose of a strong union is so you can clear things up with a phone call, and win in negotiations without a strike" (p. 69).

The very incorporation of unions consequently has led, even in the case of a relatively "militant" and "democratic" union, to the disinvolvement and pacification of workers. Workers half-recognize the severe limitations imposed by capitalists on what captive unions can negotiate about and are daily made aware on the shop floor of the union leadership's role as "policemen for the bosses" (p. 75). "A labor contract," Garson forcefully points out, "acknowledges the bosses' right to own and run the factory. A contract is the union's pledge to maintain labor peace as long as" the bosses live up to their side of the unequal bargain (p. 74).

Labor laws effectively make labor leaders, who formally bargain and sign contracts with bosses, "policemen for the bosses." Hardly coincidentally,

The very laws that facilitate union organizing make the labor union and its leadership financially and criminally responsible for strikes or other labor troubles that arise while the contract is in force. . . . In any wildcat strike the first person the manager calls is the union leader. This leader is contractually bound to scurry over and order the workers back to work. According to law the union is responsible for losses and damages due to "illegal" job actions. The union treasury can be emptied and . . . the leaders can actually be jailed for insufficiently fulfilling their obligation to keep the plant running. For these reasons they always make their appearance to stop a walkout.

But most union officials are hardly making perfunctory statements when they order the workers back to work. Today's wildcats are usually as much of a challenge to the union as to the company. Outspoken workers face reprisals from both groups (p. 74).

To make matters still worse, unions, although they have the potential to make rank-and-file members feel better about themselves by giving them some sense of participating in shaping their own destinies, tend in fact to make members feel more helpless. Again Garson hits the nail on the head:

A good union could counter some of these feelings of worthlessness and helplessness. But usually they just make it worse. And with the same motive [as the company]—control. . . .

Hoarding skills, contacts, and information is one way to hold on to power and keep other people dependent. . . . [Thus workers are prevented from developing] the confidence that comes only from "doing it for themselves." . . .

Even when the unions are actually fighting for their members, they do not encourage them to fight for themselves. If they are not trying to trick the workers, they are certainly not trying to educate or develop them.

Consciously or unconsciously, . . . [union officials] maintain individual power by fostering ignorance, creating divisions, and by exacerbating painful feelings of inadequacy. Exactly what the company does. . . .

SIX BOOKS CONSIDERED

Unless they are extraordinarily dedicated, a permanent, out-of-plant leadership eventually becomes, like the company management, another professional group with full time to devote to outmaneuvering and putting down the members.

The union itself becomes another bureaucracy before which the workers feel worthless and helpless (p. 76–79).

But even "extraordinarily dedicated" union leaders cannot alone prevent the assimilation of the union by the capitalist establishment, as Garson's own case study of the OCAW local attests. They can at best only minimize its abuses. Once institutionalized, union leaders, like foremen, have a constituted role to play in the capitalist system that (other things being equal) dominates their behavior. The only factor that can change this and reconstitute and maintain the union as a fighting force for workers is a strong, disciplined workers' movement through which workers repeatedly take collective action with the growing consciousness that capitalists' and workers' interests indeed are fundamentally antagonistic and that the workers' struggle to vindicate their interests is nothing less than an ongoing class struggle to overthrow capitalism.

In that struggle, the union organization itself is one of the prizes. If unions are not recaptured by class conscious, politically active workers, they will remain captives of capitalism. So, if *in a capitalist system any union is likely to be better than no union at all*, even the best of unions as at present constituted has in the most fundamental sense turned to collaboration—supporting and enforcing the very system that exploits the workers it purports to represent.

The UAW, which has a reputation for being a "progressive" trade union, exemplifies the problem. In contract after contract since 1955, UAW national leaders bargained with automobile companies primarily for higher wages and better fringe benefits off the job. And following contract after contract, as these union leaders ignored local, on-the-job problems, like speedup, locals all over wildcatted. The UAW did not bargain on such issues because its leaders "recognize that . . . [it is] management's prerogative to run the plant" (p. 97). Manufacturers, leaders know, "are adamant on issues affecting productivity. To GM the line speed is sacred. They will allow no arbitration on this issue." In recognition and exchange for UAW abdication

UNIONS: POLICEMEN FOR THE BOSSES

on this fundamental issue of control, corporate management has essentially said to national union leaders, " 'O.K., we'll give you the wage increase, but you can't restrict our means of getting that money right back out of you' " (p. 97).

Workers who sought to influence the speed of production, the organization of the manufacturing process, and the nature of the product would by contrast be questioning the very right of private ownership in the means of production. Such questioning is not tolerated by management or by unions. Owners and managers must maintain control of production because production is the source of capitalist profits. However, it is also the source of profound antagonism.

SIX BOOKS CONSIDERED

Working Again:
Liberal versus Marxian Understandings

BUT if production is the heart of capitalism, capitalism, not production as such, is the problem. This fact for us is as easy to miss or deny as it is crucial to understand. Richard Balzer's *Clockwork*, despite its great merits, is shaped by its author's liberal unconsciousness or basic avoidance of this fact. As such, the book is useful to consider at length, not only for its positive contributions to our understanding of what work is like, but also for its manifest and inevitable failure to understand why it is that way. The consideration of *Clockwork* also provides a fitting conclusion to my case against capitalism and liberalism, because Balzer, like me, has written a very concrete book out of and about his direct experience as a worker for five months in an electronics factory. His developed liberal understanding of the experience stands in marked contrast to my developing Marxian understanding.

Balzer never seriously explores the issue of the relationship between the quality of work and workers' lives and the nature of capitalist society. He refers to the issue, but at no point does he pause to consider it. In the last sentence of the first chapter Balzer, without comment, quotes a factory worker who directs him to "Say that I'm a cog in a capitalist system" (p. 19). Having dutifully done so, for the next three hundred pages of the book until its Conclusion there is virtually no consideration in *Clockwork* of what that remark might mean. Only in the Conclusion does Blazer belatedly ask: "Is it possible for the prevalent *us* and *them* atmosphere at work to be replaced by a feeling of *we?* Is conflict between management and labor an inherent element of capitalism? Is there a fundamental conflict between the human needs of workers and the profit needs of business?" (p. 328).

Finally driven to ask such a question, in no small part by what he personally had experienced and learned about the Western Electric factory in which he worked, Balzer in the end cannot face answering it. Rather, avoiding confronting the full implications of what he himself saw and describes, Balzer can only respond: "There are no easy answers to such questions, but if there is any possibility of genuine co-operation it will not come out of a system initiated, planned, and directed by management alone, because management and workers often have different and conflicting interests" (p. 328). This response essentially constitutes Balzer's entire consideration of capitalism's necessary implications for work.

His book, in fact, is predicated on the devout hope that somehow workers' and managements' interests are reconcilable within our capitalist system. Consequently, with a faith only somewhat shaken by his factory experience, Balzer concludes the book sincerely recommending what by now can only be called the standard list of liberal reforms to humanize and democratize capitalist work so as to reduce its destructive impact on workers' lives. The approach is predicated on the assumption, which flies in the face of historical and present reality, that management does not really understand that the workplace is dehumanizing and/or that there are acceptable methods for improving it. If management did understand, the argument goes, management would reform the workplace.

In the case of *Clockwork* this approach is central not only to how the author conceives what he experienced and to what he concludes, but also to the fact that Balzer was able to have these experiences at the Western Electric plant in the first place. For Richard Balzer worked at the plant and wrote this book with the prior permission and support of Western Electric's top management, as well as with the knowledge of his co-workers. He was introduced to management by a retired Western Electric engineer who quite correctly saw Balzer as a free-lance writer having "neither a preconceived antagonism toward industrial management" (read "capitalism"), "nor a condescending attitude toward people who earn their living by factory labor."[*] With these attractive qualities, Balzer, after being carefully screened by management, was given his temporary job as a manual worker in the plant and afforded access to statistics and management's views on worklife.

That the book still comes off as honest as well as sympathetic to the workers' plight and not uncritical of management, is a testament not simply to Balzer's integrity, but also to the acumen with which Western Electric's sophisticated management made its choice. Had management, instead, simply encouraged some public relations hack to write an in-house apology for Western Electric's version of capitalist work, the resulting book would have appeared as overt propaganda and not been very persuasive. As written, *Clockwork* is simultaneously believable, engrossing, and fundamentally unthreatening— unthreatening, that is, unless one reads it as unwittingly exposing the gross inadequacy of the liberal consciousness of work and of the reforms liberals advocate to correct the enormous problems they recognize.

LIBERALISM'S LIMITATIONS

The very title of the book and the passages in it that suggest why *Clockwork* is so named epitomize certain limitations on the liberal understanding and liberal proposals for reform of work. In contrast with the way I, for example, have dealt with the matter of work time in chapter 4, Balzer not infrequently tends to treat symptoms as if they were the disease. The problem, according to the title, appears to be not capitalist management, but the clock—which indeed, at the present level of consciousness of many workers, no doubt often does seem to them to be a major cause of their dissatisfaction. Thus Balzer says, "Probably no one thing affects and bothers shopworkers more

---

[*] "Letters to the Editor," *New York Times Book Review* (September 12, 1976), p. 49.

than the time clock" (p. 80). He refers to "the clock's control" (p. 85) and writes:

The time clock restricts personal movements by reducing the day to periods in which things are allowed and not allowed. It routinizes the day by regimenting personal needs to meet the workings of a bell. . . . As one woman told me, . . . "The bell tells us when to smoke, when to eat, when to start work, and when to stop" (p. 84).

This manner of describing the impact of a clock on human beings is not simply a matter of style. It also implies content, reflecting a way of understanding reality that Marx has called "fetishistic." Wittingly or unwittingly, it accepts appearances and diverts readers from essences, in this instance, by seemingly attributing to a machine, which in itself has no power at all to control anyone's life, the capacity to do what only living creatures—and in particular in America the capitalist owning and managerial class—can do. It is not the clock as such that regiments workers. It is rather the production relationship between capitalists and workers, within which the time clock is merely one weapon among many that management utilizes to dominate workers to achieve capitalists' ends.

Thus understood, the removal of the time clock, although it doubtless would eliminate one of the most blatant symbols of many workers' oppression, would not change the essential exploitative and dehumanizing nature of work embedded in capitalist relationships. If eliminating the time clock or allowing workers, for example, to arrange their own working hours more flexibly to suit their outside needs might for a period make workers feel better, which is not unimportant, that in itself would not fundamentally affect the quality of work or the purposes for which they must work under capitalism. In fact, to the extent that such reforms increased productivity, as nearly all liberal reformers argue they will, their net effect might well be to increase exploitation, while marginally restructuring it so that workers temporarily could enjoy it more.

In proposing such alluring reforms, *Clockwork* makes its contribution to maintaining progressive capitalism. The book, however, is not simply capitalist-serving or "pro-capitalist." Much of the book reflects Balzer's deep sensitivity to workers as human beings and his largely unarticulated awareness that the mechanisms and authority relationships at work that "alienate" workers are derived from management's ceaseless demands for productivity and profits—the legitimacy of which the author does not question. Much of the book also is a story of the ways in which many workers somehow salvage elements of dignity and satisfaction from their lives inside and outside the plant.

But Balzer's sincere humanism and the attractiveness of what he proposes, which give the appearance of doing substantial justice both to workers' and capitalists' interests, are based upon the presumption that there is no inherent, fundamental, and antagonistic class conflict between workers and capitalists. This liberal presumption precludes serious confrontation with capitalist reality and often means the questions that are unexplored about work and workers' lives are at least as important as those that are.

Balzer's introduction is indicative. *Clockwork*, Balzer aptly says, "is a testimony to the human spirit, to the capacity of people to transform and alter an environment in which they exist. It is about the richness and diversity of human beings, about people and their search for a satisfying life" (p. 12). What tends to be ignored in this "testimony" is why workers' efforts to transform their work environment in order to find some satisfaction in their lives are so desperately necessary in the first place.

Again, when Balzer tells several women he couldn't last for years in a factory because he'd probably lose his temper and get himself fired, one of the women incisively retorts: "That's a lot of bull. I watched you, and you'd do just like the rest of us. If you had to be here ten or fifteen years you'd figure out a way to do it" (p. 5). To which the author candidly responds: "She was probably right. I had assumed that I couldn't take the monotony, the sameness of the jobs, the authoritarianism. Yet experience taught me that most people can and do adjust to factory life, and if I had to I would too" (p. 5). Which is fair enough. But in the telling, why people adjust to their monotonous and authoritarian work lives almost gets lost. They "adjust" because they have to, because they have no meaningful alternative.

WORKING AGAIN

Similarly, in expressing his appreciation to Western Electric for allowing him to do what all other companies he approached had forbidden, Balzer disarmingly writes:

It is unfortunate that many companies spend vast sums advertising the products they produce, and building a corporate image, while trying to hide or at least divert attention from the workday world of the people who produce their products.

Then, as if to explain why companies do so, he continues:

The history of labor relations in the United States in this century has been dominated by an adversary relationship, with management pitted against workers. Improved working conditions, increased wages, and better benefits have largely had to be fought for. The recognition that workers are not machines, and that labor is more than a commodity, has been slow to develop (p. 11).

Indeed. But why? Why do companies try to hide the producers' reality, while making false claims in advertising about the products? Why have workers had to fight so hard for whatever they achieved? On these issues Balzer does not have very much to say. He does, however, give us hints and much evidence from which we can draw our own conclusions.

CONFINING HUMAN RELATIONS

In his chapter on "The Human Environment," Balzer writes about the daily patterns of social relations at work. Although much of what he has to say is not in this chapter explained in terms of the imperatives of production and related company rules that structure social relations in the plant, Balzer still manages to communicate the texture of workplace social life and of workers' reactions to their jobs and to each other. The reader can sense how the workday is segmented and defined according to company needs and rules and how workers, within these narrow limits, necessarily become ingenious in creating a more human social environment on the job. "Our workday," Balzer writes, "included not only the tasks we performed, but coffee breaks, lunch, coming in early, staying late, talking, teasing, joking, bitching, breaking rules, and figuring out ways to beat the system " (p. 22).

Many workers in his factory came in early to share coffee with co-workers, chat, and catch a smoke in the areas where smoking before work was permitted. Clustered in groups that usually were all male or all female, they would relax before starting work and banter with each other. Before work, as well as during their two ten-minute breaks and their half-hour unpaid lunch period, the men, like those with whom I worked, would talk about sports, swap stories about their military service, discuss problems within the plant, sometimes talk about their families, argue about current issues of political economy—inflation, the gasoline crisis, and Watergate—and watch and make comments about women, especially attractive women.

Thus legitimate socializing was confined during the workday to twenty minutes of company time. During the unpaid lunch period, people would eat, talk, kid around, smoke, play cards or chess. Some went upstairs to the cafeteria; others, especially women, took their meals in their own work area. Except for those who belonged to no informal group, workers tended to establish rigid patterns of where and with whom they would eat. Tables in the cafeteria were thought of by groups of workers as belonging to them during their lunch period. And when someone else occupied "their table," its "owners" were displeased. Those who chose to eat in their hot and crowded workplaces established similar patterns. In both cases, the author came to realize, workers were trying to stake out some "personal space" (p. 27), an area where for the moment they could "feel very comfortable" and relatively inviolable.

In the remaining seven-plus hours of the regular workday, people had very little "personal space." Most seemed "bored with and disinterested in the tasks they performed" (p. 30). Although some workers, judging from what they said, seemed to mind work less than others, the apparent differences may be attributable less to real differences in workers' personalities and in their jobs than to differences in the way they described their resignation. Take the male worker who said, "On really bad days it doesn't matter what you do, the day

334

won't hurry for you. . . . And it isn't the work. Hell, half the time I think my twelve-year-old-kid could do my job."

Or take a female worker, whom Balzer refers to as someone whom "Neither the clock nor the job seemed to get to," who said: "Oh, . . . once in a while I get bored, if I'm not feeling good . . . , then things go badly, but otherwise, really, I don't mind any of the jobs. I mean, a job is a job, and I just do it. That way I find the time goes faster." And the other woman, who declared, "When I get bored, I think of the new swimming pool we just bought from money I'm making. I think how every hour that passes means we've paid for more of that swimming pool. . . . and then I feel better" (pp. 30–31).

With such jobs and feelings about them, workers typically try to somewhat vary their own routines, to fashion "challenges" from within their tasks. But nearly always, of course, the confines are set by company demands for their performance. One worker, for example, changed the number of boards he worked on at the same time, or the pattern in which he worked on a board: "Every so often. . . . I'll work backward, and then forward. But really it doesn't help much. I hate being cooped up; sitting on my ass putting on weight doing these dumb jobs" (p. 31). Talking also helped many workers pass the day, which is really all most sought.

Since workers are not chained to their workspaces during working hours, even relatively immobilized workers usually get some chance to move around. Although again the imperatives of production and the relations of production set the bounds for what is tolerated, within those bounds there are the variations Balzer chooses to emphasize that depend on the personalities of individual workers and their supervisors:

Often during the day, some days more than others, one feels like getting up, walking around, and talking to other people. A sense of how free you are to move around depends largely on what your immediate supervisor is like. . . . some . . . made you feel uncomfortable leaving your seat at all, and . . . others . . . supposedly didn't care how much you walked around as long as you got your work done (p. 33).

But, adds Balzer,

SIX BOOKS CONSIDERED

Walking and talking in our area was something that had to be done quickly. . . . Jack, our supervisor [who was considered by workers as one of the best supervisors in the plant], didn't like to see us just standing around talking. We usually had time for only a few quick jokes or comments. Walking and talking almost became a game—watching with one eye for Jack while talking to someone else. Frequently you'd be in the midst of talking with someone when Jack would approach. He didn't have to say anything. Just a sideward glance or movement in your direction was enough to get you moving (pp. 33–34).

Some fun, these "games"—like adults playing hookey and worrying about the truant officer. Is it any wonder, then, that workers try to snatch a few extra minutes of "free" time away from the watchful supervisory eye?

"We didn't have the problem of Jack's watchful eye if we left the area, so a trip to the vending machine or the bathroom was often relaxing. The bathrooms were not just places to take care of biological needs, but places to relax, either to get away from work, to enjoy a smoke, or to hang out" (p. 34). Shades of public school, understandably so. The bathrooms in repressive institutions like factories and public schools become a kind of "no-man's land," to which people escape to relative privacy, a place where supervisory personnel by implicit agreement normally hesitate to openly or aggressively exercise their power and authority.

In addition to these "illegitimate," if tolerated, small escapes from work during the working day, there were also at Western Electric occasional legitimated escapes, such as the company-sponsored production group meeting. The way workers responded to those meetings tells as much about how they feel about their jobs as anything they might say. "Meetings," the author says, "though infrequently held, were enjoyed by most people" (p. 36). The sense in which they were "enjoyed" is revealing:

The longer the meeting, the more time we were legitimately away from our work. On more than one occasion I heard people whisper, "Ask something, ask something."

Questioned out, the meeting would end, and it would be time to return to work. The leisuerly pace of the walk back to our shop was in marked contrast to the desperate pace set when we left the plant at the end of the day.

WORKING AGAIN

About that stampede at day's end, Balzer writes:

The last of the day's activities in the plant is leaving. The three-o'clock bell rings, and there is a mad dash for the time clock, the door, and the waiting cars. . . . I wondered why people made such a mad dash to get out of the plant when they knew they were destined to be stuck in long, unpleasant lines of cars. People offered a number of explanations, reflecting a deep feeling of relief when a day of work is finished, and an anxiousness to leave the plant. Whatever the reason, once that bell rang, people wanted to get out of the plant no matter what (pp. 37–38).

One reason, we now surely can appreciate, is to escape the domination that shapes workers' work lives—even if the escape is only to the liberated zones of their own cars, backed up in bumper-to-bumper traffic in company parking lots.

On the job and under that domination, which affects all aspects of work life, human relations are complex and uneven. Writing about this aspect of work as if it were not in large part a function of what our capitalist society and capitalist work make of us, Balzer says:

The human environment at work, supportive for many, can be cruel and devastating for others. People can be very nice and very compassionate. They can also be very mean and catty. Many people enjoy the informal teasing, the constant joking, but others don't. . . . After working . . . for a while I learned that workers have mixed feelings about other workers. One day in sheer frustration Ann told me, "It kills me. We bust our butts to really produce, and it's not fair that Sylvia sits there and doesn't do anything. . . . on a farm, . . . the strong horse always [pulls] . . . extra for the weaker horse, and that's how it is in here" (p. 39).

But why, Balzer does *not* ask, did Ann feel that way? Why was it important to her that Sylvia pull her own weight? Is it only because people are "just that way"? Or more particularly, is it also because Ann and Sylvia are part of the same production group and because under Western Electric's bonus system Ann's bonus is partly dependent on Sylvia's performance? Although Balzer may not understand this, from his later chapter on the bonus system, it is apparent that Ann's frustration and anger is directly connected to how Western Electric organizes production and payment for production.

All hassles at work are not so obviously traceable to the way the

SIX BOOKS CONSIDERED

company organizes production and structures human relations to its own purposes, however. Therefore, it is ironic that two of the main examples Balzer discusses are, even though he typically fails to make the tangible connection. Continuing with his unsystematic description of "the human environment" at work, he introduces the second case:

Generally, . . . negative comments remain fairly muted but the kidding can occasionally cause serious unhappiness. Tempers can flare and a person can start crying. . . .

Most times the teasing comments are innocent—the intention . . . is to have a little fun but not to drive someone to tears. People are sometimes intentionally cruel. . . . The most graphic example I remember was. . . . [a] . . . woman, who had just transferred to the department . . . , [and] had spoiled a number of boards. The layout [the person who sets up the particular job], a woman, really chewed her out. Dale didn't say anything in her own defense. She just sat there as the woman yelled at her. When the woman left, she began crying. She continued to do her work as the tears ran down her cheeks. I went over and tried to comfort her. . . . In a halting voice she said, "What did she think, I wanted to make those mistakes? I didn't know how to do the job, no one really taught me. I didn't want to do it wrong." . . . [When she had recovered, she said:] "That's what I can't stand about this place, the way some people treat you. Nancy [the layout] treated me like a dog. I'll get her back, you just watch. I'll get even with her" (pp. 39–40).

So, worker turns upon worker, while the powers that structure and even facilitate such confrontations seem invisible. Balzer again does not ask why did Nancy treat Dale that way? Simply because that's the way "human nature" is? Because Nancy was having a bad day? Because Nancy is a cruel person? Or for some other similar personalistic reason? If we accept as adequate such superficial explanations of common occurrences, for which there is in this case no evidence at all in the book, the question still remains, why did Nancy's "cruelty" take the particular form it did? Why should "cruel" Nancy pressure inadequately trained Dale to produce better and more boards? And why was Dale inadequately trained in the first place? These questions, like so many others, cannot be meaningfully answered without recognizing the impact that capitalism has on our workplaces. If everything that happens at work cannot be explained by the connection between work and capitalism, very little of what happens can be fully understood in isolation from that connection. An appreciation of the capitalist connection is, however, nearly absent from this chapter, which Balzer lamely concludes with, "Good or bad, the human environment defines a major portion of a person's working day" (p. 41).

THE RULES AND CAPITALIST RULE

That same failure to make the capitalist connection permeates Balzer's otherwise very informative and stimulating chapter on rules in the factory. As he writes about rules, it becomes clear that prevailing patterns of authority and power relations dominate the factory's "human environment," which is earlier said to be so important in defining workers' lives. The failure in this chapter at first sight appears especially surprising, because the author is aware of the fundamental purpose of factory rules: "the company has set up an intricate set of rules designed to minimize distraction and maintain a high production schedule" (p. 90). Nevertheless, because so many of the rules about which he writes do not appear to be immediately necessary to achieve capitalism's central economic purposes, Balzer often seems to lose all sense of the frequently attenuated, complex, but remaining connections.

This loss enables the author simultaneously to recognize that the rules themselves contribute to conflict between workers and management, while still remaining unaware that the general nature of the rules, the mode in which they are enacted, and their effect upon workers must be understood as aspects of the capitalist system. The discussion of power and authority thus is so abstracted from any consideration of capitalist rule that once again what are primarily symptoms appear to be taken as causes. Rules appear as a primary source of conflict rather than as a method through which class domination is expressed and exacerbated, but also at times defused and diverted. Balzer frequently seems to blame the rules, as he does the clock, for the dictatorship of factory life in which a minority "they" rule the majority:

By setting the rules as it has, management has helped to foster an atmosphere of *we* and *they*. The company is the all-powerful source of authority, and it becomes *they*. The workers required to live within the structure the company sets, become *we*. This duality is constantly felt and expresses itself in a variety of ways (p. 90).

Of course, the "duality" is not created by, but certainly is reflected in, the rules. Rather, the duality is created by the stark fact that one class in our society owns and controls the means of production and therefore holds rule-making power and authority in the factory, while another is dependent and naturally feels dominated. So understood, much of what Balzer says about rules makes more sense.

Take the company rule against smoking, which has no obvious direct relationship to achieving the purposes of capitalist work. According to the rules, smoking "is restricted to certain areas and to certain times of day. Basically you are allowed to smoke only during the two breaks and lunch" (p. 86). The rule, however, is not strictly enforced. In part because the rule "is bitterly resented by large numbers of people. . . . the company has chosen to enforce [it] selectively" (p. 86). Many heavy smokers, for example, smoke regularly in the bathrooms, and their conduct normally is tolerated.

So workers are not legally allowed to smoke except at stated times and places, but in fact they are "allowed" to do so within much broader limits and with relative impunity. So what! How may capitalism be implicated? Surely, unlike other realms of work life we might consider, whether workers smoke or not is a matter of little economic concern for capitalists not connected with the cigarette and related industries.

Quite true. But we must recall that *capitalism is more than simply a profit-making mechanism. It is a political economy, a social system in which one class rules another for its own purposes.* And it is within the context of class dictatorship that rules and enforcement patterns on matters that in and of themselves are not of immediate economic significance to capitalists must be understood.

The company, on the one hand, makes rules not only to directly facilitate profit-making, but also to repeatedly let the worker know who's boss. As in the army and most public schools, that message comes through loud and clear: "One day Jean, who usually seems very relaxed about the rules told me, 'There are too many rules here. It's just like being in school. There's one place to smoke, one place to do this, and one place to do that. If you get out of your seat to talk to someone, you're breaking a rule' " (p. 88).

The company, on the other hand, selectively enforces many of its rules, like the one against smoking. Selective enforcement serves three additional purposes. First and most obviously, it operates as a cheap safety valve:

> Within certain limits, the breaking of rules is not very disruptive to the company. It is incredible, in fact, how infrequently major breaches of rules occur within the plant. If the company chose to enforce all of its rules strictly, workers would undoubtedly react in more negative ways toward their work. Sabotaging work . . . might become a big problem. People can be pushed only so far. To have restrictive rules that can be broken to a limited extent allows a necessary escape valve (p. 92).

Second, selective enforcement provides the company with an area of discretion within which in a particular case it may "legally" decide whether to punish rule breakers or let them off. This adds another weapon to the company arsenal, for purposes of general intimidation and for specific use against, say, those whom the company perceives as "troublemakers."

Beyond that, the setting of various rules, combined with their selective enforcement, endows certain, wholly unthreatening rule-breaking acts by workers with the illusory significance of being acts of personal assertion. It diverts workers from matters requiring collective struggle. Thus the company distracts workers from more fundamental matters and effectively shapes even some of the ways in which workers assert "personal control":

> a new worker is usually shown the "ropes" by other workers. This includes being told about rules and ways to break them. This shared, subversive information helps build a sense of solidarity among workers. The breaking of a rule represents more than the simple disregarding of an order. The action often serves to allow a worker to express some sense of personal control over

his environment, as well as to demonstrate and promote solidarity with other workers (p. 90).

Marvelous! That means, in the case of smoking in the bathroom, that the worker is effectively permitted to commit minor acts of "rebellion" which are of no consequence to capitalism. It means too that worker solidarity is somewhat enhanced in this case by the accumulated commitment of otherwise trivial acts of "resistance":

The worker has found not only a place to smoke but, more importantly, a place that has not been designated by the company. Since a worker often feels that much if not all of what he does is done in places designated by the company, under company control, finding ways to express personal freedom from this institutional regimentation is important. When the day is so structured, being able to do something illegal can become very satisfying (p. 90).

So much has "personal freedom" been degraded! It is hardly surprising, then, that to the extent the company is successful in manipulating workers' behavior to superficially satisfy their "needs not to feel powerless and impotent" (p. 92), major breaches of rules in the plant are infrequent. *The company protects its real interests in part by facilitating in a complex way rule violations that do not affect those interests.* And if, as Balzer concludes, "The need to break rules will remain as long as workers exercise little control over their immediate environment," for precisely so long will it remain in the company's interest to try by rule making and selective enforcement to influence which rules workers choose to violate and how.

Since success in manipulation and domination is limited by the current reality of class struggle, companies act to subvert whatever solidarity workers can achieve. Companies intimidate, shame, split, and coopt workers. Nowhere is this clearer than in Balzer's chapters on quality control and on the bonus system.

CONTROL: QUALITY AND HUMAN

Quality control, we know, is a serious problem today for big business. Given what capitalist work is like and how it negatively

342

shapes workers' performances, elaborate systems of control are employed by companies in an effort to mold workers and production to their purposes. The effort to control quality can be only partially successful because here too success is limited by the class conflict between workers and management. Such conflict is expressed in intricate and uneven ways.

Balzer first became aware of the company's concern with quality and of the quality control system itself at his initial orientation when a company representative said, "We have a top notch quality control system, but you can't inspect quality into a product . . . you must build it in" (p. 108). In his first week or so on the job, however, the author was preoccupied simply with learning how to do his tasks. Although initially he worked relatively slowly, he believed he was building his boards correctly until a "process checker," the lowest level of the quality control hierarchy, told him he was not and returned the boards to him for correction and resubmission.

Not until the end of his second week on the job, when he noticed "a sheet, displaying a graph, in front of . . . [his] working position," did Balzer realize there was more to quality control than that. It was then he noticed "there were similar graphs in front of everyone's positions" (p. 108). The quality control charts, he learned, graphed a worker's actual performance relative to a company-determined norm for the job. Balzer's performance, needless to say, did not measure up to standards. Alarmed, he spoke to a fellow worker who both sought to reassure him that his quality would improve as he got accustomed to the job and advised him to "Try not to pay any attention to" the chart. But Balzer was not reassured. He was "embarrassed": "Somehow it seemed that it was like displaying a low grade for everyone else to see. I couldn't understand how I could *not* be bothered by it" (p. 110).

As he talked with other workers, it turned out that most of them apparently were equally upset by the public display of the record of their mistakes. Not only that, but the process checkers, he learned, didn't even record on the charts every mistake made because they sympathized with workers who were made nervous by their public display. One process checker said, "Really, if you ask me, if the company were smart they would get rid of those darn charts. They just make people feel bad. Most people in here want to do their job correctly, and the company should work under that premise" (p. 111). The problem, then, as the checker and Balzer himself see it, is that the company doesn't understand that at least certain of its quality control methods are counterproductive.

In the shop, as time passed, increasing numbers of workers in Balzer's group complained about the quality control charts. Complaints further intensified "with news of our poor bonus." But the complaints did not develop into overt hostility until Balzer's production group was officially declared "out of control" by management. This meant that the group's accumulated demerits for poor-quality work during a particular period exceeded "a predetermined statistical limit based on production levels." Being "out of control" literally seems to mean that the normal quality control system no longer is capable of controlling production quality. Being declared "out of control" therefore subjected the group to abnormal procedures "to locate the group's problems" and to bring the group once again "under control." These procedures had serious repercussions for workers.

First, the so-called courtesy check, which by informal custom allowed a worker learning a new routine to not have initial mistakes charted on the worker's quality control chart, was eliminated. Second, process checkers were instructed by their superiors to scrupulously chart every mistake workers made. This crackdown by management made people very nervous; tempers rose. But bench workers' frustrations were taken out on the checkers, who, simply by doing their job, were caught in the middle.

With the continuing deterioration of human relations and product quality, a meeting was called with the quality control people to try to understand and resolve the group's problems. Jill, an experienced bench worker, did not expect much from the upcoming meeting: "What do you think a meeting will help to do? All that will happen, if we say anything, is we'll get in trouble. . . . They won't do anything about our complaints. They just want us to see things their way. There's no way I'm going to say anything" (p. 113).

WORKING AGAIN

The meeting was attended by engineers, time study people, the group's supervisor, and their department chief. It was chaired by Ralph, the "quality control engineer for our department, a person few of us had ever met. . . ." It was a one-sided affair, punctuated by worker outrage. Open discussion was not the name of this game.

Ralph began by saying, "I'd like to be bold enough to make some suggestions on how we can help you people improve the quality of your work. Quality is important because it's important to our customers. . . . today there is unbelievable competition from other companies in this country and from the Japanese. Now if we can't build something well and build it inexpensively, the Bell System Companies will buy elsewhere." . . . We use the quality control charts to isolate the cause of the mistakes. . . . and correct them. I know that some of you don't like these charts, but you shouldn't take them personally. We only use them to help us in isolating mistakes. . . . Now I wonder if any of you have any questions?"

Ignoring the request only for questions, Jane blurted out:

"Well, yes, I find the quality charts to be very discouraging and humiliating."

Even before Ralph got the chance to get the why out of his mouth, Jane continued, her voice full of emotion. "If I see the chart one more time, I think I'm going to scream. I've worked . . . a long time for this company and this is the first time I've ever been in this situation. I keep on making mistakes on this new job. Every day I make a mistake . . . and get so nervous I do worse. I hate that chart staring me in the face. I don't mind my supervisor seeing it, but I don't think it should be up for everyone to see."

Ralph tried to mollify her. . . . "Those charts are up there not to embarrass you, but so the supervisor can see them. We're afraid if they were just given to the supervisor they might get buried in his desk."

At which point the author had great difficulty keeping silent any longer. Aware of the shaming effect of the charts and of the transparency of the explanation for their use, he "waited for someone to say something. I was sure someone would point out that our supervisor rarely if ever went around checking the sheets, so that couldn't be the reason to have the charts up. Since no one said anything, I finally made the point." In response, the velvet glove of management peeled back to betray its iron fist:

SIX BOOKS CONSIDERED

Ralph smiled and repeated what he had just said. When Jane started complaining again about the humiliation she felt, he looked at her and in a lowered voice said, "Maybe there's nothing to say except that you aren't working well."

The room was silent again and then Grace, a woman with eleven years of service, said, "You know, as long as I've worked here I've never understood the need for those personalized charts. I remember when I began working here I was always embarrassed by them. If you ask me they aren't helpful; they just make you feel uncomfortable. I don't know why the company uses them."

Larry McNeil, our department chief, spoke for the first time. "Why do we need them? Of course we need them. How are you going to tell the bad apple in the bunch unless you have the quality charts?"

As if to recoup from that momentary display of management candor, Ralph then said, "I feel you people are taking this all too personally. Those charts are posted to help you, to help you improve your work. Look, if you know what you're doing wrong, you can improve on it. If you make work with fewer mistakes your bonus will go up." To which the author retorted: " 'If the quality control sheets are so helpful, why aren't the ratings of the supervisors posted to help them?' People laughed."

At least some people laughed. Ralph apparently did not appreciate the humor. The meeting itself seemed on the verge of going "out of control," so "Ralph, instead of answering my question, asked if there were any other questions. When none were put forth, he closed the meeting" (pp. 114–16).

On the way back to work from the meeting, workers talked about it.

Jill, the woman who had warned me to be quiet, said, "See, what did I tell you? They didn't want to hear what we had to say. They had an answer for everything, didn't they? They're not going to change anything. That's why I didn't say anything. I felt sorry for Jane, but she should have known better. She's been here long enough to know not to speak up at one of these meetings. You'll see, they're going to make it even harder on her" (p. 116).

A number of other workers also "thought Jane should have known better than to speak up." But, on the other hand, "A few people

WORKING AGAIN

thought Jane had been courageous to speak up. One fellow told me, 'I didn't say nothing because I don't speak English so good, but I feel just like Jane. But now I'm glad I didn't say nothing because all they do is bullshit with you when you tell them how you feel' " (p. 116).

The group meeting had not been much of a success for anyone, least of all management. Understandably, therefore, no more meetings of the entire group were called by management. The following month things remained about the same—the lowered bonus, the strained relations between process checkers and bench people. By the time the author had left the plant some time later, however, for some unknown reason the tension had eased. Quality control, in short, was returning to normal. What that meant was that the same "complicated and elaborate quality control system" which predated the described events was being restored. That system, to Balzer's mind, is on the whole necessary and deserves "much . . . credit" for the "high quality" of Western Electric products during a period "when there is increasing national concern about the deteriorating quality of much of our manufactured products" (p. 117). Balzer's main objection to the quality control system expectably is to the "public display of the charts," which he recognizes as "degrading" and in any event holds to be "an ineffective way of trying to improve quality" (p. 117).

In the end, he cannot really understand why events developed as they did: "One would think that, when the deleterious aspects of such a small feature as hanging the charts had been brought to the management's attention, it would have been corrected, but that isn't what happened. Lower management ignored the feelings of the bench workers and, what's worse, gave credence to the feeling in our shop that speaking up at meetings was a waste of time" (p. 118). Confused, Balzer can only conclude the chapter wishfully declaring the company "should be more sensitive to the human problems that their quality control program has created" (p. 119).

To all of which one can only respond, But, Mr. Balzer, the job of management is not to be concerned with human problems as such. And speaking up at meetings, in truth, generally is a waste of time as well as often dangerous. And besides, the entire quality control system was developed to compensate for the negative effects of the more subtle control system inherent in the capitalist division of labor that so alienates workers. Thus understood, the practice of hanging quality control charts, which in the abstract certainly could easily be discontinued without exactly endangering the capitalist system, may in the concrete context of this particular group have a function of which you seem unaware. Perhaps, for example, the practice is tied in with the operation of the plant's bonus system.

THE BONUS SYSTEM AND CAPITALIST RATIONALITY

The bonus system at Western Electric, one learns in Balzer's next chapter, is, like the one at Blancs, so complex, so inequitable, and so seemingly irrational as to appear nearly to defy human understanding. Why the bonus system is like this is not considered in *Clockwork*, though the need for the existence of some kind of bonus system in our society is more or less presumed. The need arises jointly from the fact that, as Balzer imprecisely puts it, "We are a society committed to high productivity," and from the capitalist conclusion that workers in our society generally will not produce efficiently for their masters unless they are somehow made to do so. Where production is organized along a moving assembly line, bonus systems are not very necessary since there "the speed of the line controls productivity"—which is to say, it controls workers as they produce. But where, as in Balzer's and my plants, workers are not so organized in their production, other methods must be employed to extract extra output. As a result, "piece rates are set and salaries based on productivity. At Western Electric there is a complicated system that combines an hourly wage with a bonus system based on rates and group productivity" (p. 122).

This all sounds quite straightforward, but in practice it is hardly that. In fact, from Balzer's descriptions of the inequitable, confusing, and seemingly irrational ways in which the bonus system operates at Western Electric, one is led to suspect the bonus system must serve some ulterior purposes. This is a necessary conclusion if one is to try to begin to make some sense of Balzer's own accounts of his group's experiences with that system. Balzer himself cannot really make sense of it. He therefore typically concludes a chapter rich in descriptions of what properly should be understood as intense, if formally limited class struggle with the abstract suggestion that the bonus system could be changed to operate more rationally and equitably and "could theoretically benefit both the company and the worker" (p. 131). A chapter detailing serious and largely unavoidable conflict within capitalist production thus ends with an evasive assertion of the potential for interclass harmony. The company, as usual in such analyses, is somehow implicitly taken to not quite understand what's going on.

But why should we believe that a pattern, which at once is so vital and so widespread in industry, really is not "understood" by those who have been responsible for establishing, refining and maintaining it over so long a time? Is it Western Electric or Balzer who ultimately does not understand? Let the reader judge.

The particular kind of bonus system employed at the Western Electric plant is, ironically, the sort liberal reformers often recommend. In this system, the amount of an individual worker's bonus depends upon his/her production group's overall performance. Tying individual bonuses to group performance ideally is supposed to increase group solidarity and to reduce individual "alienation." Coincidentally, it also is supposed to enhance the group's total productivity, in part through provoking the application of group pressure on less productive workers to be more efficient. Under such a bonus system the practice of hanging an individual worker's quality control chart in front of his/her workpost clearly can facilitate group pressure being applied. So understood, this practice, the continuation of which Balzer simply could not understand, appears quite "rational."

What is considered "rational," of course, always depends upon the purposes to be served. The bonus system was set up to serve the interests of the overall capitalist system in the United States— specifically and most obviously to induce workers to produce more than they otherwise would. If that were the bonus system's sole purpose, determining which practices associated with bonuses were rational would be relatively easy.

SIX BOOKS CONSIDERED

In fact, however, materially rewarding increased production does not appear to be its only purpose. But what exactly its other purposes are is not at all apparent. One thing, nonetheless, is clear. If the bonus system simply functioned as a method for directly rewarding increased productivity with increased payments to workers, management would not and could not knowingly and rationally support, or even tolerate, the system as it actually operates. Since it is undeniable that management knows how the system operates in practice, should we simply assume management is "irrational"? Or should we not, instead, question—as workers inchoately suspect—whether something else may not be involved? Are we not driven to do so in order to make sense of what otherwise appears to be an irrational bonus system?

That something else is involved is indicated by what a veteran woman worker told Balzer when they discussed the bonus system during his early training days at Western Electric. She suggested that if bonuses are tied to increased productivity they are manipulated by the company to maintain them around certain levels regardless of how much workers may increase their productivity: " 'In here . . . the company will tell you that the productivity of your group will determine your bonus. Well,' she said, 'let me tell you the company will try to keep the bonus between 24 per cent and 27 per cent. You'll see most groups in here make somewhere in that range' " (p. 122).

Thus employees are aware that the bonus system is manipulated and that the amount of their bonuses in any particular group normally tends to be a relatively constant proportion of total wages, no matter how productive the group may become. In the face of worker awareness of management manipulation, it is difficult to understand exclusively in terms of the direct incentive purposes of bonuses why management continues to manipulate their award. One would think that such recognized manipulation would only subvert the very purpose of bonuses to stimulate higher productivity. However, the matter appears to be more complex than that.

In two months on the job, Balzer had not met a single "person who worked on the floor who believed that the bonus system was directly tied to production" (p. 125). Therefore, he was taken by surprise by the anger workers displayed when Jack, the group's supervisor, at the next bonus meeting announced that workers in the previous month had earned only 5 percent and would receive only 13 percent managerial allowance, for a total monthly bonus of 18 percent. What surprised the author was not that people were angry that their total bonus had been reduced from the previous month, but "how personally a number of people took this announcement" (p. 125): "One woman said, 'I'm not going to do another thing today. I've earned my 5 per cent. This is ridiculous' " (p. 125).

In response to similar remarks, Jack tried to reassure people that "with some sincere application" to work, "the bonus would begin to climb." After the meeting, however, there was an immediate general slowdown, and complaints continued. Several veteran women grumbled about the blatant inequity of the bonus system plantwide. Why, they wanted to know, should workers like themselves, with long service records, have to work hard to earn an 18 percent bonus, "while some people in other groups with less than six months [of seniority] were making more than 27 per cent?" (p. 125). A male worker complained in a similar vein:

"You know, they come down here and . . . say if the guys don't fool around with the girls so much and if the girls don't spend so much time in the bathroom, the bonuses would go up. That's a lot of crap. You can spend equal time working in two different departments and the bonus would be different by several percentages" (p. 126).

Balzer "felt everyone's frustration," but the frustration did not truly become his own until he received *his* first bonus check, for July, a short month. He was disappointed to receive only $4.42 for the month, whereupon he learned for the first time from another worker that "new workers didn't fully share in the bonus" (p. 126).

That was bad enough, but what especially galled Balzer was the glaring unfairness of the way the system operated. Two other workers who had started at the plant when he did, had been placed in groups that were earning over 25 percent bonuses. They shared in those much higher bonuses, while Balzer was sharing in a 5 percent bonus.

SIX BOOKS CONSIDERED

Balzer "now understood how people felt. I felt insulted that all we had earned was 5 per cent" (p. 126).

With all the complaints about the bonus, Jack called another meeting, and said he knew people were working hard and that he would have some of the production rates for bonuses rechecked. Then, in a way that simultaneously partly placed blame for the problem of low bonuses on workers themselves and partly suggested to them a possible means to alleviate their predicament, Jack said,

"I think one of the big problems is that you people aren't filling out your bogies correctly. . . . I think many of you aren't putting down [on these individual performance records of your work] all your waiting time, or setup time. . . . We have to begin putting down all the time we can get credit for when you aren't producing" (pp. 126–27).

Everyone at the meeting understood just what Jack meant, except perhaps the author. After the meeting, one worker put it this way: "See, if we can't make our bonus with production, then we'll have to make it a pencil bonus" (p. 127). And when Balzer asked another worker what the first had meant, he was told:

"Look, we get certain credits for nonproduction activities like waiting time. Jack wants us to mark it all down. You'll learn to do more than Jack asks, to pad your bogey, everyone does. . . . If you finish a job in forty minutes, put down forty minutes for the job and another twenty for material handling" (p. 127).

The week after that conversation, the author began to record all his time spent more conscientiously on his bogey, though he did not pad. As a result, his individual efficiency rate went up markedly, first to 73 percent and then to 84 percent. That rise, in and of itself, made him feel good—as if he had for the first time won some kind of approval or recognition for his work. "Even though I hadn't worked harder I was surprised to see how much better I felt because my efficiency rate was up. I discovered that most people felt better as their efficiency ratings went up, even if they weren't working differently, but [were simply] using a pencil to its best advantage" (p. 127). So even a charade like this can make workers feel better about their work and themselves for a time.

WORKING AGAIN

Thereafter, the anxiety and anger in the shop increased further when news of the next month's bonus was announced. Jack announced that the group "had moved our earned bonus up to 10.3 per cent . . ., but we were only going to be given a 7.2 per cent managerial. Thus, the month's [total] bonus was 17.5, down [again] from last month's 18 per cent" (p. 128).

Jack, as usual, tried to pacify group members with assurances that the group would continue "heading up." But his reassurances failed: "People just said, 'Heading up where? No matter what we produce, we just keep losing money.' " Reassurances having failed, Jack turned to management's tried and true tactic—divide and rule.

He agreed that . . . some people were producing well, but not everyone was. Without attaching anyone's names to the figures he read some efficiency rates computed from last week's bogies, ranging from 53 to 102 per cent. Then he tried to put some group pressure on those producing at a low level by saying, "In a small group like this, if just three people don't do as well as they can, then your bonus is going to be hurt. . . ." (p. 128).

For the moment the tactic worked. "Jack seized upon this agreement and ended the meeting by stressing how important it was that we all kept marking things down" and so on. The success of Jack's tactic in reducing worker anger was short-lived. However, the tactic did apparently achieve something nearly as desirable from management's point of view: "the anger [of] . . . the group increasingly turned [in] upon itself" (p. 129). It remained so until Balzer left his job. Workers' complaints about other workers, process checkers and layouts, increased. Balzer himself felt "particularly hostile . . . when I discovered . . . another new worker . . . was receiving a bigger bonus check than I for the last month because his bogies were . . . higher. I knew that his percentages were higher not because he was more efficient but because he pushed his pencil, padding his bogey more than I did" (p. 129).

With that final indignity, the author decided to get along by going along, and began to pad his bogey as well. Frustrated by playing it straight with management, he "decided why bother. I might as well pad my bogey because there was certainly no reward for keeping an accurate record of what was actually being done. In the next few weeks my efficiency rating kept going up" (p. 129).

SIX BOOKS CONSIDERED

In understandably accommodating himself by padding to the pressures management imposed in practice through its bonus system, the author became, like most workers under bonus systems, an accomplice in the very inequitable system to which he objects. The effect of complicity on most is to undermine any sense of outrage and concern with changing what workers know to be an unjust system, and instead to refocus workers' efforts on trying to get "their due" in a system that thereby manages to tarnish and coopt all who come to play within its field.

The author, of course, does not quite understand this process. He is largely unconscious of the possibility that in devious ways management may derive unproclaimed benefits from its bonus system. He concedes that "the current bonus system [withal] . . . is effective in coaxing extra productivity" (p. 131) out of workers. But he believes that a fairer bonus system could be worked out that would benefit both sides. Balzer, therefore, simply cannot understand why the existing bonus system is allowed to operate as it does. He cannot appreciate the crass reality: the bonus system is the way it is because management for good reasons wants it that way.

If the author cannot recognize that these sorts of capitalist practices are inherent to our system of production, neither can he fully recognize that workers' responses to the bonus system, in particular, are a perverted and limited but significant form of resistance to the system as a whole. Workers cheat to reduce capitalist overreaching and manipulation within the system that enthralls them. "The bonus system is looked upon as a system used by management to manipulate higher production. *They* always want more production and are unwilling to pay for it. *We* have to protect ourselves, and that means padding bogies and not helping the time study people" (p. 130).

In the final analysis, Balzer can only find all the practices associated with the bonus system "unfortunate, . . . part of the general distrust reflected by a *we-they* feeling" (p. 130). Not seeing that this "feeling" is grounded in the nature of objective class struggle within capitalist relations of production, Balzer writes as if workers' negative feelings, beliefs, and attitudes could be eliminated and be replaced by positive ones if only management better understood its own self-interest. We have reached the limits of his, and many workers', understanding. Very little else about the bonus system seems to be understood. What other functions that system might be performing for capitalist management is barely considered.

However arbitrary the bonus system may be and however ambivalent workers may feel toward it, the system nevertheless does appear to be successful in stimulating "extra productivity." True, a system that was less arbitrary might well stimulate still greater productivity, at least for a time, but it also might fail to satisfy other capitalist objectives. If so, then the existing complex and inequitable bonus system is best thought of, not as arbitrary, but as tailored to serve multiple purposes, which cannot always be harmonized.

A system that was simpler and more obviously equitable would be intelligible to workers. The mystification connected with authoritative rules and rule-making would be reduced. More than that, an intelligible system could become the target of worker efforts aimed at making the system still more equitable. In this respect, confusion pays; it pays management.

In the first place, management, by running such a seemingly arbitrary system, daily reasserts its power and authority to determine all these matters capriciously, subject only to the constraint of strong, collective worker opposition. But strong, unified opposition is in turn made less likely by the overwhelming inducement for workers individually to cheat. So, second, this sort of system not only confuses workers but again channels their reactions along lines that do not fundamentally threaten capitalist production. Cheating at work, if I am correct, like cheating in school, is not a fundamental threat to or violation of the system. It is, rather, an expectable, even desirable part of it! A grossly unfair, despised system like this in which workers were not so implicated is a system that workers would be more likely to oppose outright.

Third, arbitrarily awarding higher bonuses for equal productivity to selected production groups provides for some disadvantaged workers the hope that they can "improve themselves," not by becoming more productive, but simply by obtaining a promotion or a transfer into a better group. The most effective way to realize such hopes, they know, is by cultivating management and union bosses, which adds to the bosses' authority. And finally, as we have seen, the bonus system turns worker against worker, as more productive workers blame less productive ones for inadequate contributions to total group performance.

Hence, if these very tentative conclusions are reasonably sound, the bonus system as it actually functions serves capitalists quite well. It does extract higher productivity from workers; it also confuses workers; in addition, it sets worker against worker; further, it implicates workers individually in its operation, thereby deflecting them from the real source of their suffering and subverting their collective capacity to oppose management; finally it enhances patterns of deference and collaboration in workers that are vital to capitalist production. Consequently, the bonus system may not be very neat in practice, but as a whole it can scarcely be considered "irrational."

If the bonus system cannot be understood as "irrational," neither can a capitalist management that employs it. On the contrary, as I have argued, management acts for the most part in extremely "rational" ways, fashioning and refashioning its means to achieve essentially unchanging capitalist ends. This is not, of course, to say that capitalist management does not make many mistakeş. It does. Nor to imply that management fully comprehends its world or acts purely rationally, even within its own terms. It does not. Nor do I mean to suggest that management can afford to sit back and rest on its accumulated laurels, satisfied simply to reproduce the patterns of conduct it produced in the past. It dares not. Capitalists must be more dynamic, are less in control, and are less perfect than such simplistic visions would imply. Nevertheless, despite these important qualifications, the primary point remains: work and the daily life of workers are "rationally" structured so as to achieve capitalist ends.

This means *the hypothesis for analyzing any aspect of work in America must be that its meaning lies embedded in its historical and contemporaneous functions for maintaining and developing capitalism.* Although this hypothesis will not in every case prove to be adequate, or even useful (obviously there will be aspects of work in particular cases that, say, can be understood best by understanding the personalities involved or the role chance has played in the case being studied), still, we must begin with it, because of the systematic and dominant capitalist nature of work in America.

Liberal analysts like Balzer, however, can only fitfully introduce the relevance of capitalism to work into their writing. Ideologically, the hypothesis must be effectively excluded, because if it were included and made primary then the pattern of minor and other atrocities capitalism daily perpetrates on workers would have to be understood somehow as "necessary" to achieving capitalism's ends. Such an understanding would confront liberal analysts with an unhappy choice: they would either have to apologize explicitly for the capitalist system, or they would have to move beyond liberalism to challenge capitalism. Eliminated in either case would be both the prevailing liberal deflection of such a direct challenge and the accompanying naiveté about prospects for reforming flagrantly abusive patterns of capitalist behavior, which within liberal ideology can be taken to be "irrational," "counterproductive," or else attributed to causes other than capitalism.

DEMEANED

In his chapter on "The Importance of Feeling Important," Balzer attributes the fact that workers in his plant are systematically made to feel insignificant at work to factors he does not conceive as related to capitalism. It is the familiar liberal litany. Within the plant, the gigantic size of the production unit; the unresponsiveness of accompanying bureaucracy; the imposition of busywork on workers who temporarily have nothing else to do; the privileged position accorded white-collar workers, which further demeans blue-collar workers. Reinforcing workplace factors that make workers feel unimportant are, Balzer says, two other societal factors, also not conceived as related to capitalism. First, America's "value system . . . relegates factory work to a relatively low status . . . , [and treats factory workers]. . . . as unskilled labor" (p. 143). And second, workers know that "the labor market for them is limited" (p. 143). Consequently, treated as degraded and aware at some level of consciousness that

they have few if any meaningful alternatives, workers sustain themselves in no small part by what Balzer frankly calls an "illusion"
about the future. The illusion comes in two, often combined and by
now all-too-familiar forms:

Many talk about not having their children end up doing the work they do,
just as many of their parents talked about them not working in the textile
mills or shoeshops [of Massachusetts] as they had. Others talk about someday leaving. . . . the company and taking other, more interesting,
challenging jobs. Relatively few of them will leave (p. 143).

At no point in discussing these interrelated factors, many of
which we already have seen are directly related to capitalism, does
Balzer consider that relation. Instead, by treating them somehow as
nonessential, Balzer sets the stage for the sorts of reforms he will
suggest at the end of the book to reduce the impersonality of production relations at work, to make workers feel they are important, and
to make company officials more responsive to workers' needs as
human beings. Let us watch the author at his work.

Balzer and many of his co-workers see the major cause of their
feeling unimportant at work in the size and impersonality of the
plant's operations.

"Me, who am I?" asked Mary Bellini. "You know, I'm not really very
much of a person. In a big organization like this I'm just a little fish in a big
sea." . . .

Mary Bellini is like most of us in her desire to feel special. She would
like to find some value in what she does. . . .

Janie Silver told me, "You're just a number here." . . . Mary Ken-
nedy echoed this feeling when she said, "They don't even know you're alive.
. . . it's your number and not you who gets paid at the end of the
week." . . .

Larry Lucchino, a man with twenty-three years of service . . . thinks
the company has gotten too big. "In here . . . they don't care about you,
it's too big. . . . With all the bullshit they give you about how important
you are, you're not part of anything. . . . You do your job and no more"
(pp. 134–35).

The company in turn sees these attitudes the system has created
as a production problem. Therefore, management "recognizes the
necessity to make people feel important" (p. 134). Management uses

various methods to "give workers a sense of personal importance." It tells new workers in its orientation programs, for example, that they are important. Management also organizes its thousands of production employees into "piecework groups. . . . to . . . foster a group feeling." In its monthly newsletters, management includes "stories that emphasize the important roles individual shop employees play in the successful operation of the plant." And management runs various programs "to help people with drinking and/or drug problems" (p. 134).

If most of these efforts, like the company's very successful family "open house," are transparently and essentially public relations gimmicks and in any event are primarily aimed at maintaining or improving production, Balzer does not seem to see them as such. He tends rather to see them as if they were primarily serious efforts to humanize production relations. But he also sees that these manifestations of management's "programmed concern" fail to achieve their ostensible purposes. He sees too that the exercise of more personalized, human concern on the part of supervisors, by contrast, succeeds in a variety of situations. A worker who had said he would never work overtime and had told Balzer, "The company owns me for forty hours a week and that's all," nevertheless agreed to come in one Saturday at the direct request of his supervisor, who persuaded him he was really needed. From this and other similar cases, the author correctly concludes that workers respond much better "to personal rather than institutional requests" (p. 136). "People want to feel needed and necessary, and they respond, almost regardless of the task, when they are made to feel that what they do matters" (p. 137). Moreover, "some top [management] officials care about the people working in the shops. Unfortunately, even their good intentions are sometimes sidetracked by the large-scale bureaucracy" within the company (p. 137). So the problem seems reducible to the allegedly unresponsive, intervening "large-scale bureaucracy."

But is that really the problem? Is it accurate to call the bureaucracy "unresponsive" and "impersonal"? Is it, for example, "impersonal" when dealing with top management? Is it "unresponsive" to the demand for profits? Or does the bureaucracy not in fact respond quite effectively to the overwhelming institutionalized concern with profits, to which end all human concerns in production consistently are subordinated whenever there is conflict, as there so often is? If so, then the inhumanity of production relations is fixed primarily by the end of capitalist production and not by the bureaucratic means. In service to that end, severe limits are placed on the exercise of human concern through the nature of the defined role supervisors and managers must play. Only within those limits can particular supervisors and managers be better and worse in their differing personnel relations.

Although Balzer typically emphasizes the differences, the limits are determinative. The inevitable result is that workers are systematically, if not constantly, treated indecently in incidents that "fade" over time but "are never totally forgotten." As a result, "some deep-seated resentment" commonly exists even among those workers with "generally positive feelings about . . . [their jobs] and the company" (p. 138). Meg Shepp, a thirteen-year veteran worker, put it pointedly: "I've never understood it—every time they pat you on the fanny they kick you in the teeth. They just make you feel there's no reason to work hard, . . . no reason why you should care." Theano Nikitas, who claims to "like this company" and believes "it's been good to me," put it still more broadly: "You talk to any person who's been here long enough and they've been screwed in some way by the company" (p. 139).

The screwing can take all forms. Sometimes it amounts to little more than being made to do busywork. That doesn't sound bad, until you've had to do it yourself. Thus the author did not "really understand how angry busywork could make you feel until one day" he experienced it. Frustrated, Balzer confided to another worker how insulted he was. She replied:

Now you know how it feels. . . . It is insulting. Almost all of us who have worked here know that feeling. It's degrading to know that you're being given work just to keep your hands busy. It's hard to feel that you're important when you know that. They let you know that you're expendable. . . . They move you around at will. That's why workers feel unimportant" (pp. 141–42).

WORKING AGAIN

Notwithstanding repeated indignities, however, the author concludes that workers still

do care about what they produce. What alienates them is the structure of the rules, the undemocratic nature of the work situation, and the gnawing feeling that they are unimportant. Work is all too frequently organized in a way that makes people feel that they are not expected to be responsible, that their contributions are unimportant, and that they are interchangeable with machines and with each other (p. 144).

Although Balzer attributes the cause of these feelings to bigness, he simultaneously recognizes the seemingly inexplicable superficiality of the company's main effort to deal with the problem of "plant size": "The company's efforts to minimize the effects of plant size have revolved primarily around the small work groups. However, these groups are artificial. They do not decide rules, production techniques, ways of doing business, handling bogies or operating procedure" (p. 144).

Those decisions and all other important decisions, needless to say, are tightly controlled by management for capitalist purposes.

That workers everywhere in the United States are demeaned and are treated as factors of production is of course a fundamental condition of work life arising directly from the fact that they live under a capitalist class dictatorship and are dependent upon their dictators to make a living. That conditions are not better in the particular Western Electric plant in which Balzer worked, where capitalist management is relatively "progressive," is also due in part to the fact that the union local there seems especially supine.

THE UNION

That plant was a "modified agency shop" while Balzer worked there. Workers did not have to join Local 1365 of the Communication Workers of America (CWA). Most did, though, if only because the amount of union dues was deducted from their weekly paychecks for union use whether or not they chose to become union members.

SIX BOOKS CONSIDERED

Balzer chose at the outset to become a member. For three months he "waited for a shop steward to introduce himself and welcome . . . [him] to . . . the union." None came. Co-workers hired with him, he learned, also had not been contacted by any union representative. So Balzer decided to find out who his shop steward was. He asked around his department. No one knew! Finally, he got his membership application through someone who knew a shop steward in an adjacent work area. His membership card arrived in the mail not long before he stopped work.

While he was in the plant, "Very little was ever said about the union." Balzer himself remembers seeing shop stewards in his area only once in the five months he worked there, and nothing came of their single observable intervention. Aside from that, he writes,

I can recall no other visible union activity. I never heard anyone talk about filing a grievance, or having a grievance handled by a shop steward. Periodically, one of the union's bulletin boards would have a notice about an upcoming union meeting. None of the people I met ever went to any of those monthly meetings (p. 240).

In trying to find out why union reps did not make their presence felt on the shop floor and why workers did not seem to be at all involved in what was supposed to be their union, Balzer learned that

Most people . . . generally agreed that the union had helped improve conditions and wages. However, many didn't think that highly of the local and the current leadership. . . . One man . . . told me, "It's not a real strong union, too many guys are hustling—trying to get ahead. A couple of [former union] big shots are working for the company." . . . in management positions (p. 241).

Reflecting that cozy reality, workers almost never went to union meetings, except when strike votes were taken. Out of more than five thousand members of the local, "fewer than forty. . . . [u]sually . . . attend [regular] union meetings" (p. 243)—less than 1 percent of the membership, and that handful doubtless primarily composed of union officials and hangers-on.

Balzer in fact "didn't hear much about the union until well after . . . [he] stopped working" in the plant, when in July 1974 there was a lot of activity around the upcoming contract negotiations. The contract was due to run out on July 17, coincidentally, no doubt, a mere four days into the annual, two-week, plantwide summer shutdown. As the first day of vacation, July 13, approached, "rumors started to circulate around the plant that a settlement wouldn't be reached . . . and that a strike would have to be called" (p. 241). Although many workers seemed prepared for a strike, feeling it unavoidable, some emphasized how much a long strike would hurt them financially: " 'You never get back the money you lose when you're out of work very long' " (p. 241). Listening to workers, Balzer realized "how economically taxing a strike would be. A long strike could wipe out much of a family's savings, and a short strike could inflict a serious strain on a family budget" (p. 241). Exercising our "rights" in practice tends to be very costly.

Nonetheless, Balzer expected a strike to occur. John Gearen, a co-worker, knew better: "He was sure . . . [all the talk about strike] was [just that,] a lot of talk, a big show the union and company were putting on. He thought they'd argue and threaten each other up to the last minute, and finally reach an eleventh hour settlement" (p. 242).

The union's negotiations for the first time were being handled that year on a national level, with the CWA simultaneously representing more than 500,000 Western Electric and Bell System workers in bargaining with AT&T. Negotiations continued into the plant shutdown period and beyond the current contract's expiration date, as "union and management agreed to a day-to-day extension of the existing contract." CWA's international president called the company's final offer "inadequate," and said the union wanted a full agency shop and an annual wage increase of about 14 percent. By the end of shutdown no agreement had been reached. And "When the plant reopened on July 29, people had only the vaguest idea of what was happening with the bargaining. . . . Negotiations were stalled, and union officials had called for a national . . . vote [to authorize a strike]" (p. 242).

During the day and night of the 29th, meetings were held for the various shifts to prepare for the local vote the following day. Balzer attended the main meeting for the day shift, held that night.

SIX BOOKS CONSIDERED

Over one thousand other workers also attended. The meeting was run by the union's current president and by a past president, who had become the International's local representative. The International rep said negotiations were stalled, that the company's offer for wage increases in each of the three years of the proposed three-year contract was inadequate and that certain expanded fringe benefits were, under the offer, to be delayed for too long. He said the International still hoped to avoid a strike, but wanted a strike vote in case it became necessary to call one. He urged everyone to vote for strike and announced that voting would take place the next day at the union headquarters between 10:00 A.M. and 9:00 P.M.

In response to that seemingly insignificant announcement, a spontaneous reaction took place among the rank and file at the meeting, which in its own small way is indicative of the quality of their relationship with union leaders. Balzer records what happened.

A fellow . . . raised his hand . . . and asked who had set the hours. Luccino [the International rep] said local officials. The guy said how come the hours had been set like that and why couldn't the hours start earlier, so people could vote on their way into work. Luccino said the times had been set and that was all there was to it, that they couldn't be changed.

Now people in different parts of the auditorium got up and started asking why they couldn't be changed. People began booing Luccino's answers. Holding his position, Luccino said first that since these hours had already been posted they had to be stuck to, and then insisted that there weren't enough people to man the desks for the earlier hours.

One man in the back stood up and said, "Who the hell is this union run for anyway? Can't you see we want the hours earlier? Why don't you change them?"

Luccino was getting madder and repeated that the hours couldn't be changed. Another man got up and said, "Hell, when there are union elections you open up early. Why can't you do it when we want it?"

The meeting, which had been going . . . [smoothly], was getting ugly. . . . [After a conference on stage between the current and former presidents, the current president] said that they'd change the hours and open up early. This announcement was greeted by long and loud applause, and several people volunteered to man the desks at the earlier times (pp. 243–44).

The next day the strike vote was overwhelmingly favorable, and people began to wait expectantly for the strike to be called. In the thirty years since the plant had been "organized" by the CWA there had been only one long strike, for six weeks. In recent decades there had been only two brief strikes. This time there was to be neither, because a settlement was reached within ten days after the strike vote. The day after the settlement was announced, Balzer "heard a number of disgruntled remarks about the proposed contract": "One woman told me, 'They [the union bosses] got the agency shop they wanted, and they sold us down the river for it.' Another person told me, 'They didn't do anything for us. All those promises, all that talk, and we didn't get anything' " (p. 245).

Bob Lamont, a worker who had been a union officer and member of the local's executive board for twenty-five years, of course felt differently:

I know a lot of people don't like this . . . contract. They think that the union got the agency shop and didn't get the wage package or benefits they wanted. But it isn't true, it's a damn good contract. It's the best contract we've ever gotten. . . . You'll see, people don't realize it now but they should see how well we did. You can't convey it (p. 245).

But Lamont's appreciation for the proposed contract does not appear to have been widely shared. Nor need it have been, since the contract was ratified at a local union meeting attended by only 600 members, at which less than half that number stayed on to vote.

The meeting itself, expectably, was characterized by hostility to the settlement from the rank and file and a defense of the settlement by local officials. It is all so familiar, a variation on the theme of union collaboration.

Some bitter and heated exchanges took place during the meeting.

Several people remarked that the contract they were now being asked to ratify, except for the inclusion of the agency shop provision, was very similar to the one they had been told was totally unacceptable before the strike vote. . . .

The hostility did not end with the ratification of the new contract:

For several weeks after the meeting I kept hearing complaints about the negotiations. Most were focused not at the local but at the International [which earlier had stirred workers' hopes]. One person summed up a lot of the ill feeling when she told me, "The International fooled us. They got us all worked up for a strike vote. They made us think we were really going to get something with this national bargaining. Then they pulled the rug out from under us. They got their agency shop, and we didn't get nothin'. You ask me this national bargaining ain't nothin'."

The shop floor was rife with bitter complaints about the contract and how "the workers" had been dealt a "dirty deal" (p. 246).

In the midst of all this Balzer was surprised to find a reaction among workers that should no longer surprise us:

a number of people . . . [had] turned at least some of their anger back on themselves. Helene Saunders told me, "It makes me purple when people say we were sold down the river. *It's our fault. We don't participate.* We don't go to church, we don't vote, and we don't go to union meetings. . . .

Another worker . . . was [still] more critical [of the rank and file]. He told me, "I was a union steward for a couple of weeks ten, twelve years ago, but I quit. I couldn't take it. The only time people in here bitch is when something happens to them personally. They don't give a shit about anyone else but themselves."

Ruth Davis, a shop steward, told me, "This is the first time in the fifteen years that I've been in the union that I don't agree with what . . . [it] did [!]. . . . [It was] wrong, *but* when I hear *these people in here* complain it burns my ass. *They had the chance, they could have rejected the contract.* I [voted against it] . . . and I can't afford to be out [either]. I know some people think this is a weak union. It isn't but if they think it is, it's because of them. They let it be that way. They want to be spoon fed, and not do anything, and *they deserve everything they get*" (pp. 246–47; emphasis added).

Is this reaction really surprising? Not at all. We have seen from Balzer's earlier accounts of workers' reactions to the bonus system a similar turning in of anger. And historically we know that in a variety of ways the oppressed of most ages have been socialized, with differing degrees of success, to substantially blame themselves for their own plight. So if, as we have seen from Sennett and Cobb, the particular reasons today's victims blame themselves for their own victimization are of necessity as different from historical reasons as our society's class structure, culture, and institutions are different from previous societies'—today we blame ourselves as individuals for "failing," because we half-believe each of us was "free" to do better— nevertheless, the essential message remains the same: "It's our fault.

WORKING AGAIN

We deserve what we get." The message only appears more disarming as a liberal refrain.

Balzer, needless to say, does not understand matters this way. As a result, he concludes his discussion of the union with evasiveness and with his typical seeming "balance," which would be commendable were he not describing a situation of such gross imbalance:

> Local 1365 is neither a militant local, constantly battling the company, nor is it a company union. By and large it maintains what both sides would call a good working relationship with the emphasis on conciliation wherever possible.
>
> Generally people on the shop floor see the need for the union, but they don't view it as a very active or strident force in handling their day-to-day work-connected problems. Whatever the . . . reasons, Local 1365 has evolved into a necessary bureacracy that deals with an even larger bureaucracy (pp. 247–48).

If this conclusion is not blatantly apologist, neither is it what one would call very penetrating or courageous. Nor does it reflect much awareness of the broader framework of political economy within which the company and union must be properly understood.

CAPITALIST FREEDOM OF CHOICE

By contrast, Balzer seems more aware of that framework when, in a chapter entitled "Fringe Benefits," he analyzes why "people choose to work in the shops at Western Electric" (p. 250). Yet here too, his awareness remains fundamentally stunted by his implicit acceptance of the choices capitalism throws up to workers. What Balzer understandably fails to consider is how *the nature and range of choice itself—including the weight given by workers to factors involved in a choice—are themselves products of history. The very choice workers have is the product of capitalism, which increasingly has provided the available alternatives and the compulsion to choose among them.* Indeed, workers can choose. In fact, they *must* choose, but only among limited capitalist alternatives. Their choice has been crucially shaped by two aspects of capitalist history: by the serious life problems confronting workers that capitalism has created (even as it solved others);

and by the inadequacy of government action and inaction to resolve those problems. These two factors in combination have meant that workers must sell their labor power to capitalists in an effort to satisfy their physical needs and to deal with the peculiar problems capitalism has inflicted upon them. Within this context of economic compulsion, however, choosing even among limited alternatives can take on real-life meaning.

Take the case of why workers choose to work for Western Electric. The reasons, Balzer finds, are all relative. Western Electric, compared to competing firms in the Merrimack Valley, has been particularly attractive regarding steadiness of employment and fringe benefits.

Steadiness of employment clearly is very important to the plant's workers. Western Electric, because of the high demand for its products, has been able to offer greater job security than most competing firms in the area. Job security means, among other things, that workers are better able to make regular payments on their various debts. Job security is especially attractive to workers in the Merrimack Valley, "a geographic area where economic insecurity—layoffs, seasonal slumps, plant closings—has long been a part of the scene" (p. 250).

That pervasive economic insecurity, which is the source of the attractiveness of Western Electric's relative job security, is itself of course a product of the unemployment caused by capitalism's continuing business cycles and uneven development. Relative job security is attractive, therefore, on the one hand, because capitalism has created job insecurity and, on the other, because the government has inadequately provided for workers whose jobs are terminated by capitalist crises. Western Electric has in this respect been attractive to workers because its employees have been less subject than others in the area to one kind of capitalist devastation. Thus is the very nature of workers' choice determined by the capitalist context. If there were no such phenomenon as capitalist unemployment, or if the government could assure full employment, then the relative steadiness of employment at Western Electric would not be of such concern to workers and would not be a significant factor affecting where they "choose" to work.

Something similar can be said of Western Electric's fringe benefits, which, Balzer recognizes, are structured to lock workers into continuing their employment with the company, whether they like their jobs or not. Western Electric's fringe benefits, in truth, look quite good by comparison with what "unorganized" and even many "organized" workers elsewhere receive. They look especially good compared to what a citizen receives through, say, Social Security. But the point to be remembered is that a monthly Western Electric pension of $221.67 for a "32 grade bench worker retiring in June 1974 at age sixty-five with thirty years of service" (p. 253) is not only grossly inadequate to sustain a decent life. It also looks relatively "good" only because what the government, not to speak of most other companies, has been willing to provide in the form of monthly retirement payments is still more inadequate. If instead the government assured all its citizens of decent minimal standards of health, education, and welfare over their lifetimes, the so-called fringe benefits offered directly by capitalists would be substantially less alluring. In that case, however, a capitalist government would be subverting the bargaining power of capitalist business, an unlikely event, unless compelled by a strong and militant working-class movement.

REFORMISM AND REALITY

The relevance and importance of such a movement is not apparent to Balzer. Neither in his earlier discussions nor in his final conclusions and reform recommendations at book's end, does he pay attention to the need for a working-class movement. For Balzer, reforms are to be realized, if at all, not through workers' potential and need for organized, self-conscious struggle, but through management's alleged self-interest and good will. Management, Balzer hopes, will come to understand what would have to be a singularly convenient coincidence, which, if true, would deny the ultimate reality of and continuing need for class struggle: that workplace reform is not only humane but also profitable. Since, however, the sorts of reforms Balzer proposes are hardly news to management, one would have thought that, if such reforms were likely to enhance profits as well as humanity, management long ago would have eagerly carried them out—if not for the sake of humans, then at least for the sake of profits. That management in fact has not as yet reformed the workplace along the lines liberals like Balzer have been proposing for years is strong evidence that management in the future is highly unlikely to do so unless forced to. On one level Balzer seems to know this, but on another he cannot face it.

Thus Balzer begins the final chapter of *Clockwork* with the recognition of several fundamental facts of American life. First, the 28 million men and women who work in our factories make a "huge economic contribution" to our society. Second, seemingly in spite of this, "American society tends to ignore or . . . denigrate factory work and blue-collar workers." And third, this very negative societal treatment of factory work and workers is "buttressed by the [internal] organization of plants," where "the basic reality" and the "message most effectively conveyed is that workers are exchangeable, replaceable components" (p. 322).

That said, however, instead of then talking about *why* all this is so—about the underlying reality of class domination and the capitalist class's search for profits—Balzer manages to backtrack into the unreality of wishful thinking. He neatly accomplishes this feat of avoidance in the very process of declaring that plant organization dehumanizes workers, by slipping in the seemingly innocuous phrase, "no matter what a company intends." This gives him an escape hatch: the notion that the organization of factories is somehow "unintended," or at least that its effect on workers is not truly understood by management. Through this escape route of his own making, Balzer quickly scrambles. Immediately upon having said that workers are in fact treated within factories as "exchangeable, replaceable components," he goes on to say—as if oblivious to the reasonable implications of his own analysis—that nevertheless "there is much that can be done to alter the existing conditions of the shop floor, to change the way jobs are done and the atmosphere in which work is accomplished" (p. 322). Upon such a liberal reformist basis, Balzer then proceeds ambivalently to construct a case for his hope that management will initiate reform.

WORKING AGAIN

What is most striking about this case and most obviously marks it effectively as ideological is the fact that it is made despite, not because of, Balzer's own experience with management, which scarcely constituted grounds for optimism about management's devotion to reform.

I promised to share what I learned at Western Electric with the local management in the hopes that such discussion would lead to changes within the plant. I made numerous suggestions, including changes in the orientation and training program, the removal of quality control charts and time clocks, permission to smoke wherever possible, a better explanation of the bonus system, less authoritarian roles for supervisors, more freedom for shop personnel to organize their work, and a much greater role in decision-making by shop employees. So far the only specific change resulting . . . has been . . . [that the quality control] charts have been experimentally removed from stands in several departments including the one in which I worked. . . . Still, Dave Hilder, general manager of the Works, has stated that my observations have helped "make a good operation better," and have made him and those around him more receptive to suggestions for change on the shop floor (pp. 322–23).

What finally came of all these proposals we do not know: perhaps a bit more than Dave Hilder's public relations flattery of Balzer's efforts. Perhaps, for example, the "experiment" of removing the quality control charts from public display has been spread and made routine practice, which at least would make an inhuman operation marginally more bearable. But, given all the circumstances surrounding Balzer's reform recommendations, one must be skeptical even about the likelihood of so modest an achievement. Management's timing and motives for suddenly initiating this particular reform, well after the earlier complaints concerning the practice it was intended to correct, must be suspect. And what removing the charts might mean in practice remains at least open to doubt.

To appreciate this, imagine yourself a member of plant management. Now imagine that someone is writing a book about your factory and has just made a series of reform proposals concerning its organization. Would you, under these circumstances, wish to unambiguously and categorically reject each and every one of the proposals? Or would you not prefer, at least until the book was in press, to implement one of them "experimentally . . . in several departments"? In any event, if the practice to be reformed was on balance useful to management for controlling workers, however much it may have frustrated them, would you in your assumed role as capitalist manager be willing to simply eliminate it before you had either improved existing control mechanisms or developed alternative ones? If not, then even the achievement of a particular piecemeal reform might have a quite different impact upon workers than an isolated focus on it would lead one to suspect. One can therefore no more assess the significance of removing the charts from public display without considering that act in relation to the whole system of control than one can assess the significance of a rise in workers' nominal wages without considering the inflation rate in the economy as a whole.

The "pieces" of the capitalist whole, and changes in those "pieces," can only be understood in their relation to that whole, particularly since class conflict is such a determining factor in how the system develops. This is so because under conditions of class conflict it is expectable that when the ruling class loses ground in a particular reform it will try to compensate for the loss by reshaping other aspects of the whole. That response has in fact proven to be an integral part of this history of class struggle under capitalism. Thus when the workers' movement achieved a legislative limit on the number of hours capitalists could legally bind workers by contract to work, capitalists responded by further intensifying work (e.g., speedup) and by shaping the means of economic coercion to effectively make workers choose "voluntarily" to do overtime.

The fact is that the political economy of work life currently is effectively organized as a dictatorship. Liberals may use softer words like "authoritarian" to characterize it; they may wish it were not so; and they may hope and strive for democratic reform. But fond hopes, euphemisms, and largely misdirected efforts are unlikely to change our reality substantially. On the contrary, they may be more likely to help maintain it.

If liberals often do not understand this, many workers do. They are more skeptical, for example, than Balzer appears to be of man-

WORKING AGAIN

agement assertions that it wants to reform jobs to make them less fragmented, less repetitive, less alienating, and more satisfying. One worker, in response to a proposal for job rotation, responded: "Terrific, they're going to give me ten boring jobs to do instead of one" (p. 326). Workers resist restructuring jobs, Balzer writes, because they have "a basic mistrust of management efforts." Workers have learned from bitter experience that "the company's interest in reshaping their jobs has less to do with their job satisfaction level than with increased productivity" (pp. 326–27). Workers know, in a nutshell, as one declared, "This company is not in business to make people happy but to make money" (p. 327).

Despite his hopes for reform, Balzer too appears to understand that profits are what counts for management. At the end of the book, he even wonders whether "conflict between management and labor [is] an inherent element of capitalism" (p. 328). Momentary doubts threaten his implicit optimism for reform within capitalism:

if one looks at the changes being discussed at Western Electric and elsewhere and realizes that these changes have their antecedents in experiments in the 1920s at Western Electric's Hawthorne plant, one must be skeptical about the pace of change. . . . Much of what was learned at Hawthorne a half century ago has been ignored and forgotten, although it periodically reemerges, repackaged and relabeled, as a new way to make workers feel better about what they do (pp. 328–30).

But this is mild skepticism indeed, in the face of a brutal capitalist reality. Before Balzer had completed his book, the many workers who had chosen to work at Western Electric for its "steadiness of employment" were dealt a severe blow:

Layoffs began in the last month of 1974. By the end of May 1975 more than 1500 hourly employees [over 20 percent] had been laid off. Nearly everyone with less than five years of service was laid off (p. 331).

SIX BOOKS CONSIDERED

Epilogue

CONFOUNDED by events of the 1960s and 1970s, I have sought to understand a world that earlier had seemed so intelligible as not to require effort to understand. That search has led me to a "new" theory and a new practice.

I read Marx and Marxian writings, because I could find no other framework of analysis that made as much sense of our lives in capitalist America. Marxian analysis had an impact on me like Cézanne must have had on his audience: my prior mode of viewing the world no longer appeared as "natural" but as conventional; the familiar aspects of social reality, I learned, could be analyzed and synthesized in a radically different and illuminating way I had not anticipated.

I chose, as had many middle-class radicals before me, to work in a factory to learn first-hand what unfamiliar mass work is like. While in the factory, I chose, as I have in the university, to test the limits of certain dominant institutions. I used myself as a probe to explore our system.

I acted in that way not only for personal but also for partly formed theoretical reasons. If I did not at the time truly understand the obvious, that goods producing labor is the *sine qua non* of social existence—that without physical production there can be no society, and without the production of a surplus there can be no schools, no mass media, no government, and so on—I at least vaguely realized that experiencing such work somehow might provide a key to understanding what America is about. If I did not then quite understand that the quality of work necessarily is indicative of the nature of society's class organization, I at least intuited that somehow the experience of doing "ordinary" rather than elite work would reveal crucial aspects of our society that had been obscured from my position in the university. And if I did not then actually understand that material reality shapes our existence and our thoughts, I nonetheless half-recognized that my intellectual work was nearly devoid of conscious involvement with the material world and with the daily lives of the masses of our people.

What I found and learned in the factory was a revelation for me. It was anticipated only in that working did indeed confirm my tentative belief that capitalism is the primary source of our problems. Before my factory experience, however, that abstract belief had very little content or texture. Working in the factory gave the abstraction meanings I could not have anticipated in my thoughts. My notion of class struggle, for example, no longer is confined to a received, romantic image of explosive conflict across a barricade. Instead, it now focuses more on the mundane, patterned conflicts between workers and bosses that constitute the breeding ground for the more convulsive form of conflict. The new meanings, in turn, have enabled me to further develop my theoretical understanding.

But I do not propose here to summarize that understanding, which is still limited, or to summarize this book. This book is intended to reflect the process of my own learning experience and, I hope, to stimulate in you an analogous process. I am not ready or willing to reduce what I have learned to a few pithy pages and definitions. This book has been a journey to a destination that does not yet exist. It is a journey to a destination that must be of our own conscious, active, and collective creation. Mere onlookers will not arrive. And so I hope you have read this book actively, reacting positively and negatively, integrating what fit with your own experiences, and in the process beginning perhaps to reshape your own understanding.

My journey is not ended, only this book. I do not honestly know if I will have the stamina and character to continue it. But I do know that along the way and still today nearly everything that has happened to me has been grist for the mill of re-understanding the world. I wish this for you.

EPILOGUE

Watching my infant learn so tangibly about her world shockingly confirmed that we all begin to learn about the world in a materialist way—biting on objects, getting burned, falling down. The continuing and decisive shaping influence of material reality on our thoughts, however, somehow is expunged from our consciousness as we develop, except perhaps at times when there are dramatic changes in our material existences. Our very conception of time and space, for example, has been conclusively influenced by the things among which we live. Baltimore, many people today would say, is about four hours from New York. That way of conceiving the distance between the two cities reflects our peculiar material existence. George Washington could not have said the same thing. Automobiles have shaped our appreciation of distance.

Seeing the fine documentary film *Harlan County, U.S.A.*, which recounts the struggles of coal miners and their families to achieve a decent life against the coal operators and their allies—the police, the troops, the courts, and the church hierarchy—decisively reinforced my understanding that the material conditions of work and the relations of production broadly determine workers' health, safety, longevity, income, living conditions, and family relations. In the case of coal mining the determination is obvious to the point of being undeniable, but not really so different from other occupations.

And what about you?

If you have a job, you probably work for capitalism yourself. Nearly all of us in the United States do, one way or another. If your job, whether blue- or white-collar, is in "the private sector" and fairly similar to those described in this book, then recognizing the reality is relatively easy, since capitalism and making a living are really about all you have to work for.

But if you are a professional, recognition comes harder. Professionals are near the top of the American class and occupational hierarchy, and have much the best of it. Indeed, although they do not generally own or control the means of production, professionals are given substantial discretion and allowed to feel important in their jobs. And they receive, a significant minority of them at least, striking benefits from their work—as lawyers with lucrative practices, who serve corporate interests; as economists, who help bankers manage the economy mainly for the profit of the few; and as doctors, who make small fortunes off treating people's physical and psychological ills. As such, professionals appear to be working primarily for themselves, not for capitalism.

Similarly, if you work in any phase of government, you may see yourself not as working for capitalism but as working for "the public." Manual laborers, clerks, semiprofessionals, and officials employed by the government, however, work for capitalism hardly less, if in different ways, than their counterparts in private industry for the simple reason that our government first and foremost serves capitalists', not the people's, interests. American capitalism could not long survive without its state. Likewise, if you teach, on the whole and wittingly or unwittingly, you probably teach what the system tolerates or demands to maintain itself and expand.

In many cases the reality of working for capitalism is disguised by factors like the professional nature of the job and by liberal ideology, which obscure the relationship of our jobs to the capitalist political economy. Professors, for example, may believe they are doing their own research, engaged in education for its own sake. Government employees may believe that under our system the social-service or administrative tasks they perform are (or at least are supposed to be) insulated from capitalist economics and politics. These are largely illusions. Even government employees who in good faith minister to the many victims of the capitalist system—the industrial cripples, the unemployed, the hungry, those on welfare, the socially maladjusted—are working for capitalism in a significant, if attenuated, sense: our system cannot function effectively when, as in the 1930s, there are too many obvious, conscious, and resentful victims who are not easily controlled because they are dependent neither on employers nor on the government. That is the bottom line for "welfare" in the so-called welfare state.

The currently popular novelists and film-makers who entertain us with nostalgia, science fiction and satanic, disaster, and monster tales also work for capitalism, not simply because they are part of a publishing, TV, and movie business whose paramount purpose is to make profits, but also because their particular creations further serve capitalist interests by diverting us from the main unremitting calamity of our lives, capitalism itself.

The fact is that capitalism every day claims more victims than do all the country's sharks, grizzly bears, earthquakes, and other spectacular disasters in an average year. Its commonplace victims are that vast majority of Americans who spend much of their waking lives on, and going to and from, jobs that for them have no meaning and who are treated as "factors of production," rather than as human beings.*

As human beings living in a capitalist society currently undergoing a historic (if zig-zagged) decline, many of us from our own experiences sense something is terribly wrong.† We sense it is not just our leaders, for whom we years ago lost enthusiasm, but also our public and private institutions that across the board are failing us. Our work does not satisfy. Our schools do not educate. Our dollar does not buy much. Our TV does not entertain. The products we purchase and consume no longer improve the quality of our lives. The economy cannot employ millions of our people. Our jails do not rehabilitate. Our families, increasingly characterized by intolerable tension, alcoholism, divorce, physical abuse, and mental illness, cannot stand the strain money making has put on them. Our ideology fails to inspire. And our government has proven incapable of turning this deteriorating situation around.

We have learned from costly experience to suspect, among others, the oil companies, the drug companies, the chemical compa-

---

* At its crassest, capitalism's victims include men and women physically injured and sickened because of their work. Most such injuries and sicknesses are avoidable, but capitalism does not care as much for humans as for profits. A front-page article in *The New York Times* of December 20, 1976, reports on a small part of this reality: "100,000 people die in the United States . . . from injuries and diseases contracted while working." Moreover, "in 1974 alone about 5.9 million workers—one in every ten . . . experienced injuries or disease resulting from work." Slightly less directly, "a significant . . . proportion of all cancers are caused by the toxic fumes seeping into the air and water from factories and other sources of pollution." Of the "365,000 people [who] died of cancer in 1975 . . . the heaviest concentrations of such deaths were near heavily industrialized areas." In the face of these facts and countless others like them, the poor performance record and political constraints placed on the operation of agencies like the federal Occupational Safety and Health Administration are nothing less than a typical capitalist scandal.

† For an enlightening, brief discussion of the historical and current dimensions of the crisis of declining capitalism, see John G. Gurley, *Challengers to Capitalism* (San Francisco: San Francisco Book Company, 1976), pp. 141–63.

EPILOGUE

nies, the food processing companies, the automobile companies, the utilities, the supermarkets, the unions, the CIA, the Pentagon, the presidency, the Congress, and the courts. But we are not comfortable with these suspicions. We do not know what to make of them. Superficially, they seem to imply some enormous, evil conspiracy is to blame for our problems. More profoundly, and still more discomforting, they imply the capitalist system may be to blame.

This underdeveloped awareness, forged in the societal contradictions shaping our daily lives, persistently impinges upon our inherited liberal consciousness and fitfully confronts propaganda to the contrary that everywhere surrounds us. Our daily lives thus threaten us with a provocative confusion—an inability to understand in liberal terms why what is happening to us is happening.

Increasingly bereft of illusions concerning America, we nonetheless have not yet achieved the alternative consciousness needed to understand and collectively change our lives. The gnawing suspicion that capitalism might be our main problem repeatedly is buried beneath our liberal world view and the avalanche of predigested information spewed out of our capitalist mass media and educational institutions. They present us with variations on a single theme: No, capitalism is not the problem. The problem is bigness, advanced technology, bureaucracy, and human nature. Indeed, restoring free market capitalism is the solution.

Capitalism becomes the solution, of course, only because understanding itself is imprisoned within the problem. Today, deregulating capitalism appears as the solution to problems of monopoly capitalism, but earlier monopoly capitalism developed as the solution to problems of competitive capitalism. Outside these confines, it is clear that since capitalism is the primary source of our problems, it cannot be the solution.

Realistically, therefore, we have a choice. We can resign ourselves to capitalism and the growing dehumanization it entails. Or we can recognize the need and actively work not only for progressive reform but also for an American socialist revolution.*

* Since the world history of socialist revolution has only just begun, and since socialist development has not taken place within advanced capitalist societies, no socialist country today

That revolution will not provide an instant cure for all of our existing problems. Nor will it be free of problems of its own creation. Socialism is not a utopia. It cannot be achieved overnight simply by overthrowing a capitalist ruling class and legally nationalizing the ownership of the means of production. Socialism, rather, is a long-term struggle in which human beings actively change nature—social, human, and physical. Like capitalism in its time, socialism represents a decisive advance in the capacity of human beings to realize their potential through history.

American socialism will be an ephochal revolutionary process through which our people collectively create a capacity to solve the otherwise insoluble, extremely severe problems of capitalism, as we definitively and positively change the way we relate to each other, to our selves, and to our material surroundings. Americans will create socialism when and because we come to understand that we have no other meaningful choice.

If this sounds "ideological" and frightening, it is supposed to.* One way society maintains the status quo is to make fundamental alternatives appear irrational and threatening, while attributing the source of existing problems to anything but the system itself. This obfuscation continues to take its toll.

As a consequence, consciousness of the immense and negative impact of capitalism on our lives and conscious resistance to the capi-

---

provides an even remotely satisfactory model for a future American socialist revolution. The Soviet Union, for example, has not carried out a thorough-going socialist transformation of the relations of production, with the result that the forces of production there are being developed within a state-capitalist framework. China under the leadership of Mao Tse-tung appears, by contrast, to have made remarkable progress in that transformation, but the forces of production there are still underdeveloped. It remains to be seen whether China can continue to progress on the twin fronts of socialist revolution and socialist construction or has, instead, reached the limits of what can be achieved in an underdeveloped country confronting a world whose markets and international relations are dominated by capitalist forces.

* The authors of a penetrating, recent book describe socialism in unthreatening terms as "an extension of democracy from the narrowly political to the economic realm." Socialism in this crucial respect is "the democratization of economic relationships: social ownership, democratic and participatory control of the production process by workers, equal sharing of socially necessary labor by all, . . . progressive equalization of incomes and destruction of hierarchical economic relationships." Samuel Bowles and Herbert Gintis, *Schooling in Capitalist America* (New York: Basic Books, 1976), p. 14.

EPILOGUE

talist system are not, I think, very widespread or advanced in the United States. For most Americans capitalism continues, on the whole, to be experienced through our daily lives as something natural, eternal, and universal. The present is perceived as omnipresent, as a given to be accepted and adjusted to.

But this perception, dependent upon minimally fulfilled expectations about daily life, is vulnerable to changed circumstances. Radical deterioration in the quality of daily life is disorienting. The deterioration that already has accompanied the ongoing economic crisis has deepened the fiscal problems of the state, undermined the present basis for continuing collaboration between unions and capitalist management, and begun to challenge the perception that life is as it has to be.

After the tumult of the 1960s, the 1970s have appeared calm. But the calm is unquiet. We are approaching a turning point. Which way we turn depends on us.

With the observable bankruptcy in the 1970s of the variant of liberalism/capitalism that developed out of the New Deal and has since dominated our thoughts and lives, a frantic search is on for another ideology and accompanying social organization suitable to current conditions and capable of legitimating and sustaining capitalism.

The accommodations of New Deal ideology, practices and coalitions have been ravaged by the growing contradictions of American capitalism. The middle ground is being eroded. We live at a time when objective conditions are escalating class conflict. The ruling class no longer can easily afford to "buy off" with higher standards of living the unionized segment of the working class. And the state no longer can afford to "pacify" other millions through expanding welfare and social services.

Today, big business and big government in fact are pressing to make the working class pay for supposed solutions to the capitalist crisis. Caught between these pressures and increasing rank-and-file dissatisfaction, national union leaders speak with greater militancy, reflecting the changed conditions and their opportune rediscovery of the reality of class conflict.

EPILOGUE

In this context, and despite passing appearances to the contrary, nineteenth-century liberalism/capitalism is no alternative. It is beyond restoring. Given the need, however, to attract working-class believers during a period of growing class conflict, some appropriate, substitute ideology is desperately needed. In response to this need two seemingly polar alternatives seem to have emerged: a backward-looking New Right; and, to date much less prominently, a forward-looking left liberalism.

Although these alternatives are quite different, both emphasize a kind of decentralization of power and authority within the capitalist system. In the case of the New Right, the devolution is conceived primarily in economic terms as a shift of decision-making from government to capitalists. In the case of left liberals, the devolution is conceived primarily in political terms as a formal extension of democracy to the workplace.

The New Right deals with the symptoms of problems—big government, high taxes, social disorder, and the like. It appeals because it promises to relieve symptoms we do indeed experience as deterioration in the quality of our daily lives. But its remedies are likely only to exacerbate fundamental, interrelated problems of our political economy, which the New Right is incapable of resolving: unemployment, poverty, gross inequality, exploitation, authoritarianism, alienation, and human and environmental pollution. Accordingly, under the aegis of the New Right the capitalist crisis can only intensify. With conditions of intense crisis and class struggle, the New Right threatens to become something more familiar—fascism.

By contrast, the left liberalism that seeks "workplace democracy" and "worker control" does deal with certain basic problems. It appeals because it promises to reduce class conflict, alienation, inequality, and authoritarianism in production and simultaneously to raise productivity and revitalize workers. But the meaningful and widespread practice of participatory control by workers stands in contradiction to capitalism and demands nothing less than the long-term revolutionary transformation of the capitalist division of labor. Left liberals, therefore, whatever their good intentions, cannot within capitalism realize the promise of worker self-management.

EPILOGUE

The capitalist choice, then, if I am correct, ultimately is between fascism and hollow liberal promises.

We cannot accept a choice so inadequate for satisfying our human needs. We, the people of the United States, must create our own solutions to the crisis of capitalism.

As the structure of human relations in the United States increasingly breaks down under the pressures of intensified crisis, we need to integrate a revolutionary consciousness into the struggle that is our daily lives. We need to experience capitalist life as a peculiar and contradictory mode of existence brought into being and maintained by a ruling class during a particular period of human development; to experience the present as a historical problem/opportunity that will be transcended, as it was created, by the thoughts and actions of men and women in interaction with their material surroundings.

Then, as we become the conscious makers of history, we will truly know that capitalism is not the end of history.

EPILOGUE

Index *

* An index, however useful, fragments the world into static, over-neat, seemingly mutually exclusive categories. This distorts reality. Cross-referencing is only some compensation.

388

France, Anatole, 233
Fred, 194-96, 198-200, 202-4
Freedom, 59, 188, 215, 218, 221, 229, 246,
264, 281, 286, 292, 295-99, 301, 302, 304,
305, 309, 310, 312, 316, 333, 334, 340,
341, 365, 370 (see also Liberalism); of
choice, 20, 56, 81, 83, 85-89, 97, 98, 100,
101, 107, 116, 132, 142, 153, 164-66, 193,
215, 218-21, 224, 228, 229, 242, 244,
246-49, 259-61, 289, 295-98, 302, 308-10,
331, 340, 341, 356, 357, 365-68, 372, 373,
378, 379, 381-82 (see also Dependent; Economic coercion); of association,
127, 184, 185, 187, 188, 191, 222, 223; of
speech, 127, 154, 155-57, 184, 185, 197,
222, 223, 320, 343-46; of contract, 223,
227-29 (see also Contract; Collective bargaining)
Fringe benefits, 125, 132, 133, 142, 143, 146,
148, 149, 152, 153, 161, 162, 187, 318,
322, 325, 332, 364-68; see also Blue
Cross/Blue Shield

Garson, Barbara, 237-45, 262-64, 317-26
General Mills, 265
General Motors (GM), 20, 240-42, 262, 274,
325, 326
Gintis, Herbert, see Bowles, Samuel
Godfather, Part II, 93
Goods-producing industry, 294, 374; see also
Manufacturing sector
Gorz, Andre, 260n
Government, see State, the
Gurley, John G., 377n

Harlan County, U.S.A., 375
Hartz, Louis, 215n
Hawthorne experiment, 372
Health, see Public welfare; Safety and health
Health, Education, and Welfare (HEW), De-
partment of, 236, 239, 255-57; see also Work
in America
Helena Rubenstein cosmetics factory, see
cosmetics factory
Helpless, see Powerless
Hidden Injuries of Class, see Sennett, Richard
Hiding, 35, 37, 38, 57, 74, 80

Hierarchy, 51, 92, 93, 268, 375, 379n; see
also Bureaucracy; Division of labor
Hooker, 245, 251-53
Hoppers, 7, 25, 30-34, 36-40, 42, 43, 45, 47,
52-57, 60, 63, 66-71, 76, 94, 108, 109, 190;
see also Work routine
Human nature, 234, 245, 282, 302, 337, 378,
379
Hyrske, Mary, 319-22

IAM, 115, 130, 131, 133, 139, 147, 165, 186,
206; see also Union
Ideology, 4, 5, 13, 75, 215, 216, 218, 233,
234, 271, 288, 293, 299, 310, 316, 370,
376, 377, 379, 380-81; see also Liberalism, Socialism
Inadequacy, 20, 96, 300-304, 306, 310, 312,
313, 324; see also Blame; Dehumanize;
Failure; Individualism; Self-doubt
Independence, 267, 308-10; see also Depen-
dence; Individualism
Indignity, see Dehumanize
Individualism, 4, 10, 52, 55, 91, 105, 116,
120, 122, 123, 173, 190, 194, 214, 215,
219, 224, 226, 229, 242, 299, 303-11, 314,
353, 354, 365, 374; see also Liberalism
Industrial efficiency, 267-72; see also
Capitalism
Inequality, 17, 227, 303, 304, 311-13, 316,
324, 347, 350, 353, 354, 381; see also
Equality
Inflation, 104, 133, 134, 142, 149, 162, 163,
169, 171, 172, 178, 180, 187; see also
Consumer Price Index
Information, 18, 55, 62, 127, 134, 193, 274;
use of by management to control, 93, 103-7,
144-46, 257, 340; use of by unions to
control, 117-21, 129, 140, 144-46, 148,
151-57, 158-92, 199, 202, 206, 324, 362;
see also Control; Rumors; Secrecy
Inspection, see Final Inspections Department
Intensification (of labor), 288, 371; see also
Speedup
Internalization, 272, 299, 308; see also Cost;
Social efficiency
International Association of Machinists and
Aerospace Workers, see IAM

INDEX

INDEX

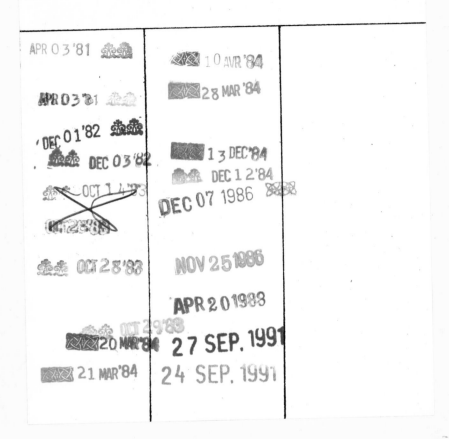